Stefan Biffl · Aybüke Aurum · Barry Boehm ·
Hakan Erdogmus · Paul Grünbacher (Eds.)

Value-Based Software Engineering

With 69 Figures and 41 Tables

 Springer

Editors

Stefan Biffl
Institute for Software Technology
Vienna University of Technology
Karlsplatz 13
1040 Wien, Austria
stefan.biffl@tuwien.ac.at

Aybüke Aurum
School of Information Systems,
Technology and Management
University of New South Wales
Sydney, NSW 2052, Australia
aybuke@unsw.edu.au

Barry Boehm
Center for Software Engineering
University of Southern California
941 W 37th Place,
Los Angeles, CA 90089-0781, USA
boehm@sunset.usc.edu

Hakan Erdogmus
Software Engineering
NRC Institute for Information
Technology
National Research Council Canada
Building M50, 1200 Montreal Rd.
Ottawa, ON, Canada K1A 0R6
Hakan.Erdogmus@nrc-cnrc.gc.ca

Paul Grünbacher
Systems Engineering & Automation
Johannes Kepler University Linz
Altenbergerstr. 69
4040 Linz, Austria
paul.gruenbacher@jku.at

Library of Congress Control Number: 2005930639

ACM Computing Classification (1998): D.2.1, D.2.8, D.2.9, D.2.10, K.6.1, K.6.3

ISBN-10 3-540-25993-7 Springer Berlin Heidelberg New York
ISBN-13 978-3-540-25993-0 Springer Berlin Heidelberg New York

Springer is a part of Springer Science+Business Media
springeronline.com

© Springer-Verlag Berlin Heidelberg 2006
Printed in Germany

Cover design: KünkelLopka, Heidelberg
Typesetting: Camera ready by the editors
Production: LE-TeX Jelonek, Schmidt & Vöckler GbR, Leipzig

Printed on acid-free paper   45/3142/YL - 5 4 3 2 1 0

Foreword

Ross Jeffery

When, as a result of pressure from the CEO, the Chief Information Officer poses the question "Just what is this information system worth to the organization?" the IT staff members are typically at a loss. "That's a difficult question," they might say; or "well it really depends" is another answer. Clearly, neither of these is very satisfactory and yet both are correct. The IT community has struggled with questions concerning the value of an organization's investment in software and hardware ever since it became a significant item in organizational budgets. And like all questions concerning value, the first step is the precise determination of the object being assessed and the second step is the identification of the entity to which the value is beneficial. In software engineering both of these can be difficult. The precise determination of the object can be complex. If it is an entire information system in an organizational context that is the object of interest, then boundary definition becomes an issue. Is the hardware and middleware to be included? Can the application exist without any other applications? If however the object of interest is, say, a software engineering activity such as testing within a particular project, then the boundary definition becomes a little easier. But the measure of benefit may become a little harder.

In this book the issues related to the value of different software engineering activities are addressed along with the benefits and opportunities in decision making under conditions of conflict of decision criteria in uncertain contexts.

Because software has many stakeholders including developers, users, and managers, it is essential that a comparative measure of the software be devised to support software decisions. This is the aim of value-based software engineering. If we can develop models and measures of value which are of use to the manager, the developer, and the user, then trade-off decisions can become possible, for example between quality and cost or between functionality and schedule. Without the comparative measures, the comparisons are impossible and the decisions regarding development alternatives can only address one criterion, such as defects or functionality, at any point in time, since we need to measure defects or functionality using the same yardstick. Value can be that yardstick.

If we were to divide the software engineering domain simplistically into the production of shrink-wrapped and other products, we could start to divide the problem. In the case of shrink-wrapped, the definition of the object of interest becomes quite clear. It is a product that is sold. The valuation of interventions in the software engineering activities in this domain appears easier than in many other domains. In this case the quality model work that has been carried out in software engineering can provide some insights into the relative value of product characteristics. It would then be possible to investigate the software engineering interventions that give rise to changes in the quality characteristics that are valued by the consumer of the software product. In this manner the link between software engineering process interventions and product characteristics allows for a value-based measure for those interventions.

Another way of looking at value in this context might be the work that has been carried out on product performance. It has been shown in many countries, for example, that outstanding product success derives from product advantage (defined as superior price/performance, customer benefits, and relative product quality), pre-development assessments, cross-functional teams, focus on markets where influence exists, and other factors. Perhaps value-based software engineering needs to understand some of these factors and then link them to substantive software quality models if value-based decisions are to be made in the software engineering context.

But how might we assess interventions in software engineering? Since software engineering is a human-intensive activity that results in a logical product that is often used as a part of a business process, the determination of value can draw from many disciplines. Perhaps one issue of interest is the assessment of the value of training of software engineers. In this case the value of human resource intervention programs may be a part of the area of interest. Can we make use of work, as given by the Brogden utility equation, for measuring the change in utility in dollars after a training program when looking at the value of project training interventions in software engineering?

Another factor that seems clearly of concern in this area is the methods we use to value information when we are making decisions under conditions of uncertainty. Methods such as the use of the expected value of perfect information (EVPI) can set the upper value bound in these conditions. The minimum can also be determined using these techniques. In this way it might be possible to consider the payoff maximization for software engineering interventions as well as the minimization of regret or loss.

Clearly these are complex, multidisciplinary opportunities for the research community, with significant potential economic impact across economies. In this book the editors have collected the current state of the art in the application of value-based approaches to software engineering activities and decisions. The book sets a framework for value, the theoretical foundations, the practices, and the application. The authors are drawn largely from the software engineering research community that is involved in the areas of software engineering decision making, measurement, and investment. This book presents an exciting collection of chapters in an area of research that will develop over the ensuing years as the importance of this work gains recognition in the wider community.

Author Biography

Ross Jeffery is Professor of Software Engineering in the School of Computer Science and Engineering at UNSW and Program Leader in Empirical Software Engineering in National ICT Australia Ltd. (NICTA). Previously he was Director of the Centre for Advanced Software Engineering Research (CAESER) at the University of New South Wales. Professor Jeffery was the founding Head of the School of Information Systems at UNSW from 1989 to 1995 and Associate Dean (Technology) for the Faculty of Commerce and Economics from 1996 to 1999. He was the founding Chairman the Australian Software Metrics Association (ASMA) where he served as Chairman from its inception for a number of years. He is Chairman of the IEAust/ACS Joint Board on Software Engineering. He has served on the editorial board of the IEEE Transactions on Software Engineering, and the Wiley International Series in Information Systems and he is Associate Editor of the Journal of Empirical Software Engineering. He has also been on the steering committee of the IEEE and ACM International Conference on Software Engineering and served as Program Co-Chair for the 1995 conference in Seattle. He is a founding member of the International Software Engineering Research Network (ISERN). He was elected Fellow of the Australian Computer Society for his contribution to software engineering research. His current research interests are in software engineering process and product modeling and improvement, electronic process guides and software knowledge management, software quality, software metrics, software technical and management reviews, and software resource modeling and estimation. His research has involved over fifty government and industry organizations over a period of 15 years and has been funded by industry, government, and universities. He has co-authored four books and over one hundred and twenty research papers.

Preface

Stefan Biffl, Aybüke Aurum, Barry Boehm, Hakan Erdogmus, Paul Grünbacher

This book tackles software engineering decisions and their consequences from a value-based perspective. The chapters of the book exploit this perspective to foster
- better evaluation of software products, services, processes, and projects from an economic point of view;
- better identification of risks for software development projects and effective decision support for them in a multicriteria and uncertain environment;
- better project management through a better understanding of the contribution of the activities and practices involved, the techniques, artifacts, and methods used, as well as the functionality, products, and systems delivered.

What Do We Mean by "Value"?

The goal of software engineering is to create products, services, and processes that add value. People who contribute to the creation of these artifacts – analysts, process engineers, software engineers, testers, managers, executives – strive in their decisions and actions to maximize some simple or complex notion of value, whether consciously or unconsciously, and whether with respect to shared goals or to satisfy personal objectives. Alas, when value considerations remain implicit, the overall effect may very well be negative. Examples of undesirable consequences of implicit and clashing value perspectives abound. A good case in point is when developers value superior design, the marketing of new, nifty functionality, quality assurance "zero defects" and the management of short time-to-market. Another example is when product quality is pursued for quality's sake with little regard to shareholder value (Favaro, 1996). Yet another is when management tries to drive development costs down by treating developers as a replaceable commodity or by evaluating them using one-dimensional performance metrics, and the development team reacts by creating knowledge silos or by "coding to rule" to protect its own interests. If value perspectives are not explicated and reconciled, everybody loses in the end.

Value-based software engineering (VBSE) brings such value considerations to the foreground so that software engineering decisions at all levels can be optimized to meet or reconcile explicit objectives of the involved stakeholders, from marketing staff and business analysts to developers, architects, and quality experts, and from process and measurement experts to project managers and executives. In VBSE, decisions are not made in a setting blind to value perspectives, whether common or differing, of these project participants.

Driven by both individual and collective goals, these stakeholders all hope to derive some benefit, whether tangible or intangible, economic or social, monetary or utilitarian, or even aesthetic or ethical. By the term value, we refer to this ultimate benefit, which is often in the eye of the beholder and admits multiple characterizations.

A *Dictionary of Canadian Economics* defines value as: *"The quantity of one product or service that will be given or accepted in exchange for another. It is therefore a measure of the economic significance of a particular good or service. This value in exchange depends on the scarcity of the good or service and the extent to which it is desired."*

While this certainly is a common definition of value and is addressed prominently in the book, it represents only one dimension. A *Modern Dictionary of Sociology* defines value more abstractly as a *"...generalized principle of behavior to which the members of a group feel a strong commitment and which provides a standard for judging specific acts and goals."*

In the same spirit, the *Oxford Companion to Law (1980)* points out that *"...value may consist of spiritual or aesthetic qualities, or in utility in use, or in the amount of money or other goods which could be obtained in exchange for the thing in question..."* although the latter, monetary sense, by virtue of being the most tangible, is the most relevant in legal contexts.

In this book, you will find many contributions that stress the more general, group-oriented, and utilitarian aspect of value alongside those that focus on the more traditional, economic and monetary aspect. Neither aspect takes precedence over the other; both aspects are relevant to tackling the wide spectrum of software engineering issues covered in this book.

A Historical Perspective

To our knowledge, the first significant text to address value considerations beyond cost models in the software development context was Boehm's Software Engineering Economics (Boehm, 1981). Boehm later focused on the relationship between value and software process. The result was the spiral model of software development, which brought to the foreground risk management as an integral component in software process (Boehm, 1986).

The value-based management movement of the early 1990s (McTaggart, 1994) inspired an *IEEE Software* essay entitled "When the Pursuit of Quality Destroys Value" (Favaro, 1996). This essay made the controversial argument that superior quality should not be a goal in itself in the absence of favorable economics. Favaro et al. used the adjective "value-based" in the software development context in a later article addressing the economics of software reuse (Favaro et al., 1998). The same year the Economics-Driven Software Engineering Research (EDSER) workshops debuted at the International Conference on Software Engineering (ICSE) as a forum to share experiences and promote VBSE-related issues among the research community. The EDSER workshops have since been collocated with this annual conference with increasing popularity, and continue to be an important source of information. Two years after EDSER's debut, Boehm and Sullivan proposed the first agenda for VBSE research at ICSE 2000.

Over time, the scope of VBSE research expanded to include aspects of value other than economic and monetary. Of particular historical interest is the WinWin model of requirements negotiation, introduced by Boehm and others in the mid-1990s" (Boehm et al., 1998). The WinWin model stressed the multi-stakeholder perspective by incorporating into the spiral model an approach for reconciling differing value propositions of project stakeholders. During the late 1990s and early 2000s, the advent of empirical and evidence-based software engineering, value-based management approaches, preference-based decision making, as well agile software development and other risk-driven methods continued to push the VBSE agenda forward and enlarge its scope. In 2003, Boehm proposed a formal VBSE agenda that captures the expanding scope of this burgeoning field (Boehm, 2003). The book both revisits and builds on this agenda.

Why Should You Care About Value-Based Software Engineering?

It is impossible to effectively address value considerations when software development is treated as an ad hoc endeavor. Much like in conventional engineering, the incorporation of value considerations requires treating software development as a purposeful endeavor, which aims at the cost-effective and reliable construction and maintenance of products that meet specific, if not always static, goals. Hence the title of the book: *Value-Based Software Engineering.*

Software admittedly has unique internal and external characteristics, in particular its highly flexible and volatile nature and its heavy dependence on collaboration among creative and skilled people, that in many instances necessitate a construction and management approach radically different from that of building a bridge or a ship, and more akin to new product development. However, basic engineering principles of discipline, economy, rigor, quality, and utility, and, to a certain extent, repeatability and predictability, still very much apply. As in conventional engineering, value considerations affect the trade-offs among these principles, but probably with much more subtlety, severity, and variety than they do in the engineering of hard products.

But why are these trade-offs so important? For no other reason than that they ultimately determine the outcome of a software project. The message of those who studied the characteristics of successful software organizations and projects is pretty strong. Both prominent business school researchers, such as Alan McCormack of the Harvard University and Michael Cusumano of the Massachusetts Institute of Technology, and software engineering thought leaders, such as Tom DeMarco, Larry Constantine, and Tim Lister, have repeatedly pointed out to the importance of value factors and the underlying trade-offs in their writings. Since the mid-1980s, the frequently cited CHAOS reports from the Standish Group have consistently identified closely related issues, such as the misalignment of IT spending with organizational objectives and user needs, as sources of failure in software projects. Our main purpose in the production of this book was to draw attention to these issues, which are impossible to reason about in a value-neutral and ad hoc setting.

The Scope of the Book

The International Organization for Standardization (ISO) defines software engineering as "the systematic application of scientific and technological knowledge, methods, and experience to the design, implementation, testing, and documentation of software to optimize its production, support, and quality" (*Information Technology: Vocabulary, Part 1, Fundamental Terms*). While the ISO definition might suffice in a value-neutral setting, we must extend the scope considerably to address value considerations effectively. Three shortcomings of this definition are remarkable from a value-oriented perspective.

First is its exclusion of economics, management science, cognitive sciences, and humanities from the body of knowledge required to create successful software systems. Value-based software engineering however cannot ignore this body of knowledge because it considers software development as a purposeful activity carried out by people for people.

The second shortcoming of the ISO definition is its delimitation of software development by technical activities such as design, implementation, and testing. VBSE in contrast must also consider, as part of the software engineering lifecycle, management-oriented activities – such as business case development, project evaluation, project planning, process selection, project management, risk management, process measurement, and monitoring – that have often been considered peripheral. VBSE as such is a multifaceted, multidisciplinary approach that covers all practices, activities, and phases involved in software development, addressing a wide variety of decisions about technical issues, business models, software development processes, software products and services, and related management practices.

The third shortcoming of the ISO definition is its failure to explicitly recognize the ultimate goal: ensuring that software systems continue to meet and adapt to evolving human and organizational needs to create value. VBSE must put these needs foremost. According to VBSE, it is not enough, or at times not even critical, for software projects to merely meet unilaterally preset schedule, budget, process, and quality objectives. Rather, it is necessary that the resulting products and services persist to increase the wealth of the stakeholders and optimize other relevant value objectives of these projects.

Who Should Read This Book?

This book is intended for those who care about the impact of value considerations in software development activities and decisions. And who should care about such considerations? Well, just about everyone: academics, managers, practitioners, and students of software engineering who recognize that software is not created in a void, that software development involves many participants – executives, project managers, business analysts, developers, quality assurance experts, users, the general public, and so on – with varying roles and stakes in both the final products and the processes used the create those products.

The book appeals particularly to readers who are interested in high-level aspects of software engineering decision making because of its focus on organizational, project-, process-, and product-level issues rather than on low-level, purely technical decisions. The target audience includes, but is not limited to:

- product managers, project managers, chief information officers who make high-level decisions;
- process experts, measurement experts, requirements engineers, business analysts, quality assurance experts, usability experts, and technical leads who participate in various lifecycle activities at key interface points and whose influence span multiple levels and phases;
- software engineering researchers, educators, and graduate students who teach or study software process, evaluate existing and new practices, technologies, methods, or products, or teach or investigate managerial, social, and economic aspects of software development.

To benefit from this book, the reader should have at least taken advanced courses or studied advanced texts on software engineering or software process, or worked in the software industry long enough to acquire an appreciation of the many trade-offs involved from beyond a purely technical perspective.

How Is the Book Organized?

We organized the book in three parts. Part 1 focuses on the foundations of VBSE and provides examples of frameworks for reasoning about value considerations in software development activities. Part 2 provides methods and techniques for VBSE that build upon the foundations and frameworks presented in Part 1. Finally, Part 3 demonstrates the benefits of VBSE through concrete examples and case studies.

While we believe that all chapters contain ideas applicable in a variety of situations, because the book addresses a wide spectrum of issues and activities, certain chapters will inevitably be more relevant to some readers than others, depending on the reader's orientation. We recommend that all readers familiarize themselves with Chapter 1 regardless of their interests, as this chapter sets the tone for the rest of the book. There are many ways to dissect the content according to particular interest areas. We hope that the following road map will help orient the reader who wishes to quickly zoom in on a specific topic.

If you are interested in project-level decisions, economic valuation of software projects and assets, and reasoning under uncertainty, make sure to read Chapters 3, 5, and 17. Readers interested in VBSE-related concepts and theories applicable to a range of software engineering lifecycle activities should start with Chapters 2, 4, 6, and 8. Chapters 7, 9, and 12 are recommended reading for those with an interest in product planning, and Chapters 6, 7, and 9 for those focusing on requirements gathering and negotiation. If the focus is on software process issues and tool adoption, Chapters 6, 8, 13, 15, and 16 discuss approaches that aid in process improvement and measurement as well as impact evaluation. Chapters 4, 10, 11, and 14 will appeal to the reader interested in product evaluation and testing-related issues. Chapters 8, 14, and 15 will appeal to those who tackle knowledge management problems. Finally, Chapters 3, 5, 6, and 13 are relevant to readers who are interested in risk management.

Whatever your orientation and interests, we hope that the book will inspire you to incorporate value considerations to your own work, or, if you have already been operating in a value-conscious setting, that you will find new insights and resources to draw upon. Good reading!

Acknowledgements

This book would not have been possible without the efforts of many. We are thankful to the authors who contributed the individual chapters and worked diligently with the editors and external reviewers to enhance the quality of the book. At least three reviewers evaluated each chapter and provided extensive feedback to improve the clarity of presentation and ensure technical coherence. Their efforts are much appreciated. We also thank Matthias Heindl, Stefan Kresnicka, Martina Lettner, Muhammad Asim Noor, Barbara Schuhmacher, Norbert Seyff, Rick Rabiser, and Markus Zeilinger for their help during this project. Finally, we thank Springer, our publisher, for trusting our vision, and in particular Ralf Gerstner for his support.

References

(Boehm, 1981) Boehm, B. W.: Software Engineering Economics (Prentice-Hall, 1981)

(Boehm, 1986) Boehm, B. W.: A Spiral Model of Software Development and Enhancement. Software Engineering Notes, 11(4)

(Boehm et al., 1998) Boehm, B. W., Egyed, A., Kwan, J., Port, D., Shaw, A., Madachy, R.: Using the WinWin Spiral Model: A Case Study. IEEE Computer, (July 1998)

(Boehm, 2003) Boehm, B. W.: Value-Based Software Engineering. Software Engineering Notes, 28(2):2003

(Favaro, 1996) Favaro, J.: When the Pursuit of Quality Destroys Value. IEEE Software (May 1996)

(Favaro et al., 1998) Favaro, J., Favaro, K. R., Favaro, P. F.: Value-based Reuse Investment, Annals of Software Engineering, 5 (1998)

(McTaggart, 1994) McTaggart, J.: The Value Imperative (The Free Press, 1994)

Table of Contents

List of Contributors

David L. Atkins
Department of Computer Science
American University in Cairo
Cairo 11511, Egypt
Email: datkins@aucegypt.edu

Aybüke Aurum
School of Information Systems, Technology and Management
University of New South Wales
Sydney NSW 2052, Australia
Email: aybuke@unsw.edu.au

Michael Berry
University of New South Wales
School of Computer Science and Engineering
Sydney NSW 2052, Australia
Email: Michael.Berry@student.unsw.edu.au

Stefan Biffl
Institute of Software Technology and Interactive Systems
Technische Universität Wien
Karlsplatz 13, A-1040, Vienna, Austria
Email: Stefan.Biffl@tuwien.ac.at

Barry W. Boehm
University of Southern California
Center for Software Engineering
941 W. 37th Place, SAL Room 328
Los Angeles, CA 90089-0781, USA
Email: boehm@cse.usc.edu

Torgeir Dingsøyr
SINTEF Information and communication technology
Department of Software Engineering
NO-7465 Trondheim, Norway
Email: Torgeir.dingsoyr@sintef.no

Alexander Egyed
Teknowledge Corporation
4640 Admiralty Way, Suite 1010
Marina Del Rey, CA 90292, USA
Email: aegyed@ieee.org

Hakan Erdogmus
Institute for Information Technology,
National Research Council Canada
M50, 1200 Montreal Rd., Ottawa, ON, Canada K1A 0R6
Email: Hakan.Erdogmus@nrc-cnrc.gc.ca

John Favaro
Consulenza Informatica
Via Gamerra 21
56123 Pisa, Italy
Email: john@favaro.net

Ann Fruhling
Department of Computer Science
College of Information Science & Technology
University of Nebraska at Omaha, USA
Email: afruhling@mail.unomaha.edu

Paul Grünbacher
Systems Engineering and Automation
Johannes Kepler University Linz
Altenbergerstr. 69, 4040 Linz, Austria
Email: paul.gruenbacher@jku.at

Michael Halling
Department of Finance
University of Vienna
Brünnerstr. 72, 1210 Vienna, Austria
Email: michael.halling@univie.ac.at

Warren Harrison
Portland State University
1825 SW Broadway
97207 Portland, OR, USA
Email: warren@cs.pdx.edu

Apurva Jain
University of Southern California
Center for Software Engineering
941 W. 37th Place, SAL Room 328
Los Angeles, CA 90089-0781, USA
Email: apurvaja@usc.edu

Sabine Köszegi
Department of Finance
University of Vienna
Brünnerstr. 72, 1210 Vienna, Austria
Email: Sabine.Koeszegi@univie.ac.at

Sebastian Maurice
Software Engineering Decision Support Lab
2500 University Drive NW
Calgary, Alberta, Canada T2N 1N4
Email: smaurice@ucalgary.ca

Audris Mockus
Avaya Corporation
Email: audris@avaya.com

An Ngo-The
Software Engineering Decision Support Lab
2500 University Drive NW
Calgary, Alberta, Canada T2N 1N4
Email: ango@cpsc.ucalgary.ca

Dietmar Pfahl
University of Calgary
Schulich School of Engineering
2500 University Drive NW
Calgary, Alberta Canada T2N 1N4
ICT Building
Email: dpfahl@ucalgary.ca

Rudolf Ramler
Software Competence Center Hagenberg GmbH
Hauptstrasse 99
4232 Hagenberg, Austria
Email: rudolf.ramler@scch.at

Donald J. Reifer
Reifer Consultants, Inc.
P.O. Box 4046
Torrance, CA 90510-4046
Email: d.reifer@ieee.org

Günther Ruhe
iCORE Professor and Industrial Research Chair Software Engineering
2500 University Drive NW
Calgary, Alberta, Canada T2N 1N4
Email: ruhe@ucalgary.ca

Omolade Saliu
Software Engineering Decision Support Lab
2500 University Drive NW
Calgary, Alberta, Canada T2N 1N4
Email: saliu@cpsc.ucalgary.ca

Harvey Siy
Lucent Technologies
Email: hpsiy@lucent.com

Rudolf Vetschera
Department of Business Studies
University of Vienna
Brünnerstr. 72, 1210 Vienna, Austria
Email: rudolf.vetschera@univie.ac.at

Gert-Jan de Vreede
Department of Information Systems & Quantitative Analysis
College of Information Science & Technology
University of Nebraska at Omaha, USA
Email: gdevreede@mail.unomaha.edu

Claes Wohlin
Department of Systems and Software Engineering
Blekinge Institute of Technology Box 520
SE-372 25 Ronneby, Sweden
Email:Claes.Wohlin@bth.se

Part 1
Foundations and Frameworks

Software companies operating within the twenty-first century will have to cope with accelerating rates of change in technology and increased levels of competition on a global scale. Within this changing business environment, in order to stay competitive software companies will be forced to constantly pursue new strategies to differentiate themselves from their competition. More than ever, software developers will need to rely upon enhanced professional and managerial capabilities to meet these new challenges. To gain competitive leverage, software developers seek to increase the efficiency and predictability of the software development process. The continuously increasing complexity of software products, as well as increasing market pressure, require a combination of carefully selected validation and verification techniques to ensure value-added and high quality product development.

The value perspective provides a good way of looking at the product development process. The ultimate aim of value propositions in software engineering is to create a strategy to achieve long-term profitable growth and sustainable competitive advantage for software companies. The implication is that software developers need to consider the key elements of value in terms of how to create value for current as well as future software products and how to deliver this value to a customer in the most profitable way. In other words, software developers should have a better understanding of the implications of the decisions they have made about the software product, the software development process, and the resources that they use.

The objective of Part 1 is to discuss the foundations of value creation for software development. This part also provides frameworks that describe how value can be added to software products through work on software project activities and production of deliverables. It also explores the interdisciplinary nature of software projects. Furthermore, it highlights existing problems of managing value propositions in software engineering, focusing on those problems that may potentially help in managing software engineering knowledge.

There are five chapters in this part that cover to the following areas:

- Chapter 1: Value-Based Software Engineering: Overview and Agenda
- Chapter 2: An Initial Theory of Value-Based Software Engineering
- Chapter 3: Valuation of Software Initiatives under Uncertainty: Concepts, Issues, and Techniques
- Chapter 4: Preference-based Decision Support in Software Engineering
- Chapter 5: Risk and the Economic Value of the Software Producer

Although it is simpler to work in value-neutral settings, the software engineering community realizes that value-neutral approaches to software engineering are one of the major causes of software project failure. In Chapter 1, *Boehm* discusses the potential benefits of integrating a value-based approach into software development engineering principles and presents a value-based software engineering agenda. Following this, in Chapter 2 *Boehm* and *Jain* provide a value-based software engineering theory which draws upon utility, decision, dependency, and control theories. Further, they discuss successful applications of this theory. Effective management of software product development contributes to competitive advantage for software companies. In Chapter 3 *Erdogmus, Favaro,* and *Halling* discuss the value-based approach from a management perspective, in the context of project-level decision making, demonstrating how economic value can influence project-level decisions through illustrative examples. Following this chapter, in Chapter 4 *Vetschera* presents the theoretical background for multicriteria decision making in software development, and then reviews several multicriteria decision making methods and discusses the applicability of these methods to decision problems in software engineering. Finally, in Chapter 5 *Harrison* discusses the fundamental aspects of valuation and the financial risk in the software development process, and shows how software risk management can be valued by using well accepted financial theory when assessing software project predictability.

1 Value-Based Software Engineering: Overview and Agenda

Barry Boehm

Abstract: Much of current software engineering practice and research is done in a value-neutral setting, in which every requirement, use case, object, test case, and defect is equally important. However, most studies of the critical success factors distinguishing successful from failed software projects find that the primary critical success factors lie in the value domain. The value-based software engineering (VBSE) agenda discussed in this chapter and exemplified in the other chapters involves integrating value considerations into the full range of existing and emerging software engineering principles and practices. The chapter then summarizes the primary components of the agenda: value-based requirements engineering, architecting, design and development, verification and validation, planning and control, risk management, quality management, people management, and an underlying theory of VBSE. It concludes with a global road map for realizing the benefits of VBSE.

Keywords: Benefits realization, business case analysis, cost-benefit analysis, investment analysis, return on investment, risk management, stakeholder values, software economics, value-based software engineering.

1.1 Overview and Rationale

Much of current software engineering practice and research is done in a value-neutral setting, in which:

- Every requirement, use case, object, test case, and defect is treated as equally important;
- Methods are presented and practiced as largely logical activities involving mappings and transformations (e.g., object-oriented development);
- "Earned value" systems track project cost and schedule, not stakeholder or business value;
- A "separation of concerns" is practiced, in which the responsibility of software engineers is confined to turning software requirements into verified code.

In earlier times, when software decisions had relatively minor influences on a system's cost, schedule, and value, the value-neutral approach was reasonably workable. But today and, increasingly, in the future, software has and will have a major influence on most systems' cost, schedule, and value; and software decisions are inextricably intertwined with system-level decisions.

Also, value-neutral software engineering principles and practices are unable to deal with most of the sources of software project failure. Major studies such as the Standish Group's CHAOS reports[1] find that most software project failures are caused by value-oriented shortfalls such as lack of user input, incomplete requirements, changing requirements, lack of resources, unrealistic expectations, unclear objectives, and unrealistic time frames.

Further, value-neutral methods are insufficient as a basis of an engineering discipline. The definition of "engineering" in (Webster, 2002) is "the application of science and mathematics by which the properties of matter and sources of energy in nature are made useful to people." Most concerns expressed about the adequacy of software engineering focus on the shortfalls in its underlying science. But it is also hard for a value-neutral approach to provide guidance for making its products useful to people, as this involves dealing with different people's utility functions or value propositions.

It is also hard to make financially responsible decisions using value-neutral methods. Let us illustrate this with an example.

Example: Automated Test Generation (ATG)

Suppose you are the manager of a $2 million software project to develop a large customer billing system. A vendor of an automated test generation (ATG) tool comes to you with the following proposition:

"Our tool has been shown to cut software test costs in half. Your test costs typically consume 50% of your total development costs, or $1 million for your current project. We'll provide you the use of the tool for 30% of your test costs, or $300K. After you've used the tool and saved 50% of your test costs, or $500K, you'll be $200K ahead".

How would you react to this proposition? The usual response for traditionally educated software engineers is to evaluate it from a technical and project management standpoint. An excellent literature review and experience paper (Persson and Yilmazturk, 2004) compiled 34 good technical and project management reasons why an ATG tool might not save you 50% of your test costs. The reasons included unrepresentative test coverage; too much output data; lack of test validity criteria; poor test design; instability due to rapid feature changes; lack of management commitment; and lack of preparation and experience ("automated chaos yields faster chaos").

Often, though, a more serious concern lies outside traditional software engineering technology and management considerations. It is that ATGs, like most current software engineering methods and tools, are value-neutral. They assume that every requirement, test case, and defect is equally important.

---

[1]http://www.standishgroup.com

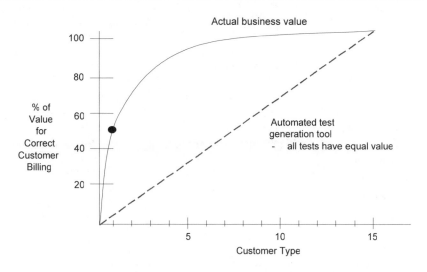

Fig. 1. Pareto 80:20 distribution of test case value

However, the more usual situation is a Pareto distribution in which 80% of the mission value comes from 20% of the software components. The data in Figure 1 are a good illustration of this phenomenon. The Pareto curve in Figure 1 comes from an experience report (Bullock, 2000) in which each customer billing type tested led to improved initial billing revenues from 75% to 90% and much lower customer complaint rates; and one of the 15 customer types accounted for 50% of the billing revenues. The straight line curve in Figure 1 is the usual result of ATG-driven testing, in which the next test is equally likely to have low or high business value.

Table 1. Comparative business cases: ATG and Pareto testing

% of Tests Run	ATG Testing				Pareto Testing			
	Cost	Value	Net Value	ROI	Cost	Value	Net Value	ROI
0	1,300	0	-1,300	-1.00	1,000	0	-1,000	-1.00
10	1,350	400	-950	-0.70	1,100	2,560	1,460	+1.33
20	1,400	800	-600	-0.43	1,200	3,200	2,000	1.67
40	1,500	1,600	100	0.07	1,400	3,840	2,440	1.74
60	1,600	2,400	800	0.50	1,600	3,968	2,368	1.48
80	1,700	3,200	1,500	0.88	1,800	3,994	2,194	1.21
100	1,800	4,000	2,200	1.22	2,000	4,000	2,000	1.00

Table 1 shows the relative levels of investment costs, business benefits, and returns on investment, *ROI = (benefits − costs) / costs*, for the value-neutral ATG testing and value-based Pareto testing strategies. Figure 2 provides a graphical comparison of the resulting ROIs. The analysis is based on the following assumptions.

- $1M of the development costs have been invested in the customer billing system by the beginning of testing.
- The ATG tool will cost $300K and will reduce test costs by 50% as promised.
- The business case for the system will produce $4M in business value in return for the $2M investment cost.
- The business case will provide a similar 80:20 distribution for the remaining 14 customer types.

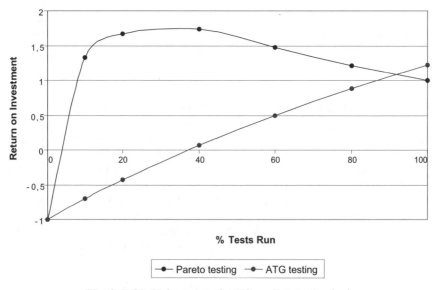

Fig. 2. ROI: Value-neutral ATG vs. Pareto Analysis

As seen in Table 1 and graphically in Figure 2, the value-neutral ATG approach does achieve a cost reduction and a higher ROI of 1.22 at the 100% tested point. But the value-based Pareto testing approach determines that a much higher ROI of 1.74 can be achieved by running only about 40% of the most valuable tests. Beyond that point, the remaining $600K of test investment will generate only $160K in business value, and is a poor investment of scarce resources. Some further considerations are:

- There may be qualitative reasons to test all 15 of the customer types. Frequently, however, the lessons learned in testing type 1 will identify a more cost-effective subset of tests to be run on the remaining 14 customer types.
- A pure focus on cost reduction can produce a poor ROI profile.

- From a cost of money standpoint, much of the benefit from the ATG strategy comes in less valuable future cash flows.
- However, appropriate combinations of Pareto-based and ATG-based testing may produce even higher ROIs.

From a global standpoint, it appears that finding out which 60% of an organization's testing budget actually produces a negative ROI would be highly worthwhile. Estimates of global software costs are approaching $1 trillion per year. If half of this is spent on testing, and 60% of the test effort can be profitably eliminated, this creates a $300 billion per year cost savings potential for such value-based testing investments.

1.2 Background and Agenda

Some VBSE Definitions and Background: Some of the dictionary definitions of "value" (Webster, 2002) are in purely financial terms, such as "the monetary worth of something: marketable price." However, in the context of this book, we use the broader dictionary definition of "value" as "relative worth, utility, or importance." This adds complications in requiring VBSE to address less rigorously analyzable situations, but enables it to provide help in addressing software engineering decisions involving personal, interpersonal, or ethical considerations, as discussed in many of the chapters.

Given that the definition of "engineering" above includes the goal of making things useful to people, it would seem that value considerations are already built into the definition of "software engineering." But since so much of current software engineering is done in a value-neutral context, we offer the following definition of VBSE: "the explicit concern with value concerns in the application of science and mathematics by which the properties of computer software are made useful to people." The resulting science includes the social sciences as well as the physical sciences, and the mathematics includes utility theory, game theory, statistical decision theory, and real options theory as well as logic, complexity theory, and category theory.

The book treats the terms "value proposition," "utility function," and "win condition" basically as synonyms. "Win condition" is primarily used in the context of stakeholders negotiating mutually satisfactory or win-win agreements, as in Chapters 2 and 7. "Utility function" is primarily used in trying to characterize the nature of a function relating a stakeholder's degree of preference for alternative (often multidimensional) outcomes. "Value proposition" is primarily used as a generic term encompassing both win conditions and utility functions.

The treatment of information as having economic value (Marschak, 1974) and the economics of computers, software, and information technology have been topics of study for some time (Sharpe, 1969; Phister, 1979; Kleijnen, 1980; Boehm, 1981). A community of interest in Economics-Driven Software Engineering Research (EDSER) has been holding annual workshops since 1999[2]. Special issues on Return on Investment have appeared in journals such as *IEEE Software* (Erdogmus et al., 2004), and books have been increasingly appearing on topics such as software business case analysis (Reifer, 2002), customer value-oriented agile methods (Cockburn, 2002; Highsmith, 2002; Schwaber and Beedle, 2002), and investment-oriented software feature prioritization and analysis (Denne and Cleland-Huang, 2004; Tockey, 2004).

A VBSE Agenda: A resulting value-based software engineering (VBSE) agenda has emerged, with the objective of integrating value considerations into the full range of existing and emerging software engineering principles and practices, and of developing an overall framework in which they compatibly reinforce each other. Some of the major elements of this agenda and example results in this book's chapters and elsewhere are discussed next.

Value-based requirements engineering includes principles and practices for identifying a system's success-critical stakeholders; eliciting their value propositions with respect to the system; and reconciling these value propositions into a mutually satisfactory set of objectives for the system. Example results include the release prioritization techniques in Chapter 12 and in (Denne and Cleland-Huang, 2004); the requirements prioritization techniques in Chapter 9 and (Karlsson and Ryan, 1997); the business case analysis techniques in (Reifer, 2002) and Chapter 6; and the stakeholder identification and requirements negotiation techniques in Chapters 6, 7, and 10.

Value-based architecting involves the further reconciliation of the system objectives with achievable architectural solutions. Example results include the multi-attribute decision support and negotiation techniques in Chapters 4 and 7; the Software Engineering Institute's Architecture Trade-off Analysis work in (Kazman et al., 2002) and (Clements et al., 2002); the concurrent system and software engineering approach in Chapter 6 and (Grünbacher et al., 2004); the software traceability techniques in Chapter 14; and the value-based software product line analyses in (Favaro, 1996) and (Faulk et al., 2000).

Value-based design and development involves techniques for ensuring that the system's objectives and value considerations are inherited by the software's design and development practices. Example results include the software traceability techniques in Chapter 14; the development tool analysis methods in Chapter 16; the process improvement ROI analysis in (van Solingen, 2004); and the customer-oriented design and development techniques in agile methods.

Value-based verification and validation involves techniques for verifying and validating that a software solution satisfies its value objectives; and processes for sequencing and prioritizing V&V tasks operating as an investing activity. Example results include the value-based testing techniques and tool investments in Chapters 10, 11, and 16; and the risk-based testing techniques in (Gerrard and Thompson, 2002).

Value-based planning and control includes principles and practices for extending traditional cost, schedule, and product planning and control techniques to in-

---

[2]http://www.cs.virginia.edu/~sullivan/EDSER-7/

clude planning and control of the value delivered to stakeholders. Example results include the value-based planning and control techniques in Chapters 6 and 8, and in (Boehm and Huang, 2003); the multi-attribute planning and decision support techniques in Chapter 4; and the release planning techniques in Chapter 12 and (Denne and Cleland-Huang, 2004).

Value-based risk management includes principles and practices for risk identification, analysis, prioritization, and mitigation. Example results include the software risk management techniques in (Boehm, 1989; Charette, 1989; DeMarco-Lister, 2003); the risk-based "how much is enough" techniques in Chapter 6; the risk-based analysis of the value of project predictability in Chapter 5; the risk-based simulation profiles in Chapter 13; the risk-based testing techniques in (Gerrard and Thompson, 2002); the insurance approach to risk management in (Raz and Shaw, 2001); and the real options analyses of intellectual property protection in Chapter 17, of modular design in (Sullivan et al., 2001), and of agile methods in (Erdogmus and Favaro, 2002).

Value-based quality management includes the prioritization of desired quality factors with respect to stakeholders' value propositions. Example results include the multi-attribute decision support techniques in Chapter 4, the quality as stakeholder value approach in (Boehm and In, 1996), the soft goal approach in (Chung et al., 1999), and the value-based approach to computer security in (Butler, 2002).

Value-based people management includes stakeholder team building and expectations management; managing the project's accommodation of all stakeholders' value propositions throughout the life cycle; and integrating ethical considerations into daily project practice. Example results include the value-based personal preferences work in Chapter 15, the approaches to developing shared tacit knowledge in agile methods, and the use of Rawls' Theory of Justice (Rawls, 1971) as a stakeholder value-based approach to software engineering ethics in (Collins et al., 1994) and Chapter 6.

A theory of value-based software engineering that connects software engineering's value-neutral computer science theory with major value-based theories such as utility theory, decision theory, dependency theory, and control theory; and that provides a process framework for guiding VBSE activities. An initial formulation of such a theory is provided in Chapter 2.

Chapter 6 summarizes seven key elements which provide further context and starting points for realizing the value-based software engineering agenda. They are:

1. Benefits Realization Analysis
2. Stakeholder Value Proposition Elicitation and Reconciliation
3. Business Case Analysis
4. Continuous Risk and Opportunity Management
5. Concurrent System and Software Engineering
6. Value-Based Monitoring and Control
7. Change as Opportunity

1.3 A Global Road Map for Realizing VBSE Benefits

Figure 3 shows a road map for making progress toward Value-Based Software Engineering and its benefits on a national or global level (Boehm and Sullivan, 2000). In the spirit of concurrent software and system engineering, it focuses its initiatives, contributions, and outcomes at the combined software and information technology (SW/IT) level. Its overall goals are to develop fundamental knowledge and practical techniques that will enable significant, measurable increase in the value created over time by software and information technology projects, products, portfolios, and the industry.

Working backward from the end objective, the road map in Figure 3 identifies a network of important intermediate outcomes. It illustrates these intermediate outcomes, dependence relationships among them, and important feedback paths by which models and analysis methods will be improved over time. The lower left part of the diagram captures tactical concerns, such as improving cost and benefit estimation for software projects, while the upper part captures strategic concerns, such as reasoning about real options and synergies between project and program elements of larger portfolios, and using the results to improve software engineering and information technology policy, research, and education.

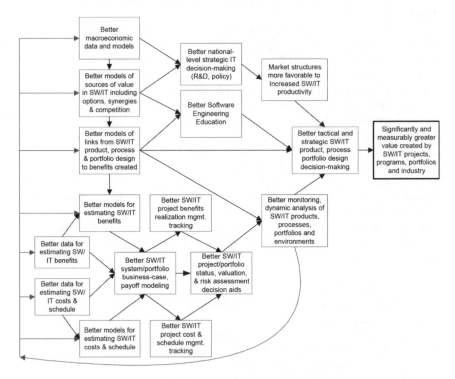

Fig. 3. Road map for realizing benefits of value-based software engineering

Making Decisions That Are Better for Value Creation

The goal of the road map is supported by a key intermediate outcome: designers and managers at all levels must make decisions that are better for value added than those they make today. Value-based decisions are of the essence in product and process design, the structure and dynamic management of larger programs, the distribution of programs in a portfolio of strategic initiatives, and national software policy. Better decision making is the key enabler of greater value added.

Value-based decision making depends in turn on a set of other advances. First, the option space within which managers and designers operate needs to be sufficiently rich. To some extent, the option space is determined by the technology market structure: which firms exist and what they produce. That structure is influenced, in turn, by a number of factors, including but not limited to national level strategic decision making, e.g., on long-term R&D investment policy, on antitrust, and so forth. The market structure determines the materials that are produced that managers and designers can then employ, and their properties.

Second, as a field we need to understand better the links between technical design mechanisms (e.g., architecture), context, and value creation to enable both better education and decision making in any given situation. An improved understanding of these links depends on developing better models of sources of value that are available to be exploited by software managers and designers in the first place (e.g., real options).

Third, people involved in decision making have to be educated in how to employ technical means more effectively to create value. In particular, they personally need to have a better understanding of the sources of value to be exploited and the links between technical decisions and the capture of value.

Fourth, dynamic monitoring and control mechanisms are needed to better guide decision makers through the option space in search of value added over time. These mechanisms have to be based on models of links between technical design and value and on system-specific models and databases that capture system status, valuation, risk, and so on: not solely as functions of software engineering parameters, such as software development cost drivers, but also of any relevant external parameters, such as the price of memory, competitor behavior, macroeconomic conditions, etc., as discussed in Section 6.6.

These system-specific models are based on better cost and payoff models and estimation and tracking capabilities, at the center of which is a business case model for a given project, program, or portfolio. Further elements of this road map are discussed in more detail in (Boehm and Sullivan, 2000).

1.4 Summary and Conclusions

As indicated in the automated test generator (ATG) example in Section 1.1, the use of value-neutral software engineering methods often causes software projects to expend significant amounts of scarce resources on activities with negative returns on investment. Just in the area of software testing, the magnitude of this wasted effort could be as high as $300 billion per year worldwide.

As indicated by the chapters in this book and related literature in the References, substantial progress is being made towards realizing the value-based software engineering (VBSE) agenda of integrating value considerations into the full range of existing and emerging software engineering practices, and of developing an overall framework in which they compatibly reinforce each other.

The seven key VBSE elements in Chapter 6 – benefits realization; stakeholder value proposition elicitation and reconciliation; business case analysis; continuous risk and opportunity management; concurrent system and software engineering; value-based monitoring and control; and change as opportunity – provide a starting point for realizing the VBSE agenda, along with the initial theory and VBSE process framework presented in Chapter 2. Evolutionary approaches for going toward VBSE practices at project, organization, national, and global levels are provided in Section 1.3.

The transition to value-based software engineering is necessarily evolutionary because it hasn't all been invented yet. There are no mature packages available on the shelf for performing software benefits analysis or value-based earned value tracking. As with everything else in information technology, VBSE is undergoing considerable change. And those who embrace this source of change as opportunity will be the first and fastest to reap its rewards.

Acknowledgements

This paper is based on research supported by the National Science Foundation, the DoD Software Intensive Systems Directorate, and the affiliates of the University of Southern California's Center for Software Engineering (USC-CSE). It owes a great deal to discussions with the USC-CSE principals, with participants in the Economics-Driven Software Engineering Research (EDSER) workshops, and with participants in the International Software Engineering Research Network (ISERN) workshops, and with the authors of the other chapters in this book. Much of Section 1.3 was co-authored by Kevin Sullivan in (Boehm and Sullivan, 2000).

References

(Boehm, 1981) Boehm, B. W.: Software Engineering Economics (Prentice Hall, 1981)

(Boehm, 1989) Boehm, B. W.: Software Risk Management (IEEE-CS Press, 1989)

(Boehm and In, 1996) Boehm, B. W. and In H.: Identifying Quality-Requirement Conflicts. IEEE Software (March 1996), pp 25–35

(Boehm and Huang, 2003) Boehm, B. W. and Huang, L.: Value-Based Software Engineering: A Case Study. IEEE Computer (March 2003), pp 33–41

(Boehm and Sullivan, 2000) Boehm, B. W., Sullivan, K., Software Economics: A Roadmap. In: The Future of Software Economics, ed by Finkelstein, A. (ACM Press, 2000), pp 319–343

(Bullock, 2000) Bullock, J.: Calculating the Value of Testing. Software Testing and Quality Engineering (May/June 2000), pp 56–62

(Butler, 2002) Butler, S.: Security Attribute Evaluation Method: A Cost-Benefit Approach. Proceedings ICSE 2002 (ACM/IEEE, May 2002), pp 232–240

(Charette, 1989) Charette, R.: Software Engineering Risk Analysis and Management (McGraw Hill, 1989)

(Chung et al., 1999) Chung, L., Nixon, B., Yu, E., Mylopoulos, J.: Non-Functional Requirements in Software Engineering (Kluwer, 1999)

(Clements et al.,2003) Clements, P., Kazman, R., Klein, M.: Evaluating Software Architecture: Methods and Case Studies (Addison Wesley, 2002)

(Cockburn, 2002) Cockburn, A.: Agile Software Development (Addison Wesley, 2002)

(Collins et al., 1994) Collins, W., Miller, K., Spielman, B., Wherry, J.: How Good is Good Enough? Communications of the ACM (January 1994), pp 81–91

(DeMarco and Lister, 2003) DeMarco, T., Lister, T.: Waltzing with Bears (Dorset House, 2003)

(Denne and Cleland-Huang, 2003) Denne, M., Cleland-Huang, J.: Software by Numbers (Prentice Hall, 2003)

(Erdogmus et al., 2004) Erdogmus, H., Favaro, J., Strigel, W. (eds.): Special Issue: Return on Investment. IEEE Software, (May/June 2004)

(Erdogmus and Favaro, 2002) Erdogmus, H., Favaro, J.: Keep your Options Open: Extreme Programming and the Economics of Flexibility. In: Extreme Programming Perspectives, ed by G. Succi et al. (Addison Wesley, 2002), pp 503–552

(Favaro, 1996) Favaro, J.: A Comparison of Approaches to Reuse Investment Analysis. Proceedings, ICSR 4, (IEEE, 1996)

(Faulk et al., 2000) Faulk, S., Harmon, D., Raffo, D.: Value-Based Software Engineering (VBSE): A Value-Driven Approach to Product-Line Engineering. Proceedings, First International Conference on Software Product Line Engineering, (August 2000)

(Gerrard and Thompson, 2002) Gerrard, P., Thompson, N.: Risk-Based E-Business Testing (Artech House, 2002)

(Grünbacher et al., 2004) Grünbacher, P., Egyed, A. F., Medvidovic, N.: Reconciling software requirements and architectures with intermediate models. In: Software and System Modeling (SoSyM), Vol. 3, No 3, (Springer, 2004), pp 235–253

(Highsmith, 2002) Highsmith, J.: Agile Software Development Ecosystems (Addison Wesley, 2002)

(Karlsson and Ryan, 1997) Karlsson, J., Ryan, K.: A Cost-Value Approach for Prioritizing Requirements. IEEE Software (September–October, 1997), pp 67–74

(Kazman et al., 2001) Kazman, R., Asundi J., Klein, M.: Quantifying the Costs and Benefits of Architectural Decisions. Proceedings, ICSE, (ACM/IEEE, 2001), pp 297–306

(Kleijnen 1980) Kleijnen, J.: Computers and Profits: Quantifying Financial Benefits of Information (Addison Wesley, 1980)

(Marschak, 1974) Marschak, J.: Economic Information, Decision, and Prediction (3 volumes), 1974

(Persson and Yilmazturk, 2004) Persson, C., Yilmazturk, N.: Establishment of Automated Regression Testing at ABB: Industrial Experience Report on 'Avoiding the Pitfalls.' Proc. ISESE 2004, IEEE, August 2004, pp 112–121

(Phister, 1979) Phister, M.: Data Processing Technology and Economics (Digital Press, 1979)

(Rawls, 1971) Rawls, J.: A Theory of Justice. (Belknap/Harvard U. Press, 1971, 1999)

(Raz and Shaw, 2001) Raz, O., Shaw, M.: Software Risk Management and Insurance. Proceedings, EDSER-3, IEEE-CS Press, 2001

(Reifer, 2002) Reifer, D.: Making the Software Business Case (Addison Wesley, 2002)

(Schwaber and Beedle, 2002) Schwaber, K., Beedle, M.: Agile Software Development with Scrum (Prentice Hall, 2002)

(Sharpe, 1969) Sharpe, W.: The Economics of Computers (Columbia U. Press, 1969)

(Sullivan et al., 2001) Sullivan, K., Cai, Y., Hallen B., Griswold, W.: The Structure and Value of Modularity in Software Design. Proceedings, ESEC/FSE, 2001, ACM Press, pp 99–108

(Tockey, 2004) Tockey, S.: Return on Software (Addison Wesley, 2004)

(van Solingen, 2004) van Solingen, R.: Measuring the ROI of Software Process Improvement. IEEE Software, May/June 2004, pp 32–38

(Webster, 2002) Webster's Collegiate Dictionary, Merriam-Webster, 2002

Author Biography

Barry Boehm is the TRW Professor of Software Engineering and Director of the Center for Software Engineering at the University of Southern California (USC). His current research interests include software process modeling, software requirements engineering, software architectures, software metrics and cost models, software engineering environments, and value-based software engineering. His contributions to the field include the Constructive Cost Model (COCOMO), the Spiral Model of the software process, and the Theory W (win-win) approach to software management and requirements determination. He is a Fellow of the primary professional societies in computing (ACM), aerospace (AIAA), electronics (IEEE), and systems engineering (INCOSE), and a member of the US National Academy of Engineering.

2 An Initial Theory of Value-Based Software Engineering

Barry Boehm and Apurva Jain

Abstract: This chapter presents an initial "4+1" theory of value-based software engineering (VBSE). The engine in the center is the stakeholder win-win Theory W, which addresses the questions of "which values are important?" and "how is success assured?" for a given software engineering enterprise. The four additional theories that it draws upon are utility theory (how important are the values?), decision theory (how do stakeholders' values determine decisions?), dependency theory (how do dependencies affect value realization?), and control theory (how to adapt to change and control value realization?). After discussing the motivation and context for developing a VBSE theory and the criteria for a good theory, the chapter discusses how the theories work together into a process for defining, developing, and evolving software-intensive systems. It also illustrates the application of the theory to a supply chain system example, discusses how well the theory meets the criteria for a good theory, and identifies an agenda for further research.

Keywords: adaptive control, benefits realization, control theory, decision theory, dependency theory, domain theories, game theory, risk/opportunity management, stakeholder win-win, Theory of Justice, Theory W, utility theory, value-based software engineering.

2.1 Introduction

The Preface and Chapter 1 provide general motivation for a value-based approach to software engineering. The particular motivation for developing and evolving a VBSE theory includes the following considerations:

- Understanding the "whys" of VBSE, as well as the "whats" and the "hows."
- Serving as an evaluation framework for VBSE practices.
- Providing principles for dealing with new software engineering situations (emergent requirements, rapid unpredictable change, commercial-off-the-shelf products (COTS), systems of systems "coopetition," global cross-cultural software development).
- Providing a unifying framework for stakeholders to reason about software investments in terms of value created.
- Helping to assess the maturity of the VBSE field (and its theory).
- Managing expectations about the universality and formality of theories involving people and unpredictable change.
- Serving as a basis for continuing improvement of VBSE and its theory.

VBSE Theory Context

A VBSE theory needs to address all of the considerations of computer science theory, plus considerations involved in the managerial aspects of software engineering, plus considerations involved in the personal, cultural, and economic values involved in developing and evolving successful software-intensive systems. Although this sounds considerably more complex, we have found that the use of success-critical stakeholder values to situate and guide technical and managerial decisions has actually made the job easier.

However, the need to deal with people considerations comes at a price with respect to the highly formalized theories of mathematics and science. These are able to be both formal and predictive because they rest on strong universal and timeless assumptions. Chances are that the flow of electricity through a conductor, the flow of air around an airfoil, or the flow of chemicals through a reactor will be the same ten years from now as they are now. However, basing a theory of software engineering on such assumptions as the flow of adoptions for a new software engineering product or the flow of data through an evolving software product being the same ten years from now will lead to theories with very short lifetimes. As a result, a VBSE theory will be less formal and, as we will see, will not be universal or timeless across a wide range of software situations, stakeholders, and products.

On the other hand, formalized theories of software engineering attempting to abstract out the people factors (e.g., programming calculi (Jones, 1980)) have tremendous difficulties in dealing with situations that are not universal (e.g., skill factors (Juristo et al., 2005)) or timeless (e.g., Maslow need hierarchies (Maslow, 1954)). A good treatment of these tensions between modernist (written, universal, general, timeless) and postmodern (oral, particular, local, timely) approaches to explanatory theories is provided in *Cosmopolis* (Toulmin, 1992).

Chapter Objectives, Approach, and Definitions

In this context, the objectives of this chapter are to: (1) *present* an *initial* theory of VBSE; (2) *illustrate* it via an example; (3) *evaluate* it with respect to criteria for a good theory; and (4) *identify an agenda* for further research.

The rest of this section will provide working definitions for "theory" and "criteria for a good theory," based on candidate definitions in the literature and our experiences in applying and evolving the stakeholder win-win Theory W (Boehm and Ross, 1989) since 1989.

A Working Definition of "Theory"

There are numerous definitions of "theory" to consider. They range from highly formal definitions such as, "A theory is a system of general laws that are spatially and temporally unrestricted and nonaccidental" (Hempel and Oppenheim, 1960; Danto and Morgenbesser, 1960), to relatively informal definitions such as "A theory is any coherent description or explanation of observed or experienced phenomena" (Gioia and Pitre, 1990). Our working definition of "theory" here follows (Torraco, 1997) from attempting to capture the strengths of both formal and informal approaches:

"A theory is a system for explaining a set of phenomena that specifies the key concepts that are operative in the phenomena and the laws that relate the concepts to each other."

Our theorems about success criteria for software-intensive enterprises will not be "spatially and temporally unrestricted and nonaccidental." This is because software-intensive enterprises and their success are subject to multiple concurrent influences, some of which are unpredictable. For example, a project that is poorly requirements-engineered and architected, poorly managed, behind schedule, and over budget can still turn into a great success with the appearance of just the right new COTS product to satisfy stakeholder needs. The reverse is true as well: "The best laid plans o' mice an' men Gang aft agley" through unforeseeable external circumstances (Burns, 1785).

Criteria for a Good Theory

Besides the references on "theory" above, we found good sets of criteria for a good theory in (Patterson, 1983) (importance, preciseness and clarity, parsimony or simplicity, comprehensiveness, operationality, empirical validity or verifiability, fruitfulness, practicality) and (Bacharach, 1989) (falsifiability, utility for explanation, and prediction). In comparing these with our previous criteria for evaluating Theory W (simple, general, specific, accurate, analytic, predictive, diagnostic, synthetic, generative), we converged on the following composite list of major criteria:

1. *Utility.* Particularly in a value-based context, does the theory favor addressing critical success factors rather than trivia?
2. *Generality.* Does the theory cover a wide range of situations and concerns (procedural, technical, economic, human)?
3. *Practicality.* Does the theory help address users' practical needs with respect to prediction, diagnosis, synthesis of solutions, generation of good practices, and explanation?
4. *Preciseness.* Does the theory provide situation-specific and accurate guidance?
5. *Parsimony.* Does the theory avoid excess complexity? Is it simple to understand, learn, and apply?
6. *Falsifiability.* Is the theory coherent enough to be empirically refuted?

We will address these criteria as we explain the VBSE theory in Section 2.2. After applying it to an example in Section 2.3, we will review how well the criteria were satisfied in Section 2.4. Section 2.5 will summarize our conclusions, and identify areas for further research.

2.2 A "4+1" Theory of Value-Based Software Engineering

Figure 4 summarizes the "4+1" theory of VBSE. Credit is due to Philippe Kruchten for originating this model form in the area of software architecture (Kruchten, 1999). The engine in the center is the success-critical stakeholder (SCS) win-win Theory W, which addresses the questions of "what values are important?" and "how is success assured?" for a given software engineering enterprise. The four additional theories that it draws upon are utility theory (how important are the values?), decision theory (how do stakeholders' values determine decisions?), dependency theory (how do dependencies affect value realization?), and control theory (how to adapt to change and control value realization?).

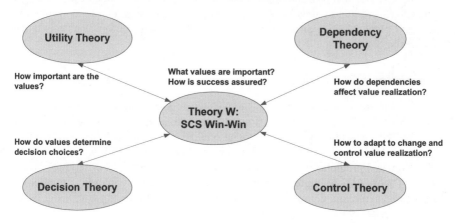

Fig. 4. The "4+1" Theory of VBSE: overall structure

The Central Engine: Theory W

The core of Theory W is the Enterprise Success Theorem: *Your enterprise will succeed if and only if it makes winners of your success-critical stakeholders.*

An informal proof follows. As discussed in Section 2.1, VBSE theorems and proofs are less formal than those in such areas as mathematics and physics.
1. Proof of "if":
2. Everyone significant is a winner.
3. Nobody significant is left to complain.
4. Proof of "only if":
5. Nobody wants to lose.
6. Prospective losers will refuse to participate, or will counterattack.
7. The usual result is lose-lose.

The proof of "if" is reasonably clear. The proof of "only if" may not be so clear, so we illustrate it in three frequently occurring examples of the primary stakeholders in an enterprise involving a customer contracting with a developer for a software system that will benefit a community of users, as shown in Figure 5.

Proposed Solution	Winner	Loser
1. Quick, cheap, sloppy Product	Developer and Customer	User
2. Lots of "bells and whistles"	Developer and User	Customer
3. Driving too hard a bargain	Customer and User	Developer

Fig. 5. Win-Lose generally becomes Lose-Lose

In Case 1, the customer and developer attempt to win at the expense of the user by skimping on effort and quality. When presented with the product, the user refuses to use it, leaving everyone a loser with respect to their expectations.

In Case 2, the developer and user attempt to win at the expense of the customer (usually on a cost-plus contract) by adding numerous low value "bells and whistles" to the product. When the customer's budget is exhausted without a resulting value adding product, again everyone is a loser with respect to their expectations.

In Case 3, the user and customer compile an ambitious set of features to be developed and pressure competing developers to bid low or lose the competition. Once on contract, the surviving bidder will usually counterattack by colluding with the user or customer to convert the project into Case 2 (adding user bells and whistles with funded Engineering Change Proposals) or Case 1 (saying, for example, "The contract specifies user-friendly error messages. For my programmers, a memory dump is a user-friendly error message and thus is a contractually compliant deliverable"). Again, everyone is a loser with respect to their expectations.

Achieving and Maintaining a Win-Win State: the Four Supporting Theories

However, the Enterprise Success Theorem does not tell us how to achieve and maintain a win-win state. This requires the Win-Win Achievement Theorem: *Making winners of your success-critical stakeholders requires (1) Identifying all of the success-critical stakeholders (SCSs); (2) Understanding how the SCSs want to win; (3) Having the SCSs negotiate a win-win set of product and process plans; (4) Controlling progress toward SCS win-win realization, including adaptation to change.*

Identifying All of the SCSs: Dependency Theory

Identifying all of the SCSs is in the province of *dependency theory*. A key technique is the Results Chain (Thorp, 1998).

Figure 6 shows a simple results chain provided as an example in *The Information Paradox* (Thorp, 1998). It establishes a framework linking Initiatives that consume resources (e.g., implement a new order entry system for sales) to Contributions (not delivered systems, but their effects on existing operations) and Outcomes, which may lead either to further contributions or to added value (e.g., increased sales). A particularly important contribution of the Results Chain is the link to Assumptions, which condition the realization of the Outcomes.

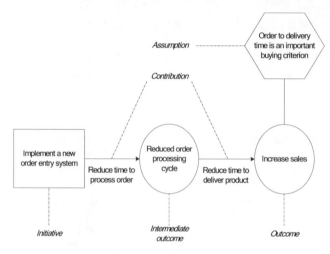

Fig. 6. Results Chain

Thus, in Figure 6, if order to delivery time turns out not to be an important buying criterion for the product being sold (e.g., stockable commodities such as soap or pencils), the reduced time to deliver the product will not result in increased sales. The Results Chain provides a valuable framework by which software project members can work with clients to identify additional non-software initiatives that may be needed to realize the potential benefits enabled by the software/IT system initiative. These may also identify some additional success-critical stakeholders who need to be represented and "bought into" the shared vision.

For example, the initiative to implement a new order entry system may reduce the time required to process orders only if an additional initiative to convince the salespeople that the new system will be good for their careers and to train them in how to use the system effectively is pursued. If the order entry system is so efficiency optimized that it does not keep track of sales credits, the salespeople will fight using it, so increased sales may also require adding capabilities to keep track of sales credits so salespeople will want to use the new system.

Further, the reduced order processing cycle will reduce the time to deliver products only if additional initiatives are pursued to coordinate the order entry system with the order fulfillment system. Some classic cases where this did not happen were the late deliveries of Hershey's Halloween candy (Carr, 2002) and Toys R US Christmas toys.

Such additional initiatives need to be added to the Results Chain. Besides increasing its realism, this also identifies additional success-critical stakeholders (salespeople and order fulfillment people) who need to be involved in the system definition and development process. The expanded Results Chain involves these stakeholders not just in a stovepipe software project to satisfy some requirements, but also in a *program* of related software and non-software initiatives focused on value-producing end results.

The Hershey's and Toys R US examples show that failing to identify an SCS such as the order fulfillment organization generally leads to failure. This makes identifying all of the SCSs essentially a necessary condition for win-win achievement. Here also, however, our informal theorems do not guarantee failure; neglectful projects can still "get lucky" and succeed if the developer or COTS vendor happens to have the additional features needed at hand. But betting on luck is not a recommended strategy.

Actually, dependency theory covers the full range of theories that help reason about how dependencies affect value realization. These include theories about product dependencies such as physics, computer science, and architectural theories (Alexander, 1979; Rechtin, 1991); theories about process dependencies, such as scheduling and concurrency theories; theories about stakeholder interdependencies, such as sociology and organization theories (Parsons, 1977; March and Simon, 1958; Argyris, 1978; Rifkin, 2004); and theories about product, process, and stakeholder interdependencies, such as economic, management, and system engineering theories (Simon, 1969; Cyert and March, 1963; Marschak and Radner, 1972; Churchman et al., 1957; Wymore, 1967; Checkland, 1981). Other examples will be provided in Section 2.4.

Understanding How the SCSs Want to Win: Utility Theory

Understanding how the SCSs want to win is in the province of *utility theory* (Dupuit, 1952; Debreu 1959; Fishburn, 1982). Misunderstanding SCS utility functions does not guarantee failure if an enterprise happens to get lucky. But again, understanding how the SCSs want to win is essentially a necessary condition for win-win achievement. Utility theory also has several branches such as the satisficing theory of bounded rationality (Simon, 1957), multi-attribute utility theory (Keeney and Raiffa, 1976), and its situation-dependent aspects such as the Maslow need hierarchy (Maslow, 1954) stating that lower level needs (food and drink; safety and security) have dominant utilities when unsatisfied and negligible utilities when satisfied.

Having the SCSs Negotiate Win-Win Plans: Decision Theory

Having the SCSs negotiate win-win plans is in the province of *decision theory*. Decision theory also has many aspects such as negotiation theory (Raiffa, 1982; Fisher and Ury, 1981), game theory (von Neumann and Morgenstern, 1944; Luce and Raiffa, 1957), multi-attribute decision theory (Keeney and Raiffa, 1976), statistical decision theory and the buying of information to reduce risk (Blackwell and Girshick, 1954), real options theory as discussed in Chapters 3 and 17, and the Theory of Justice (Rawls, 1971) discussed in Chapter 15.

Getting to a win-win decision. Navigating through all of these decision options is rather complex. One aid in the stakeholder win-win negotiation context is the win-win equilibrium theory in (Boehm and Bose, 1994) and (Lee, 1996). As illustrated in Figure 7, the win-win negotiation model begins with the success-critical stakeholders (SCSs) identifying their win conditions (or value propositions) about the system to be developed and evolved. The SCSs can include considerably more classes than users, customers, and developers. Additional SCS classes can include maintainers, administrators, interoperators of co-dependent systems, testers, marketers, venture capitalists, and, as in Section 6.8 on software engineering ethics, representatives of the least advantaged people whose health, lives, or quality of life may be affected by the system.

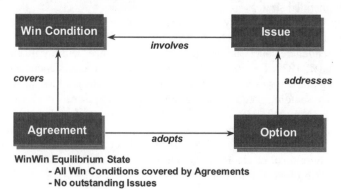

WinWin Equilibrium State
- All Win Conditions covered by Agreements
- No outstanding Issues

Fig. 7. WinWin Negotiation Model

Besides *Win Conditions*, the win-win negotiation model in Figure 7 involves *Agreements* (in which all the SCSs agree to adopt a win condition or an option), *Issues* (in which an SCS can identify a conflict between its and others' win conditions), and *Options* (proposals for resolving issues by expanding the option space). Agreements can also be reached by having the SCSs agree to adopt an option to resolve an issue.

The WinWin equilibrium state in Figure 7 holds when all the win conditions are covered by agreements, and there are no outstanding issues. At the beginning of a negotiation, this is true by default. As soon as a stakeholder enters a win condition, the other stakeholders can all accept it via an agreement, in which case the WinWin equilibrium state still holds, or some stakeholder enters an issue and an associated conflicting win condition. The negotiation then leaves the WinWin equilibrium state, and the stakeholders attempt to formulate options to resolve the issue. For example, if the conflicting win conditions are to have the system run on a Windows platform and a Unix platform, an acceptable option might be to build the system to run on Java Virtual Machine (JVM). The negotiation proceeds until all of the stakeholders' win conditions are entered and the WinWin equilibrium state is achieved, or until the stakeholders agree that the project should be disbanded because some issues are irresolvable. In such situations, it is much preferable to determine this before rather than after developing the system. And in terms of the WinWin Achievement Theorem, this also makes negotiating win-win plans a necessary condition for win-win achievement.

Controlling Progress Toward SCS Win-Win Realization: Control Theory

Controlling progress toward SCS win-win realization is in the province of *control theory*. As summarized in (Brogan, 1974) the necessary conditions for successful enterprise control are *observability* (the ability to observe the current enterprise state), *predictability* (the ability to predict whether the enterprise is heading toward an unacceptable state), *controllability* (the ability to redirect the enterprise toward an acceptable near-term state and a successful end state), and *stability* (the avoidance of positive feedback cycles that cause control systems to overcompensate and become unstable).

The application of these necessary conditions to people-intensive software enterprises does not permit the use of observability and controllability equations as precise as those in aerospace and electrical engineering, but they capture most of the wisdom provided by software management thought leaders. Examples are *"You can't control what you can't measure"* (DeMarco, 1982); *"If you don't know where you're going, a map won't help"* (Humphrey, 1989); and *"Giving people rewards for finding bugs is more likely to increase bug production than to increase software quality"* (Adams, 1995).

Particularly for VBSE, it is more important to apply control theory principles to the expected value being realized by the project rather than just to project progress with respect to plans. Traditional "earned value" systems have their uses, but they need to be complemented by business value and mission value achievement monitoring and control systems as discussed in Chapter 8 and (Boehm and Huang, 2003). These involve the use of risk management; *adaptive control* functions such as market watch and plan renegotiation; and *multicriteria control mechanisms* such as BTOPP (Morton, 1991; Thorp, 1998) and balanced scorecards (Kaplan and Norton, 1996). Particularly in an era of increasing rates of change, this makes both traditional and adaptive control (Highsmith, 2000) necessary conditions for software enterprise success in terms of the WinWin Achievement Theorem.

2.3 Using and Testing the VBSE Theory: Process Framework and Example

In this section, we present in Figure 8 a seven step process-oriented expansion of the 4+1 VBSE theory framework shown in Figure 4, and then apply it to a supply chain management system development example. In Section 2.4, we will use the results to evaluate how well it addresses the criteria for a good theory presented in Section 2.1.3.

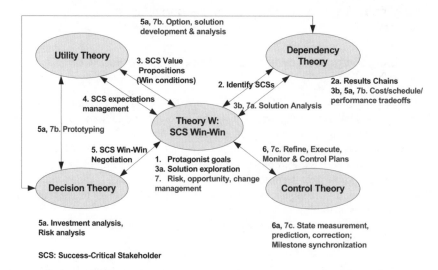

Fig. 8. Process-oriented expansion of 4+1 VBSE Theory framework

Step 1 of the process starts with a protagonist or change agent who provides the motivating force to get a new project, initiative, or enterprise started. As shown in Table 2, protagonists can be organization leaders with goals, authority, and resources, entrepreneurs with goals and resources, inventors with goals and ideas, or consortia with shared goals and distributed leadership and resources.

Table 2. Frequent protagonist classes

Protagonist Class	Goals	Authority	Ideas	Resources
Leader with Goals, Baseline Agenda	X	X	X	X
Leader with Goals, Open Agenda	X	X		X
Entrepreneur with Goals, Baseline Agenda	X		X	X
Entrepreneur with Goals, Open Agenda	X			X
Inventor with Goals, Ideas	X		X	
Consortium with Shared Goals	X	(X)		(X)

Each class of protagonist will take a somewhat different approach in visiting the seven main steps in Figure 8 to create and sustain a win-win combination of SCSs to achieve their goals. In this section, we will trace the approach taken by a leader whose goals involve a combination of opportunities and problems, who has the authority and resources to address the goals, and who is open to different ideas for addressing them. She is Susan Swanson, an experienced MBA executive, former bicycling champion, and newly hired CEO of Sierra Mountainbikes, Inc. (a fictitious company representative of two similar companies with less successful projects).

Sierra Mountainbikes Opportunities and Problems

Susan began by convening her management and technology leaders, along with a couple of external consultants, to develop a constructive shared vision of Sierra Mountainbikes' primary opportunities and problems. The results determined a significant opportunity for growth, as Sierra's bicycles were considered top quality and competitively priced. The major problem area was in Sierra's old manual order processing system. Distributors, retailers, and customers were very frustrated with the high rates of late or wrong deliveries; poor synchronization between order entry, confirmation, and fulfillment; and disorganized responses to problem situations. As sales volumes increased, the problems and overhead expenses continued to escalate.

In considering solution options, Susan and her Sierra team concluded that since their primary core competence was in bicycles rather than software, their best strategy would be to outsource the development of a new order processing system, but to do it in a way that gave the external developers a share in the system's success. As a result, to address these problems, Sierra entered into a strategic partnership with eServices Inc. for joint development of a new order processing and fulfillment system. eServices was a growing innovator in the development of supply chain management systems (in terms of Table 2, an inventor with ideas looking for leaders with compatible goals and resources to apply their ideas).

Step 2: Identifying the Success-Critical Stakeholders (SCSs)

Step 2 in the process version of the VBSE theory shown in Figure 8 involves identifying all of the success-critical stakeholders involved in achieving the project's goals. As seen in Figure 9, the Step *2a Results Chain* jointly determined by Sierra and eServices, this includes not only the sales personnel, distributors, retailers, and customers involved in order processing, but also the suppliers involved in timely delivery of Sierra's bicycle components.

The Results Chain includes initiatives to integrate the new system with an upgrade of Sierra's supplier, financial, production, and human resource management information systems. The Sierra-eServices strategic partnership is organized around both the system's results chain and business case, so that both parties share in the responsibilities and rewards of realizing the system's benefits. Thus, both parties share a motivation to understand and accommodate each other's value propositions or win conditions and to use value-based feedback control to manage the program of initiatives. This illustrates the "only if" part of the Enterprise Success Theorem. If Susan had been a traditional cost-cutting, short horizon executive, Sierra would have contracted for a lowest bidder order processing system using Case 3 in Figure 5, and would have ended up with a buggy, unmaintainable stovepipe order processing system and many downstream order fulfillment and supplier problems to plague its future.

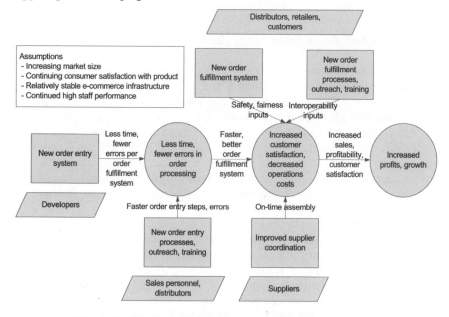

Fig. 9. Results Chain for Sierra supply chain management

In terms of the VBSE process in Figure 8, however, Sierra and eServices used the Results Chain form of Dependency Theory to identify additional SCSs (sales personnel, distributors, retailers, customers, suppliers) who also need to be brought into the SCS WinWin equilibrium state (fortunately, pollution and public safety are not major issues with bicycles, so a representative of the general public is not necessary).

Steps 3 and 4: Understanding SCS Value Propositions; Managing Expectations

As shown in Figure 10 (the first four steps in Figure 8), Step 3 (understanding all of the SCSs' value propositions or win conditions) primarily involves utility theory. But it also involves Theory W in reconciling SCS win conditions with achievable solutions (Step 3a), and various forms of dependency theory in conducting cost/schedule/performance solution trade-off, and sensitivity analyses (Step 3b).

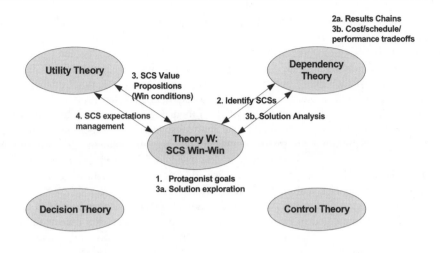

SCS: Success-Critical Stakeholder

Fig. 10. Steps 1-4 in the VBSE theory framework

For example, the suppliers and distributors may identify some complex exception reporting, trend analysis, and customer relations management features they would like to have in the system's Initial Operational Capability (IOC) in early 2006. However, the use of forms of dependency theory such as software cost and schedule estimation models may show that the dependency of IOC delivery schedule on IOC software size makes it unrealistic to try to develop the full desired feature set by the IOC date. In such a case, Sierra and eServices will have to revisit the SCSs' utility functions in Step 4 by showing them the cost and schedule model credentials and results, and asking them to expand their utility functions by prioritizing their desired features and participating in further solution exploration (a go-back to Step 3a) to achieve a win-win consensus on the top priority subset of features to include in the IOC.

It may be in some cases that the SCSs' IOC needs are irreconcilable with the IOC schedule. If so, the SCSs may need to live with a later IOC, or to declare that a SCS win-win state is unachievable and abort the project. Again, it is better to do this earlier rather than later. The particular considerations are discussed in more detail in a paper on the Schedule as Independent Variable (SAIV) process (Boehm et al., 2002).

Step 5: SCSs Negotiate a Win-Win Decision

Actually, the previous paragraph anticipates the content of Step 5, in which the SCSs negotiate a win-win decision to commit themselves to go forward. Once the SCSs have identified and calibrated their win conditions in Steps 3 and 4, the process of identifying conflicts or Issues among win conditions; inventing and exploring Options to resolve Issues; and converging on Agreements to adopt win conditions or Options proceeds as described in Section 2.2 and Chapter 7.

In a situation such as the Sierra supply chain project, the number of SCSs and the variety of their win conditions (cost, schedule, personnel, functionality, performance, usability, interoperability, etc.) means that multi-attribute decision theory will be involved as well as negotiation theory. Susan will also be concerned with investment theory or business case analysis to assure her stakeholders that the supply chain initiative will generate a strong return on investment. As many of the decisions will involve uncertainties (market trends, COTS product compatibilities, user interface choices), forms of statistical decision theory such as buying information to reduce risk will be involved as well.

User interface prototypes are actually ways of better understanding SCS utility functions, as indicated in Figure 8 by the arrow between decision theory and utility theory. The other components of Step 5a in Figure 8 involve other aspects of dependency theory, such as performance analysis, business case analysis, or critical-path schedule analysis. As also shown in Figure 8, these analyses will often proceed at increasing levels of detail in supporting steps 3a, 5a, and 7a as the project proceeds into detailed design, development, integration, and testing. Chapters 5, 10, 11, 12, 14, and 16 provide further detailed examples.

| Date | Current System | | | | New System | | | | | | | | | | | | |
| | | | | | Financial | | | | | | | | Customers | | | |
	Market Size ($M)	Market Share %	Sales	Profits	Market Share %	Sales	Profits	Cost Savings	Change in Profits	Cumulative Change in Profits	Cumulative Cost	ROI	Late Delivery %	Customer Satisfaction (0-5)	In-Transit Visibility (0-5)	Ease of Use (0-5)
12/31/03	360	20	72	7	20	72	7	0	0	0	0	**0**	12.4	**1.7**	1.0	1.8
12/31/04	400	20	80	8	20	80	8	0	0	0	4	**-1**	11.4	**3.0**	2.5	3.0
12/31/05	440	20	88	9	22	97	10	2.2	3.2	3.2	6	**-.47**	7.0	**4.0**	3.5	4.0
12/31/06	480	20	96	10	25	120	13	3.2	6.2	9.4	6.5	**.45**	4.0	**4.3**	4.0	4.3
12/31/07	520	20	104	11	28	146	16	4.0	9.0	18.4	7	**1.63**	3.0	**4.5**	4.3	4.5
12/31/08	560	20	112	12	30	168	19	4.4	11.4	29.8	7.5	**2.97**	2.5	**4.6**	4.6	4.6

Fig. 11. Expected benefits and business case

Figure 11 summarizes the business case analysis for the Sierra project; dollar values are all in millions of 2004 dollars ($M) for simplicity. The analysis compares the expected sales and profits for the current system (columns 4, 5) and the new system (columns 7, 8) between 2004 and 2008, the cumulative increase in profits, investment cost, and resulting return on investment (columns 11-13), and expected improvements in other dimensions such as late delivery and customer satisfaction (columns 14-17). The bottom line is a strong 2.97 ROI, plus good expected outcomes in the customer satisfaction dimensions. More detail can be found in Chapter 12 and (Boehm and Huang, 2003).

The negotiations converge on a number of win-win agreements, such as involving the suppliers and distributors in reviews, prototype exercising, and beta testing; having Sierra provide eServices with two of its staff members to work on the software development team; and agreeing on compatible data definitions for product and monetary exchange. At one point in the negotiation, an unfortunate go-back is necessary when an Agreement on a product definition standard is reversed by the management of one of the distributors, who discloses that it is now committed to an emerging international standard. After some renegotiation, the other SCSs agree to this at some additional cost. But it brings up another necessary condition for successful win-win negotiations (and other collaborative vestures such as agile methods): that the stakeholder representatives be CRACK (collaborative, representative, authorized, committed, and knowledgeable) participants (Boehm and Turner, 2004). Some other perspectives on win-win management are in (Waitley, 1985) and (Covey, 1989).

Steps 6 and 7: Planning, Executing, Monitoring, Adapting, and Controlling

As with the dependency analyses, project planning, executing, monitoring, adapting, and controlling proceed incrementally in increasing amounts of details, generally following a risk-driven spiral process. Questions such as "how much is enough planning, specifying, prototyping, COTS evaluation, business case analysis, architecting, documenting, verifying, validating, etc.?" are best resolved by balancing the risk exposures of doing too little or too much. As *Risk Exposure = Probability (Loss) * Value (Loss)* is a value-based concept, risk balancing is integral to VBSE. See (Boehm and Turner, 2004) and (Port and Chen, 2004), for example, "how much is enough?' analyses.

Value-based planning and control differs most significantly from traditional project planning and control in its emphasis on monitoring progress toward value realization rather than toward project completion. Particularly in an era of increasing rates of change in market, technology, organizational, and environmental conditions, there is an increasing probability that managing to a fixed initial set of plans and specifications will produce systems that are out of step and non-competitive with projects managing adaptively toward evolving value realization.

Perhaps the most provocative example is the traditional technique of "earned value management." It assigns "value" to the completion of project tasks and helps track progress with respect to planned budgets and schedules, but has no way of telling whether completing these tasks will add to or subtract from the business value or mission value of the enterprise. Example failure modes from this approach are systems that had to be 95% redeveloped on delivery because they failed to track evolving requirements (Boehm, 1973), and startup companies that failed to track closure of market windows.

If an organization has used steps 1-5 to identify SCSs, determine their value propositions, and develop business cases, it has developed the framework to monitor expected value realization, adjust plans, and control progress toward real SCS value achievement. Figure 12 shows how this is done for the Sierra project, based on the initial budgets, schedules, and business case in Figure 11. Value-based monitoring and control for Sierra requires additional effort in terms of technology watch and market watch, but these help Sierra to discover early that their in-transit-visibility (ITV) COTS vendor was changing direction away from Sierra's needs.

Milestone	Schedule	Cost ($K)	Op'l Cost Savings	Market Share %	Annual Sales ($M)	Annual Profits ($M)	Cum. Profits	ROI	Late Delivery %	Customer Satisfaction	ITV	Ease of Use	Risks/Opportunities
Life Cycle	3/31/04	400		20	72	7.0			12.4	1.7	1.0	1.8	(1)
Architecture	3/31/04	427		20	72	7.0			12.4	1.7	1.0	1.8	
Core	7/31/04	1,050											
Capability	7/20/04	1,096								2.4*	1.0*	2.7*	(2)
Demo (CCD)													
Software Init.	9/30/04	1,400											
Op. Cap. (IOC)	9/30/04	1,532								2.7*	1.4*	2.8*	
Hardware	9/30/04	3,500											
IOC	10/11/04	3,432											(3)
Deployed	12/31/04	4,000		20	80	8.0	0.0	-1.0	11.4	3.0	2.5	3.0	(4)
IOC	12/20/04	4,041		22	88	8.6	0.6	-.85	10.8	2.8	1.6	3.2	
Responsive	3/31/05	4,500	300						9.0	3.5	3.0	3.5	
IOC	3/30/05	4,604	324						7.4	3.3	1.6	3.8	
Full Op.	7/31/05	5,200	1,000							3.5*	2.5*	3.8*	(5)
Cap. CCD	7/28/05	5,328	946										
Full Op.	9/30/05	5,600	1,700							3.8*	3.1*	4.1*	
Cap. Beta	9/30/05	5,689	1,851										
Full Op.	12/31/05	6,000	2,200	22	106	12.2	3.2	-.47	7.0	4.0	3.5	4.0	
Cap. Deployed	12/20/05	5,977	2,483	24	115	13.5	5.1	-.15	4.8	4.1	3.3	4.2	
Release 2.1	6/30/06	6,250											

1. Increased COTS ITV risk, fallback identified.
2. Using COTS ITV fallback; new HW competitor; renegotiating HW
3. $200,000 savings from renegotiated HW.
4. New COTS ITV source identified, being prototyped.
5. New COTS ITV source initially integrated.
* Interim ratings based on trial use

Fig. 12. Value-based expected/actual outcome tracking

This enabled Sierra to adapt by producing a timely fallback plan, and to proactively identify and approach other likely ITV COTS vendors. The results, as shown in the ITV column and explained in the Risks/Opportunities column of Figure 12, was an initial dip in achieved ITV rating relative to plans, but a recovery to close to the originally planned value. The Risks/Opportunities column also shows a "new hardware competitor" opportunity found by market watch activities that results in a $200,000 hardware cost savings that mostly compensated for the added software costs of the ITV fallback. The use of prioritized requirements to drive value-based Pareto- and risk-based inspection and testing, as discussed in Chapter 1 and (Gerrard and Thompson, 2002), is another source of software cost savings.

The bottom-line results are a good example of multi-attribute quantitative/qualitative balanced scorecard methods of value-based monitoring, adaptation, and control. They are also a good example of use of the necessary conditions for value-based control based on control theory. A traditional value-neutral "earned value" management system would fail on the criteria of business value observability, predictability, and controllability, because its plans, measurements, and controls deal only with internal-project progress and not with external business value observables and controllables. They also show the value of adaptive control in changing plans to address new risks and opportunities, along with the associated go-backs to revisit previous analyses and revise previous plans in Steps 7a, 7b, and 7c.

2.4 VBSE Theory Evaluation

The Sierra example in Section 2.3 provides an opportunity to evaluate the VBSE theory with respect to the criteria for a good theory presented in Section 2.1.

Utility: Addressing Critical Success Factors. The Results Chain method in Step 2 identified missing success-critical initiatives and stakeholders that were the downfall of supply chain initiatives at Hershey's and Toys R US. The risk-driven inspection and test approaches in Step 6 avoid wasting inspection and test time on trivial-value aspects of the system.

Generality: Covering procedural, technical, economic, and human concerns; covering small and large systems. The seven-step process with its ability to accommodate parallel activities and go-backs was sufficient to cover the Sierra project's procedural needs. Technical and economic concerns are addressed in the use of dependency theory for cost, schedule, performance, and business case analyses in Steps 3a, 5a, and 7b. Human concerns are the essence of Theory W and utility theory, and of the SCS negotiations in Step 5. The steps in the VBSE theory have worked well for several midsized supply chain and customer relations management systems similar to Sierra; for over 100 small real-client e-services projects at USC; and as a framework for addressing very large systems of systems in such areas as defense and air traffic control.

Practicality: Supporting practical needs for prediction, diagnosis, solution synthesis, good practice generation, and explanation. The theory draws on a wide variety of dependency models (e.g., cost, schedule, performance, quality) to *predict* outcomes. In a stable, well-understood environment, managing to the predictions usually produces a self-fulfilling prophecy. In less stable and less familiar situations such as the Sierra case study, dependency theory was able to *diagnose* risks such as missing stakeholders in Step 2, Theory W was able to support *synthesis* of SCS win-win solutions in Steps 3-5, and adaptive control theory was able to generate good value-achievement monitoring practices to support in-process diagnosis and resynthesis in Steps 6-7. The control theory necessary conditions of observability and controllability were able to *explain* why traditional earned value systems would not have addressed and resolved these value domain problems.

Preciseness: Providing situation-specific and accurate guidance. The theory is no more (and no less) accurate than its constituent theories in predicting outcomes of unprecedented situations, but it is able to provide situation-specific guidance, as shown in its application to the Sierra supply chain project. Also, several examples were provided in Section 2.3 of how the theory would have generated different guidance in different situations, such as with the distributor management's reversal of a win-win agreement on a product definition standard in Step 5, and with the ITV COTS vendor's change of direction in Steps 6 and 7.

Parsimony: Avoiding excess complexity; ease of learning and application. The theory's use of risk management to determine "how much is enough" planning, specifying, testing, etc. helps avoid excess complexity and to make "everything as simple as possible, but no simpler" (Albert Einstein). Its ease of learning and use has been tested mainly on USC's over 100 e-services projects. These are developed by teams of five or six MS students who learn the technologies as they go, and have a 92% success rate of on-time, satisfied customer delivery (Boehm et al., 1998).

Flexibility: Ability to be empirically refuted. The case study identified a particular situation in which application of the theory could not produce a win-win solution, leading to a timely decision to cancel the project. This involved incompatible and nonnegotiable SCS win conditions about Initial Operational Capability content and schedule in Steps 3 and 4. A similar outcome could have resulted from the distributor management change of direction in Step 5.

Actually, there are several other classes of situations in which our experience has shown that the win-win approach may not succeed. These are:

- *People may disguise their true win conditions.* In one situation, a stakeholder rejected a COTS product for being too expensive. When the price was lowered, the stakeholder said that some essential features were missing. When the vendor offered to supply the features at no extra cost, the true reason came out: the stakeholder had had bad dealings with the COTS vendor in the past.
- *Some people like to win by making others losers.* It is best to seek other partners when you encounter such people.
- *You can't make omelets without breaking eggs.* Many large-scale dams that benefited millions of people had to drown some other people's homes and villages. Generous payment can reduce the loss, but generally not eliminate it.

- *Some situations have only one winner.* A good example involves political elections, in which political parties are motivated to discredit and demonize candidates and platforms of other parties.

However, many apparent only-one-winner or zero-sum-game situations can be turned into win-win situations by expanding the option space. A good example is provided in *Getting to Yes* (Fisher and Ury, 1981), in which a boundary-line location stalemate on ownership of the Sinai Desert between Egypt and Israel was resolved by creating a new option: the land was given back to Egypt, satisfying its territorial win condition, but it was turned into a demilitarized zone, satisfying Israel's security win condition. Other examples are provided in (Boehm and Ross, 1989).

2.5 Conclusions and Areas for Further Research

The VBSE theory presented above has been shown to apply well to a reasonably complex supply chain application. In other situations, versions of the theory have been successfully applied to over 100 small e-services applications, and to some very large software-intensive systems of systems.

The VBSE theory satisfies the main criteria for a good theory (utility, generality, practicality, preciseness, parsimony, and falsifiability) reasonably well, particularly when compared to other theories involving explanations of human behavior.

The theory identifies several fruitful areas for further research, some, such as elaborations of aspects of utility theory, decision theory, and dependency theory to address particular VBSE issues, are discussed in other chapters in this book. Others are identified in the VBSE agenda but not covered in the book, such as extensions of the theory to cover areas like programming methodology, agile methods, quality assurance, COTS-based applications, software maintenance, and combinations of these and the other areas covered.

Another area we are exploring is the extension of the current theory to provide a theory of value-based systems engineering. The systems engineering field is inherently value-based, and shares many of the same challenges as software engineering, but also brings additional considerations of hardware phenomenology and hardware-software-peopleware trade-offs into the arena.

Finally, as with all theories, the initial VBSE theory needs many more tests. The easiest tests to start with are those of its ability to explain differences between success and failure on completed projects. Other tests that can be done right away are those of its ability to generate good software engineering practices; an early example is in (Boehm and Ross, 1989).

Further analyses can be performed on its consistency with other theories, such as the chaos theories underlying agile and adaptive software development (Highsmith, 2002) or the theories underlying formal software development (Jones, 1980) and generative programming approaches (Czarnecki and Eisenecker, 2000).

Tests of utility, generality, practicality, preciseness, and parsimony basically involve trying to apply the theory in different situations, observing its successes and shortfalls, and generating improvements in the theory that enhance its capability in different situations or uncover unstated assumptions that should be made explicit to limit its domain of dependable applicability. We hope that this initial presentation of the theory will be sufficiently attractive for people to give this option a try.

Acknowledgments

The research on this Chapter has been supported by a National Science Foundation grant, "Value-Based Science of Design," and by the Affiliates of the USC Center for Software Engineering.

References

(Adams, 1995) Adams, S.: Dilbert Comic Strips, 1995

(Alexander, 1979) Alexander, C.: The Timeless Way of Building (Oxford University Press, 1979)

(Argyris, 1978) Argyris, C.: Organizational Learning (Addison-Wesley, 1978)

(Bacharach, 1989) Bacharach, S. B.: Organizational theories: Some criteria for evaluation. Academy of management review, 14 (4), pp 496–515

(Boehm, 1973) Boehm, B. W.: Software and Its Impact: A Quantitative Assessment. Datamation, May 1973, pp 48–59

(Boehm and Bose, 1994) Boehm, B. W., Bose P.: A Collaborative Spiral Software Process Model Based on Theory W. Proceedings, ICSP 3, IEEE, Oct. 1994

(Boehm and Huang, 2003) Boehm B., Huang L.: Value-Based Software Engineering: A Case Study. IEEE Computer, March 2003, pp 21–29

(Boehm and Turner, 2004) Boehm, B. W., Turner R.: Balancing Agility and Discipline (Addison Wesley, 2004)

(Boehm and Ross, 1989) Boehm, B. W., Ross, R.: Theory-W Software Project Management: Principles and Examples. IEEE Transactions Software Engineering, July 1989, pp 902–916

(Boehm et al., 2002) Boehm, B. W., Port, D., Huang, L., Brown, W.: Using the Spiral Model and MBASE to Generate New Acquisition Process Models: SAIV, CAIV, and SCQAIV. CrossTalk, January 2002, pp 20–25

(Boehm et al., 1998) Boehm, B. W., Egyed, A., Kwan, J., Port, D., Shah, A., Madachy, R.: Using the WinWin Spiral Model: A Case Study. IEEE Computer, July 1998, pp 33–44

(Blackwell and Girshick, 1954) Blackwell, D., Girshick, M.: Theory of Games and Statistical Decisions (Wiley, 1954)

(Brogan, 1974) Brogan W.: Modern Control Theory, 3rd edition (Prentice Hall, 1991)

(Burns, 1785) Burns, R.: To a Mouse, November 1785

(Carr, 2002) Carr, D.: Sweet Victory (Baseline, December 2002)

(Checkland, 1981) Checkland, P.: Systems Thinking, Systems Practice (Wiley, 1981)

(Churchman et al., 1957) Churchman, C. W., Ackoff, R., Arnoff, E.: An Introduction to Operations Research (Wiley, 1957)

(Covey, 1989) Covey, S.: The Seven Habits of Highly Successful People (Fireside/Simon & Schuster, 1989)

(Cyert and March, 1963) Cyert, R. M., March, J.G.: A Behavioral Theory of the Firm (Prentice Hall, 1963)

(Czarnecki and Eisenecker, 2002) Czarnecki K., Eisenecker, U.: Generative Programming: Methods, Tools, and Applications (Addison-Wesley, 2000)

(Danto and Morgenbesser, 1960) Danto A., Morgenbesser S. (eds.): Philosophy of Science (Meridian Books, 1960)

(Debreu, 1959) Debreu, G.: Theory of Value (Wiley, 1959)

(DeMarco, 1982) DeMarco T.: Controlling Software Projects (Yourdon Press, 1982)

(Dupuit, 1952) Dupuit, J.: On the Measurement of the Utility of Public Works, Translated by R. H. Barback, International Economic Papers 2:83–110, 1844 (1952)

(Fishburn, 1982) Fishburn, P. C.: The Foundations of Expected Utility (Dordrecht, 1982)

(Fisher and Ury, 1981) Fisher, R., Ury, W.: Getting To Yes: Negotiating Agreement Without Giving In (Houghton Mifflin, 1981)

(Gerrard and Thompson, 2002) Gerrard, P., Thompson, N.: Risk-Based E-Business Testing (Artech House, 2002)

(Gioia and Pitre, 1990) Gioia, D. A., Pitre, E.: Multi-paradigm perspectives on theory building. Academy of Management Review. **15**, pp 584–602

(Hempel and Oppenheimer, 1960) Hempel, C. G., Oppenheim, P.: Problems of the Concept of General Law. In: Danto, A., Mogenbesser, S. (eds.): Philosophy of Science (Meridian Books, 1960)

(Highsmith, 2000) Highsmith, J.: Adaptive Software Development (Dorset House, 2000)

(Highsmith, 2002) Highsmith, J.: Agile Software Development Ecosystems (Addison Wesley, 2002)

(Humphrey, 1989) Humphrey, W. S.: Managing the Software Process (Addison Wesley, 1989)

(Jones, 1980) Jones, C. B.: Software development: A rigorous approach (Prentice Hall, 1980)

(Juristo et al., 2005) Juristo, N., Moreno, A., Acuna, S.: A Software Process Model Handbook for Incorporating People's Capabilities (Kluwer, 2005)

(Kaplan and Norton, 1996) Kaplan, R., Norton, D.: The Balanced Scorecard: Translating Strategy into Action (Harvard Business School Press, Cambridge 1996)

(Keeney and Raiffa, 1976) Keeney, R. L., Raiffa, H.: Decisions with Multiple Ob-
    jectives: Preferences and Value Tradeoffs (Cambridge University Press, Cam-
    bridge 1976)
(Kruchten, 1999) Kruchten, P.: The Rational Unified Process: An Introduction
    (Addison Wesley, 1999)
(Lee, 1996) Lee, M. J.: Foundations of the WinWin Requirements Negotiation
    System PhD dissertation (University of Southern California, 1996)
(Luce and Raiffa, 1957) Luce, R. D., Raiffa, H.: Games and Decisions (Wiley,
    1957)
(March and Simon, 1958) March, J., Simon, H.: Organizations (Wiley, 1958)
(Marschak and Radner, 1972) Marschak, J., Radner, R.: Economic Theory of
    Teams (Yale University Press, 1972)
(Maslow, 1954) Maslow, A.: Motivation and Personality (Harper, 1954)
(Parsons, 1977) Parsons, T.: Social Systems and the Evolution of Action Theory
    (The Free Press, 1977)
(Patterson, 1983) Patterson, C. H.: Theories of counseling and psychotherapy
    (Harper and Row, 1983)
(Port and Chen, 2004) Port, D., Chen, A.: Assessing COTS Assessment: How
    Much Is Enough? ICCBSS 2004 Proceedings (Springer, 2004)
(Raiffa, 1982) Raiffa, H.: The Art and Science of Negotiation (Belknap/Harvard
    U. Press, 1982)
(Rawls, 1971, 1999) Rawls, J.: A Theory of Justice (Belknap/Harvard U. Press,
    1971, 1999)
(Rechtin, 1991) Rechtin, E.: Systems Architecting: Creating and Building Com-
    plex Systems (Prentice-Hall, 1991)
(Rifkin, 2004) Rifkin, S.: The Parsons Game: The First Simulation of Talcott Par-
    sons' Theory of Action PhD dissertation (George Washington University,
    2004)
(Morton, 1991) Morton, M. S.: The Corporation of the 1990s: Information Tech-
    nology and Organization Transformation (Oxford University Press, Oxford
    1991)
(Simon, 1969) Simon, H.: The Science of the Artificial (MIT Press, 1969)
(Simon, 1957) Simon, H.: Models of Man (Wiley, 1957)
(Thorp et al., 1998) Thorp, J., DMR's Center for Strategic Leadership: The Infor-
    mation Paradox: Realizing the Benefits of Information Technology (McGraw-
    Hill, 1998)
(Torraco, 1997) Torraco, R. J.: Theory-building research methods. In: Swanson,
    R. A., Holton III, E. F. (eds.): Human resource development handbook: Link-
    ing research and practice (Berrett-Koehler, 1997), pp 114–137
(Toulmin, 1992) Toulmin, S.: Cosmopolis: The Hidden Agenda of Modernity (U.
    of Chicago Press, 1992 reprint edition)
(von Neumann and Morgenstern, 1944) von Neumann, J., Morgenstern, O.: The-
    ory of Games and Economic Behavior (Princeton University Press, 1944)
(Waitley, 1985) Waitley, D.: The Double Win (Berkley, 1985)
(Wymore, 1967) Wymore, A. W.: A Mathematical Theory of Systems Engineer-
    ing: The Elements (Wiley, New York 1967)

Author Biographies

Barry Boehm is the TRW Professor of Software Engineering and Director of the Center for Software Engineering at the University of Southern California (USC). His current research interests include software process modeling, software requirements engineering, software architectures, software metrics and cost models, software engineering environments, and value-based software engineering. His contributions to the field include the Constructive Cost Model (COCOMO), the Spiral Model of the software process, and the Theory W (win-win) approach to software management and requirements determination. He is a Fellow of the primary professional societies in computing (ACM), aerospace (AIAA), electronics (IEEE), and systems engineering (INCOSE), and a member of the US National Academy of Engineering.

Apurva Jain is a PhD candidate student in the Computer Science department at the University of Southern California. His research interests include software management and economics, software architecture, and value-based software engineering.

3 Valuation of Software Initiatives Under Uncertainty: Concepts, Issues, and Techniques

Hakan Erdogmus, John Favaro and Michael Halling

Abstract: State of the practice in software engineering economics often focuses exclusively on cost issues and technical considerations for decision making. Value-based software engineering (VBSE) expands the cost focus by also considering benefits, opportunities, and risks. Of central importance in this context is valuation, the process for determining the economic value of a product, service, or a process. Uncertainty is a major challenge in the valuation of software assets and projects. This chapter first introduces uncertainty along with other significant issues and concepts in valuation, and surveys the relevant literature. Then it discusses decision tree and options-based techniques to demonstrate how valuation can help with dynamic decision making under uncertainty in software development projects.

Keywords: Software economics, valuation, net present value, discounted cash flow, uncertainty, decision tree, real options.

3.1 Introduction

Technological and economic factors put enormous competitive pressures on organizations producing software and providing services and products that rely on software. As a result, software professionals and managers at all levels have to make decisions in complex situations under uncertainty and conflicting goals. They have to take many variables into consideration. Academic research and industrial practice have by and large tackled decision making in software development by focusing on the cost side, for example, by looking for more efficient ways to develop software or by evaluating new software initiatives only in terms of development effort. However, determining the value of a new initiative requires other important dimensions, benefits, and uncertainty, to be accounted for as well. Without these dimensions, the consequences of product or process decisions cannot be properly evaluated.

Several authors have explicitly promoted value, as opposed to cost alone, as a basis for decision making in software engineering (Favaro, 1996; Favaro et al., 1998; Favaro, 1999; Biffl and Halling, 2001; Boehm and Sullivan, 1999; Port et al., 2002; Boehm 2003). In Chapter 1 Boehm identifies seven key elements for value-based software engineering (VBSE). Among these elements, valuation specifically addresses *Business Case Analysis*, *Continuous Risk and Opportunity Management*, and *Change as Opportunity*. Focusing on these elements naturally positions valuation more as a management activity than as a tool for technical decision making, although valuation concepts are relevant and have been applied to technical decisions in software engineering as well (Sullivan et al., 1999). This chapter addresses valuation from a management perspective in terms of its ability to help with decisions at the project level. The aim is to orient the reader and illustrate how economic value can be leveraged to make project-level decisions, rather than describe a specific valuation process or provide a self-contained exposition of the topic.

The chapter is organized as follows. Section 3.2 draws attention to the main issues that make valuation difficult and provides pointers to the relevant literature. Sections 3.3 and 3.4 focus on the treatment of uncertainty and dynamic decisions. Section 3.3 first discusses a decision-theoretic approach through an illustrative example and introduces the notion of an *option*. Section 3.4 then builds on this approach to explain how projects with growth opportunities and abandonment strategies can be analyzed using *real options* theory.

It is impossible to cover a topic as diverse as valuation with its rich theoretical foundations and multiplicity of underlying techniques in a single chapter. However we hope to provide a glimpse by focusing on the most thorny issues and on the techniques that we deem most illustrative and promising. For the reader who desires a deeper investigation, Section 3.4 provides many references for further reading. Finally, Section 3.5 gives a summary and discusses the difficulties regarding the adoption of the various techniques mentioned.

3.2 Issues in Valuation

Valuation is the process of determining the economic value of an asset, be it a product, a service, or a process. In simple terms, *value* is defined as the net worth, or the difference between the benefits and the costs of the asset, all adjusted appropriately for risk, at a given point in time. When the costs are disregarded, are implicit, or have been incurred before the point at which an asset is evaluated, the value may refer to future benefits or the remaining worth of the asset at that point. Several factors make valuation a difficult endeavor:

- Costs and benefits might occur at different points in time and need to be downward adjusted, or *discounted*, to account for *time value of money*: the fundamental principle that money is worth more today than in the future under ordinary economic conditions. Discounted Cash Flow and related techniques handle time value of money. These are illustrated in the earlier parts of Section 3.3.
- Not all determinants of value are known at the time of the valuation due to uncertainty inherent in the environment. Modeling uncertainty is more often an art than a science. Section 3.3 shows how decision tree and options-based approaches can help address uncertainty.
- The appropriate discount rate to use depends on the risk carried by a project and the return expected on alternative initiatives. These factors must be analyzed to determine the discount rate. Chapter 5 tackles this topic.

- Sometimes intangible benefits such as learning, growth opportunities, and embedded flexibility are the dominant sources of value under uncertainty. These benefits are hard to quantify and require more advanced techniques such as decision trees and real options analysis that are designed to deal with uncertainty. While later parts of Section 3.3 introduce decision trees, Section 3.4 discusses real options.
- Value is to a certain extent in the eye of the beholder: risk preferences of stakeholders who make resource decisions influence it. Section 3.2 briefly talks about the techniques for taking into account risk preferences in valuation.
- When assets are interdependent, it may be more appropriate to treat them as parts of a whole. This calls for a portfolio-based approach. Section 3.2 provides a short discussion on project portfolios.
- When stakeholders have clashing incentives and different information, value can be destroyed or become hard to judge. While these effects are unavoidable, incorporating them into valuation may lead to more objective results. Section 3.2 touches upon how they can affect value creation.

The remainder of this section draws attention to these issues and provides pointers for tackling them. It is impossible to do justice to all of these issues in the space allocated. Therefore, Sections 3.3 and 3.4 focus on the basic valuation concepts as well as the treatment of uncertainty, covered by the first four bullets above. The treatment of uncertainty is especially important from the VBSE perspective because uncertainty is prevalent in software development and can be a significant source of value creation or destruction depending on how it is managed. The different techniques and approaches discussed in the chapter are summarized in Table 3 at the end of the chapter.

Beyond Cost-Benefit Analysis

The valuation of software assets and projects depends on a detailed analysis of underlying costs and benefits. A prerequisite for cost-benefit analysis is the identification of the relevant value and cost drivers. While models for software development costs are well-established, comprehensive definitions of individual value drivers (e.g., performance variables that support decision making and prioritization) and frameworks for value creation in software engineering have been missing.

Models exist in economic theory for the analysis of value creation. The most prominent is the model of Porter (Porter, 1985; Porter and Millar, 1985), based on value chain analysis. The core idea behind this model is the definition of value as "the amount buyers are willing to pay for what a supplier provides them." The application of Porter's model to software projects would involve definition of strategic goals, identification of critical activities, definition of product properties, and analysis of the value of these activities and properties. The buyer perspective of value gives rise to a single-dimensional, external measure, which is more objective and easier to reason about than those given rise by multidimensional, internal perspectives.

A special challenge for cost-benefit analysis in software engineering is the assessment of intangible or soft benefits, the influence of time on the value of these benefits and costs, and the consideration of uncertainty. However these situations are not unique to software development. Comparable situations can be found in the valuation of public goods and social investments; see (Layard and Glaister, 1994) for an example.

Intangible benefits should in the long run lead to an improvement in monetary terms (Powell, 1992). These benefits include flexibility and learning, which can generate significant long-term value in software development. Traditional cost-oriented techniques (Boehm, 1984; Boehm, 2000) address only tangible benefits such as direct savings due to reduced effort. Real options analysis is a promising approach that can address this gap. Sections 3.3 and 3.4 will discuss this approach and the underlying theory.

Modeling Uncertainty

In addition to benefits and costs, the valuation process must consider uncertainty. Uncertainty arises from different sources. Natural uncertainty directly relates to variations in the environment variables (e.g., the variation in the number of defects in a software product). Parameter uncertainty relates to the estimation of parameters (e.g., the reliability of the average number of defects). Model uncertainty relates to the validity of specific models used (e.g., the suitability of a certain distribution to model the defects). Kitchenham and Linkman (1997) provide a taxonomy of uncertainty for software engineering that includes additional sources such as scope error and assumption error.

The traditional approach of handling uncertainty is by defining probability distributions for the underlying quantities, allowing the application of standard calculus. Other approaches based on fuzzy measures or Bayesian networks (Klir and Wiermann, 1998) consider different types of prior knowledge. Srivastava and Mock (2002) have successfully applied these approaches to analyze business decisions.

Main financial theories, such as the traditional portfolio theory (Markowitz, 1952, Lintner, 1965) and the Capital Asset Pricing Model (CAPM) (Sharpe, 1964, Mossin, 1966), consider both expected returns and borne risks in order to value alternative trading strategies. This means that uncertainty and resulting risks can also be seen from an opportunistic perspective. If appropriately rewarded, risks are warranted depending on the investors' risk attitudes, but an appropriate risk premium is expected for additional risk borne when uncertainty increases. The reason behind this argument is that risk, as measured by the standard deviation of expected returns, includes both positive and negative variability. The determination of this risk premium and the resulting *risk-adjusted discount rate* are central to valuation, especially in discounted cash flow models (Myers, 1974, Black, 1988).

These are briefly discussed in the beginning of Section 3.3, but elaborated in more detail in Chapter 5.

Attitudes of Decision Makers

When stakeholders take on decision making roles about allocation of limited resources, their decisions are to an extent driven by their attitudes toward risk and how they tend to respond to uncertainty. These attitudes are reflected in the decision maker's assessment of value derived from the underlying resource allocation activity. The main modeling concept here is utility. Although in software engineering economics, utility functions are often introduced to avoid assigning monetary value to benefits and costs, the concept of utility in finance has a different foundation.

Utility functions in finance mainly model investors' risk aversion. While according to traditional portfolio theory, investors directly care about the mean (expected returns) and variance (risk or volatility) of asset returns, utility functions defined over wealth offer more flexibility to account for risk. The shape of the utility function determines the intensity of the investor's risk aversion, that is, how the decision maker's attitude toward risk distorts the losses and gains of varying amounts. For example, the magnitude of the negative utility a risk-averse person would assign to a *loss* of a certain amount would be higher than the magnitude of the positive utility he would assign to a *gain* of an equivalent amount.

Furthermore, one can distinguish between absolute and relative risk aversion. Absolute risk aversion is a measure of an investor's reaction to uncertainty relating to absolute changes in wealth. Absolute risk aversion decreases with wealth, implying that a billionaire would be relatively unconcerned with a risk that might worry a poor person. Absolute risk aversion is measured by the relative change in the slope of the utility function at a particular level of wealth. Relative risk aversion in contrast is a measure of an investor's reaction to uncertainty relating to percentage changes in wealth. Absolute and relative risk aversion are connected. For example, constant relative risk aversion, a common assumption, implies diminishing absolute risk aversion (i.e., investors become less risk averse as their wealth increases).

Utility functions can be employed in a similar way to model organizational and individual attitudes toward risk in the valuation of non-financial assets as they are used in finance to model investors' risk aversion. They have also proven to be a key factor in the integration of the decision tree and real options approaches described later in this chapter (Smith and Nau, 1995).

Chapter 4 discusses the use of utility in the context of multi-attribute decision making. While Chapter 4 also surveys several other techniques that address value from a multidimensional perspective, in this chapter, we consider value only from a single-dimensional, economic perspective. Economics are considered most important in making business decisions, and as such form the basis of valuation. The multi-attribute perspective is of interest when aspects of value that cannot be reduced to monetary terms are important for the underlying decisions, but valuation is not concerned with nonmonetary definitions of value.

Project Portfolios

Interactions among multiple projects often affect value. For accurate reasoning, the valuation model must consider these interactions. This implies the use of a portfolio-based approach. In a portfolio-based approach, assets are not valued in isolation. The value of a portfolio of assets is not simply the sum of its parts.

An important concept here is diversification. Diversification refers to an investor's ability to limit the net effect of uncertainty on the value of an investment by spreading the investment over multiple risky assets. The resulting reduction in overall risk impacts the value of the portfolio. In order to quantify the risk reduction, one must know the correlation between the investment opportunities. The impact of diversification is largest if the different investment opportunities are negatively correlated and it is smallest if they are positively correlated.

While calculating correlations is straightforward for financial assets with observable prices, it is not so for a group of software projects. Projects in a portfolio can have different types of dependencies, due to shared infrastructure and resources that are hard to identify and measure. The type of dependency determines applicable valuation methods. This represents an important difference from financial portfolio theory where one-dimensional correlation structures with respect to observed prices are sufficient. Therefore existing financial methods (Markowitz, 1952) must be adapted to the software engineering context before they can be applied to relevant decision problems. Böckle et al. (2004) discuss the economics of software product lines from a portfolio perspective based on shared costs and infrastructure, but do not address the risk implications.

Seemingly disparate projects may also have structural dependencies that are deliberate or accidental. For example, successful completion of a pilot project can trigger a much larger project. Conversely, a failed project in an unproven technology can impede parallel initiatives. In these cases, again, the individual components cannot be valued in isolation. Such interactions can sometimes be modeled as a portfolio of options, and analyzed using real options techniques discussed in Sections 3.3 and 3.4.

Agency Conflicts and Information Asymmetries

It is also important to be aware of the factors that negatively affect value. Agency conflicts are concerned with misalignment of stakeholder interests, and are a potential source of value destruction at the organizational level. Measures of value at the organizational level are agreed upon by the principal stakeholders, such as the private owners, public shareholders, or the community served by the organization. Information asymmetries lead to differing stakeholder perspectives, which in turn may cause undesirable behavior that negatively affects these measures.

Problems of agency conflicts and closely related information asymmetries play a dominant role in areas such as corporate finance and microeconomics. In corporate finance, corporate governance (Shleifer and Vishny, 1997; Hirschey et al., 2003) addresses resolution of agency conflicts that arise due to the separation of ownership and management. Adam Smith more than 200 years ago concluded that "people tend to look after their own affairs with more care than they use in looking after the affairs of others." Generally speaking, agency conflicts occur if project stakeholders have private incentives that differ from the common project goals. These conflicts are exacerbated by information asymmetries, where certain stakeholders have superior or private information, that is, information more accurate than that available to others or information not available to others at all.

If different stakeholders in a software project (e.g., developers, managers, tester, clients) have different incentives and different access to information, the assessment of value on a department or company level becomes more difficult. In valuation, game theoretic techniques can be used to model these effects and highlight their impact. Sang-Pok et al. (2004) use such a technique to analyze the decision to collect data from software developers given that it takes additional effort and the data might be used to evaluate the same stakeholders who provide the data. They define different strategies and find that if every developer strives to maximize his own utility, the result of the group will not be Pareto-optimal (the best that could be achieved without disadvantaging at least one stakeholder) although a Pareto-optimal solution exists.

An example of agency effects in real options analysis concerns the exercise of abandonment options. Abandonment options that are supposed to kill non-performing projects midstream are sometimes not optimally exercised due to conflicts between short-term interests of managers and long-term corporate goals. These conflicts can be taken into account in valuation through simulation, game-theoretic techniques, and augmenting the uncertainty models.

Chapter 7 addresses agency conflicts and information asymmetries in the context of requirements negotiation.

3.3 Valuation of Uncertain Projects with Decision Trees

When information on benefits, costs and the future states of the world is available, valuation techniques of varying sophistication can exploit the information in different ways. However, most techniques rely on a foundational method called *Discounted Cash Flow* (DCF) and the fundamental concept of *Net Present Value* (NPV) to which this method gives rise.

The premise of DCF valuation is to render costs and benefits that occur at different points in the future by adjusting them with an appropriate *discount rate*. The discount rate captures the risk borne the cash flow associated with the future benefit or cost. It is applied to the cash flow just like a compound interest rate, but in reverse, to express the cash flow in *present value* terms. Then an NPV can be computed by summing the present value of all estimated cash flows. The NPV tells us the project's *net* worth in today's currency.

We assume that the appropriate discount rates are provided since their determination is beyond the scope of this chapter. Chapter 5 discusses this topic and provides a specific technique that can be used in software projects. Further resources are mentioned in Section 3.4.

In spite of the universal acceptance of DCF and NPV, managers have often hesitated to use them in practice, citing an inability to integrate the techniques into the strategic planning process. Whereas these techniques are essentially static in nature, reflecting their origins in the valuation of financial instruments, strategic planning is a dynamic process, whereby management must constantly evaluate alternatives and make decisions that condition future scenarios under uncertainty. The need to bring techniques for modeling *active management* into the valuation process has motivated the recent interest in the discipline of real options, which aims to create such a bridge between finance and strategy. We will exploit this relationship by a progression of models of increasing complexity, starting with static NPV and gradually expanding it to handle dynamic decisions and flexibility, first through a decision theoretic approach in this section and then through real options theory in the next.

An Uncertain Project with no Flexibility

As a means of getting acquainted with the principal concepts underlying the real options approach, let us consider the economic analysis of the prospects for a software research and development (R&D) project. R&D projects, by their very nature, have very uncertain prospects. Uncertainty makes the prospects vary over possible states of nature. It is not unusual to have to consider a wide spectrum of such states, or outcomes, ranging from spectacular success to spectacular failure. A value then must be attached to each possible outcome and an expected worth computed by aggregating over all the outcomes. It is not unusual to have to consider a wide spectrum of possible outcomes, ranging from spectacular success to spectacular failure.

Suppose that we are considering an investment of $200,000 in a software R&D project lasting five years. As a first step in an NPV analysis we might characterize the possible economic outcomes of the project as being Best, Normal, or Worst, and associate a best estimate and probability with each of them. This effectively models uncertainty.

- 30% probability of a *Best economic outcome* of $1 million
- 40% probability of a *Normal economic outcome* of $500,000
- 30% probability of a *Worst economic outcome* of 0

We assume that the discount rate associated with the firm's projects is 20% per year ($r_{adr} = 0.2$) and that the risk-free rate of return is 2% per year ($r_f = 0.02$). The rate r_{adr} is referred to as a *risk-adjusted discount rate*; it represents the minimum annual return expected of initiatives of comparable risk. This is the discount rate we use for calculating the present value of the project's future benefits. The rate r_f represents the return expected from an initiative with no systematic risk. This rate can be observed in the markets and given by the return on short-term government bonds. The risk-free rate is used to calculate the present value of future costs that are either certain or whose uncertainty only depends on factors internal or unique to the project.

The NPV of the economic prospects for this project is straightforward to calculate. However, before we proceed, the possible benefits are first weighted by their respective probabilities. Then the weighted benefits are added over all outcomes to calculate an *expected worth*. Having reduced the future benefits to a single cash flow, we are now ready to discount the result. Since the benefits will be realized after five years, the expected worth of the benefits is discounted back five years using the risk-adjusted rate as a compound interest rate applied in reverse to calculate a present value. The cost of $200,000 is committed upfront; therefore it does not need to be discounted. Finally the undiscounted cost is deducted from the discounted expected benefit to arrive at an NPV:

$$NPV = -200 + \frac{1000 \times 30\% + 500 \times 40\% + 0 \times 30\%}{(1 + r_{adr})^5} = \$940$$

At NPV of less than $1,000, we should be indifferent about the investment.

Accounting for Staged Outlays

Now we will begin to add some more realism to the scenario. A first step is to be more realistic about the timing of the expenses. Unlike a stock or bond, where the entire investment is made up-front, a project's resources are generally allocated in stages. For example, instead of allocating the entire investment of $200,000 in one lump sum, we might allocate progressively larger amounts such as:

- $20,000 in a first stage to develop a nonfunctional prototype to gauge concept feasibility, allocated immediately;
- $80,000 in a second stage to produce a first release to be beta tested by users, allocated after one year; and
- $100,000 in a third stage for full development, allocated after two years.

Not only is this a more realistic allocation scenario, but it also confers an extra advantage: the money for the second and third stages can sit in the bank and earn interest while waiting to be invested in the project. In fact, it would not even be necessary to have all of it available at the beginning of the project. For example, in order to have the $100,000 dollars available for the second-year investment, it would only be necessary to have $100/(1 + r_f)^2 = \$96,120$ available at the beginning – the rest would come from the interest earned while waiting. This brings us to a first important observation: an expense incurred later has an economic advantage over the same expense incurred earlier, and the degree of that advantage is linked directly to the risk-free interest rate. With this insight, the new NPV calculation for the example is given below, where the staged costs are discounted by the risk-free rate, and the benefits at the end are discounted at the firm's risk-adjusted rate as before. Again, the expected worth is computed for the benefits by aggregating over possible outcomes before proceeding with the NPV calculation. The NPV calculation itself involves discounting the resulting cash flows and summing them.

$$NPV = -20 + \frac{-80}{(1+r_f)^1} + \frac{-100}{(1+r_f)^2} + \frac{1000\times30\% + 500\times40\% + 0\times30\%}{(1+r_{adr})^5} = \$6,390$$

At this point, we can make another observation, concerning the nature of the NPV calculation. Notice that the calculated NPV would have been the same if the corresponding Best, Normal, and Worst values had been 600, 500, and 400; or 700, 500, and 300; or even 800, 500, and 200. Why is this? NPV here calculates a single, expected net worth; it throws away any information about how much the different estimates vary from this expected worth. In statistical terms, one could say that NPV calculated based on expected worth of the cash flows preserves the mean, but not the variance. Yet intuitively it seems that a decision maker might want to know something about how far the estimated values vary – if only to have an idea of how uncertain we are about those estimates: if the estimates vary widely, then intuitively this large variation must reflect our degree of uncertainty in our estimates.

One way in which we could retain this information about how far the estimates vary is by switching to a tree-like representation, as in Figure 13. The nodes mark the different funding stages, milestones, or outcomes of the project. The branches denote the state changes.

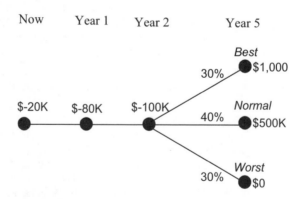

Fig. 13. Representation of uncertainty in the R&D project

This tree-like representation captures and records visually the differing estimates about the outcome, and so is more useful as an aid to understanding the uncertainty underlying the scenario.

Resolution of Uncertainty

We can further improve the realism of the R&D project scenario. After working for a while on the project – for example, after the end of a first stage – we are more likely to have a better idea of its prospects. By the end of the first stage, we may already be able to judge the prospects as being either *bright* or *dim*. In the optimistic scenario, the probabilities will have remained as we judged in the beginning; whereas in the pessimistic scenario, the probability of a Worst outcome will have increased considerably, at the expense of the probabilities of the Best and Normal outcomes.

The more refined representation in Figure 14 helps us to portray this situation visually, where we have assumed equal probabilities of the future scenario being either bright or dim after the first stage.

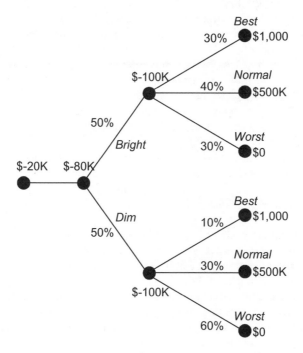

Fig. 14. Refined scenario for the R&D project

Assuming that bright and dim outlooks are equally probable at the end of the first stage, the NPV of the refined scenario now declines significantly below zero, to -

$43,450, due to the effects of the *dim* scenario. Yet here again, the NPV calculation does not preserve the extra information we have gained from the passage of time, captured in our improved estimates of the relative probabilities of the various outcomes and their variance from the expected worth. Although the passage of time delivers valuable information, traditional NPV still does not incorporate this information in the appropriate way, although our tree-like representation does express it. As a result the NPV now looks worse than ever. More importantly, with the tree-like representation, we can handle the most important element that is still missing from a realistic scenario: the ability to act upon new information. As time passes we do not only acquire information, but we can also act on it: that is, we can make *decisions*.

Incorporating Flexibility through Options

What kind of decision might we take in this scenario? The most obvious would be the decision after each stage concerning whether to continue the project or not. R&D projects notoriously rarely make it to full funding; they are canceled long before, often after the first stage. That is, management has an *option to abandon* the project. We can reflect this decision making process through a small modification to our tree-like representation, transforming it into a *decision tree*.

Decision trees go beyond NPV by not only representing the occurrence of costs and benefits over time, but by also representing the decisions taken by management in response to these occurrences. Our original, simple tree-like representation is refined by distinguishing different kinds of nodes:

- *Outcome and state change nodes* – similar to those in our original representation, they represent possible outcomes or state changes, with associated probabilities, as we have seen before;
- *Decision nodes* – these nodes represent decision points in the tree, where management can actively intervene;
- *Action nodes* – represent the actions possibly associated with a decision, such as making a further investment outlay.

We now elaborate our scenario further by making explicit the decisions that will be available to management at various stages of project execution. To begin, management has an option to either continue or stop the project after the first stage depending on the evaluation of the nonfunctional prototype. At that point, management is likely to continue the project only if the prospects are looking bright; if the prospects have turned dim, then the project could be canceled.

Furthermore, we assume that after completion of the second stage, where an initial release of the product is available, we will have accumulated enough information to have a clear idea of what the final outcome of a fully funded project would be – that is, either Best, Normal, or Worst – and be able to put a number on it. At that point, management has another option available to either continue or stop the project. Clearly, the decision will be based on whether the expectation of the final outcome, revealed after the second stage and following the beta testing on the initial release, will justify the last investment outlay necessary to carry out the project to completion.

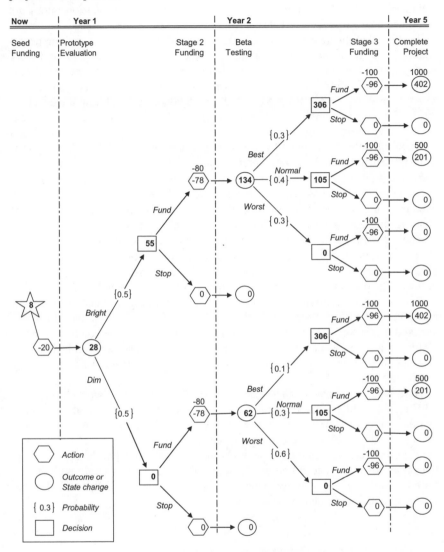

Fig. 15. Full decision tree of the R&D project

The full decision tree capturing this scenario, including all its possible decisions, actions, state changes, and outcomes together with their probabilities, is shown in Figure 15. The leaf nodes represent the final outcomes. The figures inside these nodes represent the associated benefits in present value (already discounted) terms. The corresponding future values (before discounting) are indicated above the nodes. The figures inside the action nodes represent the costs, again in present value terms, associated with the corresponding actions – in this case the additional funding required. The future values of the investment costs are indicated above the action nodes. The bold figures inside the state change and decision nodes are computed as we fold the tree back starting from the leaf nodes.

The fact that the decision tree now includes *options* for decision making necessitates a change in the way it is evaluated. We must start at the end, and work *backward* through time. At each decision point in the tree, the alternative with the higher assigned worth is chosen as the worth of the project at that decision point.

As an example, consider the $100,000 funding decision right after the beta testing in Year 2, following an optimistic (bright) evaluation in Year 1. Let us focus on the case where the outlook review in Year 2 after the beta testing predicts a Normal outcome, represented by a benefit estimate of $500,000. If the project is fully funded, the remaining net worth of the project after the beta testing will be $201,000 – $96,000 = $105,000 in present value terms. If the project is abandoned at that point, it will be $0. The optimal decision is therefore to proceed, effectively exercising the continuation option. The worth of the project at the decision node consequently equals Max ($0, $105,000) = $105,000.

The net worth of the whole decision tree is given by the computed worth of the state change node under Stage 2, minus the seed funding of $20,000. The result, $28,000 – $20,000 = $8,000, represents the dynamic project NPV with the exit options. The project looks much more attractive than it did without the options.

Remarkably, only in the worst-case scenarios is the project abandoned by exercising the exit option at Stage 3. With the given uncertainty model, the exit option at Stage 2 is never exercised. However a slight increase in the conditional probability of a Worst outcome after a pessimistic (dim) evaluation would trigger the exit option in Stage 2 because the present value of a positive funding decision would be negative.

Here what accounts for the more than $50,000 difference between the static NPV of -$43,000 and the dynamic NPV of $8,000 is the presence of the options and the ability to exercise them under the right conditions. The exercise of the options prevents the otherwise negative values from propagating toward the root of the decision tree. Consequently, the downside risk is limited, but the upside potential is not affected. The difference between the static and dynamic NPVs is referred to as the *option premium*. This premium represents the additional value, under uncertainty, attributed to managerial flexibility.

3.4 Real Options Theory

The example of the R&D project has highlighted a number of significant points:
- Options for decision making can be analyzed economically when they are modeled explicitly, as they are in decision trees.
- The passage of time resolves uncertainty and adds more information.
- Less money is needed for the same investment made later in time because of the possibility of earning interest.

- Large variations in possible outcomes make options even more valuable, because the decision maker can choose to exploit the best outcomes and discard the worst outcomes. In contrast, a small variation in possible outcomes makes the decision making process less important.

We will now see how these points relate to the discipline of *real options*.

Significance of Options

In an environment where uncertainty is high, it is important to have as many options for decision making as possible, either to exploit opportunities with good prospects or to limit the damage when prospects turn sour. Many of the activities carried out by IT organizations today are in fact targeted at acquiring and exercising strategic flexibility in various forms:

- A firm may have developed or acquired valuable infrastructure technology, such as a set of financial business objects and frameworks giving it the option to enter a new, potentially profitable market of electronic banking (Favaro and Favaro, 1999).
- The human and organizational capabilities developed by a firm may yield strategic options. If it has invested heavily in the recruitment of talented personnel, and invested heavily in training them in component-based development processes, then it may have acquired a strategic option to switch course rapidly in response to changing requirements, improving competitive advantage (Favaro et al., 1998).
- The firm may have created an equally valuable option to get out of an unprofitable market or project by employing IT resources that retain their value even if a project must be stopped. An example would be basing a development project on COTS software that could still be used in another context if the project is halted prematurely. Indeed, using COTS components may give rise to a variety of other options of which the firm can take advantage to increase the value of its IT portfolio. COTS components are not only potentially reusable assets, but they also allow upgrading to new technologies at low switching costs (Erdogmus and Vandergraaf, 1999; Erdogmus, 2001).
- When a new technology arrives on the market a firm may decide to wait and see whether the technology matures and is successful in the marketplace before investing its resources in participating in that market (Favaro, 1999; Erdogmus, 2000).

Each of the scenarios, with its various embedded options, could be modeled with the decision-tree techniques illustrated, but an alternative theory from the financial community has become available in recent years that more directly supports the analysis of strategic options and their associated flexibility: option pricing theory. One advantage over decision trees of using option pricing theory to analyze dynamically managed decisions is that the analysis can often be represented in a compact, explicit, and more easily understandable form (albeit sometimes at the

expense of loss of detail). The theory makes it both possible to classify such decisions conceptually and more straightforward to reason about their behavior. Modeling a dynamic decision explicitly as a specific type of an option improves our
understanding of the nature of that decision and how different factors affect its
value.

Option Pricing Theory and Real Options

Financial options are special forms of derivative securities – that is, their value
depends on the value of an underlying asset. A call option gives the owner the
right, but not the obligation, to buy an asset on a specified future expiration date,
at a specified strike or exercise price. Similarly, a put option gives the owner the
right (but not the obligation) to sell an asset for a specified price on an expiration
date in the future. The asset on which an option is defined is called the underlying
asset of the option.

Options have been used for nearly three centuries both for speculation and for
hedging. Despite their popularity, however, their usefulness was limited by the
lack of a rigorous theory of pricing. Such a theory was developed in 1973 by
Fisher Black, Myron Scholes, and Robert Merton (winning them the 1997 Nobel
Prize in Economics), and led to a new science of financial engineering, whereby
derivative instruments are used in many inventive ways to manage risk in investments.

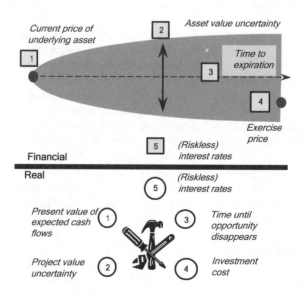

Fig. 16. Financial and real option correspondence

Option pricing theory was first developed for the valuation of income streams from traded financial assets (e.g., stocks). In contrast, real options are intended for the valuation of income streams from projects and other *real assets*. Figure 16 summarizes the parameters associated with financial options, and their mapping to real-world project parameters. Two of the parameters (1 and 4) are familiar from NPV techniques: the estimated present value of the investment's payoffs and the cost of investment.

The remaining three parameters were not as readily identifiable in the decision tree example although they had implicit counterparts:

- The level of uncertainty of the underlying asset, commonly represented by the *standard deviation of the asset's return* (Parameter 2) – the more the variation in an investment's return, the more valuable becomes the option to make decisions concerning that investment.
- The *time of the investment decision* (Parameter 3) – the passage of time affects the value of an option; the more distant the investment decision from the present time, the higher the uncertainty and the lower the impact of the future investment cost.
- The *interest rate* (Parameter 5) – the ability to make an investment later in time is like money in the bank, literally, because interest can be earned in the meantime.

Thus, option pricing theory does not *replace* NPV, which remains the point of departure for any serious financial insight, but *augments* it with new reasoning capabilities. The time parameter permits reasoning about when an investment can be made. (NPV implicitly assumes immediate investment.) The standard deviation parameter permits reasoning about the magnitude of the uncertainty of the future evolution of the investment's worth. (NPV permits only calculation of the expected worth of an investment, providing no insight on its variance.) Finally, there is another important characteristic of an option not directly reflected in the parameters: the fact that it is a contingent investment, whereby a decision point is included.

Growth Options

Consider the *growth option*, which is closely related to the option in the decision tree example, where a smaller investment may yield an option to make a larger, profitable investment at a later time. Growth has become the principal preoccupation of many IT companies today. Indeed, the high stock prices of many Internet companies such as Google have been linked to investor expectations of nonlinear growth opportunities (translating into greatly increased future revenues).

Yet many of these same companies are subject to the danger of value-destroying growth. How can a firm pursue aggressive growth strategies while retaining the financial discipline to be sure that its strategy is *increasing* value rather than destroying it?

A typical scenario in the provision of Web-based personalized services helps illustrate the point. A major retail investment advisor believes that there may be an enormous future market for customized Web-based investment services, including a variety of personalized functionalities that can be configured for each individual client. To prepare for entry into this new market, the company will have to create the infrastructure that permits such rapid configuration. The infrastructure consists of comprehensive object-oriented frameworks, components, and trained personnel, and will be created by an internal project under the code name of StockFrame.

We assume it will take two years and an investment of $800 million to create the infrastructure. At the end of two years, the decision will be made whether to enter the market with a new venture called myStocks, depending on current market conditions. Market entry would involve an investment of $800 million, with a total expected present value of revenues of $600 million. However, a high level of uncertainty is associated with this market assessment: the revenue estimates have historically been subject to an annual percentage fluctuation with a standard deviation of 40%.

This scenario is similar to the one in the decision tree example. Suppose that the StockFrame investment is a pure loss leader, that is, with no cash inflows. Then the NPV of that investment is –$80 million. To calculate the NPV of the myStocks venture, we discount the $800 million investment in two years back to the present using the risk-free interest rate (let us assume 4% for this example) to obtain about $740 million. Thus the NPV of myStocks is about $600 – $740 = –$140 million.

No value-conscious manager would even begin the StockFrame project based upon these figures. However, a standard deviation of 40% in its possible revenues means that the payoffs to myStock *might* be *much higher* than the expected worth predicted by the plain NPV. The StockFrame investment, even with its negative NPV, provides the opportunity to capture those nonlinear payoffs, and that opportunity has value that is not reflected in the NPV figure. Furthermore, the ability to block all further investment if the outlook dims for myStock is not reflected in the NPV calculation. These ideas are familiar from the decision tree example, but real options provides the opportunity for a compact representation of the scenario and calculation of the value of the option created by StockFrame.

We can make the following correspondence between the key parameters of the scenario and the parameters of the Black-Scholes formula for evaluating a call option:

- The $600 million present value of expected cash flows from the myStock venture corresponds to the current price of the underlying asset in the call option calculation (S). This represents the payoff from the venture.
- The $800 million investment required to undertake the myStock venture corresponds to the exercise price (X).
- The decision point at 2 years corresponds to the expiration date of the call option (t).

- The estimated 40% standard deviation of the payoff's annual percentage fluc-
  tuations has a direct correspondence in the standard deviation of the underlying
  stock's returns (σ).
- The risk-free rate of 4% at which all future costs are discounted also finds a direct correspondence in the Black-Scholes formula (r_f).

Assume for this discussion that we have a calculator available for the Black-
Scholes formula for a call option that must be exercised on or before the expiration date of the option. Then:

$$BS\_CALL(S = 600, X = 800, t = 2, \sigma = 40\%, r_f = 4\%) = \$89 \text{ million}$$

The call option formula is given by:

$$BS\_CALL(S, X, t, \sigma, r_f) = S \times N(d_1(\frac{S}{PV(X, r_f)}, t, \sigma))$$
$$- PV(X, r_f) \times N(d_2(\frac{S}{PV(X, r_f)}, t, \sigma)),$$

where:

$$d_1(x, t, \sigma) = \frac{\ln x + \frac{1}{2}\sigma^2 t}{\sigma\sqrt{t}},$$

$$d_2(x, t, \sigma) = d_1(x, t, \sigma) - \sigma\sqrt{t},$$

$PV(X, r_f)$ denotes the present value of X discounted using r_f, and
N denotes the cumulative standardized normal distribution function.

Thus, the execution of the StockFrame project provides the option to decide
whether to invest in the myFrame venture after two years. Since the option corresponds to an opportunity to delay a decision for two years in the hopes of exploiting the upside scenario of myFrame's future cash flows (this situation is analogous
to the best-case scenario in the decision-tree example), it has value – and the
Black-Scholes calculation puts a number on that value, at $89 million.

Adding that value to the present value of its own cash flows, we arrive at an
augmented NPV of (–$80) + $89 = $9 million. This figure only refers to the value
of the StockFrame investment, and is linked to the fact that it is part of an overall
contingent investment strategy. Nevertheless it provides the necessary justification
to undertake the StockFrame investment in order to have the strategic option to
contemplate the myStock venture two years later. Based upon this analysis, a
value-conscious manager can proceed with the initial, strategic investment with
the confidence that financial discipline has been respected.

The call option value is most sensitive to the present value of the payoff S, the
future investment cost X, and the uncertainty measure σ. For example, increasing
the present value of the payoff by 25% from $600 million to $750 million increases the option value by over 90%, from $89 to $172 million; decreasing the
future investment cost by 25% from $800 to $600 million increases the option

value by over 70% to $153 million; and increasing the uncertainty measure by 25% from 40% to 50% increases the option value by close to 40% to $123 million. The least sensitive parameters are time to investment decision t and the risk-free interest rate r_f. For example, extending the time to investment decision 25% from 2 to 2.5 years increases the option value by about 22% to $109 million, and increasing the risk-free interest rate by 25% from 4% to 5% increases the option value by only about 5% to $93 million.

Abandonment Options

The growth option represents an important class of real option involving the *expansion* of an investment. Another important class of real option involves the *abandonment* of investment. We saw one case in the decision tree example, involving staged projects. In another important case, strategic investment is oriented toward the conservation of business value if the current course must be abandoned.

One such case is COTS-based development, embodied in the notorious "build or buy" decision. The use of COTS in a project is often costlier in the initial outlay than custom development, including cost of purchase or licensing and the associated learning curve and customization issues. But these outlays also bring flexibility: the COTS-based technology can be put to other uses if the venture does not turn out to be as valuable as originally estimated. The extra investment buys a kind of insurance, an opportunity to bail out of a project if its fortunes begin to dim, without losing all of the investment.

As an example, suppose a venture is being contemplated that involves the construction of a specialized database. The present value of all future payoffs from this venture is originally estimated at $40 million, but with high uncertainty, represented by a standard deviation of 50%. Management plans to revise the venture's outlook in 18 months of operation, and decide what to do based upon the revised outlook. A current dilemma concerns whether to develop the database from scratch, specifically for the venture, or whether to purchase a license for a COTS database, and train the personnel to customize it to specifications.

If all goes well with the venture, the cheaper, custom-built solution will provide the maximum economic value; but if the market sours, management will have no choice with a custom solution but to stay the course or lose the entire investment. The cost outlays for the COTS-based solution would be higher by $3 million, a considerable amount; but management believes that the COTS technology and personnel could be redeployed to other uses worth $30 million if the decision to cancel the venture were taken. Although that is still much less than the estimated $40 million payoff of the contemplated venture, it does provide an escape route. The management dilemma essentially boils down to a trade-off between the extra expense of the COTS-based solution and the value of the option to change the course that the COTS solution makes available.

Whereas the growth option could be modeled as a *call* option, this type of scenario corresponds to a *put* option – an option that provides insurance. Assuming the availability of a calculator for the Black-Scholes formula for a put option, we have:

$$BS\_PUT(S = 40, X = 30, t = 1.5, \sigma = 50\%, r_f = 4\%) = 3.5M,$$

where

$$BS\_PUT(S, X, t, \sigma, r_f) = BS\_CALL(S, X, t, \sigma, r_f) + PV(X, r_f) - S.$$

Thus, the value of the option to decide after 18 months to abandon the project and put the COTS-based technology to another use rather than stay the course is \$3.5 million. In this case, the value of that option just exceeds the extra investment necessary to provide it. In another, less uncertain scenario, we might have found that it was better to simply build the system from scratch in the most cost-effective way possible.

Further Reading

The reader can refer to Chapter 4 for more comprehensive discussions of the basic financial concepts that underlie valuation, such as Discounted Cash Flow, Net Present Value, and the relationship between risk and return. These concepts are also discussed under the general topics of capital budgeting and risk in Brealey and Myers (1996). Steve Tockey's text on *Return on Software* (Tockey, 2004) is also a good resource that is accessible to software professionals. For a specific focus on cost-benefit analysis, see Layard and Glaister (1994).

The discussion of real options in this chapter has only skimmed the surface of the vast literature on both theory and practice. The seminal paper on option pricing is by Black and Scholes (1973), providing the original rationale for and derivation of the option pricing model. A few years later, an important alternative approach to option pricing, known as the binomial model, was developed by Cox, Ross, and Rubenstein (Cox et al., 1979). The binomial model, together with its risk-neutral approach to option pricing, is not only simpler than the Black-Scholes derivation, but also more flexible with wider application. Both the Black-Scholes and binomial models are expounded with software process examples in a chapter of *Extreme Programming Perspectives* (Erdogmus and Favaro, 2002).

Options can be modeled and valued using classical decision-tree techniques, as we have illustrated in this chapter. While this approach allows for richness in terms of handling multiple interdependent options and arbitrary, discrete models of uncertainty, the size of the underlying decision trees increase exponentially with the model complexity. Steve Tockey's text (Tockey, 2004) includes a chapter that provides an overview of decision tree analysis in the context of software engineering.

Going beyond the simplified exposition of decision trees and options, Smith and Nau (1995) explain the precise relationship between option pricing and decision trees, and demonstrate how the two models together can account for both market and private risk. This hybrid technique is exploited in an article by Erdogmus (2002) to value software projects with multiple sources of uncertainty.

On the one hand, in spite of its analytic power, real options has proved challenging to use in the context of software engineering projects. The original derivation of the Black-Scholes formula was based upon the assumption of being able to trade assets continuously – an assumption already considered by some to be questionable for financial assets, and considered by many to be untenable for real assets (such as software projects). The ensuing controversy has prompted the development of option pricing techniques, such as by (Dixit and Pindyck, 1995), which do not appeal to market-related arguments in their derivation. Techniques based on Monte Carlo simulation (Mun, 2002) later gained popularity for the same reason and for their practicality in valuing options on real assets.

On the other hand, there is a significant community that accepts the essential validity of the Black-Scholes and binomial approaches as a way to determine *idealized value* and points out the considerable advantages of these approaches, such as the avoidance of the need to specify subjective probabilities and enumerate different outcomes. The Black-Scholes model may be used in a compact fashion, with few key parameters that can often be estimated using market or historical data. The reader can consult the *Extreme Programming Perspectives* chapter (Erdogmus and Favaro, 2002) for a comparison of real and financial options and a discussion of the portability of the financial option pricing assumptions.

For a high-level treatment of real options outside the software engineering context, we recommend (Amram and Kulatalika, 1999) and (Copeland and Antikarov, 2001). (Mun, 2002) is an excellent technical resource for real options analysis that exploits numeric techniques, such as Monte Carlo simulation and optimization, that do not appeal to market-related arguments. Additional references can be found in the "Further Reading" sidebar of the IEEE Software magazine's May/June 2004 focus issue on *Return on Investment* (Erdogmus et al., 2004).

3.5 Summary and Discussion

A structured valuation process that accounts for costs, benefits, and uncertainty is required to support software professionals and project managers in making value-oriented decisions. Software projects are subject to multiple sources of uncertainty and incorporate additional complexities, such as intangible benefits, flexibility, interactions among projects, and conflicting stakeholder interests that may impact value to various extents. Different techniques including game theory, real options analysis, utility functions, and portfolio-based approaches, exist for dealing with these factors in valuation. These techniques, when appropriately used, can augment traditional methods to help assess the effects when their consequences are deemed significant.

This chapter focused on the natural tension in software projects between the cost of investment in flexibility and the value of the opportunities such flexibility provides. Much of software development is colored by this tension. Multitiered system architectures, application frameworks, modular development, and components are examples of providing insurance, of protecting that which does not change from that which does change. The value of that protection is proportional to the probability that change will occur. The real options approach to valuation reveals the underlying drivers – the costs, the benefits, the time frame of the investment, and above all, the uncertainty surrounding the investment. In doing so, it brings a rational analysis regime to a difficult problem in software engineering: gauging the benefits of flexibility and dynamic decisions in process, product, and project decisions.

This chapter tried to bridge the gap between theory and application by providing both a survey on theory related to valuation and discussing examples using selected valuation techniques beyond the traditional approaches. The chapter illustrates that value-based software engineering faces interesting challenges. Expertise already exists in selected areas, but various promising concepts from finance and economics are waiting to be tailored, integrated, and applied to the area of software development.

The challenges regarding the use of financial and economic methods, such as option pricing theory and portfolio theory, in the VBSE context are their reliance on objective historical data on observed prices of assets and the ability to buy or sell assets in arbitrary quantities. Such objective data is unfortunately often unavailable for software projects. Neither are software projects and software-based assets liquid or tradable in arbitrary proportions. Strategies to cope with these difficulties include using proxies (data on related activities or assets, thought to be correlated with the actual activity or asset of interest) where possible, using simulation-based and other numeric techniques that don not assume tradability (Mun, 2002), relying on subjective estimates where necessary, tailoring the methods to have less demanding data requirements, focusing on sensitivity analysis where reliable data is unavailable, and most importantly, understanding the implications of violating assumptions. The last point means treating the valuations obtained as reflecting *idealized* rather than *fair* values and focusing on the insights gained rather than the numbers churned.

Data availability and reliability problems however are not unique to software projects and should not be viewed as an obstacle. Table 3 summarizes the difficulties involved with different techniques and the common strategies used to address these difficulties. Examples of the use of available market or project data as proxies in software project valuation can be found in work by Erdogmus (2000, 2001, 2002).

Table 3. Applying financial and economic techniques in VBSE

Theory or technique	When to use?	How challenges alleviated?
	Main challenges with application in VBSE	
DCF and traditional NPV	Static decisions; no flexibility; no embedded options.	1. Consider multiple scenarios and aggregate. Use subjective estimates. Use sensitivity analysis for unknown cash flows.
	1. Estimation of cash flows. *2. Determination of proper discount rate.*	2. See Chapter 5.
Decision trees	Dynamic decisions; flexibility; multiple embedded options; complex structuring of decisions; able to identify discrete outcomes and associated probabilities; focus on understanding dynamics of multiple nested decisions; multiple interdependent projects with transparent interactions.	1. Same as NPV/DCF. 2. Simplify by considering only most relevant scenarios. Use sensitivity analysis.
	1. Same as NPV/DCF. *2. Modeling uncertainty.*	
Real options and option pricing theory	Dynamic decisions; flexibility; single or few embedded options; simple decision structure conforming to known templates; probability distribution of outcomes unidentifiable; able to represent uncertainty as percentage variation; quick results; focus on understanding impact of valuation parameters.	1. Use market proxies and private data from past projects when available. Use industry benchmarks. Use sensitivity analysis. 2. Interpret results as "idealized values." Model options using simple decision trees if necessary. Use simulation-based or other numeric techniques that do not assume tradability (Mun, 2002).
	1. Estimation of uncertainty due to lack of objective data. *2. Non-tradability of software assets and projects when using models with analytic, closed-form solutions such as the Black-Scholes model.* *3. Mapping projects to option pricing problems.*	3. Simplify scenarios by considering only the most significant options (earliest, with largest and most uncertain payoffs). Consider most important milestones only and fit into existing templates when possible.
Utility theory	Need to factor in decision maker preferences and attitudes for risk.	Use known techniques for eliciting utility of stakeholders when practical. Use standardized functions when necessary.
	Identification of utility functions.	See Chapter 4.

Theory or technique	When to use?	How challenges alleviated?
	Main challenges with application in VBSE	
Portfolio theory	Multiple interdependent projects whose interactions are generally identifiable as positive or negative correlations among project returns; focus on optimal allocation of resources among alternative activities.	1. Use proxies when possible. 2. Tailor to handle "all or none"-type resource allocation; use optimization techniques (Mun, 2002).
	1. Determination correlations among projects due to lack of objective data. 2. Projects resources cannot be allocated in arbitrary quantities.	

References

(Amram and Kulatilaka, 1999) (Amram and Kulatilaka, 1999) Amram, M., Kulatilaka, N.: Real options: managing strategic investment in an uncertain world (Harvard Business School Press, 1999)

(Biffl and Halling, 2001) Biffl, S., Halling, M.: A Framework for Economic Planning and Evaluation of Software Inspection Processes. In: Proc. of the Workshop on Inspection in Software Engineering (July 2001)

(Black, 1988) Black, F.: A Simple Discounting Rule. Financial Management, **17**, pp 7–11 (1988)

(Black and Scholes, 1973) Black, F., Scholes, M.: The pricing of options and corporate liabilities. Journal of Political Economy, **81**, pp 637–659 (1973)

(Boehm, 1984) Boehm, B. W.: Software Engineering Economics (Prentice Hall, 1984)

(Boehm, 2000) Boehm, B. W.: Software Cost Estimation with Cocomo II (Prentice Hall, 2000)

(Boehm, 2003) Boehm, B. W.: Value-Based Software Engineering. Software Engineering Notes, **28**(2), (2003)

(Boehm and Sullivan, 1999) Boehm, B. W., Sullivan, K.: Software Economics: status and prospects. Information and Software Technology, **41**, pp 937–946 (1999)

(Böckle et al., 2004) Böckle, G., Clements, P., McGregor, J.D., Muthig, D., Schmid, K.: Calculating ROI for Software Product Lines. IEEE Software, pp 23–31 (May 2004)

(Brealey and Myers, 1996) Brealey, R.A., Myers, S.C.: Principles of Corporate Finance, 5th Edition (McGraw Hill, 1996)

(Copeland and Antikarov, 2001) Copeland, T., Antikarov, V.: Real Options: A Practitioner's Guide (Texere, New York 2001)

(Cox et al., 1979) Cox, J., Ross, S., Rubinstein, M.: Option pricing: a simplified approach. Journal of Financial Economics, **7**(3), pp 229–263 (1979)

(Dixit and Pindyck, 1995) Dixit, A.K., Pindyck, R.S.: The options approach to capital investment. Harvard Business Review, **73**, pp 105–115 (1995)

(Erdogmus, 2000) Erdogmus, H.: Value of Commercial Software Development under Technology Risk. The Financier, **7**, pp 1–4 (2000)

(Erdogmus, 2001) Erdogmus, H.: Management of license cost uncertainty in software development: a real options approach. In: Proc. 5th Annual Conference on Real Options: Theory Meets Practice, UCLA, Los Angeles, CA (2001)

(Erdogmus, 2002) Erdogmus, H.: Valuation of Learning Options in Software Development Under Private and Market Risk. The Engineering Economist, **47**(13), pp 304–353 (2002)

(Erdogmus and Favaro, 2002) Erdogmus, H., Favaro, J.: Keep Your Options Open: Extreme Programming and the Economics of Flexibility. In: Extreme Programming Perspectives, ed by L. Williams, D. Wells, M. Marchesi and G. Succi (Addison-Wesley, 2002)

(Erdogmus and Vandergraaf, 1999) Erdogmus, H., Vandergraaf, J.: Quantitative approaches for assessing the value of COTS-centric development. In: Proc. Sixth International Software Metrics Symposium, Boca Raton, Florida, (IEEE Computer Society, 1999)

(Erdogmus et al., 2004) Erdogmus, H., Favaro, J., Striegel, W.: Return on Investment: Guest Editors' Introduction. IEEE Software, pp 18–24 (May/Jun. 2004)

(Favaro, 1996) Favaro J.: When the Pursuit of Quality Destroys Value. IEEE Software, pp 93–95 (May 1996)

(Favaro, 1999) Favaro, J.: Managing IT for Value. In: Proc. National Polish Soft. Eng. Conference, Warsaw (May 1999)

(Favaro and Favaro, 1999) Favaro, J.M., Favaro, K.R.: Strategic Analysis of Application Framework Investments. In: Building Application Frameworks: Object Oriented Foundations of Framework Design, ed by M. Fayad and R. Johnson (John Wiley and Sons, 1999)

(Favaro et al., 1998) Favaro, J.M., Favaro, P., Favaro, K.R.: Value-based software reuse investment. Annals of Software Engineering, **5**, pp 5–52 (1998)

(Hirschey et al., 2003) Hirschey, M., John, K., Makhija, A. K.: Corporate Governance and Finance. Advances in Financial Economics, Vol. 8 (Elsevier, 2003)

(Kitchenham and Linkman, 1997) Kitchenham, B., Linkman, S.: Estimates, Uncertainty and Risk. IEEE Software, pp 69–74 (May 1997)

(Klir and Wiermann, 1998) Klir, G.J., Wiermann, M.J.: Uncertainty-Based Information. Studies in Fuzziness and Soft Computing, Vol. 15 (Physica-Verlag, Heidelberg 1998)

(Layard and Glaister, 1994) Layard, R., Glaister, S.: Cost-Benefit Analysis, 2nd Edition (Cambridge University Press, 1994)

(Lintner, 1965) Lintner, J.: The Valuation of Risk Assets and the Selection of Risky Investments in Stock Portfolios and Capital Budgets. Review of Economics and Statistics, **47**, pp 13–37 (1965)

(Markowitz, 1952) Markowitz, H.: Portfolio Selection. Journal of Finance, **7**, pp 77–91 (1952)

(Mossin, 1966) Mossin, J.: Equilibrium in a Capital Asset Market. Econometrica, **34**, pp 768–783 (1966)

(Mun, 2002) Mun, J.: Real Options Analysis: Tools and Techniques for Valuing Strategic Investments and Decisions (John Wiley & Sons, 2002)

(Myers, 1974) Myers, S.C.: Interactions of Corporate Financing and Investment Decisions: Implications for Capital Budgeting. Journal of Finance, **29**, pp 1–25 (1974)

(Port et al., 2002) Port, D., Halling, M., Kazman, R., Biffl, S.: Strategic Quality Assurance Planning. In: Proc. 4th Int. Workshop on Economics-Driven Software Engineering Research (EDSER-4) (2002)

(Porter, 1985) Porter, M.E.: Competitive Advantage: Creating and Sustaining Superior Performance (Free Press, New York 1985)

(Porter and Millar, 1985) Porter, M. E., Millar, V. E.: How Information Gives You Competitive Advantage. Harvard Business Review, **63**, pp 140–160 (1985)

(Powell, 1992) Powell, P.: Information Technology Evaluation: Is It Different? Journal of the Operational Research Society. **43**(1), pp 29–42 (1992)

(Sang-Pok et al., 2004) Sang-Pok, K., Hak-Kyung, S., Kyung-Whan, L.: Study to Secure Reliability of Measurement Data through Application of Game Theory. In: Proc. EUROMICRO Conference (2004)

(Sharpe, 1964) Sharpe, W.F.: Capital Asset Prices: A Theory of Market Equilibrium under Conditions of Risk. Journal of Finance, **19**, pp 425–442 (1964)

(Shleifer and Vishny, 1997) Shleifer, A. Vishny, R. W.: A Survey of Corporate Governance. Journal of Finance, **52**(2), pp 737–783 (1997)

(Smith and Nau, 1995) Smith, J.E., Nau, R.F.: Valuing risky projects: option pricing theory and decision analysis. Management Science, **41**(5)

(Srivastava and Mock, 2002) Srivastava, R.P., Mock, T.J.: Belief Functions in Business Decisions. In: Studies in Fuzziness and Soft Computing Vol. 88 (Physica-Verlag, Heidelberg 2002)

(Sullivan et al., 1999) Sullivan, K.J., Chalasani, P., Jha, S., Sazawal, S.V.: Software Design as an Investment Activity: A Real Options Perspective. In: Real Options and Business Strategy: Applications to Decision Making, ed by L. Trigeorgis (Risk Books, 1999)

(Tockey, 2004) Tockey, S: Return on Software: Maximizing the Return on Your Software Investment (Addison-Wesley, 2004)

Author Biographies

Hakan Erdogmus is a senior research officer with the software engineering group at the National Research Council's Institute for Information Technology in Ottawa, Canada. His current research interests are centered on agile software development and software engineering economics. Mr. Erdogmus holds a doctoral degree in Telecommunications from Université du Québec's Institut national de la recherche scientifique and a Master's degree in Computer Science from McGill University, Montréal.

John Favaro is the founder of Consulenza Informatica in Pisa, Italy. In 1996 he introduced the principles of Value-based Management in software engineering in an article in IEEE Software on the relationship between quality management and value creation. In 1998 he introduced Value-based Software Reuse Investment, applying the ideas of Value-based Management and option pricing theory to the analysis of investments in software reuse. Recently he has investigated the relationship of Value-based Management to agile development processes. He is a founding member of the International Society for the Advancement of Software Education (ISASE) and is on the permanent steering committee of the International Conference on Software Reuse. He was guest editor of the May/June 2004 special issue of IEEE Software on "Return on Investment in the Software Industry." He took his degrees in computer science at Yale University and the University of California at Berkeley.

Michael Halling is an Assistant Professor at the University of Vienna. He studied Computer Science at the Vienna University of Technology and Business Administration at the University of Vienna. He holds a PhD from the Vienna University of Technology in Computer Science and completed the CCEFM Postgraduate Program in Finance. Michael Halling is currently doing research in the area of international equity markets, portfolio management, default risk modeling, and corporate finance. His industrial experience includes an employment with a leading consulting company and projects with the Austrian government, the Austrian central bank, and several Austrian banks.

4 Preference-Based Decision Support in Software Engineering

Rudolf Vetschera

Abstract: Throughout the lifecycle of a software system, complex decisions have to be made. One major source of complexity in decision problems is the need to simultaneously consider different, and sometimes conflicting, criteria. When a decision involves multiple criteria, it cannot be made in a purely objective way, but requires subjective judgement to evaluate the trade-offs between criteria. In the field of decision analysis, several methods have been developed to help decision makers to specify their preferences and apply them to a decision problem in a consistent way. In this chapter, we review several methods for multicriteria decision making, in particular additive weighting methods, methods based on aspiration levels, and outranking methods. We present the theoretical background of these methods, their specific ways of evaluating alternatives, and discuss their applicability to decision problems in software engineering. A concluding section discusses issues related to sensitivity analysis and the use of incomplete information.

Keywords: Decision analysis, subjective preferences, multiple criteria, additive weighting, aspiration levels, outranking methods, sensitivity analysis.

4.1 Introduction

The field of decision analysis is concerned with supporting people to make better, or even optimal, decisions. A decision involves the selection of one out of several possible alternatives, which are evaluated according to their outcomes. In many decision problems, finding the optimal alternative is far from trivial, because their outcomes involve several dimensions and thus cannot be compared directly. This multidimensionality of outcomes can arise for different reasons.

One possibility, on which we will focus in this chapter, is that the decision alternatives have an impact on several different attributes, which all are relevant for the decision maker. For example, a consumer chooses a particular car not only because of its price, but takes into account different attributes like performance, fuel consumption, or comfort.

Another situation, in which it is necessary to consider multidimensional outcomes, arises when alternatives lead to different outcomes in different states of the environment, and the decision maker is uncertain which state will arise. The same outcome, e.g., the same amount of profit, will have a different impact on the decision depending on whether it occurs in a likely or unlikely state of the environment. Other factors which lead to a multidimensionality of outcomes are multiple stakeholders or outcomes which occur at different points in time.

When the consequences of a decision are multidimensional, alternative courses of action can often not be compared in an entirely objective way. Whether one prefers a comfortable, but expensive car over a cheaper, but less comfortable one, or whether one is willing to accept higher risks instead of a small, but safe profit, is a matter of subjective preferences.

However, the fact that such complex decision problems necessarily involve subjective judgment does not imply that such decisions must be based on pure intuition. The aim of decision analysis is to develop methods that allow decision makers to apply their preferences to a decision problem in a logical and consistent manner. Often the sheer complexity of a decision problem is overwhelming. Methods of decision analysis help to break down such problems into small, cognitively manageable tasks, and integrate their results back into a coherent and, given the decision maker's subjective preferences, optimal decision.

All four sources of multidimensionality mentioned above are potentially relevant for decisions in software engineering. Different evaluation criteria like performance, reliability, functionality, as well as costs must be taken into account, so most decisions involve multiple criteria. Software development projects are characterized by high levels of uncertainty concerning resources required, possible technical obstacles during the development process, and so on, so they are decision problems under risk. Decisions also affect various stakeholders like users, developers, or project managers. And finally, consequences of decisions can be spread over the entire lifecycle of a software system and thus are clearly multitemporal.

Although all branches of decision analysis are therefore relevant for software engineering, this chapter will focus on multicriteria decision problems. The first reason for this focus is that multicriteria decisions are a very general class of decision problems. Decisions under risk and intertemporal decisions both involve dimensions which are more comparable to each other than entirely different attributes. While one Euro of profit in a very unlikely state is not the same as one Euro of profit in a more likely state, and one Euro of profit tomorrow is not the same as ten years from now, there is still a natural relationship between these dimensions, which can be exploited in decision making. But there is no natural and objective way of comparing additional features in a software system to shorter completion time. Thus the role of subjective preferences is most evident in multicriteria decision problems, and methods developed for this class of problems are best suited to explain fundamental concepts of decision support.

On the other hand, group decisions involve not only potential trade-offs between the different interests of stakeholders, but also "meta-criteria" like fairness, which further complicate the problem. Methods of multicriteria decision making, although they do no explicitly deal with issues like fairness, nevertheless can provide considerable support also for group decision problems. They allow us to integrate different perspectives of the problem, which can come from different stakeholders, into one consistent view. Thereby, they provide a general framework which can also assist the solution of group decision problems.

Although this chapter is focused on the field of multicriteria decision analysis, it still is not possible to give a comprehensive review of this area within one book chapter. The main objective of this chapter is therefore to provide an introduction into several methodologies, which have been developed in this field, their fundamental assumptions, and their particular strengths and problems. While it is not possible within the restricted space of one chapter to provide in-depth descriptions of the methods or their application in different areas of software engineering, some references to such applications and short illustrative examples will be provided.

The remainder of this chapter is structured as follows: Section 4.2 provides the motivation for considering multiple criteria in software engineering decisions. Section 4.3 reviews three fundamental approaches to multicriteria decision making by discussing methods based on additive weighting, on aspiration levels, and on outranking relations. Section 4.4 addresses issues of incomplete information and sensitivity analysis. Section 4.5 concludes the chapter with a short discussion on selection criteria for identifying the appropriate method for a specific decision situation.

4.2 Decisions with Multiple Criteria and Software Engineering

One important argument in several chapters of this book is that decisions in and about software engineering should focus on the value which is created by developing a software system. One might presume that value is a single, unique criterion to be considered and therefore it is not necessary to focus on multiple criteria when making decisions in software engineering. However, even when we focus on value creation as the guiding principle in software engineering, multicriteria decision methods are of considerable importance.

Firstly, the value which a software systems generates is a multidimensional concept by itself, which involves different attributes, time periods and stakeholders (see Chapter 7). The literature on information systems evaluation has developed a multitude of measures for the success of an information system (DeLone and McLean, 1992). While ultimately the impact of an information system on the organization in which it is used is the main indicator of its success, DeLone and McLean (1992) further distinguish the levels of system quality, information quality, system use, user satisfaction, and individual impact as alternative, and mostly complementary, measures of the success of an information system.

Even when impact at the level of the entire organization is considered as the main criterion for evaluating an information system, different attributes can be used to measure its value. The impact on organizational performance can range from short-run, easy to quantify cost savings to "soft" strategic advantages, which can hardly be expressed directly in monetary terms (Farbey et al., 1995). Furthermore, the direct influence of information systems on the performance of firms is difficult to determine (Boehm, 2003). Thus, it might be more appropriate to evaluate information systems using intermediate variables like inventory turnover or capacity utilization, which in turn influence profit (Barua et al., 1995). These intermediate variables can be considered as separate criteria when determining the value of an information system.

Thus the value provided by an information system is a multidimensional concept and consequently information systems should be evaluated using multicriteria methodologies. Furthermore, the concepts of value discussed so far evaluate an information system only from the perspective of the organization in which it is used. But the organization is just one stakeholder in the process of software development (Boehm, 2003).

The entity developing a software system can be part of a larger organization, which will eventually reap the benefits of the system developed, as in the case of an in-house software department. But it might as well be an entirely different organization, for example, in the development of commercial software products. Of course, a developer of commercial software also needs to take the benefits to customers into account, since they will only be willing to invest in software if they can expect a positive return. But the perceptions of benefits are still quite different. For a commercial developer, the possibility to sell a software system to a wider set of potential customers can be an important criterion, which is less relevant in an in-house development effort.

The organization introducing an information system must be distinguished from the actual users who interact with the system, and whose interests and demands on the system might be quite different (Boehm, 2003). A similar distinction can be made on the development side, where the interests of individual developers (like becoming familiar with some new technology) might be different from those of the company employing them (which could, for example, be interested in lowering development costs). Considering the diverse interests of various stakeholder groups increases the number of criteria to be used.

The criteria mentioned so far can only be evaluated after the development process is completed. But for many decisions to be made during the process, the impact of decision alternatives on attributes of the finished product or the whole process is not clear. In such cases, intermediary attributes, which can more easily be related to the decision alternatives at hand, and which serve as proxies for the desired attributes, must be used. For example, portability to future platforms might be a desirable attribute of a finished system. In selecting an off-the-shelf component, this attribute could be replaced by an attribute describing the likelihood that the supplier of the component will be available to perform the necessary adjustments several years in the future.

To summarize our arguments so far, multiple criteria should be considered in decisions during a software development process for the following reasons:
- Because the value of an information system itself is a multidimensional concept.
- Because multiple criteria make it possible to accommodate for the interests of different stakeholder groups in the development process.
- Several criteria can be used jointly as proxies for higher level goals, when the relationship between decision alternatives and those higher level goals cannot directly be established.

In all these cases, the aggregation between the different attributes is not completely subjective, but also has some objective aspects. This is different from decision problems which are typically discussed in multicriteria analysis, where the importance of attributes is determined only by the subjective preferences of the decision maker. Whether one prefers a sunny, but small apartment over a bigger and darker one, or how much space one is willing to give up for an extra hour of sunshine in the living room, is entirely a matter of personal taste.

In contrast to these personal preferences, the tradeoff between designing the feature set of a new system to closely fit the requirements of an important, long-standing customer or to open the potential for conquering new markets is a business decision. It requires subjective judgment and cannot be solved using purely objective data. But in this case, the subjective component of the decision is to a certain extent a substitute of objective information rather than a characteristic feature of the problem. In the next section, in which we discuss various approaches to solve multicriteria decision problems, we will therefore specifically focus on the question of how well these methods are able to integrate objective and subjective information when evaluating trade-offs between different attributes.

4.3 Multicriteria Decision Methods

In this section, we provide an overview of different methods which have been developed in the theory of multicriteria decision analysis. These methods differ not only in their formal mechanisms used to represent preferences and aggregate information about different attributes, but also in their fundamental concepts of the origin of preferences and the role which methods for decision support should play in the decision process. Nevertheless, they still rely on a quite common concept of what constitutes a multicriteria decision problem.

Structure and forms of multicriteria decision problems

A multicriteria decision problem can be characterized by (Keeney and Raiffa, 1976):

- a (finite or infinite) set of decision alternatives, among which exactly one is to be chosen,
- a set of criteria or attributes in which the alternatives are to be evaluated, and
- the performance of alternatives in the criteria.

An infinite set of decision alternatives can be described by continuous decision variables and constraints which are imposed on their values. A finite set of decision alternatives can be enumerated; for example, different GUI toolkits which could be used in a project can be listed as decision alternatives. Multicriteria decision problems in which alternatives are described via decision variables and constraints are often called *multiobjective programming* problems (Hwang and Masud, 1979), while problems in which the alternatives are explicitly given are called *multi-attribute* decision problems (Hwang and Yoon, 1981).

Multiple criteria are often associated with a strict conflict between criteria, where one goal cannot be achieved without sacrificing another goal. But most methods of multicriteria decision making take a more general perspective and are not restricted to this type of situation. They can also deal with other relations between criteria like mutual support, when improvement in one criterion (sometimes) leads also to improvements in other criteria. While some methods require that decision makers are able to conceptually distinguish between the impacts of different criteria on the overall evaluation of an alternative, there are also methods to avoid this condition of preferential independence.

Methods of multicriteria decision making can be classified according to different dimensions. One possibility is to consider the time at which preference information is elicited from the decision maker. This can take place before or after the main calculations of the algorithm are performed, or interactively, when preference elicitation and calculation phases are interspersed (Hwang and Masud, 1979).

Another classification, which we will use for the remainder of this chapter, is based on the different forms in which preferences are represented and distinguishes between *weights*, *aspiration levels*, and *outranking* methods. All methods for multicriteria decision making require some parameters to represent the preferences of the decision maker. In methods based on aspiration levels, these parameters are levels of the attributes themselves. Weights are more abstract parameters, which are multiplied with attribute values to obtain an evaluation. Outranking methods use yet another type of parameters.

The following notation will be used in the remainder of this chapter: we consider a multi-attribute decision problem in which alternatives are explicitly given (for example, different technologies available for a component of a software system). There are N different alternatives, an individual alternative is referred to as A_i. The alternatives are evaluated in K attributes, so each alternative can be characterized by a vector of K components:

$$A_i = (a_{i1}, a_{i2}, \ldots, a_{ik}, \ldots, a_{iK}) \tag{1}$$

where a_{ik} represents the evaluation of alternative A_i in attribute k. For simplicity, we will assume that the decision maker wants to maximize all the attributes. If necessary, the sign of an attribute can be changed to fulfill this assumption. We also assume that attributes are standardized so that the best possible value is represented by one, and the worst value by zero.

An important concept in multicriteria decision making is *dominance*. An alternative A_i dominates another alternative A_j if it is at least as good as A_j in all attributes and strictly better in at least one attribute. Formally A_i dominates A_j if the following two conditions hold:

$$\forall k : a_{ik} \geq a_{jk}$$
$$\exists k : a_{ik} > a_{jk} \tag{2}$$

Alternatives which are not dominated by other alternatives are called *efficient* or *Pareto-optimal*.

Additive weighting methods

Additive weighting methods are probably the most widely used approach to deal with multicriteria decision problems. In their simplest form, weights are directly applied to the (standardized) attribute values and alternatives are evaluated according to

$$u(A_i) = \sum_k w_k a_{ik} \tag{3}$$

The alternative with the highest value of $u(A_i)$ is chosen. While (3) is conceptually simple and seems to be an intuitive approach to handle multiple criteria, it leads to considerable problems, from both a theoretical and a practical point of view.

A major practical problem in employing (3) is the selection of the weights w_k. Intuitively, the weights reflect the "importance" of different attributes, so a decision maker might feel that if attribute k is "twice as important" to him than attribute m, then w_k should also be two times as big as w_m. But equation (3) combines weights with attribute values. When $w_k = 2w_m$, this means that going from the worst to the best possible value in attribute k contributes twice as much to the evaluation of an alternative than going from the worst to the best value in attribute m. Thus weights always refer to the importance of attributes relative to their possible range of values. Failure to take this into account might lead to an improper specification of weights, which do not reflect the true preferences of the decision maker.

Another important property of the simple additive weighting model (3) is the assumption of constant rates of substitution between attributes. This means that the decision maker is always willing to trade in a certain amount of attribute k for a constant amount of attribute m, independently of the values achieved in the two attributes. Consider, for example, the decision between several options for a crash program, in which additional resources are committed to shorten the development time for a project. The assumption of constant tradeoff rates implies that the decision maker is willing to spend just the same amount for the first week of reduction as for the fifteenth week. In many instances, preferences of decision makers do not fulfill this assumption.

Another problem of (3) is that some efficient alternatives might never be found using this approach. While this seems to be a rather abstract, technical argument, it has considerable practical consequences as illustrated in Figure 17.

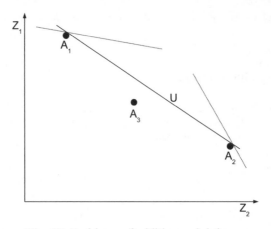

Fig. 17. Problems of additive weighting

Figure 17 shows three alternatives, which are evaluated in two attributes Z_1 and Z_2. All three alternatives are efficient, and A_3 seems to be a well-balanced compromise. But A_3 can never be selected as the best alternative in an additive weighting scheme. When the weights are chosen as in the line U in Figure 17, then A_1 and A_2 are evaluated as equal and better than A_3. Weight changes will cause either A_1 or A_2 to become the optimal alternative, but never A_3. Thus a simple additive weighting approach eliminates alternatives which are dominated by a linear combination of other alternatives, although not by any existing alternative (Chankong and Haimes, 1983).

This problem can be overcome when attribute values in (3) are transformed and (3) is modified to

$$u(A_i) = \sum_k w_k v_k(a_{ik})$$

(4)

where v_k is a partial utility function for attribute k. When v_k is a concave function, (4) represents decreasing marginal benefits, and additional improvements in an attribute which already has a high value would be valued less. In Figure 17, using concave marginal utility functions would cause A_1 to shift downward and A_2 to the left, so for some ranges of weights, A_3 could become the optimal alternative.

Equation (4) describes the basic form of multi-attribute utility functions used in Multi-Attribute Utility Theory (MAUT) (Keeney and Raiffa, 1976). MAUT provides an axiomatically founded theory of multicriteria decision making. An additive function (4) is an appropriate model of preferences when the attributes fulfill the requirement of preferential independence, i.e., when the contribution of each attribute to the overall evaluation of an alternative does not depend on the values in other attributes. This assumption is violated if an attribute requires a high value in another attribute to be useful. For example, a high resolution display is useless without adequate processing power to generate graphics within reasonable time. Thus the attributes "graphics resolution" and "processing power" of a workstation do not fulfill the assumption of preferential independence.

Interdependencies between attributes can be handled by other forms of multi-attibute utility functions, like product or multilinear functions, which contain multiplicative terms between two or more attributes.

While MAUT can overcome most of the problems of the simple additive weighting approach (3), it also considerably increases the cognitive requirements on the decision maker, who must specify the weights as well as the partial utility functions. Several methods have been developed for the elicitation of these parameters. But empirical research has shown that although these methods should theoretically lead to identical results, the results are often quite different due to various bias phenomena (Schoemaker and Waid, 1982; Weber et al., 1988). We therefore will not present the individual methods in detail here, but refer to the relevant literature (von Winterfeldt and Edwards, 1986).

A popular variant of the additive weighting model is the Analytic Hierarchy Process (AHP) developed by Saaty (1980). Instead of using a partial utility function v_k, this method directly evaluates alternatives in each attribute and then performs an additive aggregation similar to (4). The AHP also allows for a hierarchical structure of attributes: The ultimate goal of selecting a best decision alternative is first broken up into top-level goals, each of which can consist of multiple subgoals at the second level and so on until one reaches subgoals in which the alternatives under consideration can easily be evaluated. Attributes thus form a tree, to which the alternatives are added at the lowest level to provide a consistent representation of the decision problem.

The weights used to aggregate across the levels of this hierarchy are derived from pairwise comparisons of all lower level attributes with respect to the higher level. The elements are compared on a ratio scale, the comparison of elements A_i and A_j is represented by a factor c_{ij} indicating how many times alternatives A_i is considered to be better than alternative A_j. The factors c_{ij} form a comparison matrix C. By definition of the comparison factors, matrix C is reciprocal, i.e., $c_{ij} = 1/c_{ji}$.

Assume that the true performance ("priority") of alternative A_i is given by w_i. When all comparisons are performed consistently,

$$c_{ij} = w_i/w_j \tag{5}$$

and, since it is easy to verify that

$$C \cdot W = NW \tag{6}$$

the true priority vector $W = (w_1,...,w_N)$ is an eigenvector of the comparison matrix C. Since the eigenvector is robust against small disturbances of the matrix C, the eigenvector is also used to estimate the vector of priorities from a comparison matrix if the matrix is not entirely consistent.

By comparing all elements of the lower level to each other, the AHP provides for a certain level of redundancy, which is used to level out possible inconsistencies in the decision maker's judgments. There are also measures for the consistency of a comparison matrix and rules indicating when a comparison matrix can be considered as sufficiently consistent or when the comparisons should be revised.

The AHP has been proposed by several authors as a decision making tool in software engineering problems, especially concerning the selection of IS projects (Muralidhar et al., 1990; Schniederjans and Wilson, 1991; Lee and Kwak, 1999), of development tools (Kim and Yoon, 1992; Lai et al., 1999; Lai et al., 2002), of system software (Roper-Lowe and Sharp, 1990; Mamaghani, 2002), and of enterprise-wide information technologies (Sarkis and Sundarraj, 2003). It has also been used to measure the quality of information systems as a multidimensional construct (Santhanam and Guimaraes, 1995; Kim, 1998; Forgionne, 1999; Phillips-Wren et al., 2004).

A typical evaluation hierarchy for software selection problems can be found in (Lai et al., 1999, p. 225). Their hierarchy consists of four levels of attributes. The top level is formed by the single goal of selecting the optimal system, in the particular case analyzed there, of selecting an optimal multimedia authoring system. The second level consists of two still rather broad attributes, technical considerations on one hand and managerial considerations on the other hand. Technical considerations are broken up at the third level into the attributes development support, graphic support, multimedia support, and data file support. For managerial considerations, only two attributes are considered at level three, cost-effectiveness and vendor support. Each attribute at level three of the hierarchy is then represented by between six and nine rather specific and easily measurable attributes at level four, for example, the ability to import text, spreadsheet, MIDI, or other data file types are used for the level three attribute "data file support."

This example shows the important benefit of a hierarchical structure of attributes: by systematically decomposing attributes and identifying lower level attributes which contribute to the achievement of the higher level attributes, it is possible to move from rather abstract concepts like managerial considerations to easily measurable attributes like the ability to import different file types. It also shows that one indeed needs to consider all levels of attributes: without the specific attributes, it would not be possible to evaluate the alternatives in the abstract, high-level attributes, while on the other hand, decision makers would probably be overwhelmed by the task of judging the importance of a large number of specific attributes without being able to relate them to higher level concepts.

But the example also shows that in creating an attribute hierarchy, one needs to carefully consider the relationships between attributes, especially if an additive weighting approach like the AHP is used. One might question whether attributes like multimedia support and data file support really fulfill the assumption of preferential independence required by this method. The value of program features to process, for example, video data is probably not independent of the possibility to read and write video data files.

A major advantage of additive weighting methods like MAUT or the AHP is their ability to handle both quantitative and qualitative attributes. To assign a partial utility value, it is not necessary that the underlying attributes have numerical values. For example, a component technology can be rated as "innovative," "state of the art," or "outdated," and a utility value assigned to each level. At the same time, numerical attributes (for example, estimates of effort expressed in man-months) can also be accommodated in these methods, either by direct linear transformations or by using nonlinear partial utility functions v_k.

While it might be difficult for decision makers to express their preferences in the form of weights, additive weighting methods are rather well suited to accommodate objective information on the importance of attributes. Formally (assuming that the partial utility functions v_k are linear), weights correspond to the partial derivatives of the upper level goals with respect to the lower level goals. When empirical data on both levels is available, the weights could be estimated by statistical methods.

Aspiration-level Methods

Weights are abstract quantities, which do not directly relate to the decision problem at hand, making it difficult for decision makers to specify them. Methods based on aspiration levels try to avoid those difficulties and allow the decision maker to articulate preferences in a more natural way. Aspiration levels are levels of the attributes themselves, which a decision maker wants to achieve. For example, in acquiring COTS components, one could try to find components which combine a certain level of functionality, do not exceed certain resource requirements at execution time, and cost less than a certain amount of money. Such aspiration levels for attributes can be used to specify the decision maker's preferences toward the attributes, even if no alternative exists which at the same time fulfills the aspiration levels in all attributes.

The concept of aspiration levels was first used in *goal programming* introduced by Charnes and Cooper in the 1950s (Charnes et al., 1955; Charnes and Cooper, 1961). Goal programming was originally developed to solve multiobjective linear programming problems where alternatives are represented by continuous decision variables (x_j).

The goal programming model finds a solution in which the values of the objective functions are as close as possible to a prespecified goal vector $G = (g_1, ..., g_K)$. By introducing deviation variables d_k^+ and d_k^-, the problem can be formulated as a linear programming problem with a single objective function:

$$\min \sum_k \left(d_k^+ + d_k^- \right)$$
$$\sum_j c_{kj} x_j + d_k^- - d_k^+ = g_k \quad k = 1, ..., K \tag{7}$$
$$\sum_j a_{ij} x_j \le b_i \quad i = 1, ..., N$$

In model (7), there are the K linear objective functions with coefficients c_{kj}. The parameters a_{ij} and b_i represent the coefficients and limiting values of N constraints. The two deviation variables d_k^+ and d_k^- are used to measure the over-achievement and underachievement of goal k. Thus any kind of deviation from the goal level in any objective is considered to be equally undesirable.

This assumption of equal importance of goals can be relaxed by weighting the deviation variables. An important variant is *hierarchical goal programming*, where the weights differ by several orders of magnitude. Thus, it is ensured that goals with higher priority are completely satisfied before the model attempts to optimize the less important goals.

While model (7) is a linear programming model with continuous decision variables, the basic framework of goal programming is applicable to any type of multi-objective optimization problem. Goal programming models have been proposed for several decision problems in software engineering, like requirement analysis (Jain et al., 1991). Most models were developed for project selection (Lawrence et al., 1983; Schniederjans and Wilson, 1991; Lee and Kim, 2000). These models use binary (0/1) variables to represent potential projects. Setting variable x_j to 1 indicates that the project is carried out.

As an example for a project selection model, we consider a simplified version of the model in (Schniederjans and Wilson, 1991). The model uses six goals, which are grouped into three hierarchical levels. Goals at the highest (most important) level are considered as obligatory goals, like avoiding to exceed the maximum available manpower or budget. The remaining two levels are formed by flexible goals, like avoiding deviations from the expected (rather than the maximum) budget or balancing the workload on clerical staff. The entire model is formulated as follows:

$$\text{Min } P_1(d_1^+ + d_2^+ + d_3^+ + d_4^+) +$$
$$P_2(d_5^+ + d_5^-) +$$
$$P_3(d_6^+ + d_6^-)$$

s.t.

$$\sum_j hp_j x_j + d_1^- - d_1^+ = HP$$

$$\sum_j ha_j x_j + d_2^- - d_2^+ = HA$$

$$\sum_j b_j x_j + d_3^- - d_3^+ = BM \qquad (8)$$

$$x_2 + d_4^- = 1$$

$$\sum_j b_j x_j + d_5^- - d_5^+ = BE$$

$$\sum_j hc_j x_j + d_6^- - d_6^+ = HC$$

$$x_j \in \{0,1\}$$

The objective function of the model consists of three parts, which are weighted by factors P1, P2, and P3. When P1 is chosen much greater than P2, and P2 much greater than P_3, the model will first attempt to satisfy the goals represented by the first four constraints, then the fifth goal and the last goal will only be optimized when the other goals are satisfied.

The first constraint represents the obligatory goal to keep the number of total programmer hours used within the maximum available capacity denoted by HP. Here hp_j represents the number of programmer hours used for project j. The constraint contains both a lower deviation variable d_1^-, which takes on a positive value if the number of hours actually used is less than the maximum HP, and an upper deviation variable d_1^+, which takes a positive value if the capacity used exceeds the maximum. Only d_1^+ is included in the objective function, since underutilization of the maximum capacity is not considered a violation of this goal. Similarly, the second constraint relates analyst time used to the available maximum analyst hours HA and the third constraint relates total expenditures to the maximum budget BM. The coefficients ha_j and b_j represent the usage of analysts' time and budget for project j. The fourth constraint represents the fact that one particular project, x_2, must definitely be undertaken. The deviational variable d_4^+ becomes 1 when project x_2 is not included in the solution, and by including it in the objective function, this requirement becomes an obligatory goal.

The fifth constraint, like the third constraint, refers to the total expenditures for the projects undertaken. But it compares this amount not to the overall maximum, but to the overall expected budget BE, which should be attained as closely as possible. Thus for this constraint, both the positive and the negative deviational variables are included in the objective function. The same holds for the last constraint, which models the number of clerical hours used and relates their total to the target value HC.

The standard goal programming model (7) implies that the goal vector is the most attractive solution for the decision maker and that any deviation from it is considered as harmful. Thus, when the chosen goal vector is feasible, the model will select it, even when it is dominated by other solutions.

Other methods for aspiration-based decision support try to overcome this problem and always provide an efficient solution. This is achieved by using a *scalarizing function* (Wierzbicki, 1986), which provides a parameterized representation of the set of efficient solutions. In this approach, a *reference point* defined in terms of goal levels serves as control parameter of the scalarizing function and determines the efficient solution selected. One commonly used scalarizing function is the extended Tchebycheff distance to the reference point given by

$$s = \min_k (z_k - g_k) + \rho \sum_k (z_k - g_k) \qquad (9)$$

where $z_k = \sum c_{kj} x_j$ is the level of goal k achieved by a solution, g_k is the reference level for goal k specified by the decision maker, and ρ is a (typically small) technical parameter. By adding the second term in equation (9) with just a small weight, the generation of dominated solutions is avoided.

The main advantage of this approach is that the reference point $(g_1, ..., g_K)$ can be a feasible as well as an infeasible point. When the reference point itself is not feasible, maximization of (9) will generate an efficient solution to the problem which is as close to the reference point as possible. When the reference point is feasible, a solution which dominates the reference point will be found, or the reference point itself is returned when it is efficient. The decision maker can control the structure of the efficient solution by changing the reference values g_k: increasing g_k for an objective k will also lead to a solution which is better in that objective.

Different functions could be used as scalarizing functions in this approach. The main advantage of the Tchebycheff norm used in (9) is that unlike an additive weighting function, it also allows the selection of a solution which is efficient, but dominated by a linear combination of other feasible goal vectors. Thus the problem illustrated in Figure 17 is avoided. This feature makes the reference point approach particularly attractive for problems with discrete alternatives (or alternatives described by binary or integer decision variables).

Aspiration levels are often seen as a more natural way for decision makers to specify their preferences than weights (Lewandowski and Wierzbicki, 1989). A reference point approach is particularly attractive for interactive decision support systems, because it allows the decision maker to freely search the set of efficient solutions. This concept has been implemented in several systems for the interactive solution of multi-objective optimization problems (Grauer et al., 1984; Korhonen and Wallenius, 1988).

But the fact that aspiration-based methods work directly with goal levels also means that for these methods, all goals must be measured on a numerical scale. Thus it is not possible to take into account qualitative goals as easily as in weighting methods. Furthermore, while there are methods to estimate reference points from empirical data (Vetschera, 1994), their application is not straightforward. Therefore, aspiration-based methods have some disadvantages for the specific context of software engineering, where qualitative criteria and the ability to incorporate objective, rather than subjective, information are important.

Outranking Methods

Additive weighting methods and aspiration-based methods differ not only in technical terms. They are also based on rather different views about the decision maker's preferences. Additive weighting methods implicitly assume that the decision maker's preferences exist ex ante and can be elicited independently of the decision problem at hand. Aspiration-based methods take a more dynamic perspective. The reference point is constantly changed to search the set of efficient solutions. Thus preferences are seen as evolving while the decision maker finds out more about the problem, the goal levels which can be achieved, and the trade-offs between goals inherent to the problem. Clear preferences toward the different goals need not even exist at the beginning of this process.

Outranking methods take this constructivist view of preferences one step further. Their main goal is to construct preferences, based on objective information on the decision alternatives, rather than to elicit and apply preexisting preferences.

Outranking methods are used only for multi-attribute decision problems, in which a set of discrete alternatives is explicitly given. The central concept (and the main output) of these methods is the *outranking relation*. This is a binary relation between alternatives indicating that one alternative should be considered to be better than another.

As a typical example of this type of methods, we consider the ELECTRE family of methods developed by B. Roy (Crama and Hansen, 1983; Roy and Vincke, 1984; Roy, 1991), specifically the ELECTRE I method. For other types of outranking methods like the PROMETHEE family of methods (Brans et al., 1984), we refer to the literature (Roy and Vanderpooten, 1996; Pomerol and Barba-Romero, 2000).

The dominance relation between alternatives is based on objective information and thus could be used as an objective instrument to rank alternatives. The main problem of the dominance relation is its lack of discriminatory power. Since dominance is based on rather strict requirements, the dominance relation contains few elements and consequently, the set of efficient alternatives can still be quite large. The main aim of outranking methods is to provide a relation which is richer than the dominance relation, and thus eliminates more alternatives.

An alternative has to fulfill two requirements to dominate another one:

- It must not be worse than the other alternative in any attribute, and
- it must be strictly better in at least one attribute.

The main obstacle to achieving dominance is the first requirement. If this requirement is weakened, a richer relation can be established. The ELECTRE method relaxes this requirement to the condition that an alternative should not be much worse than another alternative in any attribute. This concept is formalized by the *discordance* index, which synthesizes all the evidence against establishing an outranking.

The discordance index d_{ij} between alternatives A_i and A_j is computed as:

$$d_{ij} = \frac{\max\limits_{k:a_{ik} < a_{jk}} a_{jk} - a_{ik}}{\max\limits_{k} |a_{ik} - a_{jk}|} \qquad (10)$$

i.e., the ratio of the maximum difference in those attributes where alternative A_i is worse than A_j to the maximum difference in all attributes. If this ratio is low, the differences in favor of A_j are small compared to the differences in favor of A_i, and an outranking of A_i over A_j can be established.

The second requirement of dominance is replaced in ELECTRE by the concept of *concordance*, which represents all the facts confirming that alternative A_i is better than alternative A_j. The concordance index c_{ij} between two alternatives is calculated as

$$c_{ij} = \sum_{k:a_{ik}>a_{jk}} w_k \tag{11}$$

i.e., the sum of weights of all the attributes in which A_i is better than A_j. By introducing weights, ELECTRE also enables the decision maker to specify the importance of attributes. But unlike in additive weighting, in this method the weights are not multiplied with the attribute values, so the weights are independent of the attribute ranges.

The significance of the concordance and discordance indices is determined by comparing them to a concordance threshold s_c and a discordance threshold s_d, respectively. An outranking is established between A_i and A_j if and only if $c_{ij} > s_c$ and $d_{ij} < s_d$, that is if there is sufficient evidence to consider A_i better than A_j and no sufficient evidence against this proposition. By increasing the discordance threshold or lowering the concordance threshold, the number of outrankings can be increased. This effect can be used to develop an interactive algorithm, in which alternatives are successively eliminated until only one optimal alternative remains (Vetschera, 1988).

Since outranking methods operate mainly on objective data, they seem to be quite well suited for decision problems in software engineering. Calculation of the concordance index requires only a comparison between attribute values, which is possible for qualitative attributes, too. The discordance index requires the calculation of differences and thus can be determined only for numerical attributes. For qualitative attributes, other methods would be needed to determine discordance, although this issue has not yet been discussed intensively in the literature. Although these methods seem to be quite well suited for decision problems in software development and engineering, only few documented applications exist so far (Paschetta and Tsoukias, 2000; Stamelos et al., 2000; Blin and Tsoukias, 2001).

4.4 Incomplete Information and Sensitivity Analysis

All decision methods presented so far require various types of (numerical) information describing the performance of alternatives in the attributes as well as the preferences of the decision maker. In practical applications, it is often difficult to provide this information precisely. Therefore, techniques to deal with imprecise or incomplete information were developed in the context of all the approaches discussed. These methods can broadly be classified into two main groups:

- Approaches based on sensitivity analysis first determine the optimal alternative assuming that no uncertainty exists. In a second step, the sensitivity of the decision with respect to data changes is analyzed. When small changes in the inputs

would change the decision, it is considered to be sensitive and additional information is sought.
- The second class of approaches seeks to extend the decision methods to deal directly with incomplete or imprecise information.

Both types of approaches exist for additive weighting methods. In sensitivity analysis for this type of methods, one typically studies the effects of weight changes on the selection of the optimal alternative. The impact of changes of a single weight can be analyzed by interpreting the evaluation of each alternative as a function of that weight. A plot of this function provides the decision maker with a convenient overview about how weight changes would influence the decision.

Simultaneous sensitivity analyses for several weights can be performed using distance-based approaches (Evans, 1984; Rios Insua and French, 1991), which measure the total change in parameter space leading to a different decision, or by considering the size (volume) of the region in parameter space in which the chosen alternative remains optimal (Charnetski and Soland, 1978; Vetschera, 1997).

Decision methods based on incomplete information (Weber, 1987) typically assume that instead of one precise numerical value, the information available describes a set of possible values, for example, an interval or a relationship between parameters. A decision maker could, for example, state that the weight for attribute "costs" should be larger than the weight for the attribute "performance," but not be able to give precise values for the two weights.

Methods for decision making under incomplete information determine whether, given the information available, an alternative can definitely be considered as better than another alternative and find the set of alternatives which are optimal for at least some possible parameter values.

We denote the utility of alternative A_i given some weight vector $\mathbf{w}$ by $u(A_i \mid \mathbf{w})$ and the set of weight vectors which are compatible with the information provided by the decision maker by W. To determine whether alternative A_i can ever be considered as better than alternative A_j, the following optimization model is solved:

$$\max_{\mathbf{w} \in W} u(A_i \mid \mathbf{w}) - u(A_j \mid \mathbf{w}) \tag{12}$$

When the optimal objective value of (12) is negative, no parameter vector $\mathbf{w} \in W$ exists for which alternative A_i has higher utility than alternative A_j. If only information on the weights is incomplete, model (12) is a linear programming model, which can be solved easily. For the case of incomplete information on both the weights and the performance of alternatives, transformations have been developed which allow us to represent this problem also as a linear programming problem (Park and Kim, 1997).

The problem of incomplete information on parameters has also been studied extensively in the context of aspiration level methods, mainly goal programming. Here uncertain parameters are often represented by fuzzy numbers, leading to the method of *fuzzy goal programming* (Zimmermann, 1978; Carlsson and Fullér, 2002), which deals with uncertainty in the goal values as well as the constraints.

For outranking methods, similar techniques for dealing with incomplete and imprecise information are available. Sensitivity analysis methods (Vetschera, 1986; Mareschal, 1988; Wolters and Mareschal, 1995; Miettinen and Salminen, 1999) allow us to calculate bounds for model parameters like weights or concordance and discordance thresholds within which the outranking relation remains unchanged. There are also outranking methods which use incomplete and fuzzy information. On one hand, outranking relations themselves can be considered as fuzzy (Roubens, 1996); on the other hand, specific methods were developed to use imprecise data on the various model parameters (Roy and Vanderpooten, 1996; Le Teno and Mareschal, 1998; Dias and Climaco, 1999; Dias et al., 2002).

4.5 Summary and Conclusions

In this chapter, we have surveyed a spectrum of different methods for solving multicriteria decision problems and discussed their applicability to decisions in software engineering. Obviously, the problem of selecting a multicriteria decision method is a multicriteria problem by itself, so it is not surprising that no single best method exists, which can be applied by all decision makers for all problems.

One important criterion for the selection of a method is the structure of the decision problem: the distinction between multi-attribute problems with a given set of alternatives and multi-objective optimization problems, in which alternatives are described via decision variables, provides a useful guideline. However, this distinction is not as clear-cut as it might seem on first sight. The choice of a problem representation is to some extent arbitrary. A set of constraints and discrete decision variables of a multi-objective problem can be mapped into an exhaustive list of alternatives, thus transforming the problem into a multi-attribute problem.

Apart from the representation of decision alternatives, the scale on which their outcomes are measured plays an important role. Both additive weighting methods and outranking methods are rather well suited to deal with qualitative attributes as well as with quantitative data. This factor could be important for many applications in software engineering.

Another important component in a multicriteria decision problem is the user's preferences. Here decision problems in software engineering are specific, because preferences are not purely subjective, but objective facts about the importance of criteria have to be taken into account. This can be accomplished quite easily in additive weighting models, while for the other methods techniques still need to be developed.

Thus, for different problems, different methods are most appropriate. The field of multicriteria decision making offers a large toolbox, which can help to make more rational and consistent decisions even in complex situations, as they frequently occur during the lifecycle of a software project.

References

(Barua et al., 1995) Barua, A., Kriebel, C. H., Mukhopadhyay, T.: Information Technologies and Business Value: An Analytic and Empirical Investigation. Inf Sys Research **6**(1), pp 3–51

(Blin and Tsoukias, 2001) Blin, M.-J., Tsoukias, A.: Multi-Criteria Methodology Contribution to the Software Quality Evaluation. Software Quality Journal **9**(2), pp 113–132

(Boehm, 2003) Boehm, B. W.: Value-Based Software Engineering. Software Engineering Notes **28**(2), p 4

(Brans et al., 1984) Brans, J. P., Mareschal, B., Vincke, P.: Promethee: A New Family of Outranking Methods in Multicriteria Analysis. In: Operational Research '84, ed by Brans, J. P. (North Holland, Amsterdam, 1984), pp 477–490

(Carlsson and Fullér, 2002) Carlsson, C., Fullér, R.: Fuzzy Reasoning in Decision Making and Optimization (Physica, Heidelberg 2002)

(Chankong and Haimes, 1983) Chankong, V., Haimes, Y. Y.: Multiobjective Decision Making: Theory and Methodology (North Holland, Amsterdam 1983)

(Charnes and Cooper, 1961) Charnes, A., Cooper, W. W.: Management Models and Industrial Applications of Linear Programming (J. Wiley & Sons, New York 1961)

(Charnes et al., 1955) Charnes, A., Cooper, W. W., Ferguson, R. O.: Optimal Estimation of Executive Compensation by Linear Programming. Manage. Sci. **1**(2), pp 138–151

(Charnetski and Soland, 1978) Charnetski, J. R., Soland, R. M.: Multiple-Attribute Decision Making With Partial Information: The Comparative Hypervolume Criterion. Nav. Res. Logist. Q **25**, pp 279–288

(Crama and Hansen, 1983) Crama, Y., Hansen, P.: An Introduction to the ELECTRE Research Programme. In: Essays and Surveys on Multiple Criteria Decision Making, ed by Hansen, P. (Springer, Berlin, 1983), pp 31–42

(DeLone and McLean, 1992) DeLone, W. H., McLean, E. R.: Information Systems Success: The Quest for the Dependent Variable. Inf Sys Research **3**(1), pp 60–95

(Dias and Climaco, 1999) Dias, L. C., Climaco, J. C.: On Computing ELECTRE's Credibility Indices under Partial Information. J. Multi-Criteria Dec. Anal. **8**(2), pp 74–92

(Dias et al., 2002) Dias, L. C., Mousseau, V., Figueira, J., Climaco, J. C.: An Aggregation/Disaggregation Approach to obtain Robust Conclusions with ELECTRE TRI. Eur. J. Oper. Res **138**(2), pp 332–348

(Evans, 1984) Evans, J. R.: Sensitivity Analysis in Decision Theory. Decis Sci **15**(2), pp 239–247

(Farbey et al., 1995) Farbey, B., Land, F. F., Targett, D.: A Taxonomy of Information Systems Applications: The Benefits' Evaluation Ladder. Eur. J. Inf. Systs. **4**(1), pp 41–50

(Forgionne, 1999) Forgionne, G.: An AHP model of DSS effectiveness. Eur. J. Inf. Systs. **8**(2), pp 95–106

(Grauer et al., 1984) Grauer, M., Lewandowski, A., Wierzbicki, A. P.: DIDASS –
    Theory, Implementation and Experiences. In: Interactive Decision Analysis,
    ed by Wierzbicki, A. P. (Springer, Berlin, 1984), pp 22–30
(Hwang and Masud, 1979) Hwang, C.-L., Masud, A. S.: Multiple Objective Deci-
    sion Making – Methods and Applications A State-of-the-Art Survey
    (Springer, Berlin 1979)
(Hwang and Yoon, 1981) Hwang, C.-L., Yoon, K.: Multiple Attribute Decision
    Making – Methods and Applications: A State of the Art Survey (Springer,
    Berlin 1981)
(Jain et al., 1991) Jain, H. K., Tanniru, M. R., Fazlollahi, B.: MCDM Approach
    for Generating and Evaluating Alternatives in Requirement Analysis. Inf Sys
    Research 2(3), pp 223–239
(Keeney and Raiffa, 1976) Keeney, R. L., Raiffa, H.: Decisions with Multiple Ob-
    jectives: Preferences and Value Tradeoffs (J. Wiley & Sons, New York 1976)
(Kim and Yoon, 1992) Kim, C. S., Yoon, Y.: Selection of a Good Expert System
    Shell for Instructional Purposes in Business. Inf Manage 23(5), pp 249–262
(Kim, 1998) Kim, J.: Hierarchical Structure of Intranet Functions and Their Rela-
    tive Importance: Using the Analytic Hierarchy Process for Virtual Organiza-
    tions. Decis. Support Syst. 23(1), pp 59–74
(Korhonen and Wallenius, 1988) Korhonen, P., Wallenius, J.: A Pareto Race. Nav.
    Res. Logist. 35(6), pp 615–623
(Lai et al., 1999) Lai, V. S., Trueblood, R. P., Wong, B. K.: Software Selection: A
    Case Study of the Application of the Analytical Hierarchical Process to the
    Selection of a Multimedia Authoring System. Inf Manage 36(4), pp 221–232
(Lai et al., 2002) Lai, V. S., Wong, B. K., Cheung, W.: Group Decision Making in
    a Multiple Criteria Environment: A Case using the AHP in Software Selec-
    tion. Eur. J. Oper. Res 137(1), pp 134–144
(Lawrence et al., 1983) Lawrence, K. D., Marose, R. A., Lawrence, S. M.: Multi-
    ple Goal Portfolio Analysis Model for the Selection of MIS Projects. In: Es-
    says and Surveys on Multiple Criteria Decision Making, ed by Hansen, P.
    (Springer, Berlin, 1983), pp 229–237
(Le Teno and Mareschal, 1998) Le Teno, J. F., Mareschal, B.: An Interval Version
    of PROMETHEE for the Comparison of Building Products' Design with Ill-
    defined Data on Environmental Quality. Eur. J. Oper. Res 109(2), pp 522–529
(Lee and Kwak, 1999) Lee, C. W., Kwak, N. K.: Information Resource Planning
    for a Health-Care System Using an AHP-based Goal Programming Method. J.
    Opl Res. Soc. 50(12), pp 1191–1198
(Lee and Kim, 2000) Lee, J., Kim, S.: Using Analytic Network Process and Goal
    Programming for Interdependent Information System Project Selection. Com-
    put. and Ops. Res. 27(4), pp 367–382
(Lewandowski and Wierzbicki, 1989) Lewandowski, A., Wierzbicki, A. P.: Deci-
    sion Support Systems Using Reference Point Optimization. In: Aspiration
    Based Decision Support Systems, ed by Lewandowski, A. and Wierzbicki, A.
    P. (Springer, Berlin, 1989), pp 3–20

(Mamaghani, 2002) Mamaghani, F.: Evaluation and Selection of an Antivirus and Content Filtering Software. Information Management and Computer Security **10**(1), pp 28–32

(Mareschal, 1988) Mareschal, B.: Weight Stability Intervals in Multicriteria Decision Aid. Eur. J. Oper. Res **33**(1), pp 54–64

(Miettinen and Salminen, 1999) Miettinen, K., Salminen, P.: Decision-aid for Discrete Multiple Criteria Decision Making Problems with Imprecise Data. Eur. J. Oper. Res **119**(1), pp 50–60

(Muralidhar et al., 1990) Muralidhar, K., Santhanam, R., Wilson, R. L.: Using the Analytic Hierarchy Process for Information System Project Selection. Inf Manage **18**(2), pp 87–95

(Park and Kim, 1997) Park, K. S., Kim, S. H.: Tools for Interactive Multiattribute Decisionmaking with Incompletely Identified Information. Eur. J. Oper. Res **98**(1), pp 111–123

(Paschetta and Tsoukias, 2000) Paschetta, E. and Tsoukias, A.: A Real-World MCDA Application: Evaluating Software. J. Multi-Criteria Dec. Anal. **9**(5), pp 205–225

(Phillips-Wren et al., 2004) Phillips-Wren, G. E., Hahn, E. D., Forgionne, G. A.: A Multiple-Criteria Framework for Evaluation of Decision Support Systems. Omega **32**(4), pp 323–332

(Pomerol and Barba-Romero, 2000) Pomerol, J.-C., Barba-Romero, S.: Multicriterion Decision in Management: Principles and Practice (Kluwer, 2000)

(Rios Insua and French, 1991) Rios Insua, D., French, S.: A Framework for Sensitivity Analysis in Discrete Multi-Objective Decision-Making. Eur. J. Oper. Res **54**(2), pp 176–190

(Roper-Lowe and Sharp, 1990) Roper-Lowe, G. C., Sharp, J. A.: The Analytic Hierarchy Process and Its Application to an Information Technology Decision. J. Opl Res. Soc. **41**(1), pp 49–59

(Roubens, 1996) Roubens, M.: Choice Procedures in Fuzzy Multicriteria Decision Analysis based on Pairwise Comparisons. Fuzzy Sets Syst. **84**(2), pp 135–142

(Roy, 1991) Roy, B.: The Outranking Approach and the Foundations of ELECTRE Methods. Theory Decis. **31**, pp 49–73

(Roy and Vanderpooten, 1996) Roy, B., Vanderpooten, D.: The European School of MCDA: Emergence, Basic Features and Current Works. J. Multi-Criteria Dec. Anal. **5**(1), pp 22–36

(Roy and Vincke, 1984) Roy, B., Vincke, P.: Relational Systems of Preference with One or More Pseudo-Criteria: Some New Concepts and Results. Manage. Sci. **30**(11), pp 1323–1335

(Saaty, 1980) Saaty, T. L.: The Analytic Hierarchy Process (McGraw-Hill, New York 1980)

(Santhanam and Guimaraes, 1995) Santhanam, R., Guimaraes, T.: Assessing the Quality of Institutional DSS. Eur. J. Inf. Systs. **4**(3), pp 159–170

(Sarkis and Sundarraj, 2003) Sarkis, J., Sundarraj, R. P.: Evaluating Componentized Enterprise Information Technologies: A Multiattribute Modeling Approach. Inf Sys Frontiers **5**(3), pp 303–320

(Schniederjans and Wilson, 1991) Schniederjans, M. J., Wilson, R. L.: Using the Analytic Hierarchy Process and Goal Programming for Information System Project Selection. Inf Manage **20**(5), pp 333–342

(Schoemaker and Waid, 1982) Schoemaker, P. J. H., Waid, C. C.: An Experimental Comparison of Different Approaches to Determining Weights in Additive Utility Models. Manage. Sci. **28**, pp 182–196

(Stamelos et al., 2000) Stamelos, I., Vlahavas, I., Refanidis, I., Tsoukias, A.: Knowledge Based Evaluation of Software Systems: A Case Study. Information and Software Technology **42**(5), pp 333–345

(Vetschera, 1986) Vetschera, R.: Sensitivity Analysis for the ELECTRE Multicriteria Method. Z. Oper. Res. **30**, pp B 99–B 117

(Vetschera, 1988) Vetschera, R.: An Interactive Outranking System for Multi-Attribute Decision Making. Comput. and Ops. Res. **15**(4), pp 311–322

(Vetschera, 1994) Vetschera, R.: Estimating Aspiration Levels from Discrete Choices – Computational Techniques and Experiences. Eur. J. Oper. Res **76**(3), pp 455–465

(Vetschera, 1997) Vetschera, R.: A Recursive Algorithm for Volume-Based Sensitivity Analysis of Linear Decision Models. Comput. and Ops. Res. **24**(5), pp 477–491

(von Winterfeldt and Edwards, 1986) von Winterfeldt, D., Edwards, W.: Decision Analysis and Behavioral Research (Cambridge University Press, 1986)

(Weber, 1987) Weber, M.: Decision Making with Incomplete Information. Eur. J. Oper. Res **28**(1), pp 44–57

(Weber et al., 1988) Weber, M., Eisenführ, F., von Winterfeldt, D.: The Effects of Splitting Attributes on Weights in Multiattribute Utility Measurement. Manage. Sci. **34**, pp 431–445

(Wierzbicki, 1986) Wierzbicki, A. P.: On the Completeness and Constructiveness of Parametric Characterizations to Vector Optimization Problems. OR Spektrum **8**, pp 73–87

(Wolters and Mareschal, 1995) Wolters, W. T. M., Mareschal, B.: Novel Types of Sensitivity Analysis for Additive MCDM Methods. Eur. J. Oper. Res **81**(2), pp 281–290

(Zimmermann, 1978) Zimmermann, H.-J.: Fuzzy Programming and Linear Programming with Several Objective Functions. Fuzzy Sets Syst. **1**(1), pp 45–55

Author Biography

Rudolf Vetschera is full professor of Organization and Planning at the school of Business, Economics and Statistics, University of Vienna, Austria. He holds a PhD in Economics and Social Sciences from the University of Vienna, Austria. Before his current position, he was full professor of Business Administration at the University of Konstanz, Germany. He has published three books and over 60 papers in reviewed journals and collective volumes. His research interests are at the intersection of organization theory, decision analysis, and information systems, especially in the mutual influence of these areas on each other.

5 Risk and the Economic Value of the Software Producer

Warren Harrison

Abstract: The economic worth of a commercial organization is a function of the present value of its future profits, discounted for both time and risk. Consequently, the economic value of a software firm is greatly affected by the predictability of the organization's software development projects, since unpredictable projects warrant large risk premiums. We can quantitatively approximate the value of increased predictability, and evaluate the effectiveness of efforts, such as process improvement, to improve the predictability of software development projects.

Keywords: Financial Risk, Return on Investment, Process Improvement, Capital Budgeting.

5.1. Introduction

As pointed out by Berry and Aurum in Chapter 8, "decision making within a value-based software engineering framework requires the inclusion of indicators of value." Since the primary obligation of a business organization is to increase the wealth of its shareholders, establishing a well-accepted measure of the economic worth of an organization (and consequently, its contribution to the wealth of its shareholders) is central to any discussion of valuation of the artifacts that lead to that worth.

In this chapter, we explore the components of economic value, and the effect of financial risk upon valuation, particularly within the context of commercial software producers. We divide the discussion into three parts. Sections 5.2 through 5.5 provide the fundamental concepts necessary to discussion valuation and financial risk. Sections 5.6 through 5.9 extend the concepts to the measurement of the predictability of software projects, with particular application focused on software process improvement and its effects on predictability. Sections 5.10 through 5.12 introduce the concept of "relative risk" with respect to predicting the economic contribution of software projects to the economic value of the firm and illustrate how this concept may be used to assign value to risk mitigation efforts such as process improvement efforts.

5.2. The Value of the Firm

The economic worth of a commercial organization is a function of the total profit it can generate over its remaining lifetime (Brealey and Myers, 2000). For a software company, this translates into the profits derived from its software products. Obviously, if a firm has a finite lifetime, as it ages its economic worth decreases, all other things being constant, since fewer years remain over which it can generate profits.

Because firms are usually established with the intention of perpetual operation, this concept is difficult to realize in practice. However, if we consider a somewhat contrived example we can illustrate this concept very easily.

Assume the date is January 1, 1999. We have just established a consultancy to mitigate the effect of the Y2K problem. We have contracted to provide services to a single customer for our actual costs, plus $1,000,000, payable on December 31, 1999, at the end of the contract period. These funds are in an escrow account, guaranteeing that they will be paid at the end of twelve months. Sadly, we have no plans or prospects for additional business after December 31, 1999. Our solution must be deployed before January 1, 2000, and once deployed we can claim no further revenue from the technology.

The economic value of the firm is therefore $1,000,000. Certainly, a rational businessperson would pay no more than $1,000,000 (and in fact would probably refuse to pay even that much) for our consultancy since they could expect to receive only $1,000,000 in return.

5.3. The Time Value of Money

The economic value of a firm is less if the expected profits accrue later in time rather than earlier. We call this phenomenon *the time value of money*.

For the sake of argument, let us say that we have found a wealthy entrepreneur with a desire to enter the Y2K market. Just as our investor gets ready to purchase our consultancy, he announces his intention to instead purchase our competitor who has a very similar arrangement with another customer.

Why the change of heart? We are puzzled to learn that his decision was based on the fact that while our payment was due on December 31, 1999 at the end of the contract period, our competitor had shrewdly specified that their payment was due at the beginning of their contract period on January 1, 1999.

In this case, a million dollars a year in the future is not the same as a million dollars today. Our wealthy investor cleverly noted that with our competitor, he would immediately receive his million dollars upon purchasing the company, allowing him to reinvest the proceeds at 5% interest for a year, yielding $1,050,000 at the end of the year as opposed to the $1,000,000 he would receive had he bought our company.

So how much is our company really worth, if the purchaser has to wait 12 months to receive the proceeds of the contract? Obviously if the spoiler in our earlier deal was the extra interest our investor would have forgone had he purchased our company rather than the competitor, then we would need to discount our asking price to make ourselves competitive.[3]

By how much should we discount our price? A good starting point would be to reduce our asking price by enough so the investor could buy our company, plus have enough left over to invest so at the end of the year the investment plus interest would total $50,000 (when added to our end of period return of $1,000,000, this would yield $1,050,000).

Assuming a 5% rate of return[4], the asking price for our firm could be no more than $952,380 on January 1, 1999. This would yield $1,050,000 in revenue at the end of the year. $1,000,000 would come from the contracted payment, and the $47,620 difference between $1,000,000 and the asking price of $952,380 would grow to $50,000 after being invested for one year at 5%. This is also known as our firm's *Present Value*.

In the present circumstance, all other things being equal, a rational investor would be indifferent to which investment choice – purchase our company or our competitor's – he selected. In both cases, he would invest $1,000,000 on January 1, 1999 and receive $1,050,000 on December 31, 1999.

We can compute the Present Value *(PV)* of an asset worth *FV* dollars *n* years in the future assuming an annual interest rate (cost of capital) of *k*:

$$PV = FV/(1+k)n$$

Therefore, in our previous example, the Future Value of our consultancy is $1,000,000 payable in one year *(n)*, and we assume an opportunity to invest the initial outlay at 5% per year *(k)*. Then:

$$PV = 1,000,000/1.051$$
$$PV = 952,380$$

In Chapter 17, Reifer discusses using this mechanism, among others, to value intellectual property, and Maurice, Ruhe, Saliu, and Ngo-The maximize the Net Present Value (NPV) of a software investment by sequencing feature delivery in Chapter 12.

---

[3]In actuality, the availability of our competitor's firm for purchase is irrelevant, since our hypothetical investor could simply invest his $1,000,000 in a bond or certificate of deposit at 5% interest and *still* end up with $1,050,000 at the end of the year.

[4]The reader should note a 5% return is unrealistically small for modern companies that often demand double digit ROI from their investments.

5.4. Financial Risk

In our earlier example, we assumed the $1,000,000 payment was certain. There-fore, we could determine the investment necessary at a particular cost of capital to yield the future value we wish to receive at the end of the investment period.

Risk, in a financial context, is a measure of likelihood of the receipt of a par-ticular sum of money in the future. Notably, financial risk does not consider just the likelihood of receiving *less* than a certain sum of money, but also the likeli-hood of receiving *more* than a certain sum of money. In financial circles, investors want to know exactly what they're going to receive, since underestimating can re-sult in a misapplication of funds just as easily as can overestimating.

Risk reflects the uncertainty of a given expected return. This may be due to an uncertain business environment, unresolved technical challenges, inconsistent worker performance, unknown customer needs or simply poor prediction due to inadequate effort devoted to, or incompetence at performing predictions.

Two different types of financial risk are recognized. One type of risk is shared by most, if not all, other investments. This sort of risk is known as *systematic risk*, or *undiversifiable risk*, because it cannot be mitigated by diversifying investments since all the players are affected by the same factors.

On the other hand, *unsystematic risk*, or sometimes *specific risk*, is the risk spe-cific to a single investment. The classical approach to mitigating unsystematic risk is by diversifying investments or, as it is often advised, "*avoid putting all of your eggs into one basket*" (Harrison, 2002).

Just as investors insist on discounting a future asset or revenue to account for the time period between the investment and the payout, they likewise insist on dis-counts to reflect how *risky* a given investment may be.

Ordinarily this is accomplished by adding a *risk premium* Φ to the discount rate to obtain a *risk-adjusted discount rate:*

$$k = r_f + \Phi$$

where r_f reflects the risk-free discount rate and Φ is the risk premium.

The risk-free rate represents the interest investors are willing to accept when an investment is "risk free," such as in the case of U.S. Treasury Bills, where default is simply not an option. This is obviously much lower than a rate that reflects some measure of risk, such as that represented by a dot-com investment that may have a high probability of default. The difference between the returns investors expect from a Treasury Bill and the returns investors expect from the dot-com in-vestment is reflected by the risk premium.

Adding the risk premium Φ to the risk-free rate causes a higher overall discount rate, and consequently a lower present value. This means a risky project must gen-erate greater expected returns in order to compete (i.e., provide comparable pre-sent value) with a less risky project. An alternative approach to risk premiums is further explored in Chapter 3.

5.5. Prediction and the Value of the Firm

In the case of the Y2K Company described earlier, the contracted profit, the date of its receipt and the termination date of the firm are all known in advance. More commonly, we only have predictions: predictions of the profit, predictions of when the profit will be received, and an assumption that the organization will continue in business indefinitely.

Luckily, we can dispense with the issue of how long a firm will be in business. It is simply not feasible to compute the returns of every individual project out to infinity. Therefore, in practice, we usually select a *valuation horizon* of 5-10 years.

With a modest amount of computation, we can see that there is little point in considering a lengthy valuation horizon since the present value contributed by projects far in the future is negligible, especially as the discount rate begins to reflect more realistic returns on investment demanded by modern companies and even modest risk premiums. Table 4 illustrates the Present Value of $100,000 discounted at several different rates received in the future over a number of possible valuation horizons.

As can be seen from Table 4, if a company demands a 20% return on its capital, the present value of a project that does not provide a return for ten years has shrunk to a fraction (16%) of its future returns. This effectively removes projects that do not provide returns for several years from consideration.

Table 4. Discounted value of $100,000 received *n* years in the future

Years in Future	Present Value at 5%	Present Value at 10%	Present Value at 15%	Present Value at 20%	Present Value at 25%
1	95,238	90,909	86,957	83,333	80,000
2	90,703	82,645	75,614	69,444	64,000
3	86,384	75,131	65,752	57,870	51,200
4	82,270	68,301	57,175	48,225	40,960
5	78,353	62,092	49,718	40,188	32,768
10	61,391	38,554	24,718	16,151	10,737
15	48,102	23,939	12,289	6,491	3,518
20	37,689	14,864	6,110	2,608	1,153
25	29,530	9,230	3,038	1,048	378
30	23,138	5,731	1,510	421	124
40	14,205	2,209	373	68	13
50	8,720	852	92	11	1

Since we can safely omit an analysis of revenues received more than ten years in the future using realistic discount rates, we are left with the value of the firm being a function of the returns it will realize over the next few years, discounted for time and risk.

5.6. Multi-Project Firms and Economic Value

To recap, an organization derives its economic value from its combined future profits, discounted for the delay until the specific revenue is realized and the uncertainty (risk) of receiving this revenue.

Software development organizations derive the bulk of their profits from the completion and sale of software products. Consequently, we can approximate the economic value of a software organization that has n projects underway as (Harrison et al., 1999b):

$$\sum_{i=1}^{n} PV(\text{future revenue from project}_i)$$

where the PV includes discounting for both time and risk.

For example, consider an organization that has four concurrent projects underway with certain returns at the end of each project, and an annual cost of capital of 5% (Table 5)[5].

Table 5. Four projects, returns, schedules, and present value

Project	Profit Upon Delivery	Months to Delivery	Present Value
A	$100,000	12	$95,133
B	$250,000	24	$226,256
C	$25,000	12	$23,783
D	$750,000	36	$645,732
Value of the Firm			$990,905

The value of the firm under these assumptions is $990,905. By adjusting the discount rate, we can explore the effects of lengthening schedule and adjusting the risk characteristics of individual projects.

5.7. The Economic Cost of Extended Time-to-Market

These concepts can be applied to the problem of "time-to-market" faced by most software project managers. While the impact of delayed entry into a market is of-

[5]While we are accustomed to speaking about annual cost of capital, it is more common to factor in periodic interest compounding. This is usually done on a monthly basis, so the annual cost of capital is divided by 12 to arrive at a monthly cost of capital, and the computation of Present Value $PV=FV/(1+r)n$ is interpreted such that r reflects the periodic cost of capital and n is the number of periods (12 in the case of monthly compounding).

ten explained in vague terms of market share, one measurable result of releasing a product later rather than earlier is a delay in the receipt of revenue. Given the impact of time discounted cash flows on the value of the firm, we can quite easily determine the impact of extended time-to-market.

Table 6 shows that by simply extending the schedule by 10% on the four projects shown in Table 5, the economic value of the firm decreases by $13,019 from $990,905 to $977,886.

Table 6. Four projects from Table 5 delayed by 10%

Project	Profit Upon Delivery	Months to Delivery	Present Value
A	$100,000	13	$94,738
B	$250,000	26	$224,383
C	$25,000	13	$23,685
D	$750,000	40	$635,081
Value of the Firm			$977,886

The significance of the quantified cost of schedule extension to the organization is that it provides an economic measure of avoiding extending these schedules. Taken another way, it tells us the point at which expenditures to avoid schedule extension on these four projects are no longer economically feasible.

5.8. Financial Risk and Software Projects

Profits from a software development project are the function of two primary factors: Benefits received and resources expended. To some extent, virtually every organization exists to derive the maximum benefit for its stakeholders while expending the smallest number of resources.

We might associate "benefits received" with sales, and "resources expended" with expenses when dealing with a for-profit commercial organization. However, we could just as easily associate "benefits received" with the number of clients served, and "resources expended" with the number of person hours spent servicing these clients for a social service organization that has no interest in making a monetary profit. While the details may differ somewhat between contexts, the concepts of "revenue" and "expenses" generalizes quite well.

Earlier examples assumed that the profits from a project were certain. However, experience tells us that both the projected revenue from a project and the projected costs to develop it are usually in error, often by a great amount.

Some software development organizations can avoid revenue uncertainties because they work under negotiated contracts, as did the company in our Y2K example. However, even in the case of "shrink-wrap" software companies, the accuracy of revenue forecasts is not a software engineering issue, but rather one of marketing. Therefore, we will not consider the effect of uncertain revenue in our analysis, and assume for the purpose of our discussion, that the amount of future revenue is known.

However, the heart of software engineering project management is cost and schedule. Any time the projected costs or schedule of a software development project are in question, it introduces financial risk into the project. This financial risk is subsequently reflected in the economic value of the organization through risk-based discounting – essentially with an ad hoc risk premium.

Pfahl provides a more involved discussion of assessing project risk through software process simulation in Chapter 13.

Uncertainty in project cost prediction comes from many sources. It could be that the requirements of the project are poorly defined, or the customer may be prone to requesting numerous changes along the way. There may be flaws in the cost projection process itself – through either inexperienced personnel or lack of historical data. Regardless of the source, the net effect is that we are uncertain of the cost of the project, and therefore, we are uncertain of the profit that the firm will realize from it.

Projects for which the projected costs bear very little uncertainty may have the present value of their future profits affected only minimally in terms of their contribution to the overall economic value of the firm. On the other hand, projects for which there is great uncertainty involving their future profits may see their contribution to the economic value of the firm greatly discounted to account for their financial risk.

This is illustrated in Table 7, in which the four projects shown in Table 5 are re-evaluated using risk premiums. In this example, we assume Projects A and C demonstrate very little financial risk, and consequently are assigned risk premiums of 0. On the other hand, Project B is assigned a risk premium of 5% and Project D is assigned a risk premium of 10%. As can be seen, the economic value of the firm decreases by $187,580 from $990,905 to $803,325. This is a huge effect indeed, and dwarfs the impact of extending the time-to-market by 10% that we saw in Table 6.

Table 7. Effect of financial risk on projects from Table 5

Project	Profit Upon Delivery	Months to Delivery	Risk Premium	Present Value
A	$100,000	12	0%	$95.133
B	$250,000	24	5%	$204,852
C	$25,000	12	0%	$23,783
D	$750,000	36	10%	$479,557
Value of the Firm				$803,325

5.9 Predictability and Process Improvement

The key to reducing financial risk is predictability – the ability accurately forecast the resources necessary to carry out a job. Predictability is not increased productivity. For instance, delivering a project under budget may very well indicate increased productivity. However, from the perspective of predictability, delivering a project under budget is no more desirable than exceeding the predicted budget. Poor predictability may very well mean that projects are mistakenly undertaken (i.e., the predicted costs are less than what is actually incurred) or are mistakenly rejected (i.e., the predicted costs are more than actually required).

Software producers have attempted to increase the predictability of their projects through process improvement (Harrison et al., 1999a) first goals of the Software Engineering Institute's Capability Maturity Model (CMM) is to gain predictability (Bamberger, 1997) – organizations that have scored at the CMM Level-2 process maturity are said to have "repeatable" processes.

Indeed, there have been many reports on the impact of higher levels of process maturity on predictability (Herbsleb et al., 1994; Brodman and Johnson, 1995). Several studies have been able to actually quantify the improvements:

- Raytheon reported that predictability of budget and schedule was "reduced" from an average 40% overrun to +/- 3% after advancing to a CMM Level-4 (Haley et al., 1995).
- Motorola reported that estimation accuracy on project schedule and effort improved to better than 90% in the process of qualifying for a CMM Level-5 rating (Diaz and Sligo, 1997).
- Hughes published predictability improvement data indicating that the Cost-Performance Index (CPI) went from 0.94 to 0.97 in response to SEI Maturity improvements (Humphrey et al., 1991).

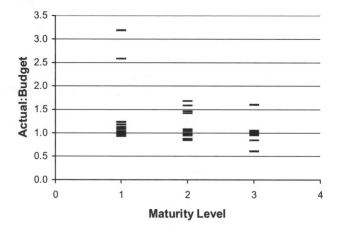

Fig. 18. Maturity level and actual budget

In particular, a study by Lawlis et al. (1995) suggests that U.S. Department of Defense contractors assessed at higher SEI Maturity Levels did a better job of meeting their target costs. In particular, the ratio of Actual to Budgeted Costs for 17 CMM Level-1 and 17 CMM Level-3 projects suggested that the Level-1 projects exhibited a mean *Actual to Budgeted cost ratio* of 1.25 while Level-3 projects exhibited a mean *Actual to Budgeted cost ratio* of 1.01.

However, even more importantly, the variability improved greatly between the Level-1 and Level-3 projects. As can be seen from Figure 18, CMM Level-1 projects exhibited a wide spread of Actual to Budgeted cost ratio outcomes with a standard deviation of 0.63. On the other hand, CMM Level-3 organizations exhibited a much tighter set of outcomes with a standard deviation of only 0.18. This reduction in variability suggests significant improvements in predictability between the maturity levels.

Of course, predictability is not the only benefit that accrues from process maturity. There are certainly many other benefits from investing in process improvement. For example, improved productivity, reduced time-to-market, increased quality, etc. (van Solingen, 2004). However, in this chapter, our focus is solely on the value enhancement that comes from better predictability when process maturity increases.

5.10 Arriving at a Risk Premium for Software Projects

The risk premium Φ reflects the "cost per unit of risk" and is based upon the variability of the expected returns. This is usually reflected as the β coefficient of the *Capital Asset Pricing Model* (Brealey and Myers, 2000), or "CAPM" as it is often called. However, CAPM assumes certain market structures that are not available at the level of a software project. Therefore, the specific techniques are not directly transferable. Nevertheless, improved predictability of costs reduces the variability of expected profits and the concepts used in CAPM are equally valid for collections of software projects.

The expected cost of a project can be expressed as a distribution with a mean (μ) and standard deviation (σ). We use this to establish relative risk among competing projects (Harrison, 2001). The relative financial risk λ between two projects, P and Q can be approximated by the ratio of the coefficients of variation (σ/μ) of their distribution of expected returns: For example, we can arrive at the relative risk of Project P with respect to Q via:

$$\lambda_{P\,wrt\,Q} = (\sigma_P/\mu_P)/(\sigma_Q/\mu_Q)$$

The relative risk of a collection of projects can be used to establish an appropriate discount rate k for Project P, relative to Project Q:

$$k_{P\,wrt\,Q} = r_f + \Phi_Q \times \lambda_{P\,wrt\,Q}$$

Based on the Lawlis, Flowe, and Thordahl data, CMM Level-1 projects with a relative risk of 0.504 appear to be 280% more financially risky than CMM Level-3 projects with a relative risk of 0.178 (Table 8).

Table 8. Relative risks of CMM Level-1 and Level-3 projects

Actual-to-Budget	Mean	Standard Deviation	Relative Risk
Level-1	1.25	0.63	0.504
Level-3	1.01	0.18	0.178

This is reflected by the relative risk premium for Level-1 projects (L1) and Level-3 projects (L3):

$$k_{L1\ wrt\ L3} = r_f + \Phi_{L3} \times 2.83$$
$$k_{L3\ wrt\ L1} = r_f + \Phi_{L1} \times 0.35$$

This technique provides a method by which an appropriate risk-adjusted discount rate can be derived for a CMM Level-3 project, given the appropriate risk premium Φ for a CMM Level-1 project (or vice versa).

While the firm's theoretical risk premium may not be directly available, an approximation can be made by observing past decision making behavior.

The *Internal Rate of Return* (IRR) is the discount rate at which the net present value (discounted returns – costs) of an investment is zero (Brealey and Myers, 2000). By computing the Internal Rate of Return for past CMM Level-1 projects and subtracting the risk free rate r_f, we can readily obtain the risk premium that is considered acceptable by decision makers (or at least the risk premium the firm is currently paying whether it likes it or not). Once this "baseline risk premium" is established, it is a simple matter to obtain the appropriate risk premium for the less variable CMM Level-3 projects.

5.11 Computing the Financial Value of Improved Predictability

A firm in the business of building software increases its value by building new products that will provide future returns. Since the inherent value of the firm is defined as the risk-adjusted present value of all its future profits, all other things being equal, a firm with a riskier future profit stream will suffer from an increased risk premium, and consequently will possess a lower inherent value.

The value of process improvement can be derived by projecting the contribution of a given project (or portfolio of projects) to the value of the firm should it be developed using either a CMM Level-1 or a CMM Level-3 process. Given the

Level-3 process will result in a more predictable cost, and subsequently a less variable profit stream, we should expect that the anticipated contribution to the value of the firm would be subject to a lower risk premium, and consequently offer a higher risk-adjusted present value.

The difference between the discounted profit projections using the Level-1 and Level-3 processes is the added value obtained from the increased maturity. The process for establishing the economic value of increased predictability is:

1. Compute NPV for Level-1 effort
2. Compute NPV for Level-3 effort
3. The difference is the added value of increased predictability

This provides a real, measurable, financial benefit that can be recognized and understood within the context of major capital budgeting decisions.

5.12 An Illustrative Example

In this section, the techniques outlined so far are applied to a hypothetical example in order to illustrate their use. The example is based upon several simplifying assumptions to improve discourse. However, these assumptions do not reduce the general applicability of the approach.

We assume a $7,500,000 fixed-price software development contract in which all revenue is realized upon delivery in Year 3. Further, we assume a predicted cost to develop of $5,000,000 million, which is all encumbered at the beginning of the project. This provides a simplified model in which all cost is incurred at the beginning of the project, and all revenue is realized at the end. We also assume a 5% risk-free cost of capital and a 5% risk premium on past Level-1 projects.[6]

The first step is to obtain the Net Profit to be received in Year 3 (in "Year 3 dollars"). In order to do this, the $5,000,000 encumbered at the beginning of Year 1 must be adjusted to reflect what the $5,000,000 would be worth after three years of being invested at the given discount rate. This consists of compounding, which is essentially the inverse of discounting:

$$FV(\$5,000,000) \text{ in 3 years @ } 5\% =$$
$$PV(1+r)n = \$5,000,000 \ (1.05)^3 = \$5,800,000$$

which yields a profit in Year 3 dollars of $7,500,000 – $5,800,000, or $1,700,000.

Given no risk at all (i.e., a risk premium of zero), we can discount the $1,700,000 profit in three years at 5% to arrive at a Net Present Value for the project:

$$NPV \text{ w/certainty} = \$1,700,000 \ /(1.05)^3 = \$1,500,000$$

---

[6]The choice of 5% for both the risk-free cost of capital and the risk premium was arbitrarily selected for ease of computation.

Given our assumption of a 5% risk premium on past CMM Level-1 projects (i.e., 5% (r_f) + 5% (Φ) = 10%), the Net Present Value for a Level-1 process will be:

$$NPV = \$1,700,000/(1.10)^3 = \$1,300,000$$

Using the Lawlis, Flowe, and Thordahl data to derive a relative risk premium we arrive at a Net Present Value for a CMM Level-3 process of:

$$\Phi = 5\% \times 0.35$$
$$\Phi = 1.75\%$$
$$NPV = \$1.7M/(1.0675)^3 = \$1,400,000$$

The hypothetical CMM Level-3 process contributes $1,400,000 to the economic value of the firm, compared to a contribution of $1,300,000 by the hypothetical Level-1 process. Consequently, the difference of approximately $100,000 reflects the value of increased predictability in this specific case. Naturally, most software development firms will have portfolios of many development projects, so the actual contribution of increased maturity would no doubt far exceed this amount. These results can facilitate the construction of business cases for process improvement since they are able to articulate the benefits of improved predictability in financially quantifiable terms that can be used in computations of return on investment and payback periods.

It is important to note that this discussion reflects only the value added by increased predictability. Improvements in productivity and reduced rework are not considered in this analysis. Obviously, they also play significant roles in any business cases used to justify investments in process improvement.

5.13 Conclusions

In this chapter, we have proposed the use of well-accepted financial theory to assess the financial benefit of increased predictability. While our discussion addressed process improvement, the underlying concepts can be used in any situation that is subject uncertain returns.

For example, the basic concept could be used to evaluate the costs of obtaining improved information for cost estimation purposes. One could compare the enhanced estimation cost vs. the value of the improved predictability. The use of these techniques can lead to better business cases for investing in any initiative intended to reduce uncertainty.

Alternately, improvements in gathering software requirements can also be viewed as reducing uncertainty. There are few things that can improve a cost or schedule estimation better than obtaining a clear idea of what you are supposed to build. Consequently, this technique can be used to financially evaluate efforts intended to pin down requirements. Naturally, other properties are also important – perhaps even more important – such as out-of-pocket expenses for rework, improved market share by releasing a product before your competitors, etc. However, it would be a mistake to focus on local expenses without noting the overall effect on the economic value of the organization.

This approach to evaluating investments is fairly mature within the financial and capital budgeting communities. However, it has had little exposure to date within the software engineering industry.

References

(Bamberger, 1997) Bamberger, J.: Essence of the Capability Maturity Model, IEEE Computer **30** (6), pp 112–114

(Brealey and Myers, 2000) Brealey, S., and R. Myers: Principles of Corporate Finance, 6th Edition, (Irwin/McGraw-Hill, Boston, 2000)

(Brodman and Johnson, 1995) Brodman, J.G., and D.L. Johnson: Return on Investment (ROI) from Software Process Improvement Measure by U.S. Industry, Software Process – Improvement and Practice **1** (1), pp 35–47

(Diaz and Sligo, 1997) Diaz, M. and J. Sligo: How Software Process Improvement Helped Motorola, IEEE Software **14** (5), pp 75–81

(Haley et al., 1995) Haley, T., B. Ireland, E. Wojtaszek, D. Nash and R. Dion: Raytheon Electronic Systems Experience in Software Process Improvement, SEI Technical Report CMU/SEI-95-TR017

(Harrison, 2001) Harrison, W.: Using the Economic Value of the Firm as a Basis for Assessing the Value of Process Improvements, Proc 2001 NASA/IEEE Software Engineering Workshop, College Park Maryland, November 2001, pp 123–127

(Harrison, 2002) Harrison, W.: "Mitigating Risk Using Portfolios in Software Development Projects", Fourth International Economics Driven Software Engineering Workshop, (EDSER-4). Orlando, Florida, May 2002

(Harrison et al., 1999a) Harrison, W., D. Raffo, and J. Settle: Process Improvement as a Capital Investment: Risks and Deferred Paybacks, Pacific Northwest Software Quality Conference, Portland, Oregon, Oct. 1999, pp 241–250

(Harrison et al., 1999b) Harrison, W., D. Raffo, J. Settle, and N. Eickelmann: Adapting Financial Measures: Making a Business Case for Software Process Improvement, Software Quality Journal **8** (3), pp 211–231

(Herbsleb et al., 1994) Herbsleb, J. A. Carleton, J. Rozum, J. Siegel and D. Zubrow: Benefits of CMM-Based Software Process Improvement, SEI Technical Report CMU/SEI-94-TR-013

(Humphrey et al., 1991) Humphrey, W. and W.S. Snyder, and T.R. Willis: Software Process Improvement at Hughes Aircraft, IEEE Softw. **8** (4), pp 11–23

(Lawlis et al., 1995) Lawlis, P.K., R.M. Flowe, and J.B. Thordahl: A Correlational Study of the CMM and Software Development Performance, Crosstalk, September 1995, pp 21–25

(van Solingen, 2004) van Solingen, R, Measuring the ROI of Software Process Improvement, IEEE Software **21** (3), pp 32–38

Author Biography

Warren Harrison is a professor of computer science at Portland State University in Portland, Oregon, and a member of the Oregon Master of Software Engineering faculty. He is currently Editor-in-Chief of IEEE Software magazine. Warren has been the North American Editor and the Editor in Chief of the Software Quality Journal, and he was co-founder and Editor in Chief of the Empirical Software Engineering journal. He serves on Motorola's Software Development Tools and Productivity Research Visionary Board and is a member of the NSF Software Engineering Research Center, an academic-industry consortium. Warren's interests include measurement and decision making, software quality, software engineering economics, and project management, as well as mobile Internet technologies and digital forensics. His academic research has involved diverse industrial partnerships, and he maintains a strong practical focus on the useful application of new techniques and technologies.

Part 2
Practices

Part 2 provides methods and techniques for VBSE that build up on the foundations and frameworks presented in Part 1. The chapters in this part present practices that help to enhance professional and managerial capabilities in applying VSBE concepts in concrete SE processes and projects.

The objective of Part 2 is to show how key practices of VBSE can help in fostering ethical behavior, managing decision making, eliciting and reconciling stakeholder value propositions, improving usability, and software testing.

The presented methods and techniques aim at improving the predictability of SE processes, such as improving the efficiency of requirements collection, structured/methodical data-driven decisions, and sharing value concepts in a work group, e.g., through knowledge management and negotiation.

There are six Chapters in this part that cover the following areas:

- Chapter 6: Value-Based Software Engineering: Seven Key Practices and Ethical Considerations
- Chapter 7: Stakeholder Value Proposition Elicitation and Reconciliation
- Chapter 8: Measurement and Decision Making
- Chapter 9: Criteria for Selecting Software Requirements to Create Product Value: An Industrial Empirical Study
- Chapter 10: Collaborative Usability Testing to Facilitate Stakeholder Involvement
- Chapter 11: Value-Based Management of Software Testing

In Chapter 6, *Boehm* presents seven key elements that provide foundations for value-based software engineering, such as: Benefits Realization Analysis, Stakeholder Value Proposition Elicitation and Reconciliation, and Value-Based Monitoring and Control. A case study outlines VBSE elements can be used to incorporate ethical considerations into software engineering practice. Following this, in Chapter 8 *Berry* and *Aurum* present a behavioral decision making model that identifies the impact of measurement products on decision making behavior to augment strictly rational decision making frameworks. In Chapter 7 *Grünbacher, Köszegi*, and *Biffl* motivate the need of methods and tools for understanding and reconciling stakeholder value propositions in software engineering. They present an example of a groupware-supported negotiation method that provides process structure and mediation to stakeholders, identify challenges of stakeholder value proposition elicitation and negotiation, and discuss possible method improvements to address these challenges. Following this chapter, in Chapter 9 *Wohlin* and *Aurum* provide an overview of the product value concept to quantify the importance of different decision making criteria when deciding whether to include a requirement in a project or release and present an industrial survey. In Chapter 10, *Fruhling* and *de Vreede* present a repeatable collaborative usability testing process supported by a Group Support System to facilitate stakeholder involvement through stakeholder expectation management, visualization, and trade off analysis, prioritization of usability action items, and a simple business case analysis. Finally, in Chapter 11 *Ramler, Biffl*, and *Grünbacher* motivate the need for value-based testing, describe practices supporting the management of value-based testing, outline a framework for value-based test management, and illustrate the framework with an example.

6 Value-Based Software Engineering: Seven Key Elements and Ethical Considerations

Barry Boehm

Abstract: This chapter presents seven key elements that provide candidate foundations for value-based software engineering:
1. Benefits Realization Analysis
2. Stakeholder Value Proposition Elicitation and Reconciliation
3. Business Case Analysis
4. Continuous Risk and Opportunity Management
5. Concurrent System and Software Engineering
6. Value-Based Monitoring and Control
7. Change as Opportunity
Using a case study we show how some of these elements can be used to incorporate ethical considerations into daily software engineering practice.

Keywords: Benefits realization, business case analysis, cost-benefit analysis, investment analysis, return on investment, risk management, stakeholder values, software economics, software engineering ethics, value-based software engineering.

6.1 Benefits Realization Analysis

Many software projects fail by succumbing to the "Field of Dreams" syndrome. This refers to the American movie in which a Midwestern farmer has a dream that if he builds a baseball field on his farm, the legendary players of the past will appear and play on it ("Build the field and the players will come").

In *The Information Paradox* (Thorp, 1998), John Thorp discusses the paradox that organizations' success in profitability or market capitalization do not correlate with their level of investment in information technology (IT). He traces this paradox to an IT and software analogy of the "Field of Dreams" syndrome: "Build the software and the benefits will come."

To counter this syndrome, Thorp and his company, the DMR Consulting Group, developed a Benefits Realization Approach (BRA) for determining and coordinating the other initiatives besides software and IT system development that are needed in order for the organization to realize the potential IT system benefits. The most significant of these features, the Results Chain, is discussed next.

Results Chain

Figure 19 shows a simple Results Chain provided as an example in *The Information Paradox*. It establishes a framework linking Initiatives that consume resources (e.g., implement a new order entry system for sales) to Contributions (not delivered systems, but their effects on existing operations) and Outcomes, which may lead either to further contributions or to added value (e.g., increased sales). A particularly important contribution of the Results Chain is the link to Assumptions, which condition the realization of the Outcomes. Thus, in Figure 19, if order-to-delivery time turns out not to be an important buying criterion for the product being sold, (e.g., for stockable commodities such as soap and pencils), the reduced time to deliver the product will not result in increased sales.

The Results Chain is a valuable framework by which software project members can work with their clients to identify additional non-software initiatives that may be needed to realize the potential benefits enabled by the software/IT system initiative. These may also identify some additional success-critical stakeholders who need to be represented and "bought into" the shared vision.

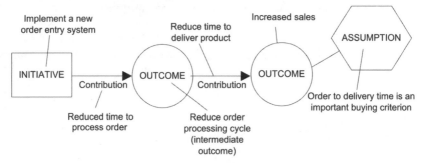

Fig. 19. Benefits Realization Approach Results Chain

For example, the initiative to implement a new order entry system may reduce the time required to process orders only if some additional initiatives or system features are pursued to convince the salespeople that the new system will be good for their careers and to train them in how to use the system effectively. For example, if the order entry system is so efficiency optimized that it does not keep track of sales credits, the salespeople will fight using it.

Further, the reduced order processing cycle will reduce the time to deliver products only if additional initiatives are pursued to coordinate the order entry system with the order fulfillment system. Some classic cases where this did not happen were the late deliveries of Hershey's Halloween candy (Carr, 2002) and Toys R Us' Christmas toys.

Such additional initiatives need to be added to the Results Chain. Besides increasing its realism, this also identifies additional success-critical stakeholders (salespeople and order fulfillment people) who need to be involved in the system definition and development process. The expanded Results Chain involves these stakeholders not just in a stovepipe software project to satisfy some requirements, but in a program of related software and non-software initiatives focused on value-producing end results.

6.2 Stakeholder Value Proposition Elicitation and Reconciliation

It would be convenient if all the success-critical stakeholders had readily expressible and compatible value propositions that could easily be turned into a set of objectives for each initiative and for the overall program of initiatives. "Readily expressible" is often unachievable because the specifics of stakeholders' value propositions tend to be emergent through experience rather than obtainable through surveys. In such cases, synthetic experience techniques such as prototypes, scenarios, and stories can accelerate elicitation.

Readily compatible stakeholder value propositions can be achievable in situations of long-term stakeholder mutual understanding and trust. However, in new situations, just considering the most frequent value propositions or success models of the most frequent project stakeholders (users, acquirers, developers, maintainers) shows that these are frequently in conflict and must be reconciled.

For example, Figure 20 shows a "spider web" of the most frequent "model clashes" among these stakeholders' success models that can cause projects to fail. The left- and right-hand sides of Figure 20 show these most frequent success models. For example, users want many features, freedom to redefine the feature set at any time, compatibility between the new system and their existing systems, and so on.

However, the spiderweb diagram shows that these user success models can clash with other stakeholders' success models. For example, the users' "many features" product-oriented success model clashes with the acquirers' "limited development budget and schedule" property-oriented success model, and with the developer's success model, "ease of meeting budget and schedule."

The developer has a success model, "freedom of choice: COTS/reuse" that can often resolve budget and schedule problems. But the developer's choice of COTS or reused components may be incompatible with the users' and maintainers' other applications, causing two further model clashes. Further, the developer's reused software may not be easy to maintain, causing an additional model clash with the maintainers.

The gray lines in Figure 20 show the results of one of the analyses performed in constructing and refining the major model clash relationships. It determined the major model clashes in the Bank of America Master Net development, one of several major project failures analyzed. Further explanations are in (Boehm et al., 2000) and (Al-Said, 2003).

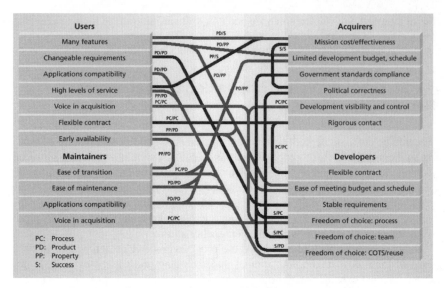

Fig. 20. Value Proposition Model-Clash spiderweb diagram

Given the goodly number of model clashes in Figure 20 (and there are potentially many more), the task of reconciling them may appear formidable. However, there are several effective approaches for stakeholder value proposition reconciliation, such as:

- *Expectations management.* Often, just becoming aware of the number of potential stakeholder value proposition conflicts that need to be resolved will cause stakeholders to relax their less critical levels of desire. Other techniques such as lessons learned retrospectives, well-calibrated cost models, and "simplifier and complicator" lists help stakeholders better understand which of their desired capabilities are infeasible with respect to budget, schedule, and technology constraints. Good examples are in Chapter 15 of this book.

- *Visualization and trade-off analysis techniques.* Frequently, prototypes, scenarios, and estimation models enable stakeholders to obtain a better mutual understanding of which aspects of an application are most important and achievable. Good examples are in Chapters 4, 8, and 10.

- *Prioritization.* Having stakeholders rank/order or categorize the relative priorities of their desired capabilities will help determine which combination of capabilities will best satisfy stakeholders' most critical needs within available resource constraints. Various techniques such as pairwise comparison and scale-of-ten ratings of relative importance and difficulty are helpful aids to prioritization. Good examples are in Chapters 7 and 12.

- *Groupware.* Some of those prioritization aids are available in groupware tools, along with collaboration-oriented support for brainstorming, discussion, and win-win negotiation of conflict situations. Good examples are in Chapters 7 and 10.

- *Business case analysis.* Determining which capabilities provide the best return on investment can help stakeholders prioritize and reconcile their value propositions. Business case analysis is summarized next, and discussed in more detail in Chapter 3.

6.3 Business Case Analysis

In its simplest form, business case analysis involves determining the relative financial costs, benefits, and *return on investment* (ROI) across a system's life cycle as *ROI = (Benefits – Costs) / Costs.* Since costs and benefits may occur at different times, the business case analysis will usually discount future cash flows based on likely rates of interest, so that all of the cash flows are referenced to a single point in time (usually the present, as in Present Value).

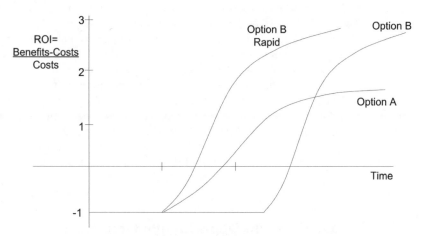

Fig. 21. Example of business case analysis results

One can then compare two decision options A and B in terms of their ROI profiles versus time. In Figure 21, for example, Option A's ROI becomes positive sooner than Option B's ROI, but its longer term ROI is lower. The stakeholders can then decide whether the longer wait for a higher ROI in Option B is preferable to the shorter wait for a lower ROI in Option A. Option Rapid-B illustrates why stakeholders are interested in rapid application development. If Rapid-B can be developed in half the time, it will be much preferable to either of Options A or original-B.

Unquantifiable Benefits, Uncertainties, and Risk

Two additional factors may be important in business case analysis. One involves unquantifiable benefits; the other involves uncertainties and risk.

In some cases, Option A might be preferred to Option B or even Rapid-B if it provided additional benefits that may be difficult to quantify, such as controllability, political benefits, or stakeholder goodwill. These can sometimes be addressed by such techniques as multiple criterion decision making or utility functions involving stakeholders' preferences for financial or non-financial returns.

In other cases, the benefit flows in Figure 21 may be predicated on uncertain assumptions. They might assume, for example, that the Option B product will be the first of its kind to enter the marketplace and will capture a large market share. However, if two similar products enter the marketplace first, then the payoff for Option B may be even less than that for Option A.

If the profitability of early competitor marketplace entry can be quantified, it can then be used to determine the relative value of the rapid development Option Rapid-B. This value can then be used to determine the advisability of adopting practices that shorten schedule at some additional cost. An example is pair programming: empirical studies indicate that paired programmers will develop software in 60-70% of the calendar time required for an individual programmer, but thereby requiring 120-140% of the cost of the individual programmer.

If the profitability of early competitor marketplace entry is unknown, this means that making a decision between the cheaper Option B and the faster Option Rapid-B involves considerable uncertainty and *risk*. It also means that there is a value in performing competitor analysis to determine the probability of early competitor marketplace entry, or of *buying information to reduce risk*. This kind of value-of-information analysis can be performed via statistical decision theory; a discussion and examples of its applicability to software decision making are provided in Chapter 1. An excellent overall introduction to software business case analysis is (Reifer, 2002). Good examples in this book are in Chapters 3, 5, 12, 16, and 17.

6.4 Continuous Risk and Opportunity Management

Risk analysis and risk management are not just early business case analysis techniques; they pervade the entire information system life cycle. Risk analysis also reintroduces the people factor into economic decision making. Different people may be more or less risk averse, and will make different decisions in similar situations, particularly when confronted with an uncertain mix of positive and negative outcomes.

For example, consider a programmer who is given four weeks to complete the development of a software module. The programmer is given two choices. One is to develop a new version of the module, which he is sure he can do in four weeks. The other is to reuse a previously developed module, for which there is an 80% chance of finishing in one week and a 20% chance of finishing in six weeks. The expected duration of this option is $(.8)(1) + (.2)(6) = 2$ weeks. This represents an expected time savings of two weeks and a corresponding savings in expected effort or cost.

Understanding and Addressing People's Utility Functions

In this situation, though, many risk-averse programmers would reject the reuse option. They do not want to be known as people who overrun schedules. Their *utility function* would assign a much larger negative utility to overrunning the four-week schedule than the positive utility of finishing ahead of schedule. In terms of expected utility, then, they would prefer the assured four-week develop a new module approach.

However, their boss may have preferred the reuse option, particularly if she had invested resources in creating the reusable components, and if she could organize the project to compensate for the uncertainties in module delivery schedules (e.g., via modular architectures and daily builds rather than a pre-planned module integration schedule). If so, she could revise the programmers' incentive structure (rewarding reuse independent of actual completion time) in a way that realigned their utility functions and success models to be consistent with hers.

Thus, understanding and addressing people's utility functions becomes a powerful tool in reducing the risk of the overall project's failure – or, from a complementary perspective, in improving the opportunity for the overall project's success. It means that value-based software engineering is not a dry "manage by the numbers" approach, but a highly people-oriented set of practices. And its treatment of uncertainty balances negative risk considerations with positive opportunity considerations. Reconciling stakeholders' utility functions involves essentially the same approaches for stakeholder value proposition elicitation and reconciliation as we discussed in Section 6.2.

Using Risk to Determine "How Much Is Enough"

A current highly debated issue is the use of plan-driven methods versus use of agile methods such as Extreme Programming, Crystal Methods, Adaptive Software Development, and Scrum (Highsmith, 2002). Recent workshop results involving plan-driven and agile methods experts have indicated that hybrid plan-driven methods are feasible, and that risk analysis can be used to determine how much planning or agility is enough for a given situation.

A central concept in risk management is the *Risk Exposure* (RE) involved in a given course of action. It is determined by accessing the probability of loss $P(L)$ involved in a course of action and the corresponding size of loss $S(L)$, and computing the risk exposure as the expected loss: $RE=P(L)*S(L)$. "Loss" can include profits, reputation, quality of life, or other value-related attributes.

Figure 22 shows risk exposure profiles for an example e-services company with a sizable installed base and desire for high assurance; a rapidly changing marketplace and desire for agility and rapid value; and an internationally distributed development team with a mix of skill levels and a need for some level of documented plans.

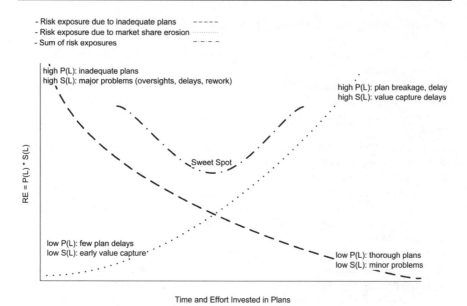

Fig. 22. Risk Exposure (RE) profile: planning detail

The downward curve in Figure 22 shows the variation in *RE* due to inadequate plans, as a function of the level of investment the company puts into its projects' process and product plans. At the left, a minimal investment corresponds to a high probability *P(L)* that the plans will have loss causing gaps, ambiguities, and inconsistencies. It also corresponds to a high *S(L)* that these deficiencies will cause major project oversights, delays, and rework costs. At the right, the more thorough the plans, the less *P(L)* that plan inadequacies will cause problems, and the smaller the *S(L)* of the associated losses.

The upward curve in Figure 22 shows the variation in *RE* due to market share erosion through delays in product introduction. Spending little time in planning will get at least a demo product into the marketplace early, enabling early value capture. Spending too much time in planning will have a high *P(L)* due both to the planning time spent, and to rapid changes causing delays via plan breakage. It will also cause a high *S(L)*, as the delays will enable others to capture most of the market share.

The upper curve in Figure 22 shows the sum of the risk exposures due to inadequate plans and market share erosion. It shows that very low and very high investments in plans have high overall risk exposures, and that there is a "sweet spot" in the middle where overall risk exposure is minimized, indicating "how much planning is enough?" for this company's operating profile.

With the example company situation as a reference point, we can run comparative risk exposure profiles of companies having different risk profiles. For example, consider an e-services company with a small installed base and less need for high assurance, a rapidly changing marketplace, and a collocated team of highly capable and collaborative developers and customers. With this profile, the major change in risk exposure from Figure 22 is that the size of rework loss from minimal plans is much smaller due to the ability of the team to rapidly replan and refactor, and thus the company's sweet spot moves to the left toward agile methods.

As another example, consider a company in the plan-driven home ground, with a more stable product line of larger, more safety-critical systems. Here, the major difference from Figure 22 is a much higher size of rework loss from minimal plans, and a resulting shift of the company's sweet spot toward higher investments in plans. Further discussion and illustration of these issues and more quantitative analyses are provided in (Boehm and Turner, 2004).

Similar analyses have shown that such risk analysis techniques can be used to determine "how much is enough" for other key software engineering levels of activity, such as testing, specification, prototyping, COTS evaluation, formal methods, or documentation. Other good treatments of risk considerations are in Chapters 5, 13, and 17.

6.5 Concurrent System and Software Engineering

As we discussed in Chapter 1, the increasing pace of change in the information technology marketplace is driving organizations toward increasing levels of agility in their software development methods, while their products and services are concurrently becoming more and more software intensive. These trends also mean that the traditional sequential approach to software development, in which systems engineers determined software requirements and passed them to software engineers for development, is increasingly risky to use.

Increasingly, then, it is much more preferable to have systems engineers and software engineers concurrently engineering the product's or service's operational concept, requirements, architecture, life cycle plans, and key sections of code. Concurrent engineering is also preferable when system requirements are more emergent from usage or prototyping than prespecifiable. It is further preferable when the relative costs, benefits, and risks of *commercial off-the-shelf* (COTS) software or outsourcing decisions will simultaneously affect requirements, architectures, code, plans, costs, and schedules. It is also essential in determining cost-value trade-off relationships in developing software product lines (Faulk et al., 2000).

Relevant Process Models

For the future, then, concurrent spiral-type process models will increasingly be preferred over sequential "waterfall"-type process models. Several are available, such as the Evolutionary Spiral Process (SPC, 1992), the Rational Unified Process (RUP) (Royce, 1998; Jacobson et al., 1999; Kruchten, 2001), and the

MBASE/CeBASE models (Boehm and Port, 2001; Boehm et al., 2002a). Some agile process models such as Lean Software Development and Adaptive Software Development (Highsmith, 2002) also emphasize concurrent system and software engineering.

An important feature of concurrent process models is that their milestone pass-fail criteria involve demonstrations of consistency and feasibility across a set of concurrently-developed artifacts. For example, Table 9 shows the pass/fail criteria for the anchor point milestones used in MBASE and RUP: *Life Cycle Objectives* (LCO), *Life Cycle Architecture* (LCA), and *Initial Operational Capability* (IOC) (Boehm and Port, 2001).

Table 9. LCO, LCA, and IOC Pass/Fail Criteria

LCO *(Life Cycle Objectives)*	LCA *(Life Cycle Architecture)*	IOC *(Initial Op. Capability)*
For at least one architectture, a system built to that architecture will:	For a specific detailed architecture, a system built to that architecture will:	An implemented architecture, an operational system that has:
• Support the core operational concept • Satisfy the core requirements • Be faithful to the prototype(s) • Be buildable within the budgets and schedules in the plan • Show a viable business case • Have its key stake-holders committed to support the Elaboration Phase (to LCA)	• Support the elaborated operational concept • Satisfy the elaborated requirements • Be faithful to the prototype(s) • Be buildable within the budgets and schedules in the plan • Show a viable business case • Have all major risks resolved or covered by a risk management plan • Have its key stake-holders committed to support the full life cycle	• Realized the operational concept • Implemented the initial operational requirements • Prepared a system operation and support plan • Prepared the initial site(s) in which the system will be deployed for transition • Prepared the users, operators, and maintainers to assume their operational roles

These milestones work well as common commitment points across a variety of process model variants because they reflect similar commitment points during one's lifetime. The LCO milestone is the equivalent of getting engaged, and the LCA milestone is the equivalent of getting married. As in life, if you marry your architecture in haste, you and your stakeholders will repent at leisure (if, in Internet time, any leisure time is available). The third anchor point milestone, IOC, constitutes an even larger commitment: It is the equivalent of having your first child, with all the associated commitments of care and feeding of a legacy system.

Another important development in this area is the Capability Maturity Model-Integrated (CMMI) (SEI, 2002; Ahern et. al, 2001). It integrates the previous software-centric Software CMM (Paulk et al., 1994) with CMMs for System Engineering and for Integrated Product and Process Development. The CMMI (and its predecessor iCMM (FAA, 1997) provides a process maturity assessment and improvement framework, which organizations can use to evolve from sequential to concurrent systems and software engineering approaches, in ways which emphasize integrated stakeholders teaming and reconciliation of stakeholder value propositions. Further good examples of concurrent system and software engineering are in Chapters 4, 7, 8, 9, 10, 12, and 14.

6.6 Value-Based Monitoring and Control

A technique often used to implement project monitoring and control functions in the software CMM or the CMMI is Earned Value Management. It works as shown in Figure 23.

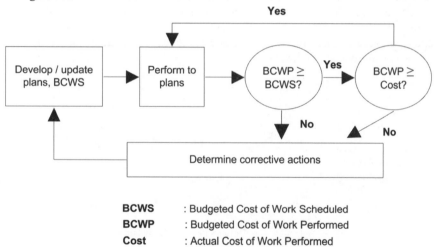

BCWS	: Budgeted Cost of Work Scheduled
BCWP	: Budgeted Cost of Work Performed
Cost	: Actual Cost of Work Performed

Fig. 23. "Earned Value" feedback process

The Earned Value Management process is generally good for tracking whether the project is meeting its original plan. However, it becomes difficult to administer if the project's plan changes rapidly. More significantly, it has *absolutely nothing to say about the actual value being earned* for the organization by the project's results. A project can be tremendously successful with respect to its cost-oriented "earned value," but an absolute disaster in terms of actual organizational value earned. This frequently happens when the resulting product has flaws with respect to user acceptability, operational cost-effectiveness, or timely market entry. Thus, it would be preferable to have techniques which support monitoring and control of the actual value to be earned by the project's results.

Business Case and Benefits Realized Monitoring and Control

A first step is to use the project's business case (discussed in Section 6.3) as a means of monitoring the actual business value of the capabilities to be delivered by the project. This involves continuing update of the business case to reflect changes in business model assumptions, market conditions, organizational priorities, and progress with respect to enabling initiatives. Monitoring the delivered value of undelivered capabilities is difficult; therefore, this approach works best when the project is organized to produce relatively frequent increments of delivered capability.

A related next step is to monitor assumptions and progress with respect to all of the Initiatives and Outcomes involved in the project's Results Chain discussed in Section 6.1 and shown in Figure 19. The suggested monitoring approach in (Thorp, 1998) involves coloring in the degree to which Initiatives and Outcomes have been realized. This can be extended to monitor Contributions and validity of Assumptions as well. For example, monitoring the Contribution, "Reduce time to deliver product" in Figure 19 could uncover the problem that speeding up order entry will create more order fulfillment delays unless a complementary order fulfillment Initiative is established.

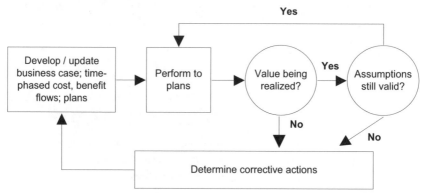

Fig. 24. Value realization feedback process

The resulting value realization feedback process is shown in Figure 24. With respect to the order entry example just above, finding out that value was not being realized via reduced delivery times would lead to some corrective action, most likely the establishment of an order fulfillment speedup Initiative. This would require updates of the overall plans and business case, and new time-phased cost and benefit flows to monitor.

A further option in the value realization feedback process involves adjusting the value function to reflect progress with respect to the product's production function as illustrated in Figure 25. The usual economic production function is an S-shaped curve in which the early "Investment" segment involves development of infra-structure and architecture which does not directly generate benefits, but which is necessary for realization of the benefits in the High-payoff and Diminishing re-turns segment of the curve. This means that tracking direct benefits realized usu-ally produces pessimistic results during the Investment segment of the curve. One can either manage stakeholders' expectations to accept low early benefit flows (as with the ROI profiles in Figure 21), or use an alternative value function (the dotted line in Figure 25), which ascribes additional indirect value to the early investments in infrastructure and architecture. (Actually, the real options techniques in (Sulli-van et al., 2001) and Chapters 3, 5, and 17 can estimate such values). The pre-ferred approach will depend on the project's stakeholders and their expectations.

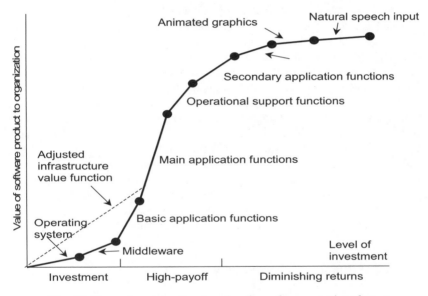

Fig. 25. Example production function for software product features

Of course, the actual and potential benefit values realized by each increment of capability need to be monitored and adjusted for changes. For example, a low-cost and user-friendly animated graphics package may increase the net value of ani-mated graphics for certain classes of applications (e.g., education and training), and limited-domain speech understanding systems have shown considerable labor-saving value.

Value-Based Monitoring and Control at the Organization Level

Several useful techniques are available for organizing and managing multi-dimensional improvement strategies. The Balanced Scorecard technique (Kaplan and Norton, 1996) organizes goals, strategies, and initiatives into four perspectives: financial; customer; internal business process; and learning and growth. The BTOPP business system (Morton, 1991; Thorp, 1998) uses five perspectives: business, technology, organization, process, and people. Both are similar; organizations can choose the one that best fits or develop an alternative as appropriate. Chapters 8 and 12 provide good examples of value-based monitoring and control.

6.7 Change as Opportunity

Expending resources to adapt to change is frequently lumped into "rework costs" and treated as a negative factor to avoid. Software change tracking systems often treat changes as defects in the original requirements. Quality cost systems often treat change adaptations as a quality cost to be minimized. These criteria tend to push projects and organizations toward change aversion.

Nowadays, changes are continually going on in technology, in the marketplace, in organizations, and in stakeholders' value propositions and priorities. And the rate of change is increasing. Organizations that can adapt to change more rapidly than their competition will succeed better at their mission or in the marketplace. Thus the ability to adapt to change has business value.

Software is the premier technology for adaptation to change. It can be organized to make the cost of changes small as compared to hardware. It can be updated electronically, in ways that preserve continuity of service as the change is being made. Thus, change as opportunity for competitive success is a key economic and architectural driver for software projects and organizations.

Examples of Change as Opportunity

The main sources of change as opportunity come from changes in technology or in the marketplace that open up new opportunities to create value. There are of course other opportunity sources such as changes in legislation, organizational alignments, and international relations.

An excellent example of technology change as opportunity has been the Internet and the Web and their effect on electronic commerce. Organizations that learned early how to capitalize on this technology made significant competitive gains. Other good examples of technology change as opportunity have been agent technology, mobile computing, and the Global Positioning System (GPS).

A good example of marketplace change as opportunity is the existence of GPS and mobile computing in automobiles as an opportunity to provide mobile location-based services. Another is the opportunity to add mobile electronic collect-on-delivery billing and collection systems at the delivery point of rapid delivery services such as Federal Express and United Parcel Service.

Techniques for Enhancing Adaptability to Change

As documented in *Microsoft Secrets* (Cusumano and Selby, 1995), the world's leading software business uses a number of techniques for enhancing its adaptability to change. Its synchronize-and-stabilize approach focuses on concurrent evolutionary development, in which each feature team has the flexibility to adapt to change, while buffer periods are built into each increment to enable the teams to synchronize their results. Nightly build techniques also accommodate flexibility in the integration schedule and adaptability to change. Also, Microsoft uses a number of techniques to enhance organizational learning and adaptation, such as customer feedback analysis, project postmortems, and technology watch and marketplace watch activities.

Project techniques for enhancing adaptability to change tend to fall into two categories: architecture-based and refactoring-based. Architecture-based techniques focus on identifying the product's most likely sources of change, or evolution requirements, and using information hiding modularity techniques to hide the sources of change within architectural modules (Parnas, 1979). Then, when the changes come, they can be accommodated within modules rather than causing ripple effects across the entire product. A related technique is *schedule-as-independent-variable* (SAIV), which uses prioritized requirements as potential sources of change to ensure delivery of the highest priority requirements within a fixed schedule (Boehm et al., 2002b).

Refactoring-based change focuses on keeping the product as simple as possible, and reorganizing the product to accommodate the next set of desired changes. A number of the agile methods discussed in Section 6.4 rely on refactoring to accommodate change, while the plan-driven methods rely on architecture. Which one is more likely to succeed for a given project is largely based on the validity of the Extreme Programming slogan, "*You Aren't Going to Need It* (YAGNI)." If the evolution requirements are knowable in advance and stable, the architecture-based approach will easily accommodate them, while the YAGNI approach will incur a steady stream of excess refactorings. On the other hand, if the requirements changes are frequent and highly unpredictable, pre-architected frameworks will continually break, and refactoring simpler designs will be preferable. Traceability tools such as those in Chapter 14 can help with change impact analysis. The value-based release prioritization approach in Chapter 12 is another good approach for addressing change as opportunity.

Economic Value of Adaptability to Change

Developing a change-anticipatory modular design can be considered as an investment in *real options* which can be exercised in the future to execute changes which enhance the system's value (Amram and Kulatilaka, 1999; Baldwin and Clark, 2000). More specifically, (Sullivan et al., 2001) uses the options pricing approach to analyze the economic value of Parnas' information-hiding technique to modularization around anticipated sources of change. This approach can also be combined with other economic approaches, such as buying information to reduce the risk of anticipating the wrong set of changes (e.g., via prototypes, user surveys, marketplace watch, or technology watch activities).

Another perspective on the value of adaptability to change comes from studies of complex adaptive systems (Kauffman, 1995). These studies show that for various "fitness landscapes" or value functions, one can tune a set of adaptation parameters so that a high value operational solution will emerge over time via the interaction of a set of adaptive agents. A too rigid set of adaptation parameters will lead to gridlock; a too flexible set will lead to chaos. (Highsmith, 2000) shows numerous parallels between software development and complex adaptive systems, including the value of relatively agile over highly rigorous approaches to software development in domains undergoing rapid change.

6.8 Integrating Ethical Considerations into Software Engineering Practice

Software engineers have increasingly many and significant opportunities to influence the outcome of software projects in ways that produce harmful or positive results for some of the stakeholders involved. The field has produced some good codes of ethics such as the ACM/IEEE Software Engineering Code of Ethics and Professional Practice (ACM/IEEE, 1998). Its content covers a number of value-intensive topics such as intellectual property, privacy, confidentiality, quality of work, fairness, liability, risk disclosure, conflict of interest, and unauthorized access (Anderson et al., 1993).

However, the codes provide only general guidelines, and it has been difficult to integrate their value-oriented objectives into the value-neutral techniques and practices constituting traditional software engineering. One of the major benefits of the value-based software engineering approaches presented in this book is the opportunity to naturally integrate value-oriented ethical considerations into daily software engineering practice.

The approach presented in this chapter follows the principles in John Rawls' seminal book, *A Theory of Justice* (Rawls, 1971). The socioeconomic aspect of this theory is based on the following principle: Social and economic inequalities are to be arranged so that they are both (1) to the greatest benefit of the least advantaged; and (2) attached to offices and positions open to all under conditions of fair equality of opportunity.

This principle recognizes the fact that some individuals are better able to increase everyone's benefits than are others. It holds that it is fair for such individuals to operate with more resources than others, to the extent that they thereby generate benefits for others, and particularly maximize the benefits of least advantaged people.

The Theory W or stakeholder win-win approach (Boehm and Ross, 1989) to value-based software engineering presented in Section 6.2 and Chapter 7 provides a way to apply Rawls' Theory of Justice to daily software engineering practice, by recognizing the class of least advantaged people as one of the success-critical stakeholders in a software project.

A good start toward this approach was provided by Collins et al. (1994). They developed an interpretation of the Theory of Justice that identifies the least advantaged class or *penumbra* as an essential stakeholder in software engineering decisions, along with the providers, buyers, and users of a prospective software system. They provide and exemplify a matrix of obligations of each of the stakeholder classes to the others, and identify techniques for addressing other aspects of the Theory of Justice. These include the concept of risking harm and the publicity test for ethical appropriateness (how would you like it if your software engineering decision were discussed on the evening news?).

Fire Dispatching Case Study

This synthesized case study includes ethical problems encountered in several urban emergency services software projects.

Several years ago, the city of Zenith suffered a major fire disaster in its central business district, causing over $300 million in property damage. An investigation concluded that much of the loss could have been avoided with a modern automated fire dispatching system instead of the current largely manual system originally developed for Zenith in the 1920s.

The Mayor of Zenith then pledged to ensure that Zenith would have a modern automated fire dispatching system in two years (just before the next election). His staff chose a consultant company to rapidly prepare specifications and a competitive procurement package for the system. In three months, the company prepared the package, including an algorithm that would dispatch fire equipment based on minimizing property damage and an $8 million cost estimate. Bidding was opened for a fixed-price contract to develop the system to the specifications, and three months later, the contract was awarded to Integrated Logistics, Inc. (ILI), for their bid price of $4.4 million. ILI was new to urban emergency services but planned to reuse an extensive library of reusable logistics software. They also indicated that their automated system would reduce Zenith's annual operating costs for fire dispatching by 50%.

ILI delivered an automated system on schedule, and demonstrated its impressive user interface to city leaders and the press with much fanfare. However, three months later, the Fire Department had discovered several problems:

- There were major delays and shortfalls in the cutover from the old system to the new system due to inadequate budgeting, planning, and preparation for conversion, installation, and training for users, administrators, and maintainers.

- The automated algorithm would send equipment to false alarms in rich people's neighborhoods while poor people's houses burned, which did not look good in the newspapers.
- The labor savings were not realized after the Firemen's Union went on a one day sick-out in protest over the potential loss of dispatchers' jobs.
- The delivered system had weak "off-nominal" capabilities that resulted in numerous dispatching delays and work-arounds (at least, these provided the extra dispatchers with things to do). The system was contractually compliant, but gave signs of being very risky to use in a crisis, requiring expensive post-delivery rework to improve safety.
- The reused logistics software was weak not only on safety but on privacy safeguards, putting confidential identity and financial information at risk.
- The English-only user interface caused numerous usage problems with the general public and multilingual hot line operators.

Clearly, these problems raise ethical concerns in such areas as fairness, quality of work, liability, risk disclosure, privacy, confidentiality, and unauthorized access. Let us see how the seven key elements of VBSE presented above can be applied to integrate ethical considerations into software engineering considerations:

1. Benefits Realization Analysis. The Results Chain approach can be used to identify missing success-critical stakeholders, particularly if maximizing benefits to the least advantaged is added to the desired outcomes.

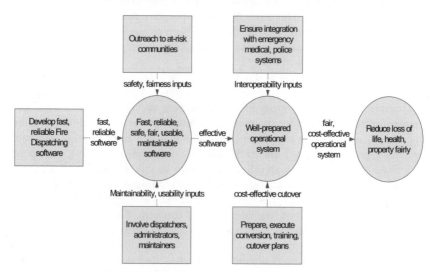

Fig. 26. Results Chain for fire dispatching system

Figure 26 provides an example Results Chain that could have been used to identify missing stakeholders and avoid the problems that happened with the Zenith Fire Dispatching System. It would start with a simple beginning Initiative to develop software on the left and a desired Outcome on the right that might initially focus on reducing property loss. By considering potential risks and pitfalls (and by considering problems lists like the one above), the customers and developers could identify and incorporate missing Initiatives and success-critical stakeholders into the system definition, development, and deployment process. As seen in Figure 26, these would include not only penumbra stakeholders, but also administrators, maintainers, and interoperators such as police and emergency medical systems.

2. Stakeholder Value Proposition Elicitation and Reconciliation. The stakeholder win-win approach to negotiating system objectives, constraints, and alternatives can be enhanced by adding representatives of the least advantaged class or penumbra, and by expanding the checklist of negotiation topics to identify the most critical system attributes for each class of stakeholder.

Table 10 shows a modification of one of the obligation matrices in (Collins et al., 1994) that provides guidance on negotiation topics. The table extends the "buyer" stakeholder to an "owner" stakeholder including not only system acquisition but also system transition, operations, and maintenance. It also adds a number of initiatives identified in the Results Chain. As with many systems, a full obligation matrix would include an additional column for interoperator stakeholders, and perhaps others such as upper management and insurance providers. The negotiation might include arrangements for Zenith software engineers to work on the developer's team, to enhance visibility and maintainability.

Table 10. Obligations of the software owner

To the provider	*To the owner*	*To the user*	*To the penumbra*
• Negotiate in good faith, recognizing the importance of provider's fair profit • Learn enough about the software to make informed decisions • Facilitate adequate communication with users, administrators, maintainers, and the penumbra	• Involve administrators, maintainers in system definition, development, and transition planning • Proactively address risks of delivery shortfalls and overruns	• Provide quality software appropriate to user's needs within reasonable budget constraints • Prudent introduction of automation • Informed consent to using software • Involve user representatives in system definition, review, and prototype exercise	• Buy software only with reasonable safeguards for the public • Open about software capabilities and limitations • Involve penumbra representatives in system definition, review, and prototype exercise

Similar example artifacts can be provided for the remaining five key elements, but space limitations constrain their description to the short summaries below.

3. Business Case Analysis. Return on investment techniques can be applied for each class of stakeholder to validate that the developed system will deliver cost-effective results, particularly for the penumbra.

4. Continuous Risk and Opportunity Management. The concept of risking harm can be expanded into a full set of risk and opportunity management techniques including risk identification, risk assessment, risk prioritization, risk planning and control, and the use of risk analysis to determine "how much is enough" of each software engineering activity.

5. Concurrent System and Software Engineering. The anchor point milestones in the WinWin Spiral Model provide a framework for controlled concurrent engineering, feasibility validation, and stakeholder concurrence on in-process software decisions and plans.

6. Value-Based Monitoring and Control. Techniques such as the Balanced Scorecard and Earned Stakeholder Value can be applied to monitor and control progress toward meeting ethical as well as product and financial goals.

7. Change as Opportunity. The pace of change in technology, organizations, environments, and stakeholder value propositions will continue to increase. Techniques such as evolution requirements, architectural encapsulation of sources of change, and agile methods can help ensure fair accommodation to change.

This partial single-thread application of the seven key elements provides an example of how VBSE techniques can integrate ethical considerations into a software engineer's daily practice. Clearly, there are many other ethical considerations for which VBSE can provide similar assistance. Besides the references (ACM/IEEE, 1998; Anderson et al., 1993; Boehm and Ross, 1989; Collins et al., 1994, Rawls, 1971), some further good treatments of software engineering ethics considerations are the books (Ermann and Shauf, 2003; Johnson and Nissenbaum, 1995; and Baird et al., 2000).

6.9 Getting Started Toward VBSE

Below are a set of steps you can take to get started toward VBSE by using the seven key elements of value-based software engineering and the VBSE guidelines for integrating ethical considerations. They are fairly compatible, and can be pursued in various combinations. The theory-driven process in Chapter 2 provides a more definitive process framework for determining when and how to invoke the seven key elements. As with most changes, it is best to start small with a receptive pilot project with good chances of demonstrating early value.

1. Benefits-Realization Analysis. Write down the name of your software initiative and its specific deliverables as its contribution as the left hand end of a Results Chain, and your stakeholders' desired outcome(s) as the right hand end. Then try to fill out the Results Chain with any success-critical assumptions, intermediate outcomes and contributions, and additional initiatives needed to fully realize the desired outcome(s). There usually will be some added initiatives, and they will often identify some missing success-critical stakeholders, such as operators, maintainers, owners of complementary systems, additional classes of users, and the general public if issues of safety, privacy, or fairness are involved.

2. *Stakeholder Value Proposition Elicitation and Reconciliation.* Use the Results Chain to interview your success-critical stakeholders to validate it and identify their additional high priority assumptions, initiatives, and outcomes. Use the Model Clash Spiderweb as a top-level checklist, and as a source for identifying model clashes that need to be reconciled among the stakeholders into a mutually satisfactory or win-win set of agreements. Summarize the results and coordinate them with the stakeholders via a Shared Vision document or its equivalent. A simple Shared Vision document would include an "elevator description" of the project and its desired outcome(s), the corresponding Results Chain, a list of the success-critical stakeholders and their roles, a System Block Diagram indicating the desired scope and boundary of the system to be developed and a list of the major project constraints. More detailed guidelines are in Section 2 of the MBASE Operational Concept Description Guidelines[7]. Other good approaches to this activity are Participatory Design (Ehn, 1990), Quality Function Deployment (Cohen, 1995), and agile methods (Highsmith, 2002).

3. *Business Case Analysis.* Do a simple (e.g., analogy-based) estimate of the costs of developing, installing, and operating your proposed system over your chosen benefits period. Do a similarly simple estimate of the resulting benefits across the benefits period. For an order processing system, for example, these could be both cost savings and increased sales and profits. Construct a chart similar to Figure 21 showing the cumulative return on investment, ROI = (benefits-costs)/costs. Also list the qualitative benefits, such as improved order fulfillment predictability and control and improved customer satisfaction. Iterate the business case with your stakeholders and ensure that they agree that it is worthwhile to proceed. Don Reifer's book, *Making the Software Business Case* (Reifer, 2002) provides further guidelines and case study examples. An example order processing case study is provided in (Boehm and Huang, 2003) and Chapter 8. Both the spiral model and its Rational Unified Process implementation are good approaches for steps 3, 4, and 5.

4. *Continuous Risk and Opportunity Management.* Any uncertainties in your business case analysis, or in your ability to realize the outcomes in your Results Chain, are sources of risk that you should eliminate early (via prototyping, user surveys, COTS evaluation, etc.), or develop plans and fallbacks for managing their future elimination. Also identify a focal point person for doing technology watch or marketplace watch activities to identify potential new risks or opportunities.

5. *Concurrent System and Software Engineering.* Rather than sequentially developing operational concepts, software requirements, prototypes, COTS and platform choices, architectures, and life cycle plans, perform these concurrently. Use the equivalent of the MBASE and Rational Unified Process Life Cycle Objectives

---

[7]http://sunset.usc.edu/research/MBASE

(LCO) and Life Cycle Architecture (LCA) milestones discussed in Section 6.5 as stakeholder review and commitment points.

   6. *Value-Based Monitoring and Control.* Use the Results Chain in step 1 to monitor the validity of assumptions, actual vs. expected contributions, and outcomes. Similarly, monitor the actual vs. estimated costs and benefits in the business case, and update the estimates at major milestones such as LCO and LCA. Also, continuously monitor the status of project risks and opportunities, and balanced-scorecard results such as customer satisfaction or fair treatment of least advantaged stakeholders. Determine appropriate corrective actions for any progress/plan/goal mismatches. Set up a simple pilot experience base for accumulating lessons learned and key metrics data (software productivity and quality metrics; balanced scorecard results) at the organizational level.

   7. *Change as Opportunity.* For small, noncritical projects with rapidly changing or highly emergent requirements, experiment with using one of the agile methods, enhanced where appropriate by the value-based steps above. For larger, more critical projects, determine the most likely sources of requirements change and modularize the system to accommodate these sources of change. Again, continuously monitor technology and the marketplace to identify and reorient the project to address unanticipated risks and opportunities. Where these are rapidly changing, experiment with hybrid plan-driven and agile methods within an architectural framework addressing the most critical and stable requirements. Process frameworks for medium and large size hybrid plan-driven and agile methods are provided in (Boehm and Turner, 2004).

The subsequent chapters in Part 2 provide more detailed guidelines on these and related VBSE techniques such as value-based requirements prioritization, release planning, usability testing, and system testing.

References

(ACM/IEEE, 1998) ACM/IEEE: The Software Engineering Code of Ethics and Professional Practice. http://www.acm.org, http://www.computer.org (1998)

(Ahern et al., 2001) Ahern, D., Clouse, A., Turner, R.: CMMI Distilled (Addison Wesley, 2001)

(Al-Said, 2003) Al-Said, M.: Identifying, Analyzing, and Avoiding Software Model Clashes PhD Dissertation (USC, 2003)

(Amram and Kulatilaka, 1999) Amram, M., Kulatilaka, N.: Real Options (Harvard Business School Press, 1999)

(Anderson et al., 1993) Anderson, R., Johnson, D., Gotterbarn, D., Perolle, J.: Using the New ACM Code of Ethics in Decision Making (Comm. ACM, February 1993), pp 98–105

(Baird et al., 2000) Baird, R., Ramsower, R., Rosenbaum, S.: Cyberethics (Prometheus Books, 2000)

(Baldwin and Clark, 2000) Baldwin, C., Clark, K.: Design Rules: The Power of Modularity (MIT Press, 2000)

(Boehm and Turner, 2004) Boehm, B. W., Turner, R.: Balancing Agility and Discipline (Addison Wesley, 2004)

(Boehm et al., 2000) Boehm, B. W., Port, D., Al-Said, M.: Avoiding the Software Model-Clash Spiderweb (Computer, 2000), pp 120–122

(Boehm et al., 2002a) Boehm, B. W., Port, D., Jain, A., Basili, V.: Achieving CMMI Level 5 Improvements with MBASE and the CeBASE Method (Cross Talk, 2002)

(Boehm et al., 2002b) Boehm, B. W., Port, D., Huang, L., Brown, A. W.: Using the Spiral Model and MBASE to Generate New Acquisition Process Models: SAIV, CAIV, and SCQAIV (Cross Talk, 2002)

(Boehm and Huang, 2003) Boehm, B. W. and Huang, L.G.: Value-based Software Engineering: A Case Study, IEEE Computer, March 2003 pp 33–41

(Boehm and Port, 2001) Boehm, B. W., Port, D.: Balancing Discipline and Flexibility with the Spiral Model and MBASE (Cross Talk, 2001)

(Boehm and Ross, 1989) Boehm, B. W., Ross, R.: Theory-W Software Project Management: Principles and Examples (IEEE Transactions on Software Engineering, 1989), pp 902–916

(Carr, 2002) Carr, D.: Sweet Victory (Baseline, 2002)

(Cohen, 1995) Cohen, L.: Quality Function Deployment (Prentice Hall, 1995)

(Collins et al., 1994) Collins, W., Miller, K., Spielman, B., Wherry, J.: How Good is Good Enough? (Comm. ACM, 1994), pp 81–91

(Cusumano and Selby, 1995) Cusumano, M., Selby, R.: Microsoft Secrets, How the World's Most Powerful Software Company Creates Technology, Shapes Markets, and Manages People (The Free Press, 1995)

(Ehn, 1990) Ehn P. (ed): Work-Oriented Design of Computer Artifacts (Lawrence Erlbaum Assoc., 1990)

(Ermann and Shauf, 2003) Ermann, M. D., Shauf, M.: Computers, Ethics, and Society 3 (Oxford U. Press, 2003)

(FAA, 1997) Federal Aviation Administration (FAA): The Integrated Capability Maturity Model (1997)

(Faulk et al., 2000) Faulk, S., Harmon, D., Raffo, D.: Value-Based Software Engineering (VBSE): A Value-Driven Approach to Product-Line Engineering. Proceedings, First International Conference on Software Product Line Engineering (August 2000)

(Highsmith, 2000) Highsmith, J.: Adaptive Software Development (Dorset House, 2000)

(Highsmith, 2002) Highsmith, J.: Agile Software Development Ecosystems, (Addison Wesley, 2002)

(Jacobson et al., 1999) Jacobson, I., Booch, G., Rumbaugh, J.: The Unified Software Development Process (Addison Wesley, 1999)

(Johnson and Nissenbaum, 1995) Johnson, D., Nissenbaum, H.: Computers, Ethics, and Social Values (Prentice Hall, 1995)

(Kaplan and Norton, 1996) Kaplan, R., Norton, D.: The Balanced Scorecard: Translating Strategy into Action (Harvard Business School Press, 1996)

(Kauffman, 1995) Kauffman, S.: At Home in the Universe (Oxford University Press, 1995)

(Kruchten, 2001) Kruchten, P.: The Rational Unified Process 3 (Addison Wesley, 2001)

(Paulk et al., 1994) Paulk, M., Weber, C., Curtis, B., Chrissis, M.: The Capability Maturity Model (Addison Wesley, 1994)

(Parnas, 1979) Parnas, D.: Designing Software for Ease of Extension and Contraction (IEEE Transactions on Software Engineering, 1979), pp 128–137

(Rawls, 1971) Rawls, J.: A Theory of Justice (Belknap/Harvard U. Press, 1971)

(Reifer, 2002) Reifer, D.: Making the Software Business Case (Addison Wesley, 2002)

(Royce, 1998) Royce, W. E.: Software Project Management (Addison-Wesley, 1998)

(Morton, 1991) Morton, M. S.: The Corporation of the 1990s: Information Technology and Organization Transformation (Oxford University Press, 1991)

(SEI, 2002) Software Engineering Institute (SEI): Capability Maturity Model Integration (CMMI), Version 1.1 (CMU/SEI-2002-TR-012, 2002)

(SPC, 1992) Software Productivity Consortium (SPC): The Evolutionary Spiral Process. SPC Technical Report (Herndon, VA, 1992)

(Sullivan et al., 2001) Sullivan, K., Cai, Y., Hallen, B., Griswold, W.: The Structure and Value of Modularity in Software Design. Proceedings, ESEC/FSE, 2001 (ACM Press, 2001), pp 99–108

(Thorp and DMR) Thorp, J., DMR: The Information Paradox (McGraw Hill, 1998)

Author Biography

Barry Boehm is the TRW Professor of Software Engineering and Director of the Center for Software Engineering at University of Southern California (USC). His current research interests include software process modeling, software requirements engineering, software architectures, software metrics and cost models, software engineering environments, and value-based software engineering. His contributions to the field include the Constructive Cost Model (COCOMO), the Spiral Model of the software process, and the Theory W (win-win) approach to software management and requirements determination. He is a Fellow of the primary professional societies in computing (ACM), aerospace (AIAA), electronics (IEEE), and systems engineering (INCOSE), and a member of the US National Academy of Engineering.

7 Stakeholder Value Proposition Elicitation and Reconciliation

Paul Grünbacher, Sabine Köszegi and Stefan Biffl

Abstract: This chapter motivates the need of methods and tools for understanding and reconciling stakeholder value propositions in software engineering. We present EasyWinWin, an example of a groupware-supported negotiation method that provides process structure and mediation to stakeholders. We identify challenges of stakeholder value proposition elicitation and negotiation and discuss possible extensions to EasyWinWin that address these challenges.

Keywords: Stakeholder value proposition, requirements negotiation, groupware, negotiation analysis.

7.1 Introduction

Eliciting and reconciling stakeholder value propositions is an integral element of value-based software engineering. Dealing with different people's utility functions or value propositions is fundamental to overcome the limitations of a value-neutral approach and for making software products useful to people (see Chapter 1). Software engineering is highly collaborative and relies on involving different people in many project situations such as project planning, risk management, requirements definition, testing (see Chapter 11), or COTS selection.

In particular, the success or failure of system development efforts rests on requirements elicitation and negotiation. Many of the failures, delays, and budget overruns in software engineering can be traced directly to shortfalls in the requirements process (StandishGroup, 2001). Hence, eliciting stakeholder interests, understanding conflicting positions, and negotiating mutually satisfactory agreements are integral elements of value-based software engineering (VBSE, see Chapter 1). Facilitating the active participation of stakeholders in requirements negotiations is crucial for project success as it helps to understand the organizational and social context of the system to be developed (Macaulay, 1993). Requirements emerge from a process of cooperative learning in which they are explored, prioritized, negotiated, evaluated, and documented to achieve mutually satisfactory agreements that accommodate different stakeholder interests and expectations. During a requirements negotiation, developers learn more about the customers' and users' worlds, while customers and users learn more about what is technically possible and feasible. In this complex process, negotiation techniques and support tools for identifying, analyzing and resolving conflicting requirements play a critical role. Shortcomings in eliciting and reconciling stakeholder value propositions can lead to severe problems (Halling et al., 2003):

- Missing or ill-defined capabilities leading to unusable systems, unreliable estimates, or infeasible architectures;
- Ill-defined interfaces to other systems or to the user making integration into the target environment infeasible;
- Miscommunication caused by language problems due to missing, unclear, or wrong terms;
- Hidden conflicts among stakeholders leading to mistrust;
- Misunderstood project constraints such as staffing, required technology, budget, and schedules causing project delays, frustration, and confusion; or
- Inconsistent or infeasible quality objectives negatively impacting the choice of feasible architecture and unnecessarily increasing development costs.

Numerous methods and tools have been developed by researchers and practitioners for eliciting, negotiating, documenting, and validating requirements (Antón and Potts, 1998; Sutcliffe et al., 1998; Robertson and Robertson, 1999). Negotiation is seen as particularly important in software engineering for analyzing and resolving conflicting positions.

The objectives of this chapter are to discuss challenges in eliciting and reconciling stakeholder value propositions, to show how the EasyWinWin requirements negotiation method deals with these challenges, and to discuss possible and necessary extensions to EasyWinWin that address these challenges.

Our research method was to first survey literature from requirements engineering and negotiation theory to gather frequent challenges in requirements elicitation and negotiation. We then evaluated the strengths and limitations of EasyWinWin. EasyWinWin has been chosen as it combines several approaches that have been reported as useful in stakeholder value proposition elicitation and negotiation. The theory behind EasyWinWin is Theory W, which plays a central role in VBSE theory (see Chapter 2, Figure 4). EasyWinWin supports expectations management, adopts prioritization techniques, and is supported with groupware tools. Based on the results from the literature review and our experience with teams using EasyWinWin we suggest useful extensions. In Section 7.2, we discuss negotiation challenges in general. Section 7.3 discusses EasyWinWin, a groupware-supported approach based on the win-win negotiation model. Section 7.4 discusses EasyWinWin with respect to the negotiation challenges and outlines how it can be complemented by integrating concepts, theories, and tools from negotiation theory. The chapter closes with conclusions and research directions in Section 7.5.

7.2 Negotiation Challenges

Negotiation is vital to support the reconciliation of stakeholder value propositions. Negotiation can be viewed as a process of interaction where debate about conflicting interests, needs, or values is the central activity. Negotiation starts when participants begin communicating their goals, and ends (successfully) when all concur on a specified set of agreements. Providing effective negotiation support is challenging. We have identified four types of potential threats for successful requirements negotiations: (1) conflicting stakeholder interests; (2) constraints with respect to stakeholders such as ability, availability, or reduced willingness to cooperate; (3) uncertainties about stakeholder preferences; and (4) the complexity of the problem at hand (e.g., the high number and interdependencies of requirements).

Conflicting Stakeholder Interests

Major system stakeholders are typically users, acquirers, developers, and maintainers, who have role-specific needs and preferences. For example, users are typically interested in many features, high level of service, and availability; acquirers generally look at cost-effectiveness, compliance with standards, or budget/schedule; developers often want flexible contracts and stable requirements. It is obvious that such value conflicts are present in most real-world projects. The key is thus to help determine how these conflicts can be reconciled.

Many approaches in software engineering can be characterized as "consensus-based," i.e., they are implicitly based on the assumption that stakeholders pursue the same principal goals and emerging conflicts can be resolved through facilitation of information and know-how exchange. Thus, existing tools for requirements negotiations are based on cooperative group support systems, which aim at facilitating group processes and reduce communication barriers. Examples are *Theory-W* (Boehm and Ross, 1989) and various generations of win-win negotiation support environments (Boehm et al., 2001).

However, the assumption that conflict in requirements negotiations can be resolved using a consensus-based approach may not always hold. In many instances, it is more reasonable to assume that stakeholders are facing actual conflicts of interests and needs which cannot simply be resolved through information exchange. In such cases, it is a promising strategy to complement the consensus-based approach with methods from negotiation theory (Pruitt and Carnevale, 1993). Typically, the preferences of different stakeholders vary considerably; it is important to understand these differences and how they can be reconciled for optimizing the overall value among stakeholders.

Negotiation theory differentiates between two types of conflicts in terms of conflict representation and potential outcomes (Pruitt and Carnevale, 1993): distributive (non-cooperative) and integrative (cooperative) conflicts. The former type of conflict can be classified as zero-sum game, where the gain of one party represents a loss of the other party. The simplest case is a negotiation where involved parties are concerned with the division of a single asset. The interest of parties is to get a bigger share of the disputed value. Distributive negotiations are the opposite of integrative negotiations, where the parties' interest is 'enlarging the pie' instead of 'dividing the pie'. They engage in a problem solving processes by integrating the parties' capabilities and resources to generate more value. In reality, many situations comprise both types of conflicts, i.e., they include integrative and distributive elements and, hence, represent mixed-motive conflicts (Pruitt and Carnevale, 1993). Facing such conflicts, stakeholders of requirements negotiations may not use exclusively a problem solving approach but also apply distributive strategies and tactics to increase their share of the disputed values. This in turn may lead to inefficient solutions for software projects. In such a setting, a mere process facilitation to encourage open information sharing can hardly be successful.

What is more, the valuable knowledge of the different stakeholders and their individual evaluation of tradeoffs between alternatives and options should not be ignored. For effective requirements negotiation support, there is not only a need to facilitate information exchange but also to guide stakeholders through difficult phases of interest consolidation with a normative negotiation support.

Stakeholder-Related Difficulties

In an ideal world, stakeholders involved in requirements negotiation would be collaborative, representative, authorized, committed, and knowledgeable to avoid a negative impact on the quality and sustainability of the negotiation outcome. However, there might be situations where one or several of these criteria are not fulfilled.

For example, stakeholder might not always be as collaborative as expected. In the literature, there are several basic strategies identified, depending on the negotiator's focus on his own, the opponent's, or joint interests (Pruitt and Rubin, 1986). The most important distinction is made between competing and problem solving strategies. By applying a competing strategy, negotiators pursue their own goals and try to persuade the other party to concede. The problem solving strategy involves a joint effort in which the parties work together, exchange information about needs and priorities, and try to find solutions, which consider needs and interests of all involved parties (see also Chapter 4 for tradeoff examples). Again, framing requirements negotiations as a collaborative group task requires that stakeholders always pursue problem solving strategies. As discussed before, conflicts can give rise to strategic or even opportunistic behavior of stakeholders. Actors could, for instance, withhold important information to gain advantages during negotiations.

Apart from potential strategic (or opportunistic) behavior of stakeholders, there are several other risks affecting the outcome of requirements negotiations. Typically, stakeholders are embedded in a social and political network within organizations. This may cause socio-emotionally motivated dysfunctional behavior when stakeholders abuse their role in the project to pursue personal goals.

Another challenge of software engineering negotiations constitutes the fact that stakeholders often represent a large body of individuals (e.g., governmental systems). They might not have the power to make commitments to other stakeholders, or they might not be able to integrate diverse preferences within a stakeholder group. What is more, in some instances, personal relationships, personal sympathies and antipathies, or the demonstration of power could receive more attention than the substance of the underlying tasks. Additionally, cognitive limitations and biases (Tversky and Kahnemann, 1978; Bazerman and Carroll, 1987) can impose a considerable threat to the success of software development associated with high complexity and uncertainty.

Additionally, the number of stakeholders may challenge communication because often stakeholders come from very different cultures, education, and experience with varying understanding of competence in the project content, and different interpretations of project terminology. In international projects there is the risk of misunderstandings and conflicts due to cultural differences . Additionally, the diversity of stakeholders often causes ill-defined semantic precision in negotiations. Hence, there is a need to reduce communication barriers between members of different groups by developing a project-specific discourse (e.g., shared glossaries).

A further important issue is the availability of stakeholders. At negotiation time, critical stakeholders may not yet be known or available to the project. In any negotiation process that needs face-to-face meetings, there are time constraints to be considered to get important stakeholders together (often no more than one full day in a quarter year).

Uncertainties about Stakeholder Preferences

Stakeholders are typically unsure about their own needs and even more unsure about the needs of others. For a long time, researchers have tried to cope with the IKIWISI problem ("I Know It When I See It"), and have proposed iterative approaches and prototyping to detect uncertainties about stakeholder preferences early on. Chapter 10 presents a collaborative approach addressing this problem. Uncertainties about preferences however do not affect only GUI characteristics. Other examples are COTS capabilities, technology maturity, and degree of achievability within cost and schedule constraints.

These introduce the need for concurrent negotiation of requirements and exploration of the solution space, with the attendant challenges of synchronizing requirements negotiations and solutions explorations, and determining how much solution exploration is enough.

Preference elicitation and the analysis of negotiators' needs and interests are crucial phases of requirements negotiations. Furthermore, a thorough discussion of potential conflicts in the differentiation phase allows preventing negative consequences in later stages of software development.

Existing support tools for software requirements negotiation such as Easy-WinWin are focused on the elicitation and consolidation of preferences through facilitation of stakeholder discussions. However, there are other negotiation tools available that also support evaluation of tradeoffs among options as well as the reconciliation of conflicting interests and consensus building (Grünbacher and Seyff, 2005). Kersten discusses several levels of tool support ranging from passive support systems that only provide an infrastructure for negotiation to proactive interventive support systems that are capable of coordinating the activities of stakeholders and critiquing their actions (Kersten, 2004). The implementation of multicriteria decision making methods, as discussed in Chapter 4, could also enhance the identification of possible areas of bargaining and efficient group solutions (Vetschera, 1990). Furthermore, such techniques can also be used to provide technical mediating facilities (Jarke et al., 1987).

Problem Complexity

Many software development projects face enormous complexity in decision making and negotiation. Even moderate projects have to deal with many interdependent requirements and with conflicting stakeholders interests. Limited information processing abilities and cognitive biases of involved parties are considerable obstacles for developing efficient solutions in software projects. Additionally, any substantial software project has to deal with changing requirements, stakeholders, and their preferences, resulting in iterative refinement of negotiation results in a project life cycle.

Effective negotiation support therefore has to not only enhance cognitive and information processing capabilities of stakeholders but also provide enough flexibility to deal with changing requirements. Although existing decision support systems (DSSs) offer opportunities to facilitate complex decisions, there is still only limited software-specific decision making support available. There is a wide variety in support features such as simulation models for prediction or choice models for aggregation of multiple criteria through knowledge-based systems and quantification techniques that could be adapted to specific contexts in requirements negotiations.

Requirements negotiations involve many different stakeholders with diverse interests and a variety of complex tasks, both challenging the successful course of a project. Therefore, these negotiations need a thorough understanding of the software process to focus on the right issues, and to structure the negotiation process in an efficient way.

7.3 The EasyWinWin Requirements Negotiation Support

This section presents the EasyWinWin approach which combines several approaches that have been reported as useful in stakeholder value proposition elicitation and negotiation (see also Chapter 2 for theory foundation). It supports expectations management, adopts prioritization techniques, and is supported with groupware tools.

EasyWinWin (Boehm et al., 2001) is a requirements negotiation methodology that builds on the win-win negotiation approach and leverages a Group Support System (GSS) to improve the involvement and interaction of key stakeholders. Using EasyWinWin, stakeholders are guided through a step-by-step win-win negotiation where they collect, elaborate, and prioritize their requirements, and surface and resolve issues to come up with mutually satisfactory agreements.

The major area of application for EasyWinWin are software requirements negotiations although experiences have also been gained in other domains (e.g., negotiation of company strategies, negotiation of innovative business processes). According to the spiral model of software development, teams can use EasyWinWin throughout the development cycle, e.g., to develop a shared project vision, to negotiate more detailed requirements about capabilities, desired properties, or requirements concerning the development process. The elicitation of stakeholder preferences is strongly supported with brainstorming and electronic voting tools. The actual negotiation of agreements relies on a facilitator. EasyWinWin assumes a collaboration-oriented conflict resolution. It does not limit the number of stakeholders, typical groups using the approach have between seven and 15 participants. Most groups have used EasyWinWin in same time (synchronous or asynchronous) settings.

Negotiation Model

The foundation for the WinWin approach is the Management Theory-W (Boehm and Ross, 1989). According to its fundamental principle a necessary and sufficient condition for a successful enterprise is that the enterprise makes winners of all its success-critical stakeholders. Key activities include (1) the identification of success-critical stakeholders; (2) the elicitation of the success-critical stakeholders' primary Win conditions; (3) the negotiation of mutually satisfactory win-win solution packages (requirements, architectures, plans, critical components, etc.); and (4) value-based monitoring and control of the WinWin equilibrium throughout the development process.

WinWin is based on a negotiation model for converging to a WinWin agreement, and defines a WinWin equilibrium condition to test whether the negotiation process has converged. The negotiation model (see Chapter 2, Figure 7, "WinWin negotiation model") guides success-critical stakeholders in elaborating mutually satisfactory agreements. Stakeholders express their goals as *Win conditions*. If everyone concurs, the Win conditions become *agreements*. When stakeholders do not concur, they identify their conflicted Win conditions and register their conflicts as *issues*. In this case, stakeholders invent options for mutual gain and explore the option tradeoffs. *Options* are iterated and turned into agreements when all stakeholders concur. Unresolved issues represent potential project risks that need to be addressed. Additionally, a domain taxonomy is used to organize win-win artifacts. Important terms of the domain are captured in a glossary. The Win-Win equilibrium condition tests if all Win conditions are covered by agreements or if there are any unresolved issues.

The context of a requirements negotiation is defined by the spiral model of software development (Boehm, 1988; Boehm 1996). The spiral model is a life-cycle model that repeatedly iterates a set of key development processes and emphasizes risk management. The WinWin Spiral Model (Boehm et al., 1998) emphasizes stakeholder involvement and complements the original Spiral Model with negotiation activities that are performed in each spiral cycle.

The input to a WinWin workshop is typically a mission statement describing the objectives of a project and a negotiation purpose statement specifying the objectives of a negotiation within a project. A WinWin negotiation is often carried out in a series of workshops (collocated or dispersed), involving all identified success-critical stakeholders. A facilitator follows detailed guidelines as described in the EasyWinWin process guidebook and moderates the negotiation process.

Before entering a negotiation, the facilitator has to identify and engage the success-critical stakeholders. A success-critical stakeholder is any individual whose interests must be accommodated in order for the project to succeed (Kotonya and Sommerville, 1998), i.e., the people who can make agreements about the requirements. Involving the right people is critical: If low-level representatives negotiate requirements, the success-critical stakeholder may subsequently disallow any agreements they reach. Such repudiation means more negotiations, which may again end with the repudiation of agreements by superiors. Involving only success-critical stakeholders can short-circuit the negotiate-repudiate-renegotiate cycle. The WinWin spiral model demands the identification of success-critical stakeholders whenever a new cycle is entered. The set of success-critical stakeholders therefore typically changes throughout a project. For example, stakeholders negotiating a contract are different from stakeholders planning and performing the deployment of a system to the target environment.

EasyWinWin Process

EasyWinWin provides a repeatable and tool supported process for requirements negotiations (Boehm et al., 2001) and helps a team of stakeholders to attain consensus by jointly discovering, elaborating, prioritizing, and negotiating their value propositions. EasyWinWin uses a *Group Support System* (GSS), a collection of collaborative software tools stakeholders use to focus and structure their mental effort as they work together toward a goal (Nunamaker et al., 1997). Briggs et al. (2003) show how a GSS can be used to create repeatable patterns of group interaction and to create collaborative methodologies that produce deliverables of consistent quality and detail. Extensive research in the lab and in the field reveals that, under certain circumstances, teams can use GSSs to become substantially more productive than would otherwise be possible (Fjermestad and Hiltz, 2001). Because a GSS allows a team to focus and structure their interactions in predictable ways, a GSS can become the foundation for developing and refining a repeatable, efficient requirements process.

Figure 27 (adapted from (Grünbacher et al., 2004a)) gives an overview about EasyWinWin activities and deliverables with relationships to important work products in the life cycle. Major deliverables of an EasyWinWin negotiation are (1) negotiation topics organized in a domain taxonomy, (2) definitions of key project terms, (3) agreements providing the foundation for further plans, (4) open issues addressing constraints, conflicts, and known problems, as well as (5) further decision rationale showing the negotiation history (such as associated comments, Win conditions, issues, and options).

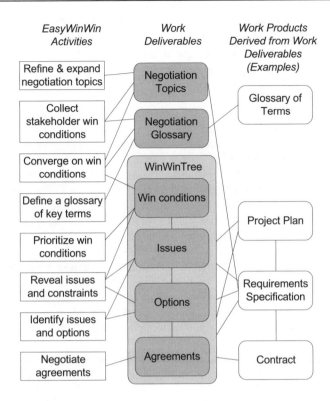

Fig. 27. EasyWinWin activities and deliverables

EasyWinWin aims at reducing the cognitive load associated with the sources and causes of complexity in requirements definition without losing or overlooking any of the richness of interrelationships among the many concepts incorporated in the requirements deliverables. According to our experience typical negotiations models created by 10+ stakeholders result in 300+ brainstorming ideas, 100+ Win conditions, 50+ issues, 50+ options, and 100+ agreements.

The following sections summarize each step of the methodology and describe how conflicting interests, stakeholder-related challenges, and task complexity are addressed during those steps.

Refine and Expand Negotiation Topics

Requirements deal with various stakeholder concerns including the system's capabilities, interfaces, properties, development, and evolution. Stakeholders are typically unaware of all the different aspects for which requirements must be written and thus tend to arrive with a narrow understanding of what they want and need from the proposed system. By reviewing and revising a shared taxonomy of negotiation topics, they often come to understand that the scope of project is much bigger than they had originally expected. In this step, the stakeholders collaboratively elaborate a shared outline containing a taxonomy of system requirements such as functional requirements, quality aspects, or evolution requirements (Robertson and Robertson, 1999). Participants review this outline and make suggestions on how to tailor it to the specifics of their project.

Collect Stakeholder Win Conditions

Stakeholders often arrive with, at least, a vague understanding of what they want from the system for themselves and their constituents. However, they often have only little knowledge of what other stakeholders expect from the system. Complexities of preferences can only be addressed when stakeholders understand one another's interests. This step accomplishes three main purposes: (1) stakeholders record first-draft statements of what they want from the proposed system, (2) stakeholders learn what others want from the system, and (3) stakeholders expand and clarify what they want from the system by reading what others want. The GSS provides an electronic brainstorming tool to surface as many different Win conditions as possible in a short period of time. Rather than interviewing stakeholders one-on-one or in small groups, many stakeholders can be brought together to contribute simultaneously, thus reducing the frequency and intensity of interactions required.

In an iterative life cycle the source of Win conditions can also be negotiation results from earlier cycles that are to be refined and elaborated. This includes unresolved issues needing attention.

Converge on Win Conditions

The contents of the brainstorming session in the previous step tend to be free ranging, wordy, partially redundant, and occasionally irrelevant. In this step, the team tries to converge on a concisely worded, nonredundant, unambiguous list of Win conditions by using an oral conversation supported by two GSS tools. There is typically about one third to half as many Win conditions as there are brainstorming comments. One tool divides the brainstorming comments among the participants so each sees a different set. This reduces complexity for stakeholders by enabling them to work in parallel on smaller chunks of their data. The other tool provides participants with a shared list which all can see on their screens. Drawing from the brainstorming comments on the screen, each participant in turn proposes orally a clear, concise statement of a Win condition to be posted on the shared list. Stakeholders continue to swap raw brainstorming comments and post new Win conditions to the shared list until nobody can find anything new to add. The group discusses each Win condition aloud to create a shared understanding of its meaning. At this time, participants may argue about the meaning of any Win condition, but they may not object to or raise issues about any Win condition. Key terms surface during these conversations which may take on special meaning for the project, or which the team may find vague or confusing. These terms are captured to a keyword list for further processing in the next step.

Define a Glossary of Key Terms

In any system development project, there are key terms that become insider jargon for project members. This step helps to develop a mutual understanding of language and to eliminate ambiguous concepts and terms. Insider jargon can simplify communication among those who know the jargon, but it can hinder communication with others. This step captures knowledge about project-specific terms: all key terms derived from the brainstorming session are posted to a shared list. The team breaks into pairs and each pair works out a definition of several key terms and posts the definitions to the shared list. Then the pairs report their definitions to the group orally, which usually provokes spirited debate. The team negotiates an agreed meaning for each term and usually finds there are other key terms, which should be added to the list and defined. The captured definitions are valuable throughout the project, especially as the composition of the team changes over time. There is, however, additional value in the spirited debate. As people negotiate the meanings of words, key project constraints emerge, assumptions surface, and the team frequently identifies new stakeholders who should be included in the requirements process. This step may be repeated several times throughout the project as the team collects new terms. Once the terms have been defined, the team goes back and restates the Win conditions more precisely.

Prioritize Win Conditions

A key to value-based software engineering is to better understand the preferences and value propositions of stakeholders. Prioritizing the Win conditions are therefore an important step in EasyWinWin. During brainstorming, convergence, and definitions of key terms, the stakeholders can post any Win condition that comes to mind, regardless of its potential impact on other Win conditions. Stakeholders learn about one another's interests, but not necessarily about how important one Win condition is compared to another, nor about what a given Win condition might cost in time, effort, and aggravation. This is the first step where participants are allowed to express their opinion about the merits of the Win conditions. Participants rate each Win condition along two criteria:

- *Value* (Business Importance), the degree to which the success of the project depends on this Win condition being realized, and
- *Feasibility* (Ease of Realization), the degree to which a Win condition is technologically, socially, politically, or economically feasible.

During this assessment, the participants are instructed, "If you do not know, do not vote." Customers and users often decide not to render opinions about the ease of realization. For example, programmers frequently choose not to rate the business importance of a given Win condition. Some people offer no assessment of Win conditions in which they have no stake, focusing instead on the ones about which they care.

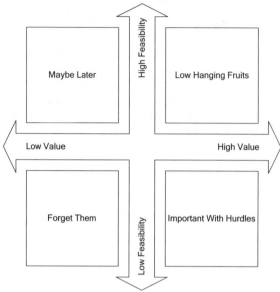

Fig. 28. Portfolio of Win conditions

Aggregated voting results can be displayed in a simple portfolio that organizes the Win conditions in the four categories as shown in Figure 28.

Reveal Issues and Constraints

The voting results are not used to drop any Win conditions. Rather they are used to provoke a well structured, tightly contained exploration in the next step. Moreover, the step allows the individuals to see how their own opinion compares to that of the group, and this in turn helps them to learn about expectations and perhaps to identify unreasonable expectations of their own.

Any given Win condition may, on its own, raise issues for any given stakeholder. The purpose of the previous step was not to eliminate low rated Win conditions, but rather to surface differences of opinion about individual Win conditions. Different stakeholders often have different reasons for the opinions they register, and those reasons originate in their differences of experience, interest, and purpose. Those differences often relate to unarticulated and unexamined project constraints. This step focuses exclusively on the areas of highest disagreement among the ballots cast in the previous step. When the results are displayed, items with high consensus display with a green background, while items with low consensus display with a red background.

This step focuses on situations where consensus is low. Stakeholders use this graph as a stimulus to explore the reasons behind their differences in opinion about a Win condition. The group holds a structured oral conversation and tries to explore possible reasons for high or low item ratings. Key information cues about the project emerge from these discussions, such as project constraints, assumptions, unshared information, or hidden agendas.

Identify Issues and Options

In this step, the team posts a shared outline with all Win conditions as main headings. The team makes two passes through this outline. On the first pass, each person reads each Win condition. If the Win condition raises any issue with a stakeholder, the stakeholder may write the issue as a subheading to the Win condition. This step also allows stakeholders to argue their case against any given Win condition, should they have an issue with something proposed by someone else. Any Win condition may have interdependencies with other Win conditions. One key purpose of this step is to identify and deal with those issues. The participants may not discuss the issues aloud at this time. Stakeholders can report risks and uncertainties as comments to a Win condition. The facilitator then helps the team to converge on the key issues for each Win condition in an oral discussion. On the next pass, each participant reads each issue. If a participant can think of any option for resolving the issue, the participant may write the option as a comment to the issue. The facilitator then helps the team to converge on the key options for each Win condition in an oral discussion. Once the issues and options have been articulated, the group is ready to begin negotiating agreements.

Negotiate Agreements

There are usually no issues on about one third of the Win conditions. After a quick review, the group usually declares these items to be agreements. They become commitments the team must fulfill. Then the group addresses each issue in turn with a traditional oral negotiation. Sometimes one or more of the options posted with an issue turn out to be the basis for an agreement. Other times the stakeholders engage in protracted discussions of an issue. During that conversation, more assumptions and constraints, key terms, options, issues, and Win conditions emerge. Each of these is captured in the tool. Every time a team member proposes an agreement out loud, somebody types it as an option on the tree. As people argue for and against options, someone captures pros and cons as electronic annotations to the options. Eventually, the group fashions an agreement with which they can live. They write the agreement on the WinWin Tree. When every Win condition and every option has an agreement, the state of WinWin equilibrium has been achieved. In an iterative development process unresolved issues are treated in a subsequent negotiation if the WinWin equilibrium cannot be reached.

Keeping Negotiations on Track

In practice, precision is traded off against speed in most negotiation situations. A major challenge for the facilitator is to watch the trade-off between generating many ideas and delivering consistent high quality negotiation results. It is also important to keep the participants focused on the right level of detail according to the negotiation purpose in order to elicit as complete and consistent information as possible in a given negotiation situation.

Negotiation artefacts are statements written in natural language and therefore error prone. Some typical examples of defects that we have identified in individual statements are unclear statements or missing information, ambiguous terms, incorrect statements, and unverifiable statements. Defects in a requirements negotiation can appear on the statement level or on the negotiation level. Typical faults we have experienced are vague or ambiguous statements, missing information, wrong level of detail, or inconsistencies. An ill-defined capability defect that can be easily fixed during requirements elicitation and negotiation can become a major problem if it cannot be realized with the chosen system architecture. Consequently, before refining the negotiation results to other life cycle artifacts like contracts, specification, project plans, or architectural models, defects should be eliminated to reduce both the effort and probability of rework stemming from undetected defects.

EasyWinWin relies on several quality checks in the stages of pre-negotiation, actual conduct of the negotiation, and post-negotiation (Grünbacher et al., 2004a).

Pre-Negotiation: The facilitator has the responsibility to ensure that the preconditions of a negotiation are satisfied. It is crucial to develop a statement summarizing the major purpose of the negotiation, context information, and major objectives of the system to be developed. The second central issue is to get all success-critical stakeholders to attend and contribute. There are some additional success factors for selecting stakeholders for a negotiation. They should be empowered and have the official authority or legal power to negotiate agreements. They should be committed to the decisions that are jointly developed. Stakeholders should be representative when serving as a delegate or agent for a team or organization. They should be collaborative and have the willingness and perceptiveness required for developing mutually satisfactory solutions in a team process. Stakeholders should also be knowledgeable and well informed about the negotiation domain.

Conduct of Negotiation: We have developed joint and rapid checking activities to be performed by a team to spot and resolve defects during a negotiation. At certain points in the process, all participants step back from the negotiation and check the quality of the products to eliminate defects that have been identified. Fixing defects in the process is typically straightforward as it is possible to clarify issues with the author. The process is not an inspection as the participants (and authors) themselves review the products.

Post-Negotiation: In addition to the joint and rapid checks performed by the stakeholders described in the preceding section, a more formal inspection process can be applied. This process involves (1) Inspection preparation to check the entry criteria of completeness and sufficient quality for understanding the inspection context; (2) Individual reading supported with reading techniques optimized for negotiation results; (3) Meeting of inspectors or some other form of defect collection; as well as (4) Report and rework to clarify the issues raised with the author if possible, or to document the problem and the resolution in a traceable way.

7.4 Possible Extensions to the EasyWinWin Approach

In this section, we assess strengths and weaknesses of the EasyWinWin approach and derive important directions for possible extensions to the EasyWinWin approach. The goal is to assess the maturity of EasyWinWin in a more general negotiation context.

Conflicting Stakeholder Interests

The most important assumption currently underlying the EasyWinWin methodology is that requirements negotiation is a collaborative group task where stakeholders – in principle – pursue the same goal. The major strength of the Easy-WinWin technique can therefore be seen in its attempt to guide various stakeholders through the difficult phases of preference elicitation and discussion of possible points of contention in order to consolidate different perspectives. From a negotiation analysis approach, this assumption is, however, risky. It is more plausible to assume that stakeholders envision real conflicts of interests: while users, for instance, are interested in high functionality and performance of the software, constituents want to minimize costs. Hence, stakeholders participate in requirements negotiations in order to defend their own interests rather than to pursue a shared goal. The following suggestions to extend the EasyWinWin approach could facilitate efficient conflict resolution in software engineering negotiations.

Individual Preference Elicitation

There are numerous approaches available for the elicitation and modeling of goals in requirements engineering (Lamsweerde et al., 1998). Preferences and objectives of individual stakeholders, however, often differ considerably and the reconciliation of diverging interests and expectations is not considered adequately so far. Tools for documenting, modeling, and managing requirements implicitly assume that stakeholders are in consensus in the trade-offs of different alternatives and hence the individual objectives and preferences of stakeholders can be aggregated to a joint problem representation. In contrast, it is more reasonable to assume that, because of the valuable knowledge of the different stakeholders, the evaluation of trade-offs between decision attributes will differ considerably and should not simply be ignored (see also Chapter 4). Existing techniques for eliciting requirements do not provide support important negotiation concepts such as 'Best Alternative To Negotiated Agreement'[8] (BATNA), aspiration levels, or reservation levels. Such concepts, however, are crucial in order to determine efficient negotiation results (Fisher and Ury, 1999).

This would require tools that enable stakeholders (a) to elicit their individual preferences in a more systematic way (e.g., by defining utility functions), and (b) to assess subjective judgments of trade-offs between decision alternatives in the pre-negotiation phase as suggested in Chapter 4. While this information can be generated by each negotiator individually and kept privately, the EasyWinWin GSS should also support the process of stakeholder identification, agenda setting, and the definition of the set of issues to be negotiated for the whole team.

Integrative Negotiations and Efficiency Analysis of Results

As indicated above, stakeholders of software projects may face actual conflicts of interests and needs. Theoretically, such situations can be framed as mixed-motive negotiations, where parties experience partly common ground (joint goals and objectives of the project) but also face considerable differences in preferences for specific issues. To resolve these differences, an integrative negotiation approach (i.e., strategy) is most promising. Integrative negotiations involve
* problem solving behavior instead of competitive behavior,
* the discussion of holistic decision alternatives, reflecting trade-offs among issues, instead of single issues
* the development of new decision alternatives (enlarging the pie),
* the reframing of the negotiation problem,
* logrolling and concession making.

Unsupported negotiators tend to negotiate sequentially, one issue at a time, neglecting the integrative potential of 'package deals' (i.e., the formulation of complete decision alternatives). The main disadvantage of sequential issue negotiation, as also proposed in the EasyWinWin framework, is that tradeoffs among issues cannot be considered adequately. A user may for instance be prepared to abandon some features of a software for a higher speed and at the same time value-specific features of the software more than others. Or a user may feel strongly about user interface and indifferent to technology alternatives, while a developer is (in the design phase) indifferent to user interface, but has a strong opinion on the technical implementation issues. This situation helps to find win-win opportunities for both stakeholders. *Negotiation Support Systems* (NSSs) are capable of managing the complexity of multi-issue negotiation problems and are therefore superior to mere face-to-face negotiation settings (Rangaswamy and Shell, 1997). Furthermore, systems based on multicriteria decision methods consider economic deci-

---

[8]This is the baseline, the best alternative a stakeholder could obtain in case the current negotiation terminates without agreement (i.e., breakdown of negotiations). Any alternative that is higher than the BATNA is better than an impasse and no alternative should be accepted that is worse than the BATNA.

sion concepts such as efficient frontier and Pareto efficiency (Raiffa et al., 2002). Hence, it seems useful to extend EasyWinWin with a combination of economic theory and practical negotiation processes to support requirements negotiation.

The convergence of individual preferences to a joint group decision during the actual negotiation phase can again be facilitated through specific support features. On the individual level, the system should assist negotiators to assess and formulate negotiation packages (decision alternatives). The system could suggest for instance different decision alternatives, which have similar aggregated utility values. This enables negotiators to compare different alternatives easily and in turn can encourage concession making and logrolling while considering tradeoffs between decision attributes. Joint improvements can be achieved by considering interests of all stakeholders and seeking for alternatives 'enlarging the pie' instead of 'dividing the pie' (Kersten and Noronha, 1999). Graphical support for the negotiation helps the stakeholders to identify their actual positions and possible solutions. Examples are described in (Beroggi, 2000) and (Kersten and Noronha, 1999).

Process-Related Challenges

Effective negotiation support has to define a process, which enhances the cognitive and information processing capabilities of stakeholders. This represents a variety of challenges to the applied negotiation processes including the representation and handling of complexity, the precision of project language, the management of negotiation history and information, and the organization of distributed negotiations in order to involve all relevant stakeholders.

Complexity and Identification of Goal Hierarchies and Dependencies

Even in small to moderate projects, problem complexity can be hard to handle and reaching consensus becomes difficult and time consuming. The implementation of multicriteria decision analysis could assist stakeholders in software projects in omitting inefficient decision alternatives and moving collectively towards the efficient frontier.

Due to high complexity of decision attributes and interdependencies between decision attributes and between objectives, methods need to be developed to reduce and to manage complexity in software projects. For instance, the analytic hierarchy process (AHP), discussed in Chapter 4, and similar techniques could help to construct appropriate goal hierarchies and to preselect promising decision alternatives (Saaty, 1980; Maiden, 1998).

The EasyWinWin process and current implementations offer only basic facilities to handle the complexity of a number of stakeholders, preferences, and Win conditions, options, and issues. The evaluation of constraints as well as of hierarchical relationships between criteria, however, has to be resolved through heuristics and intuition. The development of algorithms and powerful heuristics to rank and converge different criteria to a manageable problem could further enhance requirement negotiations. For example, by defining goal hierarchies, stakeholder negotiations could be restrained to main goals and agreement on details could be delegated to experts.

Precision of the Project Language

In software engineering negotiations, semantic precision is typically insufficient. Users are, for instance, often impatient with detailed wordsmithing and leave developers with the job of converting informal negotiation results into more formal requirements. In turn, developers often use lingo not easy to understand by outsiders. Before all stakeholders can assess different options, they need to precisely understand the meaning of the terms used. Currently no or only simple approaches such as electronic shared glossaries are in place. The glossary implemented in EasyWinWin is, for example, useful to avoid misunderstandings. It is important, however, to develop practical means to further improve the semantic precision in software engineering negotiations by considering mechanisms such as semantic modeling. Additionally, a precise and clear definition of key terms constitutes a crucial prerequisite for knowledge management.

Negotiation History and Iterative Negotiations

Today's software development projects have to deal with a dynamically changing environment. Preferences and alternatives of stakeholders are constantly influenced by environmental changes such as new requirements, changing technologies, etc. Appropriate management of these changes requires that the stakeholders have traceability from their initial negotiation to the project requirements, designs, and final deliverables to support impact analysis. Therefore, an important challenge for negotiation processes and support tools is the appropriate management of negotiation histories and iterative refinement of negotiation in a project lifecycle (e.g., the impact of change requests at a certain project stage). Currently, there is only weak support for refining and tracing negotiation results in iterative life cycles (Medvidovic et al., 2003).

We therefore suggest extensions negotiation support to the post-negotiation phase and to develop ways that will allow the consistent evolution of negotiation results and the management of multiple related negotiations in a project or across projects. In this context, approaches for consistently evolving requirements and architectures are needed (Grünbacher et al., 2004b). Further support is needed to allow the effective/efficient generation of packages for optimal negotiation results, and development of models that enable effective/efficient elicitation of negotiation input information from the project context.

Distributed Negotiations

The current EasyWinWin solution is optimized for face-to-face meetings. Organizations might be, however, unable to involve all system stakeholders during critical negotiation and collaboration activities in distributed systems engineering processes. These economic constraints call for the development of tools for distributed requirements negotiations. In this case, possible negative effects of electronic communication have to be taken into account: Lack of immediate feedback, the absence of social cues, or discipline problems may complicate the negotiation process. It is therefore an important further research direction to enhance the EasyWinWin methodology with appropriate tools to support distributed negotiations. Initial steps are presented in (Grünbacher and Braunsberger, 2003).

7.5 Conclusions

In this chapter, we propose an integrated approach to software engineering negotiation support by considering ideas of existing software engineering support philosophies (Theory W), economic theory and concepts from conflict resolution, and negotiation research. We discussed the EasyWinWin approach for eliciting and reconciling stakeholder value propositions. EasyWinWin is a consensus-based approach and assumes that stakeholders are willing to jointly solve problems and gain agreements. In this chapter we challenged this assumption and contend that stakeholders' value propositions can often not be resolved by simply facilitating information exchange. Negotiation techniques to reconcile conflicting value propositions are therefore necessary to VBSE. After analyzing strengths and weaknesses of EasyWinWin we come to the conclusion that while the system supports large parts of stakeholder preference elicitation it lacks features to systematically evaluate, compare, and negotiate decision alternatives – all prerequisites for efficient negotiation outcomes. We believe that the suggested extensions to EasyWinWin would improve negotiations in software engineering substantially.

References

(Antón and Potts, 1998) Antón, A.I. and Potts, C.: The Use of Goals to Surface Requirements for Evolving Systems. In: International Conference on Software Engineering, Colorado Springs, Colorado, USA, 1998 (IEEE Computer Society, 1998), pp 157–166

(Bazerman and Carroll, 1987) Bazerman, M.H. and Carroll, J.S.: Negotiator Cognition. Research in Organizational Behavior 9, pp 247–288

(Beroggi, 2000) Beroggi, G.E.G.: An Experimental Investigation of Virtual Negotiations with Dynamic Plots. Group Decision and Negotiation 9, pp 415–429

(Boehm, 1988) Boehm, B. W.: A spiral model of software development and enhancement. IEEE Computer 21(5), pp 61–72

(Boehm, 1996) Boehm, B. W.: Anchoring the software process. IEEE Software 13(4), pp 73–82

(Boehm and Ross, 1989) Boehm, B. W. and Ross, R.: Theory-W Software Project Management: Principles and Examples. IEEE Transactions on Software Engineering 15(7), pp 902–916

(Boehm et al., 1998) Boehm, B. W., Egyed, A.F., Kwan, J., Port, D., Shah, A. and Madachy, R.: Using the WinWin Spiral Model: A Case Study. IEEE Computer (7), pp 33–44

(Boehm et al., 2001) Boehm, B. W., Grünbacher, P. and Briggs, R.O.: Developing Groupware for Requirements Negotiation: Lessons Learned. IEEE Software 18(3), pp 46–55

(Briggs et al., 2003) Briggs, R.O., de Vreede, G.J. and Nunamaker, J.F.: Collaboration Engineering with ThinkLets to Pursue Sustained Success with Group Support Systems. J. of Management Information Systems 19(4), pp 31–63

(Fisher and Ury, 1999) Fisher, R. and Ury, W.: Getting to YES (Random House, Sydney 1999)

(Fjermestad and Hiltz, 2001) Fjermestad, J. and Hiltz, R.: Group Support Systems: A Descriptive Evaluation of Case and Field Studies. Journal of Management Information Systems 17(3), pp 115–160

(Grünbacher and Braunsberger, 2003) Grünbacher, P. and Braunsberger, P.: Tool Support for Distributed Requirements Negotiation. In: Cooperative methods and tools for distributed software processes. ed by A. Cimititle, De Lucia, A. and Gall, H. (FrancoAngeli, Milano, Italy 2003): pp 56–66

(Grünbacher et al., 2004a) Grünbacher, P., Halling, M., Biffl, S., Kitapci, H. and Boehm, B. W.: Integrating Collaborative Processes and Quality Assurance Techniques: Experiences from Requirements Negotiation. Journal of Management Information Systems 20(4), pp 9–29

(Grünbacher et al., 2004b) Grünbacher, P., Medvicovic, N. and Egyed, A.F.: Reconciling Software Requirements and Architectures with Intermediate Models. Journal on Software and System Modeling 3(3), pp 235–253

(Grünbacher and Seyff, 2005) Grünbacher, P. and Seyff, N.: Requirements Negotiation. In: to appear: Engineering and Managing Software Requirements,. ed by A. Aurum and Wohlin, C. (Springer Verlag, 2005)

(Halling et al., 2003) Halling, M., Biffl, S. and Grünbacher, P.: An Economic Approach for Improving Requirements Negotiation Models with Inspection. Requirements Engineering Journal, Springer(8), pp 236–247

(Jarke et al., 1987) Jarke, M., Jelassi, M.T. and Shakun, M.F.: Mediator: Toward a Negotiation Support System. European Journal of Operational Research 31, pp 314–334

(Kersten, 2004) Kersten, G.: E-negotiation Systems: Interaction of People and Technologies to Resolve Conflicts. InterNeg Research Papers INR 08/04

(Kersten and Noronha, 1999) Kersten, G.E. and Noronha, S.J.: WWW-based Negotiation Support: Design, Implementation, and Use. Decision Support Systems 25(2), pp 135–154

(Kotonya and Sommerville, 1998) Kotonya, G. and Sommerville, I.: Requirements Engineering: Processes and Techniques (Wiley, 1998)

(Lamsweerde et al., 1998) Lamsweerde, A.v., Darimont, R. and Letier, E.: Managing Conflicts in Goal-Driven Requirements Engineering. IEEE Transactions on Software Engineering 24(11):1998

(Macaulay, 1993) Macaulay, L.: Requirements Capture as a Cooperative Activity. In: First Intl. Symp. On Requirements Engineering, San Diego, 1993 (IEEE Press, 1993), pp 174–181

(Maiden, 1998) Maiden, N. A. and Ncube, C.: Acquiring COTS Software Selection Requirements. IEEE Software Vol. 15, No. 2(2):1998

(Medvidovic et al., 2003) Medvidovic, N., Grünbacher, P., Egyed, A.F. and Boehm, B. W.: Bridging Models across the Software Lifecycle. Journal of Systems and Software 68(3), pp 199–215

(Nunamaker et al., 1997) Nunamaker, J.F., Briggs, R.O., Mittleman, D.D., Vogel, D.R. and Balthazard, P.A.: Lessons from a Dozen Years of Group Support Systems Research: A Discussion of Lab and Field Findings. Journal of Management Information Systems 13(3), pp 163–207

(Pruitt and Carnevale, 1993) Pruitt, D.G. and Carnevale, P.J.: Negotiation in Social Conflict (Open University Press, Buckingham 1993)

(Pruitt and Rubin, 1986) Pruitt, D.G. and Rubin, J.Z.: Social Conflict. Escalation, Stalemate, and Settlement (Random House, New York 1986)

(Raiffa et al., 2002) Raiffa, H., Richardson, J. and Metcalfe, D.: Negotiation Analysis, The Science and Art of Collaborative Decision Making (Belknap Harvard, 2002)

(Rangaswamy and Shell, 1997) Rangaswamy, A. and Shell, G.R.: Using Computers to Realize Joint Gains in Negotiations: Towards an "Electronic Bargaining Table". Management Science 8, pp 1147–1163

(Robertson and Robertson, 1999) Robertson, S. and Robertson, J.: Mastering the Requirements Process (Addison-Wesley, 1999)

(Saaty, 1980) Saaty, T.L.: The Analytic Hierarchy Process. (McGraw-Hill, New York 1980)

(StandishGroup, 2001) StandishGroup: Extreme CHAOS Report. The Standish Group, 196 Old Townhouse Road, West Yarmouth, MA 02673 – http://www.standishgroup.com, 2001

(Sutcliffe et al., 1998) Sutcliffe, A.G., Maiden, N.A.M., Minocha, S. and Manuel, D.: Supporting Scenario-Based Requirements Engineering. IEEE Transactions on Software Engineering 24(12), pp 1072–1088

(Tversky and Kahnemann, 1978) Tversky, A. and Kahnemann, D.: Judgment under Uncertainty: Heuristics and Biases. In: Uncertainty in Economics. ed by P. Diamond and Rothschild, M. (Academic Press, New York 1978), pp 17–34

(Vetschera, 1990) Vetschera, R.: Group Decision and Negotiation Support – A Methodological Survey. OR Sprektrum 12, pp 67–77

Author Biographies

Paul Grünbacher is an Associate Professor at Johannes Kepler University Linz and a research associate at the Center for Software Engineering (University of Southern California, Los Angeles). He received his MSc (1992) and PhD Degrees (1996) from the University of Linz. In 1999 Paul received the Erwin-Schrödinger research scholarship and worked as a visiting professor at University of Southern California in Los Angeles. In 2001 Paul received his Habilitation degree (Venia Docendi in Angewandte Informatik) for this work on software requirements negotiation. His research focuses on applying collaborative technologies to support and automate complex software and system engineering activities such as requirements negotiation or software inspections. He is a member of ACM, ACM SIGSOFT, IEEE, and the Austrian Computer Society.

Sabine Köszegi is an Assistant Professor at the School of Business, Economics, and Statistics at the University of Vienna. In 2000 she received her PhD in Economics and Social Sciences at the University of Vienna for her work on the trust building process in a virtual context. Sabine's current research focuses on processes of electronic negotiations. Since 1999 she is member of the InterNeg research team (http://www.interneg.org) where she is involved in the research on the humanistic, social and technical aspects of negotiations of people and people-software systems as well as the design and implementation of resources (learning objects) for negotiation teaching, training, and self-learning. The research team aims to develop and test systems capable of negotiation support, interpretation of interactions, and participation.

Stefan Biffl is an Associate Professor at the Technische Universität Wien. He studied Computer Science and Business Informatics and holds a PhD from the TU Wien in Computer Science. His research focuses on empirical software engineering applied for project and quality management in software engineering. Stefan Biffl was a visiting scientist at the Fraunhofer Institute for Experimental Software Engineering (IESE, Head Prof. Dr. Dieter Rombach) where he gained further experience with empirical software engineering, in particular with survey planning. Ongoing projects with the IESE are simulation of software product lines and the distributed ISERN inspection experiment. Stefan Biffl was the principal investigator of Erwin-Schrödinger J1948 (Software Inspection Techniques to Support Project and Quality Management) project supported by the Austrian Science Fund. He is a member of ACM, ACM SIGSOFT, IEEE, the Austrian Computer Society, and the IFIP Technical Committee on Software Engineering.

8 Measurement and Decision Making

Michael Berry and Aybüke Aurum

Abstract: Value-Based Software Engineering requires the capability to measure and analyze value in order to make informed decisions. The difficulty experienced by many organizations in measuring concepts that are even simpler than value suggests that this requirement will be hard to meet. The goal of this chapter is to build an understanding of measurement and decision making and the relationship between them. A multi-view model of measurement is presented as a way to cope with the complexity of measuring concepts such as value. A behavioral decision making model is presented that identifies the points at which measurement products impact the decision making behavior of a manager or software engineer. This model attempts to satisfactorily account for the idiosyncrasies of human behavior, while preserving some elements of the rational model of decision making. The chapter concludes with an application of these models to a case study in which achieving value is a key goal.

Keywords: Decision making, decision support system, image theory, measurement and analysis.

8.1 Introduction

This chapter is intended to be of interest to people involved in software engineering, from programmer to project manager, needing an introduction to measurement and decision making. As the reader progresses through the chapters of this book, we suggest that he examines the nature of the decisions made in a VBSE framework and thinks about the role of measurement in those decisions. Whether the chapter is describing VBSE best practice or detailing useful techniques, consider the measures that will need to be collected and analyzed in order to carry out the practice or be used in the technique. From our perspective, if you can not measure value, you can not manage it.

Value-Based Software Engineering (VBSE) is a framework for improving the systems delivered to the clients by incorporating value considerations into the technical and managerial decisions that are made during system development and maintenance. The term, "incorporating value considerations," is managerial jargon for measuring (or estimating) value-related attributes and producing information from those measures that can aid decision makers. Adopting VBSE will present challenges for both software engineers and software measurement specialists. It is simpler to measure and make decisions in a client-value neutral setting, especially when technical and project issues fully consume management attention. It is simpler to assume that the specifications of functional and nonfunctional system requirements constitute all the client's expectations. Unfortunately this simplicity is gained at the client's expense in that the delivered systems cannot provide the best possible outcome to the stakeholders. Of course, the best system developers are never client-value neutral; but such developers are in short supply and we must turn to frameworks that enable ordinary people to achieve equivalent outcomes. VBSE provides such a framework by informing software engineering decisions with considerations of value.

In this chapter, we will focus on decision making and measurement within a VBSE framework. Because informed decision making is based on information, we will discuss the relationship between decision making and software measurement and analysis. We will use two models for the discussion that cope well with the intangible, multi-attributed nature of *value*. The decision making model provides a non-deterministic, behavioral model for the way managers make decisions with the help of indicators of *value*, quality, satisfaction, motivation, productivity, and effectiveness. The common element in these models is the metaphor of mental images as ill-defined, ephemeral, and highly personal constructs. The goal of measurement and analysis is to create these images in the mind of the decision maker; the goal of the decision maker is to process these images in order to arrive at an optimal course of action. These models are not specifically concerned with the measurement of *value* and decision making based on *value*. However, throughout this chapter, issues relating to *value* will be addressed.

In the next Section (8.2) these models are discussed in detail. Because software engineering typically occurs in an organizational context and the discussion to this point has been concerned with individual decision makers, the following Section (8.3) discusses the applicability of the model to group decision making. Section 8.4 presents a descriptive model of the process by which a person is stimulated to make a decision as a result of receiving a set of indicators derived through measurement and analysis. Section 8.5 explores the relationship between measurement and decision making. The concepts are brought together in Section 8.6 by a practical example of a decision making support system with associated measurement and analysis.

8.2 Models of Measurement and Decision Making

Software engineers often build systems that address the information needs of people in other business units but they pay less attention to their own information needs. A framework for software measurement and analysis has the characteristics of an information system, the goal of which is to deliver information products that satisfy the information needs of a software engineer. Information needs arise from the managerial and engineering tasks that people routinely carry out in order to deliver and maintain software-based systems. Decision making within a VBSE framework requires the inclusion of indicators of *value* in the information products on which software decisions are made. In the jargon of measurement specialists, *Value* is a measurable concept, that is: something that is not tangible but can still be measured using an appropriate scale. Some measurable concepts are simple: for example, productivity is a concept that is measured by evaluating the amount of product for a given amount of resource using a well-defined algorithm. Other measurable concepts such as value, quality, and risk are multi-attributed and the algorithms for combining the attributes are rarely well defined. The ISO/IEC standard 15939: *Software Measurement Process* (ISO/IEC 15939, 2002) provides definitions for some of the terms used above:

3.10 *indicator:* a measure that provides an estimate or evaluation of specified attributes derived from a model with respect to defined information needs

3.11 *indicator value:* numerical or categorical result assigned to an indicator

3.12 *information need:* insight necessary to manage objectives, goals, risks, and problems

3.13 *information product:* one or more indicators and their associated interpretations that address an information need (for example, a comparison of a measured defect rate to planned defect rate along with an assessment of whether or not the difference indicates a problem)

3.16 *measurable concept:* abstract relationship between attributes of entities and information needs

The difficulty for measurement and analysis is that *value* cannot be directly measured in the way that mass, volume, and time can be measured. This is partly because it is a multi-attributed, but more importantly because it is context dependent and because each person has his own concept of value for a particular context. Measuring *value* is clearly, therefore, about changing its nature from a personal construct to a group construct (often called a stakeholder value proposition) through a process of elicitation, discussion, and consensus. Once that is done, base measures can be collected using agreed upon methods and scales and combined with other base measures according to an agreed upon algorithm to produce derived measures that, by agreement, act as indicators of *value*.

In Figure 29 we illustrate the relationship between measurement and decision making with a conceptual model. To make it less abstract, imagine that a software process engineer (the *brain* in Figure 29) is interested in improving the *Project Monitoring and Control Process* (PMCP).[9] The principal object of interest is PCMP and other objects of interest might be Project Planning and Requirements Management. The *Measurement and Analysis process* (M&A, shown as a pair of scales) has two main activities: evaluating the objects of interest and evaluating (a) the improvement actions stemming from a decision and (b) the outcome of those improvements. Decision making is shown as a single process that consists of three activities: stimulating a decision, making a choice from a set of alternatives, and monitoring and controlling the choice.

---

[9]The terms used are taken from the Capability Maturity Model® Integration (CMMI[SM]), Version 1.1 Copyright 2002 by Carnegie Mellon University.

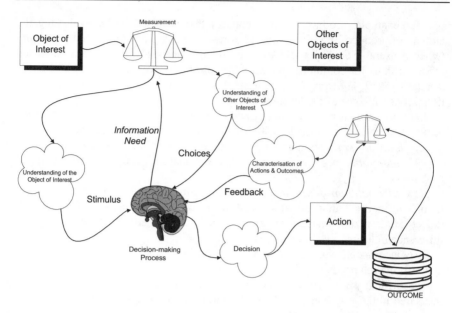

Fig. 29. Overview of measurement and decision making

In our example, stimulating the decision to improve PMCP might be measures showing the number of projects being delivered late because of failure to update the size of work products following revisions to requirements. The process engineer obtains additional information from M&A in order to understand his choices. A decision is made to revise PMCP and the appropriate actions are carried out (e.g., making more time available for PMCP, changing the process definition, revising interfaces with other processes). The revisions have outcomes for the objects of interest that are measured by M&A, providing the process engineer with feedback that may stimulate further changes.

A Model of Measurement

The process of characterizing an *object of interest* with respect to a *chosen model* consists of collecting and analyzing measures to understand the object at the *chosen level of abstraction* (Fenton and Pfleeger, 1997). The *object of interest* is whatever you are interested in measuring. Common objects of interest in software engineering are systems, projects, processes, and work products (e.g., software, specifications, designs). The term *chosen model* highlights that it is a matter of choice which properties of the *object of interest* will be evaluated and how those properties will be evaluated. Characterization occurs when values are assigned to the properties of the *object of interest* through an act of measurement that maps empirical observations of each significant property onto the *chosen model*. The term *chosen level of abstraction* is used to emphasize that people select the appropriate level of understanding of the *object of interest* based on their need for information, their background knowledge, and their degree of interest in the object. That is, the user of the model must determine a level of detail that suits his purposes.

In VBSE, the chosen model is referred to as the *stakeholder value proposition* and it is the guiding principle for decision makers who want to ensure that their chosen courses of action are aligned with generating value for the stakeholders. Chapter 3 of this book presents processes drawn from financial management that can assist with the definition and instantiation of a model of project based on stakeholder value propositions. Chapter 4 offers methods for evaluating stakeholder value propositions in situations where there are multiple stakeholders or many possible outcomes. Chapter 12 provides an industrial case study in which a decision support system assists the choice of the most promising software product release plans by integrating the various stakeholder value propositions. The chosen model of value is derived through a process of consultation and negotiation; Chapter 7 presents a method for negotiating the value model in the context of the software requirements process.

The evaluation of measurable concepts such as *value, project risk,* and *product quality* requires multiple views into the object of interest. These views are then synthesized into an overall characterization of the object of interest. For example, software quality is a familiar concept for which there are many views that need to be considered. A software quality model might state, for example, that:

Quality is a function of:
quality in use, process quality, product quality,
benefits obtained, resources consumed, context of use

If the object of interest is defined as *project value*, then the *chosen model* would show how value is a function of a particular subset of the project's attributes. This model might be expressed, for example, as:

Project value is a function of:
acceptance of technology $* w_1$, *exploitation of technology* $* w_2$,
cost of technology $* w_3$, *benefit of technology* $* w_4$,
strategic impact of technology $* w_5$

The terms w_1-w_5 express the weights that are to be applied to each attribute to derive a number for the indicator of *project value* based on their relative impact. There are many models of project value that could be chosen since there are many individual stakeholder value propositions. In this example, the chosen model of project value states that there are five important factors that collectively produce a particular value for the project:

1. Probability of users accepting the technology provided by the object of interest.
2. Probability of users being able to use the technology.
3. Cost of constructing and deploying the technology in the organization
4. Economic benefits for the organization from using the technology.
5. Impact the technology will have on the way the organization does business in the future.

Each of these factors must therefore be measured (or estimated) using an appropriate scale, and these measures then used to derive an understanding of the project's value based on the relative impact of each factor and the nature of the cause/effect relationship between the factor and value. Having developed the chosen model, it needs to be instantiated by assigning values to the factors in the model. The measurement and analysis process (ISO/IEC 15939, 2002) begins with a measurement plan that states how these values are obtained. Planning includes specifying the measurement models that enable empirical observations of each factor in the chosen model to be mapped onto a framework that enables characterization of the object of interest. There are standards that specify the measurement model for certain attributes (e.g., time, cost, functional size); but for many other attributes (e.g., technology acceptance, strategic impact), the measurement models must also be defined through a process of research and negotiation with stakeholders.

The analysis of project value requires multiple views that are painted using multiple measurement models. Each measurement model is like a lens where each *lens* is used by an observer in order to make inferences about the properties of an object of interest. These inferencing rules enable the observer to develop a sufficient, although incomplete, view of the object of interest based on incomplete information. Observers may construct the rules through personal experience or they may use rules that are formalized in standards. A key property of each *lens* is the ability to filter the properties of the object of interest that are believed to be irrelevant. This enables people to avoid being overwhelmed by the volume of data being presented. This filtering is defined in the *chosen model* for measurement which controls the filter. Each *lens* constructs a *view* of the object of interest by capturing and interpreting some properties of the object. The *chosen model* and the *chosen level of abstraction* determine which views are constructed, which properties, how the properties are evaluated, and how the property values are interpreted.

Views provide the ability to structure measurable concepts such as value, quality, and risk and help people to focus on different aspects of the object of interest at a time. They provide a way to summarize the impact of a large number of factors and to highlight areas for improvement. Some models will include a social view of the object of interest. The social view is created by the decision maker examining each of the other views for its ethical, legal, and political implications. These implications are then mapped onto the ethical, legal, and political norms for one or more social groups. Differences between the social view and the norms present opportunities for improving the object of interest.

A Model of Decision Making

Having introduced a model of measurement in the preceding section that was concerned with developing views, we continue with the visual metaphor and describe a behavioral model of decision making based on Image Theory. Two types of decision making models may be distinguished: A) prescriptive models which assert that, on balance over a period of time, if one follows the procedure then the decision outcomes are more likely to be successful, B) behavioral models which seek only to describe the behavior without specifying any particularly desirable pattern of behavior. Our behavioral model is based on Image Theory (Beach and Mitchell, 1990; Beach, 1990; Beach, 1996) developed by the psychologists Beach and Mitchell in response to a pattern of criticism of rational decision making beginning with Allais in 1953 (Edwards, 1967). In his Nobel Memorial Lecture in 1979 (Simon, 1979), Simon concludes that assumptions of rational decision making "are contrary to fact" and offers *Bounded Rationality* as a "superior alternative." Beach and Mitchell state that Image Theory is a broad theory accommodating elements of classical theory such as self-interest while integrating other attempts to develop an adequate theory of decision making. As such it is just one of many empirically based theories within the genre of *Bounded Rationality*.

The Image Theory model is based on the notion that a person simultaneously holds multiple discrete mental images of various abstract and concrete objects. These images are the means by which that person understands and responds to the world around him. The words, *mental image,* convey the idea that the image is a unique model of the object constructed by the decision maker for his own cognitive purposes. As a mental model, it is inaccessible to other people; however, to a limited extent, others may influence the development of the images. For example, the role of a specialist in software measurement is to assist the managers and software engineers to develop clear, well-formed, and valid images of the objects of interest typically found in software engineering. In a VBSE framework, the scope of the objects of interest is enlarged to include objects of interest from the client's domain. In the Beach and Mitchell model (Beach and Mitchell, 1990), there are three basic images based on: (1) The decision maker's values, ethics, beliefs, etc., (2) A projection into some desirable future, and (3) Plans made by the decision maker. In the model used here, these three images are expanded for completeness to include: (4) An image of what happened in the past, (5) An image of the current situation, and (6) a probable future that is distinct from the desirable future.

Table 11. Components in the Image Model of decision making

View of the World	Image Component
How things are.	Reality
How things are expected to be.	Expectation
How things were.	Experience
How things will be unless someone acts.	Probable Future
How things could be if something is done to change the situation.	Desirable Future
How things should be.	Beliefs and Values

The model proposes that a decision maker's view of the world is the result of six interacting and complementary images, each of which is unique to that individual. Table 11 shows the components of the model, and the particular view of the world that the component supports. The component images are discussed in more detail below.

- *Reality* is the image that the decision maker has of his present situation. *Reality* is constantly changing as new data is acquired, items of data are re-weighted in importance, and previously acquired data is found to be invalid.
- *Expectation* is an image of the future that sets bounds on the projections of the likely and desirable futures. This image is a function of the current reality, experience, and the values and beliefs and the personality of the decision maker.
- *Experience* is the decision maker's perception of how things were. It is a blend of data, selective memory, and wishful thinking. However, it strongly influences the formation of the other images.
- *Probable Future* is the image of the outcome if the current situation persists and the current plan is adhered to. This is the most volatile image as reality continually forces changes to the probable future and changes are made to the plans underlying the image.
- *Desirable Future* is the image of the preferred outcome and is an expression of the goals of the person. Note that in a team or organizational setting, it is expected that the personal goals and values of the decision maker and the goals and culture of the enterprise and stakeholders will be congruent, but that may not always be true.
- *Beliefs and Values* provide the framework within which the other images are constructed and constantly acts as a standard against which the other images are evaluated.

The challenge in Value-Based Software Engineering is to ensure that the concept of value is a dominant factor in the construction of these images. Indicators of value must be provided to the decision maker to construct *reality*. Project objectives need to be measurable in terms of value to build expectations. Post-implementation reviews need to be held to provide evidence of the value generated in order to develop *experience*. Simulators that produce projections of probable and desirable futures should include value as a dependent variable. And, finally, organizations need to inculcate the notion of delivering value as a primary *belief and value* for software engineers.

8.3 Decision Making Behavior

In this section, using the Image model, we describe the process by which a person is stimulated to make a decision as a result of receiving a set of indicators derived through measurement and analysis that characterize a particular object of interest. Figure 30 shows the decision maker combining his understanding of the object of interest with other cues and sensations to develop his perception of *reality*. This perception is influenced by the person's beliefs and values, his expectations and his experience. The image of *reality* is then extrapolated to create an image of a *probable future*. This forms the stimulus for the decision making process shown in

Figure 31 where the decision making process is highlighted to illustrate how the person's decision making process arrives at a response to the original decision stimulus.

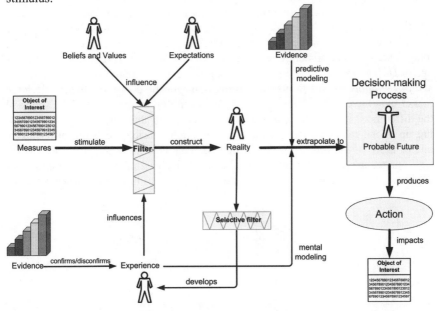

Fig. 30. Stimulating a decision

In Figure 30 the starting point is the Decision stimulus, which stems from measurement of an object of interest being filtered by the recipient. After filtering, the measures are combined to create an image of the current reality. Drawing on his experience, and often aided by predictive models, the person creates his image of what the future situation will be. Predictive models draw on evidence, rules, and policy to estimate the values of dependent variables given the state of the independent variables. This image of the future is then considered through a decision making process, the outcome of which is likely to be a *Decision response* (see Figure 3). The filtering of information about the object of interest is referred to as *decision framing* and is an essential element of decision making. Framing, according to Beach and Mitchell, is an attempt to endow a particular situation with meaning. The decision maker identifies which elements of an image are relevant in the situation and attempts to place the situation in a historical context. This, then, involves selecting aspects of the situation that are perceived to be relevant with respect to *Expectation* and *Beliefs and Values*; and with searching *Experience* to find previous goals and previous plans. If the decision framing is inappropriate, then the consequences will be an impaired control process, since the resulting *Reality* will be flawed. Note that an additional filter is involved in the development of experience: people selectively incorporate elements of their reality into their experience image. This suggests that the filtering and the mental modeling of the future based on their experience may be unreliable.

Models of decision making based on Image Theory state that a decision must be made when there is a significant dissonance between the multiple images of the decision maker. The decision maker is stimulated to act to remove the tension created by that dissonance. In effect, decision makers are continuously deciding whether they need to make a decision. Their decision may be to simply revise one of their images. And/or they decide to choose a course of action that will bring the images back into alignment over time. To do this, they must first form a new image of *Desirable Future* and the difference between this image and the current image of *Probable Future* forms the starting point for the decision. Often, a decision maker may have only a vague image of his desirable future and it is the shock of the difference between the reality and his expectations that triggers the strengthening up of the image of the desirable future. Each possible decision must change one or more of the images to be considered. This is an iterative process in which new images are tested against each other and which terminates when a course of action is chosen that delivers a satisfactory alignment of the various images.

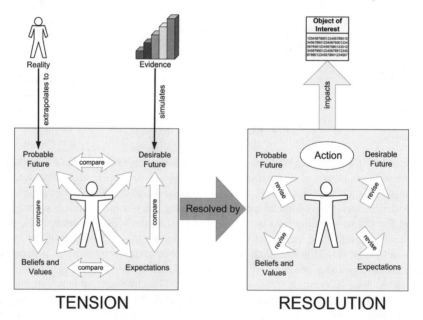

Fig. 31. Decision making process

Once a decision is made, the decision maker will need to monitor and control the chosen course of action. In contrast to other models of decision making, this model includes monitoring and control as part of the decision making process because of the need to analyze feedback and make adjustments to the chosen course of action. The decision maker must constantly monitor the difference between the previously defined *Desirable Future* and *Probable Future*. When the initial decision is made, the difference would be accounted for by the lead time to implement the plans. However, over time, additional information is received and, when viewed through experience, a new image of *Probable Future* is created. This then stimulates a new round of decision making in which the initial aim is to realign the desirable and probable futures through adjustments to the chosen course of action, but which may also lead to a revision of the desirable future.

To give an example of a decision that might need to be made, assume a software development project is being managed in a VBSE framework according to the following model:

Project value is a function of:

acceptance of technology, exploitation of technology, cost of technology, benefit of technology, strategic impact of technology.

The software process group (SPG) advises the project manager that there is an opportunity to improve the processes for building the technology being developed for the client. The SPG asks him to participate in a pilot study that will involve process appraisals, new process definitions, and developer training. The SPG presents some data collected by the Software Engineering Institute (SEI) of the benefits that could be achieved.[10] The opportunity to reduce the cost of technology to the client stimulates the project manager to consider this advice and decide if he wants to act on it. He first filters the advice based on their previous experience of process improvement, his beliefs about the SPG and the SEI, his values with respect to being involved in advanced technology, and his expectations with respect to what is possible on their particular project. From integrating all these factors, the project manager has a revised sense of the reality facing him. He has to extrapolate from this state to a set of desirable futures that will depend on whether which, if any, of the management, infrastructure, and engineering processes are improved. To do this, the project manager will use his own mental models based on their experience and explicit models that enable them to simulate various scenarios. This is where the model of project value is used. As long as the model includes views of the stakeholder value propositions, the manager can consider the impact of the recommendation of the SPG. It is even better if these views are framed in measurable terms so that each scenario is evaluated. The project manager is now in a state of tension: he has evaluated desirable scenarios that are contrasted with the image of the future that probably faces him if he does nothing. He has his beliefs and values and his expectations which contrast with the other images and he must make a choice. His skill lies in being able to choose the action that will have the best outcome in terms of the model of project value. In all but the most trivial decisions there will be multiple factors impacting the outcome, delivering many possible futures of varying degrees of desirability. Alternative courses of action can often not be compared in an entirely objective way. Refer to Chapter 4 for an example of how the project manager may choose a course of action.

Using the *Image* model, we have discussed the behavior of decision makers. The model is also consistent with the reality that many decisions must be made

---

[10]http://seir.sei.cmu.edu/seir/

collaboratively with two or more decision makers. This is discussed in the following section.

8.4 Decision Making Behavior in Groups

A group decision is expected to be an optimum course of action that is determined through collaborative activities involving idea generation, information exchange, argument and decision making. It may be argued that there is no such thing as a group decision: instead there are a set of individual decisions to accept a course of action that is arrived at through a group process. However, it is clear that when an individual participates in a group decision, he may behave differently as a group member than he would if they were acting as an individual. For example, groups have been consistently found to induce attitude polarization (Isenberg, 1986). Of particular interest are the studies that demonstrate that group decisions tend to be riskier than individual decisions. Furthermore, there is evidence that computer mediated groups will make riskier decisions than individual members (Valacich et al., 2002). Two coexisting and concurrent mechanisms are believed to be active in group decision making that result in attitude polarization (Isenberg, 1986): social comparison processes and persuasive argument.

Social comparison suggests that people are strongly motivated to perceive and to present themselves to others in the group in a "socially desirable light." When an individual detects a socially desirable group norm, he will attempt to exceed the group norm. When everyone in the group is behaving in a similar fashion, the group norm is pushed to levels higher than its members would have maintained individually. In terms of the Image behavioral model, the individual enters the group setting with his beliefs and values, his expectations, his desirable future, and his probable future. In the group setting there is a new tension in that one element of values and beliefs; that the individuals see themselves, and want to be seen by others, in a socially desirable light, is now important. The beliefs and values must change so that the individual does not care about what the group thinks (unlikely!), or the desirable future must change. Democratic civilizations acknowledge that while many core values will be held in common, voting and referenda will be necessary to resolve decisions when beliefs and values differ. Military and commercial organizations tend not to be democratic in their operation but both recognize the power of shared values and beliefs and attempt to foster them in order to make clear the socially approved direction that group decisions should follow. The other explanatory mechanism, persuasive arguments theory, suggests that the "perceived validity and perceived novelty of an argument determine how influential that particular argument will be in causing a choice shift" (Isenberg, 1986). In terms of the Image behavioral model, the individual must revise his images of his expectations, the probable future, and the desirable future based on the argument presented.

Group decisions are easier where individual members share images based on shared information. Organizations spend much effort on attempting to develop shared situational awareness, expectations, and visions of the future through shared information systems and knowledge bases. As hierarchies are the dominant structure for organizations, most group decision making is conducted in a context where the group of individuals each with specific knowledge advises a single person who has the power to authorize the chosen course of action. In this context, information exchange is seen to be the key element of group decision making (Dennis, 1996; Winquist, 1998). In terms of the Image behavioral model, a tension is created when the decision makers revise their images of their expectations, the probable future and the desirable future based on the information presented. This tension is resolved by the recommendation of a course of action. Unfortunately, information exchange in group decision making is often incomplete leading to suboptimal decisions (Dennis, 1996; Winquist, 1998). This is another example of irrational behavior in decision making and serves to emphasize the utility of behavioral decision making models.

Negotiation is a form of group decision making in which an optimal course of action is required that will benefit a number of stakeholders whose interests are often in conflict. They may have quite different values and beliefs and have conflicting images of a desirable future. Information hiding may be more frequent than information exchange and the socially desirable norm of the subgroups may be to win at the expense of other subgroups. A critical negotiation is the development of the stakeholder value propositions that will guide future decision makers. In this case the participants in the group decision making process are choosing the value model to be used during the project. For a discussion of how to facilitate the active participation of stakeholders in negotiations refer to Chapter 7.

8.5 Measurement and Analysis for Decision Making

In this section we make recommendations to improve the relationship between software measurement and decision making. The section is particularly aimed at assisting those people who specialize in software measurement to become more aware of how their information products impinge on their clients' decision making processes.

Strive to Build Images

The goal of the measurement specialist is to deliver measures to decision makers that stimulate clear images in the mind of the decision maker. The Image model of decision making provides an insight into optimizing the impact of measurement products. Visual representations are often the most powerful way of communicating a message. Modes of presentation that are effective in image-building range from presentations employing graphics (in preference to numbers or words), to simulations and role-playing. Edward Tufte's book (Tufte, 1983) is recommended for readers who may want to follow this topic further. Assimilation of the message is also easier if it fits into a familiar framework that has meaning for the person receiving the message. For example, in a society where most adults drive a car, the dashboard is a familiar concept for assembling the key performance indicators for controlling the vehicle. Transferring the dashboard model into corporate management within a car driving culture required little new learning for managers.

Match Information to the Level of Decision Making

To identify information needs, it is useful to distinguish between three classes of decisions, i.e., operational, tactical, and strategic. There is a diminishing degree of structure between operational and tactical decision making and between tactical and strategic decision making. A high degree of structure means that the nature of the decision and its information needs are predictable. A low degree of structure means that it is difficult to predict what decisions will need to be made. The implications of this with regard to measures, benchmarks, and performance indicators are that they must be appropriate for the class of decisions that must be made. Furthermore the clarity of the images declines as the decisions to be made change from operational to strategic and the information to support the decision changes from quantitative to qualitative. As the image of *reality* becomes more obscure and the futures become confused, the decision maker may compensate by relying more on *Beliefs and Values* when confronted with the need to choose a course of action, thus introducing greater subjectivity.

Match Information to Goals

It is necessary to provide the appropriate information for the decision makers' goals. In terms of the decision making model presented above, the decision maker's *desirable future* is the starting point for identifying the information needs. Unless this is done, any mismatches between *reality*, *probable future,* and *desirable future* are unlikely to be apparent. Software process assessment is measurement where the measurable concept is process capability. The popularity of process assessment based on the Software Capability Maturity Model may be explained by its ability to provide a simple summative evaluation on an ordinal scale of 1 to 5 that meets the goals. For a software acquirer it provides a clear image of what the capability of the organization is likely to be and thereby provides a means for reducing acquisition risk. For the IT manager, it provides a clear and easily communicated goal – if the organisation is now rated as a *Two*, it needs to become a *Three* on the Maturity scale.

Use Performance Indicators

A performance indicator is a measure of some relevant aspect of past performance where there is an implicit or explicit model of performance which holds that one value for the indicator is to be preferred over another value. Each performance indicator provides insight into one aspect of performance and together they contribute to the image of performance. Indicators are selected for their relevance and contribution to the image and also for their ability to help predict some future outcome. By itself, an indicator merely draws attention to a particular aspect of performance. However, that particular aspect of performance is chosen because it is believed to be associated with the outcome. The concept of Key Performance Indicators (KPIs) provides a structure for a set of indicators. The Balanced Score Card (Kaplan and Norton, 1993; Kaplan and Norton, 1992) encourages the selection of performance indicators from frames of reference covering financial aspects, customer satisfaction, process effectiveness, and innovation and learning in order to produce a more holistic view for the decision maker at various levels of the organization. There have been a number of publications dealing with adopting the Balanced Scorecard within information technology (Becker, 1999; Edberg, 1997; van Grembergen and Saull, 2001).

Performance indicators are often used to set benchmarks which are points of reference with respect to an attribute of an object of interest. For an IT manager, the choice of benchmark depends on its validity for the purpose to which it is to be applied and the quality of the data used to calculate the benchmark. Using the wrong benchmark may lead to inappropriate comparisons being made and invalid choices being made. The data set of IT measures from which the benchmarks are calculated may be internal or external with respect to an enterprise.

Improve Information Quality

Information of higher quality produces better images in terms of relevance, completeness, persistence, clarity, and contrast. The better the images, the better should be the quality of the decision. Characteristics of information used by researchers to assess information quality have included content, availability, accuracy, timeliness, reliability, completeness, appearance, conciseness, convenience, and relevance (Garrity and Sanders, 1998). However, objective assessment of information quality is problematic as the most important outcome of information quality is its impact on the individual. If the information fails to affect the individuals in an organization, then there can be few beneficial outcomes for the organization. This underlines the importance of selecting and providing measures that are found to have the most individual impact. The image theory model provides an explanation for how individual impact may be achieved. The ability to relate two or more measures to each other (e.g., number of defects compared to size of product) provides a richer view of the object of interest and can increase the impact on the decision maker. However, a balance needs to be struck – attempts to instrument every software process and to characterize every product have been failures, generating large numbers of measures, overloading the decision maker, and imposing excessive costs of data collection and analysis (Hall and Fenton, 1994).

8.6 Decision Support in a VBSE Framework

In this section we outline the components of a decision support system (DSS) that operates in a value-based framework. At this stage in the development of VBSE there is insufficient evidence to allow us to make firm recommendations on how to establish decision support in a VBSE framework. However, it is possible to take a case study and use it as the basis for an example of what the DSS might be like. The goal is to demonstrate the practical feasibility of the VBSE approach. We discuss the requirements for the DSS and suggest a measurement plan and associated algorithms that will provide the information for the DSS. The DSS and measurement plan are based on a case study published in IEEE Computer (Boehm and Huang, 2003).

> *Summary of the Case.* A manufacturer of mountain bikes has a failing order-processing system. The symptoms are (a) delivery delays and mistakes, and (b) poor synchronization between order entry, confirmation and order fulfillment. A new order-processing system is to be developed and integrated with the company's financial, production and human-resource information systems. The new system is to be developed in partnership with an external systems developer. The partnership is structured so that both parties share in the responsibilities and rewards flowing from the new system. This provides a powerful motivation for the systems developer to practice value-based software engineering in order to understand, and satisfy, their partner's value propositions. In addition to the partnership, the company's leading distributors are participating in definition and testing of the new system.

To operate in a VBSE framework, the project team requires a decision support system (DSS) that will help them to incorporate a value perspective with other more traditional perspectives such as product quality, process efficiency and project risk. The DSS will assist understanding of the project, the work products, the processes and the value that are produced. The required information for the value perspective will consist of indicators of the extent to which the client's and the developer's goals are being met. The design of the DSS must provide significant dissonance between the multiple images of the decision maker so that decisions are stimulated and informed. The challenge is to ensure that the developer's images are sufficiently coloured by the client's values. This will be achieved by choosing a model of value that incorporates both the developer's and the client's value models. This model will then be used to construct the images through indicators that characterise the system under development.

Requirements for the DSS

Key issues for the DSS: These must be satisfactorily addressed in the design of DSS as follows:

- Decisions made by developers must not be client-value neutral,
- Hundreds of tasks may progress concurrently during development,
- The client and the developer will have some conflicting goals and will therefore have some conflicting value propositions.

Goals to be incorporated: These goals of the developer's principal stakeholder for the case study must be incorporated into the project DSS in order to promote value-based software engineering management:
- Sense, evaluate, and adapt to changing value propositions in a competitive market-place,
- Avoid wasteful misuse of the organization's scarce resources.

These goals that developers traditionally have used to drive their decision making must also be incorporated:
- Deliver a software product that assists the client to achieve their goals,
- Avoid wasteful misuse of the developer's scarce resources,
- Be available to provide a service to other clients,
- Improve the capability of their software processes in order to increase efficiency and software product quality.

Scope of the DSS: The range of software development activities that need to be supported by the project's DSS are requirements engineering, architecting, design and development, verification and validation, planning and control, risk management, quality management, and people management.
Requirements for a value-based approach: This highlights the expectations for a DSS that is designed for the needs of VBSE.
- Be sensitive to return on investment factors
- Monitor the cost, schedule and progress of a complex project
- Focus on the real stakeholder value being earned
- Elicit and reconcile value propositions from stakeholders
- Reconcile value propositions with architectural solutions
- Propagate value propositions into design and development.

Chosen model of Value: Table 12 shows the model of value that will be adopted for this project and incorporated into the DSS. Once the value model is adopted, it means that every significant decision within the scope of the DSS needs to be considered with reference to the value model. The attributes of value in the model are identified from the value propositions of the client, the other stakeholders and the goals of the system developer.

Table 12. The model of value

Proposition of	Objects of Interest	Attributes
Manufacturer (Client)	Order processing, order delivery, sales	Current time and effort to process order, current delivery time, sales for the current period
Sales Staff (User)	Salesperson credits for commission	Sales credits for the current period
Distributors (User)	Order fulfillment	Filled and unfilled orders
System developer	Client service, project, processes, work products	Client satisfaction, software production, resource use, work backlog, process improvements

Required images: Multiple images based on indicators of value need to be generated in order to stimulate and inform the decision making process.

1. How things are (*reality*): For each of the attributes in the Value model, measures need to be provided of the current state.
2. How things are expected to be (*expectation*): For each of the attributes in the Value model, targets need to be established for the client's new system and for the developer's business.
3. How things were (*experience*): Where possible, it is important for the decision maker to have a sense of the historical state of each of the attributes in the Value model.
4. How things will be unless someone acts to change the situation (*probable future*): Predictions are required for each of the attributes in the Value model. The prediction is based on extrapolating the current state into the future by using the current knowledge: that is, the value propositions, the project plan, the budget, the system architecture, the requirements and the design. Predictions are qualified by expressions of confidence that will depend on such factors as the distance into the future for which the prediction is required, the variability of the development process and the quality of current knowledge.
5. How things could be if something is done to change the situation (*desirable future*): This image of future value is constructed through simulation. The most rational future image is the result of systematically varying the independent variables that determine the values of the attributes in the chosen Value model. For example, the value propositions, the project plan, the budget, the system architecture, the requirements and the design may be changed and the impact on the Value model attributes evaluated and optimized.
6. How things should be (*beliefs and values*): This image is the most subjective, being constructed by and for each individual involved in the acquisition, development and operation of the system. This image might be constructed from the following attributes:
   - *Client organisation values and beliefs*: Customer satisfaction, corporate reputation, personal reputation, environmental impact, community perceptions, stakeholder recognition.

- *User values and beliefs:* Satisfaction, staff remuneration, staff development.
- *System developer's values and beliefs:* Client satisfaction, staff satisfaction, staff remuneration, staff development, progress, challenge, technology, peer recognition.

Measurement Plan

The measurement plan describes how the information required for the DSS is constructed through the process of measurement and analysis. For each component in each model, how that component will be measured or estimated must be specified. In software measurement (ISO/IEC 15939, 2002), we distinguish between base measures, derived measures and indicators. For a base measure, for example, functional size, we need to specify only the method and scale. For a derived measure, for example, productivity, we must also specify the algorithm that is used to combine two or more measures. For an indicator, for example, earned value, we also need to state the model that attaches significance to the value of the indicator.

In Table 13 we have suggested some indicators of a measurement plan that might be appropriate for this case study. In Table 14, we have suggested the algorithms to produce these indicators for the measurement plan. Depending on the image being created, the values of the indicators will depend on estimation and will be associated with error. Even measures of existing processes, artifacts and sentiments will be associated with measurement error. We also remind measurement specialists that, because of the nature of the information needs they are trying to satisfy, formal and frequent assessment of software measurement and analysis is required to ensure that the measurement framework is meeting the requirements of its clients' information needs (Berry and Jeffery, 2000; Berry and Vandenbroek, 2001).

8.7 Conclusion

In this chapter we have presented a model of measurement and a behavioral model of decision making that we believe are appropriate for measurement and decision making in a VBSE framework. We have used these models to show how the products of measurement (measures, benchmarks and performance indicators) are applied to generate images in the mind of the decision maker and stimulate and support the decision making process. We have demonstrated how measures can be used to better inform the decision maker. Measurement in the software engineering domain has been an active topic for the last twenty years. During this time the main debate has been about the technology – for example: How to measure functional size? How to measure program complexity? How to assess product quality? The authors contend that we have yet to focus adequately on the application of the measures to achieve optimal outcomes for organisations.

Finally, we have demonstrated, through the illustration of a DSS based on a case study, that VBSE is practical although decision making is more complex in a value-based management context and the requirement for performance indicators is necessarily wider in scope. This will have major implications for people who specialize in software measurement who may have been chosen for their technical and numeracy skills. They will need to also have skills in business performance measurement if they are to adequately service the information requirements of software engineers and managers in a value-based software engineering world.

Table 13. Measurement plan

Indicator	Significance of the Indicator
Change in order processing costs	The added value to the client of the new system is a function of the decrease in the order processing costs.
Change in the order processing efficiency ratio	The added value to the client of the new system is a function of the increase in the order processing ratio (Cost of processing the order / Revenue earned from the order). The rate of change in the ratio over time would indicate whether the organisation had received all the benefits available from the new order processing system.
Change in sales commissions rate	The added value to the user of the new system is a function of the increase in sales commissions.
Change in mean and variance for time to fulfill an order	The value to the organisation of the new system is dependent on the capacity of the order fulfillment process. An increase in the mean suggests that the order fulfillment process is not coping. An increase in the variance suggests that the order fulfillment process is moving out of control.
Change in satisfaction	The job satisfaction of the manufacturer and distributors is directly related to the satisfaction of their customers.
Change in satisfaction indicators	The future of the organisation is directly related to the satisfaction of their customers.
Degree of stakeholder recognition	Organisation morale and rewards are functions of the extent to which stakeholders recognize the quality of the service provided.
Change in resource productivity rate	The value to the system developer of the new system is a function of productivity achieved on the development project.
Work backlog	The value to the system developer of the new system is reduced by the opportunity value of the backlog.
Development improvements	The value to the system developer of the new system is increased by the extent to which improvements can be introduced.
Challenge	The job satisfaction of the system developers is increased by the extent to which the new system represents a challenge.

Table 14. Measurement algorithms

Indicator	Measurement Algorithm
Change in the order processing efficiency rate	1) Measure duration of each order transaction 2) Measure dollar value of each order 3) Derive measure as ratio of sum of order values and sum of transaction duration 4) Derive indicator as the percentage change from one period to the next.
Change in sales commissions	1) Measure sales commission paid, by sales member 2) Measure hours worked by sales member 3) Derive measure as ratio of sales commission and hours worked 4) Derive indicator as the percentage change from one period to the next.
Change in mean and variance for time to fulfill an order	1) Measure duration of time in hours to fulfill each order 2) Calculate mean duration and variance for all orders by priority category 3) Derive indicators as the percentage change from one period to the next.
Change in customer satisfaction	Measure customer satisfaction by a) survey b) number of complaints and c) amount of repeat business
Stakeholder recognition	Measure the number of positive and negative comments made about the organisation in external publications
Change in productivity rate by period	1) Measure resource effort expended on the system 2) Measure resource effort expended on rework 3) Measure lost effort due to client-induced delays 4) Measure production during the period in function points 5) Derive productivity rate and express as a rate of change over previous period
Work backlog	Measure the number and potential value of service requests by other clients
Development improvements	Measure the improvements in processes, tools, technologies and staff skills
Challenge	Measure the degree of challenge in meeting the client's requirement and the amount of innovation required.

References

(Beach and Mitchell, 1990) Beach, L.R. and Mitchell, T.R., Image Theory: A Behavioral Theory of Decision Making in Organizations, Research in Organizational Behavior, 1990, 12, pp 1–41

(Beach, 1990) Beach, LR. Image Theory: Decision-making in Personal and Organizational Contexts. (Wiley Chichester 1990)

(Beach, 1996) Beach, LR. (ed), Decision Making in the Workplace – a Unified Perspective (Lawrence Erlbaum Associates, Mahwah, New Jersey 1996)

(Becker, 1999) Becker, S. A., Aligning Strategic and Project Measurement Systems. IEEE Software. May/June 1999

(Berry and Jeffery, 2000) Berry, M. and Jeffery, R. An Instrument for Assessing Software Measurement Programs. Empirical Software Engineering. An International Journal, 2000; 5(3), pp 183–200

(Berry and Vandenbroek, 2001) Berry, M. and Vandenbroek, M.: A Targeted Assessment of the Software Measurement Process. Proc. 7th International Software Metrics Symposium; London.(IEEE Computer Society Los Alamos, California 2001)

(Boehm and Huang, 2003) Boehm, B. W. and Huang, L.G.: Value-based Software Engineering: A Case Study, IEEE Computer, March 2003, pp 33–41

(Dennis, 1996) Dennis, A. R., Information Exchange and Use in Group Decision Making: You Can Lead a Group to Information, but You Can't Make It Think. MIS Quarterly December 1996

(Edberg, 1997) Edberg, D. T.: Creating a balanced IS measurement program. Information Systems Management; 14 (2), p. 32

(Edwards, 1967) Edwards, W.: The Theory of Decision-making, Decision Making ed by Edwards and Tversky, Penguin Modern Psychology 1967

(Fenton and Pfleeger, 1997) Fenton, N. and Pfleeger, S. L., Software Metrics – A Rigorous and Practical Approach. 2nd Edition (International Thomson Computer Press ; PWS Publishing Co; London, Boston, Mass.1997)

(Garrity and Sanders, 1998) Garrity, EJ and Sanders, GL (eds.). Information Systems Success Measurement (Idea Group, Hershey, 1998)

(Hall and Fenton, 1994) Hall, T. and Fenton, N., Implementing Software Metrics – the Critical Success Factors, Software Quality Journal, 3 (4), pp 195–208, (1994)

(Isenberg, 1986) Isenberg, D.J., Group Polarization: A Critical Review and Meta-Analysis. Journal of Personality and Social Psychology. 1986, 50(6), pp 1141–1151

(ISO/IEC 15939:2002) ISO/IEC 15939:2002 Information Technology – Software Measurement Process (Int. Organization for Standardization, Geneva, 2002)

(Kaplan and Norton, 1992) Kaplan, R. S. and Norton, D. P. "The Balanced Scorecard – Measures that Drive Performance", Harvard Business Review, Jan 1992, pp 71–79

(Kaplan and Norton, 1993) Kaplan, R. S. and Norton, D. P. "Putting the Balanced Scorecard to Work", Harvard Business Review, September-October 1993, pp 134–149

(Simon, 1979) Simon, H. A.: Rational Decision Making in Business Organization. American Economic Review, Sept. 1979, 69(4), p. 493

(Tufte, 1983) Tufte, E. R.: The visual display of quantitative information, (Graphics Press, Cheshire, Conn. 1983)

(Valacich et al., 2002) Valacich, J.S., Sarker, S. and Pratt, J., Computer-Mediated and Face-to-Face Groups: Who Makes Riskier Decisions? Proceedings of the 35th Hawaii International Conference on System Sciences (IEEE, 2002)

(van Grembergen and Saull, 2001) Van Grembergen, W. Saull, R. Aligning business and information technology through the balanced scorecard. System Sciences. Proceedings of the 34th Annual Hawaii International Conference. (IEEE, Jan. 2001)

(Winquist, 1998) Winquist, J.R. Information Pooling: When it Impacts Group Decision Making. Journal of Personality and Social Psychology. 1998, 74(2), pp 371–377

Author Biographies

Michael Berry is a PhD candidate at the University of New South Wales, Australia and is located at National ICT Australia (NICTA). He has a bachelor's degree in Business Administration. He is in final stages of completing his thesis on the assessment of software measurement. He has experience as a practitioner (1967-1991), as an academic (UNSW 1992-1996), and as a researcher (CSIRO 1996-2001). His interests are in software process in general and software measurement in particular. He was a member of the working group that wrote the international standard, ISO/IEC 15939:2002 "Software Measurement Process".

Aybüke Aurum is a senior lecturer at the School of Information Systems, Technology and Management, University of New South Wales. She received her BSc and MSc in Geological Engineering, and MEngSc and PhD in Computer Science. She is the founder and group leader of the Requirements Engineering Research Group (ReqEng) at the University of New South Wales. She also works as a visiting researcher in National ICT, Australia (NICTA). Her research interests include management of software development process, software inspection, requirements engineering, decision making and knowledge management.

9 Criteria for Selecting Software Requirements to Create Product Value: An Industrial Empirical Study

Claes Wohlin and Aybüke Aurum

Abstract: Product value is based on which requirements are included in a specific release of a software product. This chapter provides an overview of the value concept and presents an empirical study conducted as an industrial survey. The objective of the survey was to quantify the importance of different decision making criteria when deciding whether to include a requirement in a project or release. The results reported from the survey are based on responses from two companies. It was discovered that there were similarities in responses at a company level, although major differences existed between individual respondents to the survey. The most important criteria were found to be those related to specific customers or markets and criteria, such as development cost-benefit, delivery date, and resources. The least important criteria were those related to development and maintenance. The results also indicate that a better balance between the most important and least important criteria ought to be achieved in the future.

Keywords: Decision support, decision making, requirements selection, product management, empirical software engineering.

9.1 Introduction

Organizations operating in a knowledge-based economy are facing new challenges. There is incredible pressure on software companies to achieve and sustain competitive advantage. To remain competitive in an era of increasing uncertainty and market globalization it is important to focus on the value of different customers and markets when developing products. Software companies, like many other organizations, are forced to adapt to the strategic challenges and opportunities presented by the new economy where technological advances cause dramatic changes in business processes, products, and services.

According to economics and management science, an organization's ability to create value (in relation to its goals) depends on the utilization of intellectual capital (Drucker, 1998; Prahalad and Hamel, 1990). Intellectual capital is the sum of organizational knowledge which includes ideas, inventions, technologies, software programs, designs, processes, and creativity – which all can be converted to profit, create value, and give organizations a competitive edge (Alwis et al., 2003; Sullivan, 1998). Alwis et al. (2003) list several potential approaches that enable organizations to create value from intellectual capital, e.g., profit generation from products through sale, strategic positioning through market share, and innovation technology, customer loyalty, cost reductions, and improved productivity. Effective management of the product development process contributes to sustainable competitive advantage for software companies. This requires that software developers firstly consider customers' requirements, business requirements, and technological opportunities when making decisions. Secondly, they need to have a sound understanding of both technical and business implications of decisions that have been made throughout the development process. Thirdly, it is essential to understand the business dynamics that drive software development in terms of cost, time, and product quality as well as how software processes and products interconnect.

The real challenge for software developers is to understand factors that drive organizational value creation and how to influence them. Value depends on the relationship between customer needs and the benefits of products that satisfy those needs. Value is created when software developers provide products that satisfy customer needs (Alwis et al., 2003). However, focusing on value to a specific customer may lead to the exclusion of considering value to other stakeholders, including other customers, different markets, software developers, and project managers. This may jeopardize the long-term viability of the software company. Since customers have different needs and desires that vary with time, software companies are forced to create value along many dimensions, including economical, physical, emotional, social, cognitive and political dimensions (Nunamaker et al., 2001). There is a vast amount of literature in the management, economics, and marketing fields that has recognized the need to make product development decisions in light of their overall effect on value (Browning et al., 2002; Deaton and Muellbauer, 1980; Park, 1998; Urban and Hauser 1993).

Software developers need to know early on what the economic implications of their decisions will be in the development process, particularly when developing new products with attributes that are complex and difficult to characterize during the initial development process (Faulk et al., 2000; Harmon et al., 2003). Analyzing the economic value of a software product is complex. As such, analysis cannot be carried out simply by understanding the functionality and characteristics of software technology alone. An appreciation of the connection of this technology to business as well as to all aspects of the national and international economy is also desirable. Such an analysis must portray the future demand for software product usage accurately. This requires estimation of productivity increases from technical changes as well as estimation of economic growth and cost of software technology. Chillarege (2002) argues that in the last two decades several software product businesses announced gross profit margins of around 80%, however, there is no guarantee that this will continue into the next 20-30 years. During a software product's life cycle, market values change and different characteristics become dominant and drive business. If we can understand how market values vary during the life cycle, it would be easier to identify process models with attributes that highlight market values in a particular stage.

There has been progress made over the years in integrating value-oriented perspectives into the software engineering discipline; a discipline which includes requirements engineering, architecture, design and development, verification and validation, planning and control, risk management, quality management, people management, and principles and practices (Boehm, 2003; Boehm and Huang, 2003). A detailed discussion of the value concept in software engineering is also provided in Chapters 1, 2, and 3. A value-based approach aims to align software development with customer requirements and strategic business objectives (Faulk et al., 2000). Understanding the customer value aspects brings together domain and application engineering within a common framework.

This chapter incorporates the concept of a value-based approach in requirements engineering. It is written based on the understanding that software requirements need to be bundled together such that they are aligned with business and product objectives to create value for the user of the software product. This chapter addresses criteria for how to decide which product requirements will be included in specific software projects. In particular, the chapter presents an empirical survey into two companies where the criteria for including a specific requirement in the next project or release are prioritized. The main research question addressed is: "What defines whether a requirement will be included in a specific release/project?"

The chapter is outlined as follows. Section 9.2 describes the background and context of the value concept from three different perspectives: management, software engineering, and requirements engineering, and also presents some related works. Section 9.3 describes the design of the empirical study aimed at identifying which criteria are important when deciding whether to include a specific requirement in the next project or release. The results of the study are presented in Section 9.4. Finally some conclusions and further work is discussed in Section 9.5.

9.2 Background

This section presents the value concept for products from three different perspectives: management, software engineering, and requirements engineering. Note that a detailed discussion on valuation can be found in Chapters 1, 2, and 3. It also positions the chapter in relation to research conducted in software requirements engineering related areas, in particular release planning and prioritization.

Value Concept in Management

The *Oxford English Dictionary* defines value as "the ability of a thing to serve a purpose or cause and effect." Value creation is related to achieving desired outcomes. Thus, value can be defined as anything that one might consider useful, convenient, or essential (Nunamaker et al., 2001).

In the context of product development, value includes both product and process attributes. Browning et al. (2002) argue that product value is affected not only by the presence of necessary activities in the product development process, but also by the way those activities work together to ensure that they use and produce the right information. The value of a product to a customer depends on customer preferences and alternatives, as addressed in economics, marketing, and value engineering literature (Browning, 2003; Deaton and Muellbauer, 1980; Park, 1998; Urban and Hauser, 1993).

Customer value has two aspects (Browning, 2003): (a) Absolute value, which illustrates how well the attributes of a product address customer needs and (b) Relative value, which implies that the change in a product's value depends on alternative solutions to customer needs. There are a vast amount of studies in marketing literature that determine the vector of product values and specify the optimum level of each attribute. For example, Weinstein and Johnson (1999) define absolute value as *Value = perceived benefits/perceived price*, where perceived benefits and price are both measured relative to competing products. Browning (2003) points out that product value is essentially equal to benefit / cost. The author argues that a change in any of these factors can cause a change in the value of product. The question is how to balance these with the preferences of customer or market. Although companies put a great amount of effort into increasing customer value in their product development process, determining *how* and *when* value is added is still a challenge even in marketing and management science. Some of the strategies include focusing effort on eliminating the critical risk in a project, where the removal of the critical risk assists in adding value into product development, or using methods such as multi-attribute utility theory, where a change in value/utility typically implies a change in demand for a product (Browning et al., 2002).

Value Concept in Software Engineering

Keller (1995) argues that value of software is viewed very differently from most other kinds of objects. Thus, it is difficult to define the concept of value in software engineering, as the development process involves many stakeholders where each defines value from his own point of view. The author points out that "*Software is not something that you can hold it, yet it can be duplicated very quickly. ... As more and more software becomes "available" on public networks, the range of value will be extended even more.*" An interesting fact is that, the value of a product for a customer is expressed in terms of benefit and cost, whereas to a software company it is expressed in terms of the profit (return) from the product sold. This profit promotes economic value, determined by the net present value of future benefits that ownership of an item brings to its owner (Browning et al., 2002; Alwis et al., 2003).

In the context of software engineering, value creation involves gaining new insights or discovering new patterns of knowledge at the process level, product level, or resources level. Information and knowledge transfer to stakeholders facilitates value creation. The ability to assess the impact of changes in a software product, process, or resources during the development life cycle is an important aspect in software product management. Alwis et al. (2003) point out that the value of a product increases in proportion to its advantages over competitive products, and decreases in proportion to its disadvantage. Thus the value of any product to a customer is a function of its performance and price, relative to other products in the market.

The notion of integrating insights from customer value analysis into the software development process and the difficulties that are associated with the practical application of this have been addressed in software engineering literature. According to Harrison (2001) the software engineering community lacks the ability to quantitatively measure the benefits of reduced uncertainty in a software development project. He proposes evaluating investments in software engineering infrastructure using well-accepted economic and financial models. These models are based on a theory that the inherent value of the organization is defined as the value of all its future profits. The author argues that usage of these techniques can lead to better business cases for investing in software process improvement.

Tanaka et al. (1998) emphasize that there are various existing analysis tools and techniques for quality measurement of software product value throughout the life cycle, however many of them are not fully utilized by software developers. Firstly, it is not easy for managers to understand and utilize analyzed results. Secondly, it is time consuming to evaluate the tools and prepare the environment needed to apply them practically. Thirdly, it is important to acquire the know-how for using tools and measurement data effectively and to incorporate this into the software development process in a timely fashion. Erdogmus et al. (2004) attack the problem from an education point of view. The authors point out that, although the software engineering community has put in an enormous amount of work in the areas of metrics and cost-benefit analysis, they have failed to cover valuation and competitive strategy in a business context. According to the authors, the problem starts from the software engineering education, which ignores the need to investigate the role of technical projects in the context of overall business requirements

Faulk et al. (2000) emphasize the importance of communication between the business and technical sides of an organization, so that decision makers with different roles can have a better understanding of the software engineering implications of their decisions. The authors point out that current software development models do not support such communication. Furthermore, value creating units such as product management, marketing, and development are separated by culture, language, and perception of overall goals. Since the software development process does not link business objectives with software design decisions, the outcome is often a mismatch between technical capabilities and business goals. The authors provide a process framework that links strategic business goals, process improvement, and the application of domain engineering to software product lines and refer to this approach as a "Value-Based Software Engineering" approach. A value-based approach to software engineering is further discussed in Chapter 1

The fact that software is different than other types of products only serves to complicate matters. Software is easily changed (in many cases, too easily) and released in several releases. Thus, it is not only a matter of looking at the short-term value of the next release. The long-term evolution of a software product has to be taken into account. There is a constant tradeoff between short-term business goals to satisfy customers and different markets, and long-term evolution of the software to ensure that the software product is competitive in both the short- and long-term.

Value Concept in Requirements Engineering (RE)

It is critical that software developers integrate insights from customer value analysis into the requirements process. Several researchers emphasize how important it is for managers to understand the implications of their decisions in relation to a cost-benefit analysis, in particular during early life cycle activities (Boehm, 2003, Faulk et al., 2000). Furthermore, it is crucial to ensure that the requirements meet business goals. System engineering and management, and in particular risk management literature, stress the importance of including effort, schedule, cost, and risk assessment as part of project planning. Goal modeling techniques in requirements engineering is another approach that serves as a mechanism by which to link requirements to strategic objectives anchored in the context of an overall model of business strategy.

Gordijn and Akkerman (2003) argue that requirements engineering approaches neglect the value proposition of information systems, despite an understanding of this value proposition being key to the development of e-commerce applications. The authors focus on the use of RE and a conceptual modeling approach to articulate, analyze, and validate Internet enabled value propositions in an e-business context. They also develop an economic value perspective (called e3-value) by representing an e-commerce idea using principles and techniques which stem from RE.

Favaro (2002) points out that a full cost-benefit analysis of requirements requires investment in time and resources and is more difficult than design and implementation, as there are more unknown factors in the early stages of the life cycle. Thus it takes a full development cycle before the complete economic impact of a requirement is known. Favaro argues that software developers may add value to requirements in several ways, such as by learning to create reusable requirements that enclose cost-benefit analysis or by studying the new generation of agile development processes to enable them to understand strategic possibilities for adding value to the requirements process over the full product cycle. Furthermore, by learning more about the new tools and financial analysis, they can better understand how strategic flexibility in the requirements process adds value.

The bottom line is that software development companies are faced with the challenge of deciding which requirements to include in a specific project or release, and which requirements to reject or postpone to later releases. Thus, an empirical study was conducted to increase our understanding of which criteria are in fact the most important to include in the next project or release. It was assumed that each project handles one release. The study was conducted as a survey and results are presented from two companies.

Related Work in Release Planning and Prioritization

Market-driven (as opposed to customized) incremental product development and delivery (release) is becoming increasingly commonplace in the software industry (Ruhe and Greer, 2003; Greer and Ruhe, 2004; Carlshamre 2002). Incremental product development is planned and executed with the goal of delivering an optimal subset of requirements in a certain release (version of a product that is distributed to customers). The idea is to select what a release should contain (requirements), when it should be released (time), and at what cost (effort) this should be achieved. Decisions about which customers get which features, at what level of quality, and at what point in time, have to be made, making these activities a major determinant of the success of a product. All of these activities are vitally dependent on product requirements and are elicited/captured, analyzed, and specified before any planning and development activity can commence. Decision support in a release planning context is further discussed in Chapter 12.

The contributions in this area include addressing different aspects of requirements management, such as prioritization (Karlsson et al., 1998; Regnell et al., 2001a; Ruhe et al., 2003) and dependencies between requirements (Dahlstedt and Persson, 2003; Carlshamre et al., 2001). Moreover, researchers have worked on connecting the requirements engineering process to decision making (Regnell et al., 2001b; Aurum and Wohlin, 2002; Aurum and Wohlin 2003). Some work has also been done on release planning. In (Ruhe and Greer, 2003; Greer and Ruhe 2004), a genetic algorithm approach has been used to plan for different releases, while the work in (Carlshamre, 2002) is focused on understanding release planning.

Thus, work has been conducted on release planning and, as such, there are investigations into prioritization of requirements and dependencies between them. However, to the best of our knowledge no studies have actually looked into the criteria used in decision making about whether to incorporate a specific requirement into a software project or release. The study presented below is the first step towards filling this gap, and is needed to understand how value is created for software products.

9.3 Research Approach

This section provides an overview of the design of the survey and, in particular, the questionnaire used. The main objective is to provide insight into the following research question: "What defines whether a requirement will be included in a specific release/project?" This is closely related to understanding the underlying decision process related to requirements. Decision support is further discussed in Chapters 2 and 4. Another related issue is negotiation, which is further discussed in Chapter 7. Situations where it must be decided whether to include a specific requirement in a project or release are often not straightforward and may even involve negotiations. Negotiations are not further discussed here.

Development of the Survey Questionnaire

A survey was designed to understand and evaluate the importance of different decision making criteria when determining whether or not to include a specific requirement in a project or release. Industry representatives were asked to prioritize the importance of the different criteria in their decision making process. The following procedure was chosen to design the survey instrument, i.e., a questionnaire:

- A brainstorming session was held to identify suitable criteria to include in the survey. The session included three researchers involved in requirements engineering research. All three have close industrial contacts.
- Based on the outcome of the brainstorming session, a questionnaire was designed by the main author of this chapter.
- The questionnaire was reviewed by the participants of the brainstorming session, and one additional independent researcher, to further improve the selection of criteria.
- The questionnaire was updated based on feedback from the reviewers, and then sent to a contact person at different companies.

The brainstorming session and the review process included some in-depth discussion about whether it was possible to identify orthogonal criteria. It was concluded that it would only be possible if the criteria were kept at a high level of abstraction. This would mean that very few criteria would be evaluated and prioritized by the subjects in the study. The discussions led to a removal of some all embracing criteria, such as risk, that are related to basically all other criteria; however it also was decided to retain a number of criteria despite dependencies, since it is basically impossible to avoid all dependencies. The intention was for subjects to prioritize without thinking too much about dependencies, and instead focusing on what they viewed as the main criteria. In summary, the objective was that importance should be judged from the individual importance of the criteria and not as consequences of other criteria. The actual outcome points to three different behaviors with respect to this issue. This is further elaborated in Section 9.1.

Criteria Covered in the Questionnaire

After several iterations the questionnaire was narrowed to include 13 criteria for assessment by subjects. Many of the criteria were general in the sense that they were not solely factors relevant for selecting requirements. They were often referred to in literature discussing software success more generally (Wohlin et al., 2000). Moreover, it was also stated clearly that additional criteria could be added by the subjects. This was done to avoid subjects feeling that missing criteria hindered their completion of the questionnaire. Moreover, the questionnaire was designed this way to capture any additional criteria that were missed in the brainstorming session. It was agreed among the researchers that the 13 criteria covered three important dimensions or stakeholder groups, although this grouping was not communicated to the subjects (respondents). The three groups were: external market/customer, company management, and development/maintenance personnel. The 13 criteria included in the study are as follows. The text is exactly as communicated to the subjects in the questionnaire, including a short explanation and motivation for each criterion.

External market/customer

1. *Competitors*
   Explanation: The status of the competitors with respect to the requirement. In other words, it is taken into account whether a competitor has the implied functionality implemented or not.
   Motivation: We may feel forced to include a requirement if our competitors have the functionality, or we may want to implement something that is considered to be leading edge functionality (functionality competitors do not have).
2. *Requirement's issuer*
   Explanation: The actual issuer of the requirement is taken into account, i.e., which stakeholder (internal or external) generated the requirement.
   Motivation: We may judge some issuers as more important than others, for example, a very important customer or representative for an important market.
3. *Stakeholder priority of requirement*
   Explanation: The priority of the requirement is taken into account.
   Motivation: We may want to prioritize the requirements that our customers or markets think are of particular importance.
4. *Requirement's volatility*
   Explanation: This criterion is related to whether the requirement is likely to change or not.
   Motivation: We may want to handle highly volatile requirements differently.

Company management

5. *Support for Education/Training*
   Explanation: The ability and possibility to provide technical support, education, and training to customers, markets, and so forth with respect to the requirement.
   Motivation: We may not want to implement functionality unless we could provide the appropriate technical support, education, and training in relation to the requirement.
6. *Development cost-benefit*
   Explanation: The actual cost-benefit for implementing the requirement.
   Motivation: We may not want to include a requirement if the implementation cost is judged to be high in relation to the expected benefit.
7. *Resources/competencies*
   Explanation: The availability of resources with the right competencies to implement the requirement.
   Motivation: We may not want to implement a requirement unless we are sure that we have the right people available for the job.

8. *Delivery date/Calendar time*

   Explanation: The ability to meet the project deadline.

   Motivation: We may not want to introduce a requirement that may affect the deadline of the project negatively.

Development / maintenance personnel

9. *System impact*

   Explanation: The impact of the requirement on the existing system.

   Motivation: We may not want to implement a requirement if we judge that the actual impact in terms of changes to the existing system is too large.

10. *Complexity*

    Explanation: The estimated complexity of the requirement and the associated challenges in implementing it.

    Motivation: We may not want to include a requirement that is judged to be very complex to implement and as a consequence the risk of failure as too high.

11. *Requirements dependencies*

    Explanation: The dependencies between this specific requirement and other requirements, either already implemented or other posed requirements.

    Motivation: The dependency to other requirements (already implemented, scheduled to be implemented, or deferred to later release) may affect our decision regarding the current requirement.

12. *Evolution*

    Explanation: The impact on the future evolution of the system.

    Motivation: We may not want to implement a requirement if it is believed to make long-term evolution of the system more complicated.

13. *Maintenance*

    Explanation: The impact on the maintenance of the current system.

    Motivation: We may not want to implement a requirement if it is believed that the requirement may cause many problems in terms of maintenance.

Conducting the Survey

The above 13 criteria were included in the questionnaire as follows. First, the subjects were given a short introduction. This included positioning the survey within a larger industry-academia collaborative research project and highlighting the value of participating in the survey, the target audience for the survey (important since the communication was done through a contact person at each company), the main research question, and the estimated time for the questionnaire; and finally the subjects were also guaranteed anonymity. It was clearly stated both in the questionnaire and in an e-mail that the target audience was personnel included in the decision making process. It was expected to include the following types of management personnel: product management, project management, and line management.

The second part contained an introduction to the 13 criteria as listed in Section 9.2. The third part included a characterization of the context in which the subject responded. This included company name, unit within company, type of application, whether development was market- or customer-oriented, type of product, and the role of the subject within the organization. Contact details were also asked to ensure that each subject could be contacted for clarification purposes, although no data in the analysis will be connected to specific individuals.

The third and final part was the actual survey. The 13 criteria were listed in a table and the subjects were asked to fill out three columns with respect to the criteria. First, the subjects were asked to answer yes or no regarding whether each criterion was relevant when deciding to include a requirement in a project or release. For the other two columns the subjects were asked to provide relative weights regarding the importance of the criteria. The subjects had 1,000 points to spend among the 13 criteria (or more if they chose to add some criterion). A higher number of points meant that a criterion was relatively more important. For example, a criterion obtaining twice as many points as another criterion was viewed to be twice as important. The subjects were allowed to distribute the points as they wished, i.e., there were no requirement that each criterion should be allocated a weighting. In other words, a subject could have given all 1,000 points to one criterion.

The second column was concerned with the way different criteria are valued today, and the third column was focused on how the criteria ought to be valued in the future. The objective was to capture both the current state of practice and any changes that industry would like to make in the future. The latter may be viewed as a more ideal situation.

9.4 Survey Results and Analysis

The questionnaire was initially sent to two companies, although the intention was to send the survey to more companies. This approach was chosen for two reasons. First, it provided a means of validating that the survey was understandable and that no major problems existed with the questionnaire. Secondly, conducting the study these particular companies became a priority because they had scheduled requirements engineering-related workshops, presenting the perfect opportunity to present and discuss the survey. Later, six more companies responded to the survey, however this data has still not been analyzed and hence the results presented here are based on the two first companies only.

Unfortunately, both companies compressed their workshop schedules, which meant that the presentation and survey discussion was removed from the agenda. Feedback has hence only been sent via e-mail.

The two companies are referred to as Company A and Company B respectively. Company A is a major international company, and the responses are provided by one part of the business. This part develops hardware and software solutions for process control systems. Products from the company are sold to a world market.

Company B is part of an international enterprise. The company develops hardware and software products for automatic guided vehicles. Their products are also sold on a world market.

In total, 13 subjects responded from these two companies, i.e., seven subjects represent Company A and six subjects work at Company B. The observations, results, and analysis presented in this section are based on an analysis of the responses of these 13 subjects. This may be viewed as few respondents; however, it should be remembered that the number of responses was naturally limited by virtue of the fact that the survey targeted key personnel and roles in each organization. Given that company workshops were planned in advance, it was known that only 15 responses could be expected if all relevant people responded. Thus, 13 responses must be viewed as a very positive outcome, given the workload of the people targeted with the survey.

In this section, some general observations from the survey are presented together with the results and analysis of the data collected with respect to the criteria used in relation to the main research question.

Observations from the Questionnaire

The issue identified earlier, i.e., that the criteria were not fully orthogonal, was also identified by some of the subjects, and mentioned in their e-mail communications when submitting the questionnaire. As mentioned above, it resulted in three different approaches. One subject took a rather extreme standpoint and only gave points to two criteria, including assigning a high weighting to development cost-benefit, which is arguably related to many of the other criteria. Some subjects divided the criteria into subgroups, either based on judged importance or as a way of handling the inevitable dependencies between some of the criteria. They then assigned the criteria in a subgroup the same number of points. Finally, a third group approached the criteria without really taking the dependencies into account too much. Basically, they filled out the questionnaire from a "main criteria point of view" as was intended by the research design. In other words, they focused on each criterion's own value rather than considering its connection to other criteria.

It was also observed that one subject allocated more than 1,000 points to the criteria (1,020 points), thus the points given by the subject were rescaled so that their sum became 1,000. Four of the thirteen subjects suggested new criteria for the decision. These four subjects also provided points for the new criteria. The new criteria are further discussed in the following subsection; however it should be noted, given that only 25% of the subjects suggested new criteria, and that there was only a minor overlap between their suggestions, it was hard to include these new criteria when comparing how subjects allocated points to the same criteria. Thus it was decided that, in the case of the subjects who suggested new criteria, the points for the 13 criteria should also be rescaled to ensure comparability. The proposed new criteria are handled separately below.

Relevant Criteria

The responses provided by the subjects were related to whether the 13 criteria were relevant for this type of decisions or not. Most subjects regarded the criteria as relevant. More precisely, all subjects regarded seven of the criteria as relevant. For the remaining six criteria, the following results were obtained:

- Requirement's issuer: 12 subjects out of 13 viewed this criterion as relevant
- Requirement's volatility: 10
- Support for training/education: 10
- System impact: 12
- Complexity: 12
- Maintenance: 12

We have not further explored the above four situations in which only one person has felt that a particular criterion has no relevance, because we feel that more responses to the survey are needed before any further conclusions can be drawn. It is more interesting to look at the two criteria where three subjects state that the criteria are not relevant. While this is not a definitive answer in general, it should be noted that it probably is easier to say "yes" than "no." The subjects know that the researchers regard these criteria as relevant since the criteria appear in the list, and hence it is easier to agree that they are relevant than to object. Thus, it is interesting when three subjects disagree with the researchers.

The volatility of a requirement is not a relevant criterion according to three of the subjects. This may seem surprising. On the other hand, it may show that requirements are included for other reasons and that volatility has to instead be handled as part of the development project, for example, by postponing the implementation as long as possible until more is known about the requirement.

It is probably not as surprising that the support for education/training is depicted as a criterion that may not be relevant. The inclusion of a requirement is decided based on other criteria and if education/training is needed then this can be provided later.

The other interesting issue is that four subjects proposed new criteria. In total, five new criteria were proposed. One of them obtained two votes. The subjects only provided the names of the criteria and hence comments with respect to the criteria are based on interpretations of the researchers. The comments are not meant to imply that the newly proposed criteria should not be used, for example, in future surveys, although the criteria have relations to the criteria used in the survey as indicated below. The following five new criteria were proposed:

- Strategic importance/alignment (it is assumed that the subjects meant the same criterion, although one used importance and the other alignment)
  Comment: This criterion seems to be related to competitors (criterion 1), i.e., strategic positioning in relation to other competing products on the market.
- Customer value
  Comment: This value is probably partially related to stakeholders' priorities of

a requirement (criterion 3), since if a requirement is highly prioritized by a stakeholder, then it ought to have a high value for that stakeholder.
- Product cost
  Comment: This cost is most likely closely related to the development cost-benefit (criterion 6), although there may be differences.
- Market technology trends
  Comment: This is related to competitors (criterion 1), and in particular the text in the motivation above regarding criterion 1 where it is stated that the criterion may be important in relation to leading edge functionality.
- Function is promised/sold
  Comment: This criterion is partially related to the requirement's issuer (criterion 2). It may be viewed as more important to keep a promise to some issuers than others.

The above list of proposed new criteria illustrates that it is very difficult to formulate an exhaustive set of criteria, particularly if criteria should be reasonably independent. For future studies, it must be decided whether any of the 13 criteria included in this study should be removed and if any of the above five new criteria should be incorporated into the list.

Importance of Criteria Today

The assignment of points for the criteria was divided into two parts: 'today' and 'future'. In this section, the outcome regarding the situation 'today' is reported. The results are presented for the two companies separately. A comparison between the companies is provided in Section 9.6.

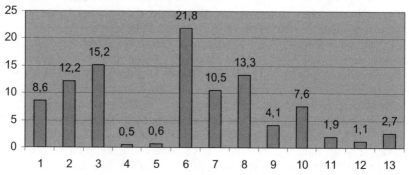

Fig. 32. Importance of current criteria at Company A

The results for each company were aggregated by taking the sum of the points provided by each subject. The sum was then normalized to a percentage figure, which makes it possible to, for example, state which criteria contribute more than X% to the decision. The results for Company A are shown in Figure 32. The list of the criteria can be found in Section 9.2.

It is worth noting that five criteria have percentage values above 10% and six criteria have values below 5%. The results from Company A indicate that some criteria are clearly more important than others. The five most important criteria are (in order): Development cost-benefit, customer/market priority of requirement, delivery date/calendar time, requirement's issuer, and resources/competencies. This indicates that issues related to specific customers/markets are important, as are traditional management aspects such as cost-benefit, delivery date, and resources. The development/maintenance aspects have low influence on the decision. It is worth noting that for both companies, it has not been possible to identify any relationship between the actual job role of the respondents and their views on which criteria should be taken into consideration.

The outcome for Company B is presented in Figure 33. The results are similar from an ordering point of view, although the actual percentage figures differ slightly. For Company B, four criteria have a value above 10% and five criteria have a value lower than 5%. The values are slightly more evenly distributed for Company B, which may be explained by the fact that one of the subjects for Company A gave almost all points to "Development cost-benefit."

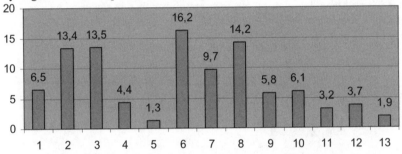

Fig. 33. Importance of current criteria at Company B

The figures for the two companies become even more similar when this subject was removed from the data set. The four criteria with a value above 10% for Company B are (in order): Development cost-benefit, delivery date/calendar time, customer/market priority of requirement, and requirement's issuer. Basically, the only difference between the top five (except for smaller differences in the percentage values) was that criteria 2 and 3 were swapped in order of importance. However, the actual difference in percentage value is small. The patterns are very similar for the two companies when it comes to the least important criteria.

In summary, it is quite clear that the two companies have very similar opinions regarding what is important when deciding whether or not to include a specific requirement in the next project or release. This makes the results even more interesting than if the companies had differing opinions, because it points to the possibility of a pattern, or common trend in views, across the software development industry. This could be a first step towards identifying key criteria in the decision making process with respect to including requirements in software projects or new releases.

As a final note, it is worth stressing that this is the picture that emerges when aggregating the prioritization from the subjects. However, at an individual level the subjects actually have quite different opinions, which are further discussed in Section 9.6.

Importance of Criteria in the Future

A similar analysis for Company A and Company B was conducted to examine how the subjects wanted to see the use of the criteria in the future. The objective was to capture what the subjects believed would be a better balance between the criteria than the situation today. The results for Company A are presented in Figure 34, where it can be seen that only three criteria had a percentage value at or above 10%. The three criteria are among the five ranked the highest in the previous section. The development cost-benefit is still viewed as most important, and the customer/market priority of a requirement is second. However, the gap between the two top criteria is smaller. The development/maintenance criteria (criteria 9-13) still have low values, but they are higher than in the previous section. In general, it seems like the patterns of today will remain in the future, although other criteria will be valued slightly more than today.

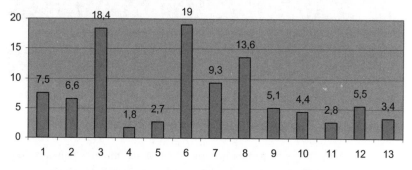

Fig. 34. Importance of future criteria at Company A

The results with respect to the future judgment of the criteria at Company B are shown in Figure 35.

The trends found for Company A are also visible for Company B, although four criteria have a value of 10% or higher. In addition to the three found for Company A, the first criterion has a high score. The first criterion is related to competitors. Moreover, the order between the two highest ranked criteria has changed. Company B would like to have the main focus to lie on the customer/market priority of a requirement rather than focusing on development cost-benefit, although the latter is still very important. At the lower end, it is also possible to see for Company B that the percentages are closer to each other. In other words, more criteria ought to be used in the future than are used today. There are differences, but the patterns are similar and the differences may very well be the results of having few subjects after all.

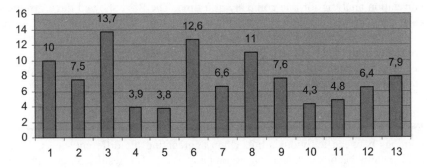

Fig. 35. Importance of future criteria at Company B

Analysis of Stakeholder Groups

The 13 criteria were divided into three groups in Section 9.2. It is interesting to see how the balance is between these groups and if there are any differences between the situation today and how the subjects say that it ought to be in the future.

In total, 13000 points have been awarded by the 13 subjects (1,000 each). The division of these points is shown in Table 15. In this case, the main interest is to study how the importance of the different areas was judged in relation to each other.

Table 15. Division of points between different dimensions of criteria

	Today	Future
External market / customer	4,824.0	4,503.5
Company management	5,722.0	5,157.0
Development / maintenance	2,454.0	3,339.5

The results presented in the table show that the criteria related to company management issues are, and will continue to be, most important. The main difference observable from Table 15 is that there is a general opinion that the development/maintenance-oriented criteria should be valued higher than it is today when it comes to decisions regarding which requirements to include in a project or release.

Individual and Company Comparison

An analysis at an individual level also has been conducted. The analysis points to the fact that there are large differences in opinions between individuals. This is supported both by a visual inspection of the collected data and a statistical analysis. The latter analysis included both a principal component analysis (PCA) and correlation analysis for one company at a time. The PCA showed three groups at each company, which indicates that the subjects represent different views. A correlation analysis yielded similar findings. Correlations between some individuals are rather high (and positive). However, some correlations between individuals are negative, although not high, which shows that there are quite different opinions among the individuals.

Based on the analysis of the opinions and views of the individuals, it is rather surprising to see common patterns at both companies as discussed in relation to Figure 32 to Figure 35. A possible explanation is that there are quite different opinions between individuals but, when aggregating the different views, a common pattern becomes visible on a company level. The results on an individual level point to a need to align the opinions of what is important when deciding what to include in a specific project or release.

Validity Threats

As for any empirical study, there are some threats to the validity of the findings. The first threat is related to what the two companies represent in terms of population. The two companies have several things in common, such as development of real-time systems for control purposes on an international market. This means that the companies may not be representative of all types of companies, and hence the results must be interpreted with some caution when moving away from the characteristics of the two studied companies.

On an individual level, there is a risk that it is easier to agree on relevance of the criteria than to disagree. However, this is partially taken care of by allowing the subjects to assign zero points to some criteria if they so wish. Moreover, it is easier to stick to the stated criteria than propose new criteria. This means that important criteria may be missing, for example, the criteria mentioned by two subjects related to strategic importance/alignment.

Another potential threat is related to the questionnaire. It is always difficult to know whether the respondents have understood the questions as intended and in a similar fashion to one another. This threat is somewhat addressed by providing the outcome of the survey to the respondents so that the results can be discussed both at the respective companies and with the researchers.

The threats point to the need to analyze the other companies included in the study, although the number of subjects for the other companies vary considerably. Moreover, the threats also highlight the need for replication of this type of study.

9.5 Conclusions and Further Work

In this chapter, the value-based concept has been discussed and studied from the viewpoint of decision making in requirements engineering. We have analyzed the determinants of whether or not a specific requirement should be included in a specific project/release. The inclusion or exclusion of specific requirements affects the value of the final product and hence the actual criteria for making these decisions are important to understand when discussing value-based software engineering.

The results from a survey conducted at two companies with 13 subjects representing roles such as product managers, project managers, and line managers are reported. It is demonstrated that the patterns from both companies were quite similar in terms of the judged importance of different criteria, although individuals had quite different opinions of what is most important. Overall, it is agreed that *who* states a requirement is important, as is his and their priority of that requirement. Moreover, issues such as development cost-benefit, delivery date, and resources available are also important. Criteria related to development and maintenance aspects, such as complexity and system impact, have lower importance. When comparing the situation today with a judgment of how it ought to be in the future, subjects expressed the desire to weight the criteria slightly differently in the future, although the general pattern remains the same. Subjects felt that criteria related to development and maintenance ought to be more important in the future than they are today.

Future work should include improving the set of criteria based on the feedback from this study or similar studies. Replications are also needed to uncover whether the findings provide a general picture of how decisions are made in the software industry with respect to which requirements to include in a project or release.

Acknowledgments

We would like to extend our thanks to Patrik Berander, Tony Gorschek, and Per Jönsson for their contribution to the brainstorming session and for reviewing the survey material. We are also grateful to the companies that have shared their experiences with us. We are particularly grateful to the contact champions and the respondents at the companies. Finally, we would like to express our gratitude to Irem Sevinc for helping us improve the English.

References

(Alwis et al., 2003) Alwis, D., Hlupic, V., Fitzgerald G.: Intellectual capital factors that impact of value creation. 25th Int. Conf Information Technology Interfaces, ITI, Cavtat, Croatia, pp 411–416, June 16–19, (2003)

(Aurum and Wohlin, 2002) Aurum, A., Wohlin, C.: Applying decision-making models in requirements engineering. Proceedings of Requirements Engineering for Software Quality, Essen Germany, December 9–10, (2002)

(Aurum and Wohlin, 2003) Aurum, A., Wohlin, C.: The fundamental nature of requirements engineering activities as a decision-making process. Information and Software Technology, **45**(14), pp 945–954, (2003)

(Boehm, 2003) Boehm, B. W.: Value-based software engineering. ACM SIGSOFT, Software Eng. Notes, **28**(2), pp 1–12, March, (2003)

(Boehm and Huang, 2003) Boehm, B. W., Huang L.G.: Value-based software engineering: A case study. IEEE Computer Society, Computer, pp 33–41, March, (2003)

(Browning, 2003) Browning T.R.: On customer value and improvement in product development processes. Systems Engineering, **6**(1), pp 49–61 (2003)

(Browning et al., 2002) Browning, T.R., Deyst, J.J., Eppinger S.D., Whitney, D.E.: Adding value in product development by creating information and reducing risk. IEEE Transactions on Engineering Management, **49**(4), pp 428–442, (2002)

(Carlshamre, 2002) Carlshamre, P.: Release planning in market-driven software product development: Provoking an understanding. Requirements Engineering **7**, pp 139–151, (2002)

(Carlshamre et al., 2001) Carlshamre, P., Sandahl, K., Lindvall, M., Regnell, B., Natt och Dag, J.: An industrial survey of requirements interdependencies in software product release planning. Proceedings Fifth IEEE International Symposium on Requirements Engineering, IEEE, Los Alamitos CA, pp 84–92, (2001)

(Chillarege, 2002) Chillarege, R.: The marriage of business dynamics and software engineering. IEEE, Software, November, pp 43–49, (2002)

(Dahlstedt and Persson 2003) Dahlstedt, Å., Persson, A.: Requirements interdependencies – Moulding the state of research into a research agenda. Proceedings Ninth International Workshop on Requirements Engineering (REFSQ'03), Klagenfurt/Velden, Austria, pp 71–80, (2003)

(Deaton and Muellbauer, 1980) Deaton, A., Muellbauer J.: Economics and consumer behavior. New York, Cambridge University Press, (1980)

(Drucker, 1998) Drucker, P.F.: Management's new paradigm. Forbes, **162**(7), pp 152–177, (1998)

(Erdogmus et al., 2004) Erdogmus, H., Favaro, J., Strigel, W.: Return on investment. IEEE Software, pp 18–22, (2004)

(Faulk et al., 2000) Faulk, S.R., Harmon, R.R., Raffo D.M.: Value-base software engineering: A value-driven approach to product-line engineering. 1st Int. Conf on Software Product-Line Engineering, Colorado, August, (2000)

(Favaro, 2002) Favaro, J.: Managing requirements for business value. IEEE Software, **19**(2), pp 15–17, March/April, (2002)

(Gordijn and Akkerman 2003) Gordijn, J., Akkerman H.: Value-based requirements engineering: Exploring innovative e-Commerce ideas. Requirements Engineering, **8**(2), pp 114–134, July (2003)

(Greer and Ruhe, 2004) Greer, D., Ruhe, G.: Software release planning: An evolutionary and iterative approach. Information and Software Technology **46**, pp 243–253, (2004)

(Harmon et al., 2003) Harmon, R., Raffo, D., Faulk, S.: Incorporating price sensitivity measurement into the software engineering process. IEEE, Portland International Conference on Technology Management for Reshaping the World, PICMET'03, pp 316–323, 20–24 July, (2003)

(Harrison, 2001) Harrison, W.: Using economic value of the firm as a basis for assessing the value of process improvements. Proceedings of 26th Annual NASA Goddard Software Engineering Workshop, pp 123–127, (2001)

(Karlsson et al., 1998) Karlsson, J. Wohlin, C., Regnell, B.: An evaluation of methods for prioritizing software requirements. Information and Software Technology, **39**(14–15), pp 939–947, (1998)

(Keller, 1995) Keller, E.: The value of software. Manufacturing Systems, ABI/INFORM Global, **13**(1), 16, January, (1995)

(Nunamaker et al., 2001) Nunamaker J.F, Briggs R.O., De Vreede G.J., Sprague R.H.: Enhancing organization's intellectual bandwidth: The quest for fast and effective value creation. Special issue: Journal of Management Information Systems, **17**(3), pp 3–8, (2001)

(Park, 1998) Park, R.J.: A plan for invention. New York, St Lucie Press, USA, (1998)

(Prahalad and Hamel, 1990) Prahalad C.K., Hamel G.: The core competence of the corporation. Harvard Business Review **68**(3), pp 79–81, (1990)

(Regnell et al., 2001a) Regnell, B. Höst, M. Natt och Dag, J., Hjelm, T.: Case study on distributed prioritisation in market-driven requirements engineering for packaged software. Requirements Engineering **6**, pp 51–62, (2001)

(Regnell et al., 2001b) Regnell, B. Paech, B., Aurum, A. Wohlin, C., Dutoit, A., Natt och Dag, J.: Requirements mean decisions! – Research issues for understanding and supporting decision-making in requirements engineering. Proceedings of First Swedish Conference on Software Engineering Research and Practice, Ronneby, Sweden, pp 49–52, (2001)

(Ruhe and Greer 2003) Ruhe G., Greer D.: Quantitative studies in software release planning under risk and resource constraints. Proceedings of International Symposium on Empirical Software Engineering (ISESE), IEEE, Los Alamitos CA, pp 262–271, (2003)

(Ruhe et al., 2003) Ruhe, G., Eberlein, A., Pfahl D.: Trade-off analysis for requirements selection. International Journal of Software Engineering and Knowledge Engineering, **13**(4), pp 345–366, (2003)

(Sullivan, 1998) Sullivan P.H.: Profiting from intellectual capital: Extracting value from innovation. New York: John Wiley and Sons, (1998)

(Tanaka et al., 1998) Tanaka, T., Aizawa, M., Ogasaware H., Yamada, A.: Software quality analysis and measurement service activity in the company. IEEE Proceedings of the 20th International Conference on Software Engineering, pp 426–429, 19–25 April, (1998)

(Urban and Hauser, 1993) Urban, GL., Hauser, J.: Design and marketing of new products. Englewood Cliffs NH: Prentice Hall, (1993)

(Weinstein and Johnson, 1999) Weinstein A., Johnson, W. C.: Designing and delivering superior customer value: concepts, cases, and applications. St. Lucie Press, Boca Raton, FL, USA, (1999)

(Wohlin et al., 2000) Wohlin, C., von Mayrhauser, A., Höst, M. and Regnell, B.: Subjective evaluation as a tool for learning from software project success. Information and Software Technology, **42**(14), pp 983–992, (2000)

Author Biographies

Claes Wohlin is a professor in Software Engineering at the School of Engineering at Blekinge Institute of Technology in Sweden. Prior to this, he has held professor chairs in software engineering at Lund University and Linköping University. He has an MSc in Electrical Engineering and a PhD in Communication Systems both from Lund University, and he has five years of industrial experience. Dr. Wohlin is co-Editor-in-Chief of the journal of Information and Software Technology published by Elsevier. He is on the editorial boards of *Empirical Software Engineering: An International Journal*, and *Software Quality Journal*. Dr. Wohlin is the recipient of the Telenor Nordic Research Prize in 2004 for his achievements in software engineering and improvement of software reliability for telecommunication systems.

Aybüke Aurum is a senior lecturer at the School of Information Systems, Technology and Management, University of New South Wales. She received her BSc and MSc in Geological Engineering, and MEngSc and PhD in Computer Science. She is the founder and group leader of the Requirements Engineering Research Group (ReqEng) at the University of New South Wales. She also works as a visiting researcher in National ICT, Australia (NICTA). Her research interests include management of software development process, software inspection, requirements engineering, decision making and knowledge management.

10 Collaborative Usability Testing to Facilitate Stakeholder Involvement

Ann L. Fruhling and Gert-Jan de Vreede

Abstract: Stakeholder involvement is an essential part of Value-Based Software Engineering. A critical part of the software engineering life cycle concerns usability testing. System usability refers to the effectiveness, efficiency, and satisfaction with which users can use the system for their relevant tasks. Unfortunately stakeholder involvement in usability testing is costly and challenging to organize. This chapter presents a repeatable collaborative usability testing process supported by a Group Support System that was developed and evaluated in a series of workshops involving a real system. The results show that the collaborative usability testing process facilitates stakeholder involvement through stakeholder expectation management, visualization and tradeoff analysis, prioritization of usability action items, the use of advanced groupware tools, and a simple business case analysis. Furthermore, the process can be considered productive and stakeholders reported substantial levels of satisfaction with it.

Keywords: Usability, usability evaluation, usability testing, collaboration, Group Support System, stakeholder value proposition elicitation, thinkLet, facilitation.

10.1 Introduction

Today, one of the major influencers of most systems' cost, schedule, and value are software decisions that are inextricably intertwined with system-level decisions (Boehm, 2003). Among these system-level decisions is the system's usability. System usability is the extent to which a system can be used by specified users to achieve specified goals with effectiveness, efficiency, and satisfaction in a specified context of use. System usability is linked to all stages of the software engineering process (Mayhew, 1999). The Usability Engineering Lifecycle, proposed by Mayhew (1999), is a holistic view of usability engineering and illustrates how various usability tasks such as user profile, task analysis, prototyping, and usability evaluation, are integrated into traditional software engineering approaches, agile methods, and object-oriented software engineering (Jacobson et al., 1992).

Systems with a high level of perceived usability are easy to learn and to use (Nielsen and Mack, 1994). System usability concerns various aspects such as the consistency and ease with which users can manipulate and navigate a Web site, the clarity of the interaction, ease of reading, arrangement of information, speed, and layout. Prior research overwhelmingly suggests that system usability is associated with many positive outcomes, such as a reduction in the number of errors, enhanced accuracy, a more positive user attitude toward the system, increased system use, and increased user productivity, see e.g., (Lecerof and Paterno, 1998; Nielsen, 1993). Furthermore, a recent study also found that system usability factors are essential elements in conveying the trustworthiness of a Web-based system and do affect users' perception of trust in personal relationship-based information exchanges (Fruhling and Lee, 2004). In summary, system usability is a key indicator for software engineering success.

A system's perceived usability level is determined using usability evaluations. Usability evaluations consider the users, the tasks, the equipment, the environment, and the relationships among them (Bevan and Macleod, 1994). Examples of usability evaluation methods include observations, cognitive walk-throughs, interviews and surveys, heuristic evaluations, focus groups, usability testing, and laboratory testing (Nielsen and Mack, 1994). These methods are not mutually exclusive. In fact, using more than one method provides richer analysis and results. As pointed out earlier, usability evaluation can occur throughout the software engineering cycle (Nielsen, 1993). For example, Rubin (1994) classifies three types of usability testing according to the point in the software engineering process:

1. Exploratory testing occurs early in the software engineering process. Its main objective is to evaluate the preliminary design concepts.
2. Assessment testing occurs after the high-level system design has been established. It seeks to evaluate how effectively the system functions have been implemented.
3. Validation testing occurs prior to the release of the system. It compares system performance to benchmark standards in time and effort required to complete a task.

A common reason why system usability breaks down is lack of user input (i.e., a value-oriented shortfall). Collaborative software engineering methods are one way to increase the solicitation of user input in a cost-effective and efficient manner (Dean et al., 1998). System developers often execute usability evaluation methods in a group setting as this may increase stakeholder input and reduce bias; a single stakeholder's own behavior in using the system may not be representative of that of the general user population. Collaborative usability evaluation can involve different types of stakeholders, often simultaneously – current and target users, usability experts, system designers, and system owners – and, thus, capture valuable insights from all stakeholders throughout the software engineering process.

The purpose of this research was to design a collaborative usability testing process, called e-CUP, and evaluate it in the field. The e-CUP process enables usability practitioners to actively involve different stakeholders and solicit their input and build consensus through synthetic experience techniques, i.e., use scenarios and prototypes. The collaborative usability testing process is an example of how usability practitioners can begin to operationalize stakeholder value proposition elicitation and reconciliation, one of the value-based software engineering approach elements (Boehm, 2003), and in this case, also improve the likelihood that the usability value of the system is considered throughout the software engineering cycle. Boehm suggests five approaches that are most effective for stakeholder value proposition reconciliation which include 1) expectation management, 2) visualization and trade-off analysis techniques, 3) prioritization, 4) groupware, and 5) business case analysis. As we will demonstrate, the collaborative usability testing process that we present in this chapter aligns well with these five approaches and successfully accommodates stakeholder value proposition elicitation.

The remainder of this chapter is structured as follows. The next two sections provide an overview on usability testing and collaboration tools and techniques that support collaborative usability testing. Section 10.4 discusses the research approach. Section 10.5 presents detailed information on e-CUP, the collaborative usability testing process, followed by Section 10.6 which discusses the application of the e-CUP process. Lastly, Section 10.7 concludes with a discussion on key insights from this research that relate to value-based software engineering.

10.2 Usability Testing

Whitefield et al. (1991) classify different usability evaluation methods based on how the user and system components are presented in the evaluation process (Figure 36). The system components can be *real* or *representational*. A real system concerns the physical presence of the computer and software system or an approximation of it, such as a prototype. Thus a system, prototype, or simulation all count as a real presence in the evaluation. A representational system refers to the specifications of the user's mental representation. For example, in questionnaires, interviews, or during code inspection, users work with their symbolic mental representations of the system. Users can also be *real* or *representational*. Real users refer to actual users or approximations of them, such as student subjects. Representational users concern descriptions or models of the user, such as a usability expert.

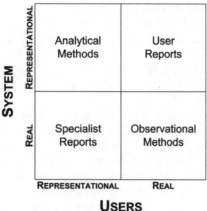

Fig. 36. Different usability evaluation methods

Based on these two dimensions, Whitefield et al. (1991) distinguish four categories of usability evaluation methods:

1. Analytical methods, where both system and user are representational. An example of an analytical method is a cognitive walk-through.
2. Specialist reports, which involves one or more people who are not real users assessing a version of the real system. It could be Human Computer Interaction (HCI) specialists who evaluate the design of a prototype using relevant handbooks, guidelines, or their own experiences. Typical methods include checklists, guidelines, walk-throughs, or heuristic evaluations by specialists.
3. User reports involve real users and their mental representations of the system. Methods typically involve questionnaires, interviews, or ranking methods.
4. Observational methods involve real users interacting with a real system. There are many such methods, ranging from informal observation of a single user to full-scale experimentation with appropriate numbers of subjects and control variables. Observations can be conducted in a real working environment (Newman and Lamming, 1995) or in usability laboratories (Nielsen, 1993). Other examples of observational methods include "thinking aloud logging" measuring actual user usage, and scenario-based usability evaluations.

The usability of many systems predominantly depends on the usability of the user interface. This is the part of the system through which the user interacts with the system either physically, perceptually, or conceptually (Nielsen and Mack, 1994). User interfaces are most commonly critiqued using the following four usability evaluation methods: heuristic evaluation, usability testing, software guidelines, and cognitive walk-throughs (Jeffries et al., 1991). In the HCI field, heuristic evaluation is one of the most commonly used methods. Compared to other methods, the heuristic evaluation method is a relatively low-cost quick method. Usability heuristic factors are a common set of criteria used to evaluate software usability. Heuristic evaluation involves having a user interface expert or a group of experts with internalized knowledge of good user interface design principles study an interface and, based on experience and training, identify potential areas of difficulty (Jeffries et al., 1991). Research has found that heuristic evaluation is the most effective among several evaluation methods in identifying large numbers of usability problems and serious problems, especially when conducted by usability specialists (Jeffries et al., 1991). However, heuristic evaluation can also be conducted by various stakeholders themselves after receiving a brief training (Lowry and Robert, 2003; Nielsen, 1993).

A number of researchers have addressed collaborative aspects of usability evaluation methods, especially with respect to heuristic evaluation. For example, Muller et al. (1998) propose a 'participatory' extension to Nielsen's heuristic evaluation technique. They argue that users (work domain experts) should be involved in the usability evaluation team. Nielsen and Molich (1990) found that a more comprehensive list of heuristic usability problems is identified when the number of evaluators consists of three to five people, rather than individuals working in isolation, who find significantly fewer usability problems. Lowry and Roberts (2003) illustrated how collaborative software can support heuristic evaluation in groups. They found that a group supported with collaborative software shared more information, generated fewer duplicate heuristic usability problems, and achieved consensus earlier. In addition, the usability evaluation results were in a format from which system developers could identify and respond to the more important problems sooner. However, Lowry and Roberts (2003) also note that it appears that the use of collaborative software does not reduce the number of heuristic evaluation errors or improve heuristic error categorization.

Like heuristic evaluation, it appears that usability testing could also benefit from a collaborative perspective. Usability testing aims to identify and correct system usability deficiencies prior to release to ensure that the systems are easy to learn and to use, that they are satisfying to use, and that they provide utility and functionality that are highly valued by the target user (Rubin, 1994). During usability testing, various stakeholders in a software engineering project such as future end users, usability experts, or developers may identify and plan to resolve usability problems collaboratively. Although several authors present general outlines and practical tips on collaborative usability testing, see e.g., (Hammontree et al., 1994; Lockwood, 2004), there appears to be a paucity of research in this area. In particular, the literature offers very few concrete guidelines or step-by-step directions on how to perform a collaborative usability evaluation workshop. What does the agenda of a usability evaluation workshop look like? Which meeting tools would be useful? How does one moderate such a workshop? Which brainstorming and discussion techniques are expected to yield useful feedback? In this chapter, we attempt to answer these and other questions by providing a detailed description of a collaborative usability testing process that enables usability experts to actively involve different stakeholders during usability testing workshops using state-of-the-art collaboration tools and techniques. Before presenting the actual process, we first discuss the collaboration technologies and techniques we used as a basis as well as the way in which the process was developed.

10.3 Collaboration Tools and Techniques for Usability Testing

Collaboration is the joint effort toward a goal (Kolfschoten et al., 2004). Collaboration is a fundamental part of organizational life. Organizations face problems so complex that no individual has the information and experience to solve a problem alone. Individuals form teams and work groups to share information, solve problems, make decisions, and monitor actions. Unfortunately, group work is often fraught with challenges that can lead to unproductive processes and failed efforts (Nunamaker et al., 1991). The difficulties of teamwork are many, from poor preparations to vague follow-through, from inarticulate goals to conflicting goals among the team members, from loud talkers to free riders.

To address such challenges, many organizations and work groups turn to groupware, technologies that support collaborative work (Ellis et al., 1991). Such technologies range from e-mail to video conferencing and workflow management systems. Group Support Systems (GSSs) are a special type of groupware. A GSS is a suite of collaborative software tools that can be used to focus and structure a team's deliberation, while reducing cognitive costs of communication and information access and minimizing distraction among teams that may consist of various stakeholders working collaboratively towards a goal (Davison and Briggs, 2000). GSSs are designed to improve the efficiency and effectiveness of meetings by offering a variety of tools to assist the group in the structuring of activities, generating ideas, and improving group communications (Nunamaker et al., 1991; Nunamaker et al., 1997). Although many commercial GSSs support distributed, anytime anyplace collaboration, most groups use the technology to support face-to-face workshops guided by a facilitator.

Groups can reap many potential benefits from using GSSs, for example broader and more equal participation, faster input to discussions, and less individual inhibitions to participate. Such benefits are often attributed to specific GSS functionalities: anonymity, parallel input, and group memory (Fjermestad and Hiltz, 1998):

1. *Parallel communication:* By using their own keyboard, participants can enter ideas in parallel. In other words, every participant can talk at the same time.
2. *Anonymous communication:* A GSS does not indicate which participant submitted which ideas or votes. In other words, participants communicate anonymously.
3. *Group memory:* During the meeting, the GSS stores all ideas and votes electronically.

There is a large body of research that shows that when used under the right conditions, work groups can translate the potential benefits of GSSs into real organizational value. For overviews of this research see (Fjermestad and Hiltz, 1998; Nunamaker et al., 1997). Previous studies on GSSs in general have reported labor cost reductions averaging 50% and reductions of project calendar days averaging 90% (Grohowski et al., 1990; Post, 1993; Vreede et al., 2003b). Within the domain of software engineering, GSSs have demonstrated their value to support such activities as requirements negotiation (Boehm et al., 2001; Grünbacher et al., 2004), prototype evaluation (Dean et al., 1998; Vreede and Dickson, 2000), software code inspection (Grünbacher et al., 2003, Genuchten et al., 2001), heuristic evaluation (Lowry and Roberts, 2003), and data modeling (Dean et al., 1998).

However, successful applications of GSSs are not a given. GSS represent a complex technology to assure success (Briggs et al., 2003a). There are many issues that may undermine the success of a GSS intervention (Vreede et al., 2003a; Vreede and Bruijn, 1999). The technology by itself is not the answer. What is needed is the purposeful design of effective collaboration processes followed by the selection or design of appropriate collaboration technologies to support these processes (Vreede and Briggs, 2005). To this end, many groups rely on experienced facilitators to design and conduct a GSS-supported collaboration process (Griffith et al., 1998; Niederman et al., 1996).

When people collaborate, they move from one group activity to another, and they accomplish the activity by moving through some combination of patterns of collaboration (Briggs et al., 2003a). Therefore, the design of an effective collaboration process should be based on the specific patterns of collaboration that one wants a group to go through so that it completes a particular group activity. We distinguish between five general patterns of collaboration (Briggs et al., 2003a):

1. *Diverge:* To move from a state of having fewer concepts to a state of having more concepts. The goal of divergence is for a group to create concepts that have not yet been considered. Brainstorming is an example of a divergence process.

2. *Converge:* To move from a state of having many concepts to a state of having a focus on, and understanding of, fewer concepts worthy of further attention. The goal of convergence is for a group to reduce their cognitive load by reducing the number of concepts they must address. A convergence process has at least two components. The first concerns filtering – eliminating some concepts from consideration. Filtering may be accomplished by eliminating concepts from consideration or by abstracting multiple specific concepts into a more general concept. The second concerns understanding – establishing shared meaning for the concepts under consideration. This is important as different people frequently understand the same term to represent different concepts.

3. *Organize:* To move from less to more understanding of the relationships among the concepts. The goal of organization is to reduce the effort of a follow-on activity. The group might, for example, organize a mixed list of ideas into a number of categories or arrange them into a hierarchical structure.

4. *Evaluate:* To move from less to more understanding of the benefit of concepts toward attaining a goal relative to one or more criteria. The goal of evaluation is to focus a discussion or inform a group's choice based on a judgment of the worth of a set of concepts with respect to a set of task-relevant criteria. For example, an evaluation process may involve having a team use a five-point scale to rate the merits of a set of alternatives.

5. *Build Consensus:* To move from having less to having more agreement among stakeholders on courses of action. The goal of consensus building is to let a group of mission-critical stakeholders arrive at mutually acceptable commitments. For example, a consensus building process may allow a group to exchange arguments on a disputed issue leading to an outcome that all members subscribe to.

When recording a design of a collaboration process that invokes a sequence of these patterns of collaboration, the specific facilitation interventions to create these patterns should be packaged such that they can be successfully recreated. This can be achieved by recording the collaboration process as a sequence of thinkLets (Vreede and Briggs, 2005). ThinkLets are the smallest unit of intellectual capital required to create a single repeatable, predictable pattern of collaboration among people working toward a goal (Briggs et al., 2003a). Each thinkLet captures everything a facilitator has to prepare and do to invoke a particular pattern of collaboration. A thinkLet frames a facilitation intervention in terms of three components: a tool, a configuration of that tool, and a script (Briggs et al., 2003a). The tool concerns the specific technology used to create the pattern of collaboration – this can range from "post-it" notes and pencils to sophisticated collaboration technologies such as GSSs. The configuration defines how the tool is prepared (e.g., projected on a public screen), set up (e.g., configured so all contributions are anonymous), and loaded with data before the start of the thinkLet (e.g., a set of questions to which people must respond). The script concerns everything a facilitator would have to do and say to a group to move it through the thinkLet.

Table 16. Examples of thinkLets

Pattern	ThinkLet	Purpose
Diverge	DealersChoice	To have a group generate ideas on assigned topics.
	LeafHopper	To have a group brainstorm ideas regarding a number of topics simultaneously.
	TheLobbyist	To let people briefly advocate their position on complex issues before casting their vote.
Converge	FastFocus	To have the group members extract a list of key issues from a broad set of brainstorming results and assure that they agree on the meaning and phrasing of the items on the resulting list.
Organize	RichRelations	To have a group uncover possible categories in which a number of existing concepts can be organized.
Evaluate	StrawPoll	To have a group evaluate a number of concepts with respect to a single criterion.
Build Consensus	MoodRing	To continuously track the level of consensus within the group regarding a certain issue.
	CrowBar	To have the group identify and discuss the reasons for a lack of consensus on certain issues.

ThinkLets can be used as building blocks in the design of collaboration processes (Kolfschoten et al., 2004). A sequence of thinkLets represents a design for a collaboration process. The collaborative usability testing process was developed using a limited set of thinkLets (see Table 16 for some examples). Before presenting this process in detail, the next section describes the way in which we designed and fine-tuned it.

10.4 Research Approach

The development and fine-tuning of our collaborative usability testing process was executed following an action research strategy. Action research has the dual intention of improving practice and contributing to theory and knowledge (Argyris et al., 2004; Checkland, 1981). We followed the action research process proposed by Zuber-Skerritt (1991) that states that an action research study may consist of four activities that can be carried out over several iterations. The first activity, 'Plan', concerns exploration of the research site and the preparation of the intervention. Next, 'Act' refers to the actual intervention made by the researcher. The 'Observe' activity concerns the collection of data during and after the actual intervention to enable evaluation. Finally, the 'Reflect' activity analyzes the collected data and infers conclusions regarding the intervention that may feed into the 'Plan' activity of a new iteration.

Action research was employed for several reasons. First, action research is especially appropriate to address 'how to' research questions. Our research aimed to explore and develop ways in which collaboration techniques and tools could support collaborative usability testing. We wanted to develop a collaboration process and evaluate its application in practice. Second, the continuous design and evaluation of a collaboration process was considered too complex to be studied in a constructed setting. Third, action research is very well suited for continuous learning. It allows researchers to evaluate and improve their problem solving techniques or theories during a series of interventions. In our research, we ran a number of usability testing workshops using the repeatable collaboration process. The experiences from each workshop resulted in minor and major changes to the collaboration process that were effectuated immediately. Finally, as far as we knew at the initiation of the project, very little work had been conducted on the use of GSS, thinkLets, and designing a repeatable collaboration process in the context of usability testing.

To allow for analysis and reflection on our research activities, we collected data from a number of quantitative and qualitative sources:

- *Direct observation.* The researchers notes of incidents, participants' remarks, and events that conveyed critical information.
- *Interviews.* The researchers held short open-ended interviews with a number of workshop participants.
- *Questionnaires.* Each workshop participant was asked to fill out a questionnaire afterward in order to measure this perception on a number of issues.
- *Session data.* The results of each group session were stored electronically. These files were used to trace the flow of information exchange during the sessions, typical meeting behavior, and other events.

Observation notes, interview results, and questionnaire data were kept in a research diary. Both researchers contributed personal insights to this diary as well. The variety of data sources gave a rich representation and enabled an in-depth reflection on our experiences with the collaboration process. The role of the researchers was that of observer and facilitator. Both researchers worked together in designing and refining the collaborative usability process. One researcher facilitated each of the workshops. This included preparing an agenda for each workshop and moderating it. The other researcher provided content expertise on the application that was the topic of the usability test. This researcher guided the application's development and could therefore readily answer any application-related questions during the workshops.

10.5. The e-CUP process

The collaborative usability testing process we developed is called e-CUP (electronic-Collaboration Usability Process). E-CUP is a repeatable process that a usability practitioner can execute to perform and facilitate collaborative usability testing. The process is executed in two steps: Preparation and workshops. During the preparation, the usability practitioner has to determine two issues (see Figure 37):

- *Determination of relevant usability aspects.* The usability practitioner has to decide which usability aspects to include in the usability testing process, e.g., ease of use, user control and freedom, consistency and standards, or help and documentation (Nielsen, 1993). This decision is informed by literature on usability and the characteristics of the system under investigation.
- *Determination of use scenarios.* The usability practitioner has to develop one or more use scenarios that the stakeholders will execute during the usability testing. Their execution of these scenarios will trigger the stakeholders' usability feedback.

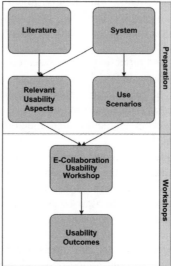

Fig. 37. The collaborative usability testing process

The workshop part of e-CUP consists of a series of thinkLets that lead the group of stakeholders through a structured sequence of activities in which the stakeholders test the system's usability and provide detailed feedback. The process is depicted in Figure 38. Each activity is represented by a rectangle that identifies the activity (bottom-right part), the thinkLet used (top part), and the pattern of collaboration that is created (left part). Arrows represent the direction of the process flow.

problem phase   **solution phase**

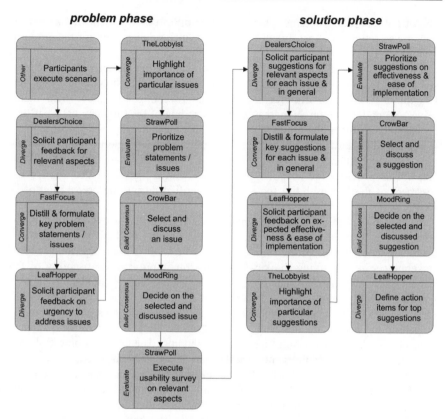

Fig. 38. The e-CUP workshop process

An e-CUP workshop consists of two phases. The *problem phase* starts with the stakeholders executing a use scenario (i.e., testing the system) with the system under investigation. Next their feedback is solicited with respect to relevant usability aspects that the usability practitioner has determined in advance. To this end, the stakeholders are presented with a sequence of brainstorming questions, each addressing a particular usability aspect. Each time they enter a response, a new question is presented to them. During the course of this activity, earlier responses are visible for stakeholders for ideas.

During the next activity, stakeholders identify the key usability problems based on the brainstorming results. This is done by having individual stakeholders distill the key usability problems from a subset of the brainstorming results. The description of each usability problem is discussed and fine-tuned resulting in a meaningful, concise statement of the problem that all stakeholders understand. The resulting list of usability problems is then prepared for prioritization. To this end, two activities take place. First, the stakeholders get the opportunity to share their thoughts through the GSS on the urgency with which these problems have to be addressed. Second, each stakeholder is allowed to briefly and verbally lobby for one of the usability problems. Then the group prioritizes the identified key problems by selecting the most urgent ones. The results are displayed for the group to review.

Based on the results, differences of opinion among the participants are addressed during two consensus building activities. First, the stakeholders are triggered to explore reasons for disagreements without revealing how they voted themselves. Second, based on an increased understanding of the (urgency of) a particular usability problem, the group takes a new vote on it. Finally, the problem phase is concluded by having the participants fill out a usability questionnaire that collects the stakeholders' assessment of the system's usability in a number of relevant areas. This provides the usability practitioner with a high-level quantitative assessment of the key usability focus areas identified during the preparation of e-CUP.

In the problem phase of e-CUP stakeholders can identify which usability problems have to be fixed. Often there are different solutions available to resolve these problems. The purpose of the *solution phase* of e-CUP is to engage the group of stakeholders in identifying the key directions for improving the usability of the system under investigation. The phase starts by asking the stakeholders to identify possible usability improvements in a number of relevant areas. These may be directly related to the usability problems identified in the previous phase. From the brainstorming results, the stakeholders converge on the key improvement suggestions and work on establishing shared understanding. The brainstorming and convergence procedures are the same as at the start of the problem phase.

Next, the stakeholders' feedback is solicited regarding the expected costs and benefits of implementing each improvement – to the extent that the stakeholders are capable of making such an assessment. They give their feedback by entering it as comments to the individual improvements. Before they actually prioritize the improvements in terms of expected effectiveness and ease of implementation, each stakeholder has the opportunity to verbally highlight the improvement he favors most. The results are displayed for all stakeholders to see. Differences of opinion are addressed using the same two consensus building activities as in the problem phase. The solution phase is concluded by having the stakeholders identify a number of further action items for the top priority improvements. They do this by entering the action items as comments to the particular improvements.

Overall, e-CUP has three distinct features. First, it moves the stakeholders from identifying *problems* to thinking about *solutions*. Yet, a usability practitioner can also decide to start the process in the solution phase if certain usability problems are defined beforehand. Second, both phases move the stakeholders from *divergence* (brainstorming) to *convergence* (clearly defining key contributions). The reason for this is allowing stakeholders to share all the information they wish to, yet at the same time making sure that the usability practitioner will leave the workshop with a clear understanding of what the group as a whole thinks are the key issues. Finally, in both phases, the usability practitioner has the possibility to let the group not only *identify* key issues, but also *prioritize* them. This enables the usability practitioner to walk away with a prioritized 'to-do' list.

10.6 Application of e-CUP

In this section we first introduce the application that was evaluated using the e-CUP process. Then we present background information on the series of workshops that were executed following the e-CUP process. Finally we reflect on the experiences and findings from these workshops.

The Application: STATPack

The e-CUP process was evaluated in the field by testing the usability of STAT-Pack: the *S*ecure *T*elecommunications *A*pplication *T*erminal *Pack*age. STATPack is an ongoing effort to address critical health communication and biosecurity needs in Nebraska. STATPack is a secure, dedicated, HIPPA-compliant, Web-based network system that supports telecommunication connectivity of clinical health laboratories in Nebraska to the Nebraska Public Health Lab (NPHL). Based on client/server technology, the system operates in a distributed environment connecting state-wide health laboratories. This connectivity allows for immediate communication and data transfer of urgent health information by transmitting images and text. For example, when a rural laboratory is processing a "suspicious" organism growing from a culture, STATPack allows for immediate consultation with the NPHL. The system was intended to help clinical laboratories in Nebraska become more prepared for a bioterrorism event or other public health emergencies.

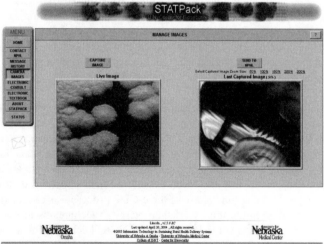

Fig. 39. STATPack can transmit images of cultures

STATPack consists of a computer terminal which includes a flat screen, a virtually indestructible and sanitizable keyboard, speakers and a high-resolution digital camera that can capture images of specimen. Along with descriptive text, these images can be sent to the NPHL for consultation (Figure 39). Should a serious situation need to be communicated to the labs, STATPack enables NPHL to send notices to each lab including an audible computer alarm. It was critical that STATPack provide an easy to learn user interface for the health laboratorians and the NPHL staff. Currently, STATPack has been deployed to six Nebraska health laboratories.

The STATPack Usability Workshops

A series of three workshops was organized to evaluate various usability aspects of STATPack using e-CUP (Table 17). Each workshop had its own agenda and purpose, but all three followed a continuous part of the e-CUP process. Each workshop was facilitated by the same facilitator (one of the researchers).

Table 17. Background information on the workshops

Workshop	Stakeholders	Focus	Number of stakeholders	Length (hrs)
1	Usability analysts	Problems	12	1.25
2	System Advocates and Developers	Solutions	6	2.00
3	End Users	Solutions	4	1.50

The three workshops involved different types of stakeholders. Stakeholders in the first workshop were undergraduate students enrolled in an HCI class. They represented usability analysts as they had received considerable training in usability guidelines and evaluation techniques and had completed four usability assessments before looking at STATPack. Given the stakeholders' expertise, the first workshop focused on the identification of key usability problems with STATPack, based on the execution of three use scenarios. Therefore, only the first phase of e-CUP was executed.

Stakeholders in the second workshop consisted of people working at the NPHL and people responsible for the development of STATPack. The goal of the second workshop was to identify functional and presentation enhancements from a high-level perspective. At the beginning of the workshop, the stakeholders went through a general use scenario as most of them were familiar with the application. Given time constraints and the technical and domain expertise of this group of stakeholders, only the second phase of the e-CUP process was executed.

The stakeholders in the third workshop were lab technicians in a regional hospital health lab who had some knowledge of STATPack. The goal of this workshop was to identify functional and presentation enhancements from an end user perspective. At the beginning of the workshop, stakeholders went through a short general use scenario to refresh their memory of using the application. As we felt that the end users were better equipped to provide solutions in their own language and terminology that would fit their work environment best, only the second phase of the e-CUP process was executed.

Fig. 40. STATPack e-CUP workshops

The first two workshops were executed at the University of Nebraska at Omaha (Figure 40). A meeting room with a horseshoe-shaped table was equipped with ten networked laptops running a GSS (GroupSystems Workgroup Edition 3.4) and with four STATPack clients. An additional laptop was attached to a projector, displaying aggregated information from the group. Stakeholders were seated one per laptop for GSS use and approximately two per STATPack client for scenario execution. The third workshop was conducted in an actual lab environment (Figure 40). The stakeholders shared the single STATPack client that was present in the lab. Each stakeholder had a laptop for GSS use. There was no projector to display group results, as the workspace where the STATPack client is located was too small.

Experiences from the Workshops

During the execution of the workshops, a number of observations were made with respect to the structure of the process and specific thinkLets that were chosen. Some of these insights led to minor modifications in the process after the first and second workshop. Thus, we stayed true to the action research cycle: observation and reflection occurred before a new intervention was planned and executed.

From the stakeholders' perspective the e-CUP workshops appeared to be successful. Their feedback indicated that they were satisfied and considered the workshops to be very useful. The stakeholders in all workshops liked working with the GSS, although in some instances there was some (initial) apprehension. For example, the stakeholders in the third workshop were a little hesitant at first. However, after a few minutes of exposure they appeared to enjoy working with the GSS. We used a validated meeting satisfaction questionnaire (Briggs et al., 2003b) to measure the stakeholders' perceived satisfaction in each workshop on a scale of 1-7, 7 most positive. The reported values in Table 18 are compound values for four questions per satisfaction construct.

Table 18. Satisfaction in the e-CUP workshops

		Workshop		
		1	*2*	*3*
Satisfaction with process	Avg	5.3	5.8	6.6
	Std	*1.2*	*1.0*	*0.5*
Satisfaction with outcomes	Avg	4.7	5.5	6.3
	Std	*1.1*	*0.8*	*0.6*

As the results show, the stakeholders had rather positive levels of satisfaction. Especially the end users in the final workshop were very satisfied with the process and outcomes of their meeting. They felt empowered as they had been able to share all feedback that they considered relevant and crucial. The results further show that satisfaction levels, both with process and outcomes, are higher for stakeholders that have a personal interest in the application, i.e., stakeholders in workshops 2 and 3. Stakeholders in the second workshop especially applauded the efficiency of the process and their ability to address all issues they felt strongly about.

From the developers' perspective, the workshops yielded valuable feedback that was both detailed and actionable. Table 19 gives an overview of the productivity in each of the three workshops in terms of the number of usability contributions that were generated by the stakeholders.

Overall, the stakeholders provided a fair number of contributions in the relatively short time that was provided during the workshops. Especially the number of unique contributions is encouraging. Upon closer examination of the productivity figures, it appeared that there is a relatively small difference between the total number of contributions and the number of unique contributions. Our observations and stakeholders' feedback suggest that this was probably due to the fact that the stakeholders brought different perspectives and opinions to the workshop. Stakeholders indicated that they had had sufficient time to share their feedback. It also appeared that the stakeholders' productivity increased with increased familiarity with the application. The stakeholders in the second workshop had been involved most directly in the development of the STATPack and hence had the most thorough understanding of it.

Table 19. Productivity in the e-CUP workshops

	Workshop		
	1	*2*	*3*
Total contributions	84	88	33
Total per stakeholder	*7.0*	*14.7*	*8.3*
Unique contributions	76	79	27
Total unique per stakeholder	*6.3*	*13.2*	*6.8*
Converged contributions	16	22	5
Converged per stakeholder	*1.3*	*3.7*	*1.3*

It was also interesting to see that the number of converged contributions represents a considerable reduction compared to the number of unique contributions. Stakeholders' feedback and analysis of the workshop data suggest that this was due to a number of reasons. First, some converged ideas were formulated on a higher level of abstraction, thereby encompassing several unique brainstorming contributions. Second, the converged contributions did not cover the complete range of unique contributions caused by the somewhat limited time for the convergence activity during the workshops (especially workshop 1). Third, the stakeholders indicated that they did not find each unique contribution important enough to become part of the set of 'key' (converged) contributions. Yet from the experiences in the three workshops, it appears that the convergence activities are the most crucial part of the process with respect to creating high quality results. Although most of the brainstorming contributions were very useful, they were also often very sketchy and somewhat hard to understand. The convergence activities took care of these shortcomings by allowing the group to arrive at a joint focus and joint understanding of key usability issues or suggestions. It may not be surprising that the convergence activities took the most time in the process. Also, it was felt that it required the most 'facilitation skill' as it often involved animated discussions between stakeholders.

Finally, in terms of the applicability of the e-CUP process it was interesting to find confirmation that the process can accommodate different usability perspectives. The first two STATPack workshops focused on different usability aspects: the first dealt with more general usability aspects, whereas the second focused more on a number of detailed issues. The general structure of the e-CUP process allows for a set of relevant usability aspects to be selected during the preparation step for a particular workshop and 'inserted' into the process flow by the usability practitioner. In other words, the e-CUP process appears to be useful in collaborative settings to test a broad range of usability aspects. However, we also found that the usability practitioner has to exercise considerable care in this part of the preparation: Analysis of the brainstorming contributions revealed that stakeholders' feedback on specific (detailed) usability questions appeared to be more actionable for the STATPack development team than feedback on more general issues. This implies that usability practitioners have to pay sufficient attention to formulating detailed or descriptive questions during the preparation of the workshop.

10.7 Conclusion

Evaluating a new application's usability is crucial in systems development. It is often done collaboratively, involving groups of current or future users, usability experts, systems designers, and/or system owners. This presents an interesting challenge: what should a repeatable collaborative usability testing process look like? The goal of our research was to design such a collaborative usability testing process, called e-CUP, and evaluate it in the field. We did so in the context of a series of usability workshops focused on the evaluation of a particular application,

STATPack. The results indicate that e-CUP is promising in terms of workshop productivity, stakeholder satisfaction, and applicability for a broad range of usability aspects.

Moreover, e-CUP substantiates Boehm's (2003) five approaches for effective stakeholder value proposition elicitation in different ways:

- *Expectation Management*: During the e-CUP workshops, various stakeholders have the opportunity to get acquainted with other stakeholders' suggestions and requests. E-CUP facilitates awareness of each stakeholder's desired usability capabilities of the system. This awareness is further enhanced by allowing stakeholders to lobby for and debate over the priority with which certain usability problem statements and improvements should be dealt with. The results of the collaborative prioritization of the usability problems and improvements helps the stakeholders to understand which action items will receive precedence over others.

- *Visualization and Trade-off Analysis*: e-CUP is executed using scenarios and prototype of the system under usability investigation. This way, comments and issues regarding the system that are raised by the stakeholders can immediately be corroborated. For example, the STATPack prototype's presence during the workshop allowed stakeholders to obtain a mutual understanding of which aspects of the application were the most important and achievable. One illustration concerns the need for improvement of the images captured by the camera. This was clearly visible to all. This improvement need 'bubbled up' during the discussion and ended up as one of the top improvement priorities. Using a common scenario and the stakeholders' possibility to actively interact with the tested system provides a foundation for discussing the key usability problems and more achievable usability improvements. With e-CUP this is further supported by allowing the stakeholders to vote on prioritizing improvements in terms of necessity (effectiveness) and ease of implementation (cost). This allows stakeholders to identify the 'low hanging fruits' (Boehm et al., 2001).

- *Prioritization*: e-CUP, as stated above, accommodates the expression of preferences by stakeholders. The individual preferences are combined so that all stakeholders can observe areas of sufficient or insufficient consensus. This insight facilitates clarification and consensus building through discussion. The process results in an agreed upon priority list of usability action items.

- *Groupware*: The workshop part of e-CUP is completely supported with GSS. The thinkLets that together make up the process specify exactly which GSS tools have to be used and how they have to be configured. The use of a GSS enables productive brainstorming, discussion, and win-win negotiation of conflict situations during the session. This is consistent with earlier research on GSS in value-based software engineering; see, e.g., (Boehm et al., 2001; Dean et al., 1998).

- *Business Case Analysis*: As stated above, e-CUP accommodates the stakeholders to take both expected effectiveness and ease of implementation into account when stating their preferences. The results provide stakeholders with a quick and efficient way to consider the best return on investment of proposed action items.

Notwithstanding the promising results, there are a number of limitations that have to be considered when interpreting our findings. First, the e-CUP process was designed in an evolutionary fashion. After each workshop, slight changes were made that were effectuated in the next workshop. Therefore, the process presented should be considered to be a first release. Future modifications and enhancements are expected. Second, we were only able to evaluate e-CUP in a limited number of workshops and with a limited number of end users (workshop 3). It may well be that future evaluation with more end users will lead to additional insights and changes to the process. Third, we have only been able to test the process with a single system, STATPack. Usability tests of other systems will have to be performed to allow for a more substantial evaluation of the process. Finally, the e-CUP process itself should not be considered to be without limitations. The quality of the process depends on the quality of the workshop participants. It is recommended to combine e-CUP with other, complimentary, usability testing approaches to accomplish a thorough evaluation of a system's usability.

We envision the following directions for future research. First, we are planning to explore the applicability of the e-CUP process for other applications and systems. Second, it would be interesting to study the e-CUP process' outcome quality compared to 'traditional' usability testing approaches. This could, for example, focus on content analysis of the results of a usability test of the same application using e-CUP and other approaches.

References

(Argyris et al., 2004) Argyris, C., Putnam, R., MacLain Smith, D.: *Action science.* (Jossey-Bass, San Francisco 2004)

(Bevan and Macleod, 1994) Bevan, N., Macleod, M.: Usability measurement in context. Behavior and Information Technology. **13**(1&2), pp 132–145 (1994)

(Boehm, 2003) Boehm, B. W.: Value-Based Software Engineering. Software Engineering Notes. **28**(2), pp 1–12 (2003)

(Boehm et al., 2001) Boehm, B. W., Grünbacher, P., Briggs, R.O.: Developing Groupware for Requirements Negotiation: Lessons Learned. IEEE Software. **18**(3), pp 46–55 (2001)

(Briggs et al., 2003a) Briggs, R.O, Vreede, G.J. de, Nunamaker, J.F. Jr.: Collaboration engineering with thinkLets to pursue sustained success with Group Support Systems. Journal of MIS. **19**(4), pp 31–63 (2003)

(Briggs et al., 2003b) Briggs, R.O., Vreede, G.J. de, Reinig, B.A.: A Theory and Measurement of Meeting Satisfaction. In: *Proceedings of the 37th Hawaiian International Conference on System Sciences,* ed by Sprague, R.H. Jr. (IEEE Computer Society Press, Los Alamitos 2003), pp 25–32

(Checkland, 1981) Checkland, P.B.: *Systems thinking, systems practice.* (Wiley, Chichester 1981)

(Davison and Briggs, 2000) Davison, R.M., Briggs, R.O.: GSS for Presentation Support. Communications of the ACM. **43**(9), pp 91–97 (2000)

(Dean et al., 1998) Dean, D.L., Lee, J.D., Pendergast, M.O., Hickey, A.M., Nunamaker, J.F. Jr.: Enabling the effective involvement of multiple users: methods and tools for collaborative software engineering. Journal of Management Information Systems. **14**(3), pp 179–222 (1998)

(Ellis et al., 1991) Ellis, C.A., Gibbs, S.J., Rein, G.L.: Groupware: Some issues and experiences. Communications of the ACM. **34**(1), pp 38–58 (1991)

(Fjermestad and Hiltz, 1998) Fjermestad, J., Hiltz, S.R.: An assessment of group support systems experimental research: Methodology and results. Journal of Management Information Systems. **15**(3), pp 7–149 (1998)

(Fruhling and Lee, 2004) Fruhling, A., Lee, S.: Examining HCI usability factors affecting consumers' trust in e-health services. In: *Proceedings of the Hawaii International Conferences on Computer Sciences*, ed by Gregson, T., Yang, D., Burg, E. (Hawaii International Conferences on Computer Sciences, ISSN #1545–6722 2004), pp 141–158

(Genuchten et al., 2001) Genuchten, M. van, Dijk, C. van, Scholten, H., Vogel, D.: Using group support systems for software inspections. IEEE Software. **18**(3), pp 60–65 (2001)

(Griffith et al., 1998) Griffith, T., Fuller, M., Northcraft, G.: Facilitator Influence in GSS. Information Systems Research. **9**(1), pp 20–36 (1998)

(Grohowski et al., 1990) Grohowski, R., McGoff, C., Vogel, D., Martz, B., and Nunamaker, J.F. Jr.: Implementing electronic meeting systems at IBM: Lessons learned and success factors. MIS Quarterly. **14**(4), pp 327–345 (1990)

(Grünbacher et al., 2004) Grünbacher, P., Halling, M., Biffl, S., Kitapci, H., Boehm, B. W.: Integrating Collaborative Processes and Quality Assurance Techniques: Experiences from Requirements Negotiation. Journal of Management Information Systems. **20**(4), pp 9–29 (2004)

(Grünbacher et al., 2003) Grünbacher, P., Halling, M., and Biffl, S.: An empirical study on groupware support for software inspection meetings. In: *Proceedings of 18th IEEE International Conference on Automated Software Engineering*, Montreal, Canada, (IEEE CS Press, Los Alamitos 2003), pp 4–11

(Hammontree et al., 1994) Hammontree, M., Weiler, P., Nayak, N.: Remote Usability Testing. Interactions. July. **1**(3), pp 21–25 (1994)

(Jacobson et al., 1992) Jacobson, I., Christerson, M., Jonsson, P., Overgaard, G.: *Object-Oriented Software Engineering – A Use Case Driven Approach*. (Addison-Wesley, Harlow, UK 1992)

(Jeffries et al., 1991) Jeffries, R., Miller, J.R., Wharton, C., Uyeda, K.M.: User interface evaluation in the real world. Communications of the ACM. **44**(3), pp 199–124 (1991)

(Kolfschoten et al., 2004) Kolfschoten, G.L, Briggs, R.O., Appelman, J.H., Vreede, G.J. de: ThinkLets as Building Blocks for Collaboration Processes: A Further Conceptualization. In: *Proceedings of CRIWG2004*, ed by Vreede, G.J. de, Guerrero, L., Marin, G., Costa Rica, Lecture Notes in Computer Science vol 3198 (Springer, Berlin Heidelberg New York 2004)

(Lecerof and Paterno, 1998) Lecerof, A., Paterno, F.: Automatic support for usability evaluation. IEEE Transactions on Software Engineering. **24:** pp 863–887 (1998)

(Lockwood, 2004) Lockwood, L.: Collaborative Usability Inspections: Finding Usability Defects Efficiently and Cost-Effectively. In: *Proceedings of the 2004 Usability Professionals' Association Conf.* (2004)

(Lowry and Roberts, 2003) Lowry, P., Roberts, T.: Improving the usability evaluation technique, heuristic evaluation, through the use of collaborative software. In: *Proceedings of the 9th Americas Conference on Information Systems (AMCIS)*. 2203–2211 (2003)

(Mayhew, 1999) Mayhew, D.J.: *The Usability Engineering Lifecycle* (Morgan Kaufman, San Francisco 1999)

(Muller et al., 1998) Muller, M., Matheson, L., Page, C., Gallup, R.: Participatory Heuristic Evaluation. Interactions. September–October, pp 13–18 (1998)

(Newman and Lamming, 1995) Newman, W.M., Lamming, M.G.: *Interactive system design* (Addison-Wesley, Cambridge, MA 1995)

(Niederman et al., 1996) Niederman, F., Beise, C.M., Beranek, P.M.: Issues and Concerns about Computer-Supported Meetings: The Facilitator's Perspective. MIS Quarterly. **20**(1), pp 1–22 (1996)

(Nielsen, 1993) Nielsen, J.: *Usability Engineering* (Academic Press, New York 1993)

(Nielsen and Mack, 1994) Nielsen, J., Mack, R.: *Usability inspection methods* (Wiley, New York 1994)

(Nielsen and Molich, 1990) Nielsen, J., Molich, R.: Teaching user interface design based on usability engineering. ACM SIGCHI Bulletin. **21**(1), pp 45–48 (1990)

(Nunamaker et al., 1991) Nunamaker, J., Dennis, A., Valacich, J., Vogel, D., George, J.: Electronic Meeting Systems to Support Group Work. Communications of the ACM. **34**(7), pp 40–61 (1991)

(Nunamaker et al., 1997) Nunamaker, J.F. Jr., Briggs, R.O., Mittleman, D., Vogel, D., Balthazard, P.A.: Lessons from a Dozen Years of Group Support Systems Research: A Discussion of Lab and Field Findings. Journal of MIS. **13**(3), pp 163–207 (1997)

(Post, 1993) Post, B.Q.: A Business Case Framework for Group Support Technology. Journal of MIS. **9**(3), pp 7–26 (1993)

(Rubin, 1994) Rubin, J.: *Handbook of Usability Testing* (Wiley, New York 1994)

(Vreede and Briggs, 2005) Vreede, G.J. de, Briggs, R.O.: Collaboration Engineering: Designing Repeatable Processes for High-Value Collaborative Tasks. In: *Proceedings of the 38th Hawaiian International Conference on System Sciences,* ed by Sprague, R.H. Jr. (IEEE CS Press, Los Alamitos 2005) p 17c

(Vreede and Bruijn, 1999) Vreede, G.J. de, Bruijn, H. de: Exploring the Boundaries of Successful GSS Application: Supporting Inter-Organizational Policy Networks. DataBase. **30**(3–4), pp 111–131 (1999)

(Vreede and Dickson, 2000) Vreede, G.J. de, G.W. Dickson: Using GSS to Support Designing Organizational Processes and Information Systems: An Action Research Study on Collaborative Business Engineering. Group Decision and Negotiation. **9**(2), pp 161–183 (2000)

(Vreede et al., 2003a) Vreede, G.J. de, Davison, R., Briggs, R.O.: How A Silver Bullet May Lose Its Shine – Learning from Failures with Group Support Systems. Communications of the ACM. **46**(8), pp 96–101 (2003)

(Vreede et al., 2003b) Vreede, G.J. de, Vogel, D.R., Kolfschoten, G., Wien, J.S.: Fifteen years of in-situ GSS use: A comparison across time and national boundaries. In: *Proceedings of the 36th Hawaiian International Conference on System Sciences,* ed by Sprague, R.H. Jr. (IEEE Computer Society Press, Los Alamitos 2003), pp 9–17

(Whitefield et al., 1991) Whitefield, A., Wilson, F., Dowell, J.: A framework for human factors evaluation. Behavior and Information Technology. **10**(1), pp 65–79 (1991)

(Zuber-Skerritt, 1991) Zuber-Skerritt, O.: *Action research for change and development* (Gower Publishing, Aldershot 1991)

Author Biographies

Ann L. Fruhling is an Assistant Professor in the Computer Science department in the College of Information Science and Technology at the University of Nebraska at Omaha (UNO). Dr. Fruhling's research includes human-computer interaction usability, user interface design, software engineering methodologies, e-health trust issues, and software engineering solutions for biosecurity decision support applications. Previously, she was the Director of the Computer Information Management and Telecommunications Systems Management programs at College of Saint Mary (CSM). Prior to her academic career, Dr. Fruhling was an information technology professional at Texas Instruments, Mutual of Omaha, Commercial Federal Savings Bank, and AT&T.

Gert-Jan de Vreede is a Professor at the Department of Information Systems & Quantitative Analysis at the University of Nebraska at Omaha where he is director of the Peter Kiewit Institute's Consortium for Collaboration Engineering. He is also affiliated with the Faculty of Technology, Policy and Management of Delft University of Technology in the Netherlands from where he received his PhD. His research focuses on the application, adoption, and diffusion of collaboration technology in organizations, the development of repeatable collaboration processes, facilitation of group meetings, and the application of collaboration technology in different socio-cultural environments.

11 Value-Based Management of Software Testing

Rudolf Ramler, Stefan Biffl and Paul Grünbacher

Abstract: Testing is one of the most resource-intensive activities in software development and consumes between 30 and 50% of total development costs according to many studies. Testing is however often not organized to maximize business value and not aligned with a project's mission. Path, branch, instruction, mutation, scenario, or requirement testing usually treat all aspects of software as equally important, while in practice 80% of the value often comes from 20% of the software. In order to maximize the return of investment gained from software testing, the management of testing needs to maximize its value contribution. In this chapter we motivate the need for value-based testing, describe practices supporting the management of value-based testing, outline a framework for value-based test management, and illustrate the framework with an example.

Keywords: Value-based software engineering, value-based testing, cost of testing, benefits of testing, test management.

11.1 Introduction

Testing is one of the most important and most widely used approaches for validation and verification (V&V). V&V aims at comprehensively analyzing and testing software to determine that it performs the intended functions correctly, to ensure that it performs no unintended functions, and to measure its quality and reliability (Wallace and Fujii, 1989). According to IEEE 610.12 (1990) testing is defined as "an activity in which a system or component is executed under specified conditions, the results are observed or recorded, and an evaluation is made of some aspect of the system or component."

Testing is widely used in practice and plays a central role in the quality assurance strategies of many organizations. As software pervades more and more critical tasks and affects everyday life, security, and well being of millions of people (Ferscha and Mattern, 2004), the importance of testing will increase in the future. Studies show that testing already consumes between 30 and 50% of software development costs (Beizer, 1990). Even higher percentages are not uncommon for safety-critical systems. Finding more efficient ways to perform effective testing is therefore a key challenge in testing (Harrold, 2000).

Managing software testing based on value considerations promises to tackle increasing testing costs and required effort. Value-based test management could also provide guidance to better align testing investments with project objectives and business value. In Chapter 1, Boehm presents an impressive example of potential test cost savings (on project level as well as on global scale) by focusing testing on the most valuable aspects. The example illustrates that with an investment-oriented focus on testing 7% of the customer billing types (1 in 15) achieved 50% of the benefits of testing the software. Completely testing the system requires a constantly increasing effort and, due to decreasing marginal benefits, results in a negative return on investment. Although a "100% tested" status is not a practical goal, there is still room for a considerable amount of improvement and savings by better adjusting testing to its value contribution.

The motivation for value-based software engineering comes from the fact that "much of current software engineering practice and research is done in a value-neutral setting, in which every requirement, use case, object, and defect is treated as equally important" (Boehm, 2003). This is especially true for testing, where its indirect contribution to product value leads to a value-neutral perception of testing. The common separation of concerns between development and testing exacerbates the problem. Testing is often reduced to a purely technical issue leaving the close relationship between testing and business decisions unlinked and the potential value contribution of testing unexploited.

The objectives of this chapter are to motivate the need for value-based management of testing, to explain its underlying elements, to discuss existing practices that support value-based testing, and to outline a general framework for value-based test management. The remainder of this chapter is thus structured as follows. In Section 11.2 we discuss test management under the light of its value contribution. In Section 11.3 we describe existing practices that support value-based testing. Section 11.4 depicts a value-based test management framework using an example for illustration. An outlook on further research directions closes the chapter.

11.2 Taking a Value-Based Perspective on Testing

The objectives of value-based verification and validation are defined as "*ensuring that a software solution satisfies its value objectives*" and "*organizing V&V tasks to operate as an investment activity*" (Boehm and Huang, 2003). What are the contributions of testing if we look at it from a value-based perspective? Fundamentally, we can consider two dimensions: The internal dimension of testing covers costs and benefits of testing. The external dimension emphasizes the opportunities and risks of the future system that have to be addressed. The key challenge in value-based testing is to integrate these two dimensions, i.e., align the internal test process with the value objectives coming from the customers and the market.

It becomes clear that a pure focus on the technical aspects of testing (e.g., the testing methods and tools) is inappropriate to align the internal and external dimensions. Instead, test management activities need to adopt a value-based perspective.

Figure 41 illustrates the external and internal dimensions of test management and their interdependencies. The internal dimension is similar to the scope of control of the test manager in the project. This dimension addresses costs from software testing practice as well as short-term and long-term benefits of testing. The external dimension considers stakeholders and parameters outside the scope of control of the test manager. Value-based test management organizes testing to satisfy value propositions of the stakeholders and to focus the team on the most worthwhile testing targets.

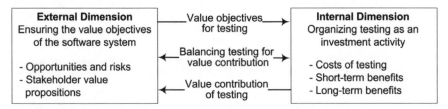

Fig. 41. Balancing external and internal stakeholder value propositions

The key question coming from the external view of software testing is: "How can we ensure the value objectives of the software system?" The goal is to reconcile stakeholder value propositions by focusing testing efforts on the most worthwhile parts of the software, the most important quality characteristics, and the most urgent symptoms of risks that threaten the value contribution of the project. Answering this question involves market opportunities and threats, project-specific customer value propositions, as well as costs and benefits. Please refer to Chapter 1 for details about opportunities and risks and to Chapter 7 for elicitation and reconciliation of stakeholder value propositions.

The internal view builds on the stakeholder value propositions and the test budget that represents the possible level of testing effort in a project. The key question in this view is: "How can we organize testing as an investment activity?" The goal is to achieve effective and efficient testing considering changes in development and budget reductions. Internal project stakeholders consider how plans for software development and associated testing activities can contribute to stakeholder value propositions by supplying system functionality and performance, but also by limiting the impact of project-relevant risks.

Appropriate communication is necessary to balance the external and internal dimensions of testing to assure the consistency of testing objectives with stakeholder value propositions.

Value Contribution of Testing

Compared to other development activities such as coding or user interface design, testing does not create immediate product value. Instead, testing informs and supports other value generating tasks in software development. A key to understanding the value contribution of testing is the contribution chain of testing (see the benefits realization approach described in Chapter 1). The contribution chain establishes the relation of testing to the final product that ultimately creates value for the stakeholders. Usually, the contribution chain of testing is complex and involves several different "clients," who benefit from testing.

Direct clients of testing are developers and project managers, who directly interact with the testing team (representing the internal dimension). However, in the spirit of value-based software engineering important parties for testing are customers and users (representing the external view). Customers and users are the source of value objectives (see Chapter 7), which set the context and scope of testing. Within this context testing informs developers and project managers to what extent value objectives are met and where improvement is required.

Clients of Testing

Developers, project managers, quality managers, customers, analysts, end users, or maintenance staff benefit from a thorough analysis of the software system and rely on feedback for detecting problems, reducing uncertainty, making decisions, or improving products and processes. The following examples show the kind of feedback from testing required by different groups:

- *Customers and users* get information as to what extent mutually agreed requirements are satisfied and to what extent the software meets their value propositions. Testing also provides visibility and insights about project progress. Passed tests reduce the odds of misbehavior and acceptance decisions are thus frequently based on the results of tests. When acceptance tests are impractical or fail to reveal hidden problems that become visible only in real-world conditions, alpha and beta testing provide a more solid foundation for acceptance decisions.
- *Marketing and product managers* require information from testing for planning releases, pricing, promotion, and distribution. A gap between the actual quality and the quality expected by customers and users most certainly leads to misleading expectations and wrong assumptions that diminish or prevent value realization (Boehm, 2000b). In order to successfully manage these expectations and to satisfy individual and organizational objectives, reconciling customer needs with product design has to consider quality in addition to functionality.
- For *project managers* testing supports risk management and progress estimation. The focus is on identifying and eliminating risks that are potential value breakers and inhibit value achievements. Early detection of severe defects that significantly reduce project performance is a major objective. Ideally, testing reduces uncertainty and helps project managers to take better, more informed decisions, e.g., for defect removal, system stabilization, and release decisions.
- *Quality managers* are interested in the identification of problems and in particular problem trends. Results from testing are the input for the assessment of development performance and provide the basis for quality assurance strategies and process improvement. Rosenberg (2003) discusses how testing contributes to quality assurance and shows that problems need to be documented, corrected, and can then be used for process improvement; after assessing problem reports for their validity corrective actions are implemented in accordance with customer-approved solutions; developers and users are informed about the

problem status; and data for measuring and predicting software quality and reliability is provided.

- *Developers* require feedback from testing to gain confidence that the implementation is complete and correct, conforming to standards, and satisfying quality requirements. For stabilization, testing provides details about defects and their estimated severity, information for reproducing defects, and support for revealing the cause of the failures. Besides, testing provides feedback for improvement and learning from defects. For example, throughout maintenance a detailed and reproducible description of problems contributes to the efficient implementation of changes and regression tests ensuring that these changes do not break existing functionality.
- For *requirements engineers*, testing is valuable to validate and verify requirements. Gause and Weinberg (1989) point out that "… one of the most effective ways of testing requirements is with test cases very much like those for testing a complete system." Deriving black-box tests from requirements helps to assure their completeness, accuracy, clarity, and conciseness early on. Tests thus enhance requirements and enable development in a test-driven manner.

To summarize, testing helps to realize benefits by reducing planning uncertainty, mitigating risks, making more informed decisions, controlling efforts, and minimizing downstream costs (the internal dimension). More importantly, it helps to realize the expected stakeholder value propositions (the external dimension).

These benefits, however, do not come for free and the costs of testing are often significant. Testing can be perceived as buying information and can be considered as an investment activity as it reduces the costs of risks, uncertainties, and the reward of taking risks. Making sound decisions about the investment in testing requires understanding their implications on both costs and benefits. The underlying questions therefore are: What are the costs of testing, and what are the benefits of testing for value generating activities?

Costs of Testing

Evaluating test cost-benefit ratio of testing activities is difficult in most organizations as only little is known about the actual costs of testing, and similarly about the costs of inadequate testing (Burnstein, 2003). The "Cost of Quality" model (Gryna, 1998; Slaughter et al., 1998) helps to analyze testing costs. The model distinguishes *costs of conformance* incurred in achieving quality and *costs of nonconformance* incurred because of a lack of quality. Costs *of conformance* are

- *prevention costs* for preventing errors, e.g., through extended prototyping, use of modeling tools, process inspection, and training and
- *appraisal costs* for assessing the product through verification and validation activities like test planning and setup, test data generation, test execution, results analysis, and reporting.

Costs of nonconformance are

- *internal failure costs* associated with defects found prior to release, e.g., cause analysis and debugging, development of temporary workarounds, defect fixing, inspection of rework, retesting and regression testing, and
- *external failure costs* as a direct or indirect result of defects found after the product is released, e.g., technical and field support, maintenance due to defects, service releases and upgrades, reimbursements for returned products, warranty expenses, liability claims, penalties, lost sales, or market shares.

The costs of testing comprise appraisal costs and internal failure costs. Appraisal costs, such as test planning, test design and implementation, setup of the test environment, and (initial) test execution occur independently from actual defects since tests need to be run at least once to assess the state of the product. All testing costs that are a consequence of defects, such as retesting and regression testing, are internal failure costs.

Approaches to estimate the costs of testing are discussed by Burnstein (2003) and Pinkster et al. (2004). These approaches are based on cost estimation models, testing tasks, tester/developer ratios, or expert judgment. Estimations of actual costs such as the nature of the software product under test, the level of tester ability, or the level of tool support depend on test cost impact items (Burnstein, 2003).

Benefits of Testing

We structure this discussion by distinguishing between short-term benefits mostly dealing with one project and long-term benefits affecting multiple projects in an organization. The assessment of benefits and applicable valuation models (see also Chapters 3, 4, and 5) depend on stakeholder role and project context. The book provides a number of models to describe stakeholder value propositions. It remains challenging to reconcile the different stakeholder views and to negotiate priorities for testing (see Chapter 7).

Short-term benefits

Within a project, the groups requesting information from testing are mainly concerned about short-term effects and, hence, testing is usually treated as a short-term investment. Cost, schedule, scope, and quality are usually the boundaries of planning and control within a project. An analysis of testing costs and (short-term) benefits has to weigh the influences of testing on overall project costs, schedule, scope, and quality to determine an optimal investment. Commonly reported benefits of testing include:

- *Reduction of planning uncertainty:* Testing provides feedback on the quality of key deliverables early in the development process and helps project management to assess risks and to increase project predictability.
- *Saved rework:* Finding major defects often avoids costly rework and reduces the size and frequency of risks which negatively affect value achievement. An

investment in testing can considerably speed up development by reducing downstream efforts for debugging and fixing defects (internal failure costs). "Getting the product right the first time so that you don't waste time reworking design and code" is one of the fundamentals for rapid development (McConnell, 1996).

While quality assurance costs are usually measured in person hours (Biffl et al., 2001) or their monetary equivalent (Reifer, 2002), benefits address different aspects of software projects and are harder to quantify. For cost-benefit evaluation, test costs must be compared to benefits. This gets complicated, particularly if test costs are measured in different units. Typically short-term benefits come from risk reduction, a lower the variance of quality, and from performance indicators allowing more informed decisions.

Long-term benefits

The "Cost of Quality" model proposes an inverse relationship between conformance costs and nonconformance costs. Increasing prevention and appraisal (conformance costs) lead to reduced costs of failure (nonconformance costs). Typically, finding and fixing defects after delivery is often 100 times more expensive than during early phases (Boehm and Basili, 2001). Black (2002) illustrates the return on investment in testing through savings in cost of nonconformance, in particular, cost of external failure. He argues that "… the costs of conformance plus the costs of nonconformance related to internal failures will be less than the costs of nonconformance related to external failures" if investment in testing and quality assurance is budgeted wisely.

Furthermore, testing leads to insights in the strengths and weaknesses of the development process and fosters learning from previous errors. Increasing knowledge and improved processes help to prevent defects and reduce further appraisal costs. The cost of quality is minimal in a situation of zero defects. At the point where savings from reduced nonconformance costs outweigh conformance costs, quality is considered "free" (Crosby, 1979), at least in the long run. Quality initiatives that aim to improve the development process build on this thought (Slaughter et al., 1998; Hauston, 2002).

Testing contributes to the achievement of the "quality is free" idea by providing information and services in each stage of improvement. Hence, the view of testing changes over time as people better understand its role. Beizer (1990) describes the "phases in a tester's mental life" and argues that the attitude toward testing matures along the following line of thinking: (0) testing is debugging, (1) testing demonstrates that the software works, (2) testing demonstrates that the software does not work, (3) testing reduces the perceived risk of not working to an acceptable value, and – ultimately – (4) testing is the mental discipline that results in testable, low-risk software without much testing effort.

Expected long-term benefits of testing can make it reasonable to increase the test budget beyond the project's short-term needs (see also Chapter 5 on financial benefits of risk reduction and improved process ratings). Long-term benefits are realized later and therefore need to be discounted when compared to current costs (see Chapter 3 on valuation).

Balancing Testing for Value Contribution

Our discussion of short-term and long-term costs and benefits emphasized the internal dimension of testing. In order to be "value-based," testing has to be aligned with the external dimension and show how it supports stakeholder value propositions and how it considers arising opportunities and perceived risks.

Risk can be used to answer a central question in making these investment decisions (Boehm, 2003): How much testing is enough? Projects that are under heavy time-to-market pressure, e.g., when exploiting the first-mover advantage of implementing a new standard, working against fixed drop-dead dates, or coping with constantly eroding market shares all bear the risk of not completing in time and failing to realize benefits. This risk has to be balanced with the risk of delivering a product that fails to meet customer expectations.

The level of effort driven by risk considerations has been illustrated by Boehm (2000a) for pre-ship testing (see also Chapter 1). Take, for instance, the risk exposure profile for a project developing a new, improved version of an established shrink-wrapped product, e.g., an accounting application. Failing to meet quality expectations or time-to-market goals may result in losses of profits or reputation. On the one hand, shipping the product early allows only minimal investments in testing and severe defects may remain undetected. Spending more on testing reduces the risk exposure, as fewer and less critical defects remain in the product. On the other hand, the risk exposure increases due to market share erosion caused by delayed shipping. Customers waiting for promised new features might switch to the products of competitors. In order to minimizing overall risk exposure one has to optimize the investment in testing.

Investment decisions, however, should not only consider the total testing effort. They also have to distribute the testing efforts across the different clients of testing to improve the value contribution of testing. In a project dealing with medical devices the highest value may be earned through high reliability. Time-to-market will be the main focus for a consumer electronics product where testing would mainly support the release planning decision.

Optimal distribution of testing also has to consider budget, schedule, or resources constraints. The range of time and resources allocated for testing depends on the project type and the desired level of quality. Compare, for example, the different quality requirements for a flight control system, an electronic banking application, or a movie player. Despite the huge impact of system-specific requirements, the actual budget of testing often depends on the negotiation skills of the test manager (Bullock, 2000). Inadequate budgets for quality assurance and testing are reported throughout the software industry, ranging from local small companies to large-scale NASA initiatives (Rosenberg, 2003).

Furthermore, the dynamic environment of many projects renders test strategies based on an initial, optimal cost-benefit analysis invalid. As complex projects take complex paths, "the goal is often not to achieve what you said you would at the beginning of the project, but to achieve the maximum possible within the time and resources available" (McConnell, 1996). Continuously monitoring and replanning of testing activities are vital to consider changing opportunities and risks, as are new findings from earlier test results (Boehm, 1988).

11.3 Practices Supporting Value-Based Testing

Although the concept of value is often neglected as guiding principle to manage software testing, several practices and approaches are available for testing that already support value-based software engineering. In this section we discuss selected practices, which we consider as essential for value-based testing. These practices can be used as a starting point to endorse the value contribution of testing and to implement testing as an integral part of a value-based software engineering strategy:

- *Requirements-based testing*: As requirements capture mutually agreed stakeholder value propositions it is essential to organize testing based on the requirements of the software system.
- *Risk-based testing*: Risks need to be constantly monitored and considered when organizing testing activities and allocating resources.
- *Iterative and concurrent testing*: The ability to adapt to changing requirements and risks is vital for testing to provide timely and accurate information.
- *Stakeholder involvement in testing*: To overcome the separation of concerns key stakeholders need to contribute to the testing effort.
- *Testing managed as investment*: This practice comprises value-based test planning, monitoring, and control.

Requirements-Based Testing

Value-based testing has to be anchored in the requirements. Requirements capture mutually agreed upon stakeholder needs. Requirements-based testing helps to assure that the system satisfies these needs and realizes the intended value for the stakeholders. Requirements-based testing usually traces tests to requirements. Usually there is at least one test for every requirement. This traceability helps to demonstrate that the system conforms with the requirements and to infer whether the stakeholders' needs are satisfied (see also Chapter 14).

An important aspect is requirements prioritization. Changes in the urgency of needs result in different priorities for testing. Requirements implementing high priority needs need to be tested earlier and with higher intensity. As a result, requirements-based testing typically shows some degree of risk orientation. Also, requirements-based testing encourages a test design that can be used early to verify requirements (Gause and Weinberg, 1989) and to uncover defects even before implementation has started. This can lead to considerable time and effort savings, given that "current software projects spend about 40 to 50% of their effort on avoidable rework" (Boehm and Basili, 2001).

Risk-Based Testing

The risk orientation of requirements-based testing should be extended beyond priorities and also consider the probability of failure and the resulting loss. *Risk Exposure = (Probability of Loss) * (Size of Loss)* can be used to focus testing on the highest value capabilities and on the most critical types of failures. Risk exposure takes into account the estimated intensity of usage (e.g., the frequency of execution), the probability of a failure, the priority of the affected requirement, and the severity of a failure (not every failure will cause a total loss of functionality).

Bach (1999) criticizes a common pitfall in requirements-based testing: "We incur risk to the extent that we deliver a product that has important problems in it. The true mission of testing is to bring that risk to light, not merely to demonstrate conformance to stated requirements." The ability of risk-based testing goes beyond mere prioritization of testing according to required functionality. Risk considerations are also essential to identify areas potentially containing errors. Examples are components implemented with a new programming language, by inexperienced personnel, or without adequate tool support. Exploring the sources of risk identifies defects more directly and more likely than by basing tests on requirements solely. A risk-based approach should therefore be taken in all aspects of testing, from test planning and test management (Redmill, 2004; Amland, 1999) to test design (Kaner et al., 2002).

Iterative and Concurrent Testing

Risks as well as requirements and business needs are typically volatile and evolve over time. Changes become necessary either because new insights arise from development and testing, or because shifts occur in the business environment. The ability to quickly respond to changes and to easily accommodate the consequences provides a competitive advantage (Chapter 1). Most modern development processes are therefore highly iterative to better handle changing requirements and risks. Testing needs the flexibility to promptly support changes. With requirements and quality attributes becoming moving targets, instant feedback from testing is a prerequisite for making well-timed and well-informed decisions.

An illustrative example of how testing supports change in agile development is given by Wells (2002). He describes the contribution of testing as a continuous change monitoring and control activity as follows: "Acceptance tests define the functionality to be implemented during an iteration. A unit test is just a plan for what code you will write next. Tests give feedback by defining exactly when a task is done. Tests give feedback by announcing when a requirement has been violated. Tests watch over all integration activities and give feedback on integration problems. Altogether, tests form a concrete and decisive form of planning and give enormous amounts of feedback ...."

Stakeholder Involvement in Testing

The traditional separation of concerns in testing – "A programmer should avoid attempting to test his or her own program" (Myers, 1979) – has obfuscated the contribution of testing to value generation. Developers throw their code "over the wall" to testers who throw back bug reports. Direct interaction is discouraged and leads to communication overhead, misunderstandings, organizational gaps, information loss, and conflicts (Cohen et al., 2004; Weinberg, 2003). Testers become the messengers of bad news. The organizational distance between technical groups (e.g., development or testing) and business-centered groups (e.g., product management or marketing) also impedes effective communication. In many organizations, these groups are not only separated organizationally, they are separated by culture, language, and perception of goals.

Value-based software engineering requires that testing fosters cooperation and efficient communication between all involved parties (see Section 11.2 on clients of testing). Testing has to gather and negotiate value propositions from all involved stakeholders to assure a balanced testing focus. For example, customers and users have to be integrated in testing activities as they are the primary source of value objectives. Testing should be working hand in hand with development to provide information for cost-effective defect location, while development has to design for testability to ensure cost-effective testing. Involving people in testing who are also involved in related activities, (e.g., requirements engineering or development) provides a great potential to link testing more closely with value creating activities. In emphasizing people and communication, agile methods have demonstrated that these synergies, which currently often lie idle, can be activated.

Testing Managed as Investment

Testing supports monitoring and control of projects and should also apply the concepts of value-based monitoring and control to guide the testing effort. The goal of managing testing is to perform testing effectively and efficiently from a value-based perspective. However, decisions in testing are often made from a purely technical viewpoint. As a result, testing does not provide the information that is valued most and the return of the investment in testing is not satisfactory.

An interesting example that illustrates the need for balancing investments in testing is the decision to automate tests. Test automation has the potential to reduce time and costs, especially in highly iterative processes. However, automated tests require a fairly high initial effort, the time for developing the test scripts. Thus, test automation pays off only if the costs of automatically running the tests plus the initial effort are lower than the costs of running the tests manually. Tests have to be run a number of times to break even. The exact number depends on factors such as how easy it is to implement the tests or how often tests can be executed until they have to be adapted or re-implemented.

Nevertheless, this example shows the investment in test automation in a value-neutral context, taking only technical considerations into account. Such a value-neutral investment may reduce the ability of testing to efficiently adapt to changes in the design of the system under test (Kaner et al., 1999). Furthermore, the initial effort for automating tests may be better invested in manually running different tests, e.g., by increasing the diversification of tests or focusing tests on the most critical parts of the system. Boehm and Basili (2001) report: "About 80% of the defects come from 20% of the modules, and about half the modules are defect free" and "About 90% of the downtime comes from, at most, 10% of the defects. " Value-based test management therefore provides a great potential to optimize testing by focusing the effort of testing on the 20% of high-risk modules instead of testing everything automatically.

Test management frequently has to make investment decisions, e.g., when selecting appropriate test design methods, defining coverage criteria, prioritizing tests, or deciding on test automation. All of these decisions should be guided by the concept of value in order to optimize the overall testing performance.

11.4 A Framework for Value-Based Test Management

Existing development standards define the core activities of testing. According to ESA's PSS-05 (1991) and IEEE 610.12 (1990), for example, the testing process consists of test planning, test design, test case specification, test procedure definition, test procedure execution, and analysis of the results. While these activities provide a pragmatic framework for a systematic test process, they are not focused on delivering optimal value for the involved stakeholders.

The purpose of the framework presented in this section is to integrate our discussion of the value contribution of testing in Section 11.2 and the presentation of practices supporting value-based testing in Section 11.3. The proposed framework emphasizes test planning activities, considers testing as an investment, and covers decision making and test prioritization. The test framework is compatible with iterative development processes, such as the Rational Unified Process (Kruchten, 2003), in which iterations drive recurring test planning and builds are suggested as frames for test cycles. The proposed framework draws on concepts from software requirements negotiation (Boehm et al., 2001) and release planning (Ruhe and Ngo-The, 2004). While requirements negotiation and release planning approaches aim at delivering the most efficiently realizable and sufficiently important requirements first, value-based test planning focuses tests based on desired system parts, quality attributes, and project risks.

Framework Overview

The framework relies on three main tasks: Eliciting and reconciling stakeholder value propositions, test priority negotiation, and propagating stakeholder value propositions to the technical domain. It consists of three consecutive stages that propagate the value objectives to operational testing activities. The framework aims at strengthening the ties between testing and stakeholder value propositions, the transformation of value objectives to testing priorities, and their application in test construction and execution.

The stages also represent different levels in decision making, ranging from decisions on general objectives of testing linked to business value down to detailed decisions on optimizing test execution sequences. Throughout all stages, the scope of the decisions is defined by the previous stage and continually narrows down on technical issues. The link back to business value is established by basing decisions on the input from the previous stage. Testing generates information for its internal and external clients. This information can also be used as feedback for managing testing activities. The feedback from test execution to the previous stages of test management establishes a control loop.

In more detail, the three stages of the framework, as depicted in Figure 42, are:

- *Initial overall planning:* The purpose of the first stage is to bring the stakeholders together to consolidate their value models and to negotiate testing objectives.
- *Test cycle construction:* The purpose of the second stage is to elaborate the testing objectives defined in Stage I into a sequence of test cycles.
- *Test cycle execution optimization:* The purpose of the third stage is to optimize and schedule the execution of the planned tests within the current test cycle.

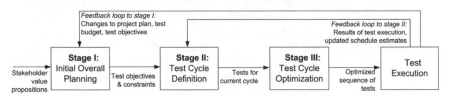

Fig. 42. Stages in test framework

Stage I – Initial overall planning. At first, a road map for testing the future system is developed. Success-critical stakeholders participate in deriving test objectives from their value propositions and negotiate priorities for testing. Test objectives are risks, requirements, and quality attributes that should be addressed. Furthermore, as testing is usually restricted in terms of time and resources, the stakeholders define the scope and intensity of testing, often involving cost-benefit analysis and trade-off negotiations.

The selection of stakeholders determines the scope of test benefits to be addressed. Clients of testing that are closely involved in development will emphasize short-term benefits within the project; stakeholders that are responsible beyond a single project will focus on long-term benefits of testing (e.g., understanding problem trends). Stakeholders translate more general benefit models (e.g., assumptions on "good practice for software development") into testing priorities for the more specific project context.

Key decisions that have to be made in this stage include:

- Testing priorities for key features, quality attributes, and system parts
- Budget and resources invested in testing aligned to value objectives
- Timeline and major milestones coordinated with development

The first stage incorporates many of the practices considered important for value-based testing (see Section 11.3): It relies on the involvement of stakeholders, it establishes a link from testing to high-level requirements and risk as proposed in requirements-based and risk-based testing, and it manages testing as an investment.

Stage II – Test cycle construction. The practice of iterative and concurrent testing is emphasized in the second stage. The testing objectives defined in the previous stage are evolved into a sequence of test cycles and the available test budget is allocated to the test cycles according to cost-benefit considerations. The corresponding test cycles are then constructed based on stakeholder value propositions from Stage I and on test cycles successfully passed previously. Each test cycle moves testing progress forward one step on the road planned in stage I. Within a cycle all effort is put in accomplishing the test objectives. After the cycle has finished, testing returns to Stage II. The test manager evaluates the situation in the light of the results and plans the next cycle.

Release planning approaches as described in Chapter 12 and (Ruhe and Ngo-The, 2004) aim at delivering the key requirements or the most efficiently realizable and sufficiently important requirements first. Similarly, value-based testing focuses the effort of testing on requirements, quality attributes, and system parts with a high-risk exposure. Optimizing the sequence of test cycles (e.g., by running the cycles addressing the most valuable testing objectives first) makes the value contribution of testing less sensitive to a reduction of the test budget. The end of a test cycle results in a checkpoint with consolidated results. Thus, whenever the testing budget is cut back and no further cycles are possible, the status of the last finished cycle is the final result of testing. Long cycles, therefore, also bear the risk that testing has to be stopped without a value-supporting result. The uncertainty of assumptions made about project attributes (independent from the validity of the assumptions) mainly drives the need for revisions of the test cycle sequence.

Key decisions that have to be made in this stage include:

- *Test targets for the test cycle.* What specifically will be tested in order to gain a high return on investment. Examples are untested new capabilities, fixes that have to be re-tested, or existing capabilities that have to be regression tested to reveal possible side effects.
- *The length of the test cycle.* From the viewpoint of testing, a test cycle should be long enough to provide sufficient new data indicating testing progress (e.g., old errors corrected, new errors found, and new functionality implemented). A small number of long test cycles requires less planning overhead but sacrifices more frequent adaptation of the testing strategy to changes.

Stage III – Test cycle execution optimization. In this stage the execution of the planned tests is scheduled to maximize testing effectiveness, i.e., to accommodate the planned work within the fixed time frame. Thereby, the fixed test cycles create time boxes for testing, which provide a simplified and temporarily static context for optimizing the execution schedule. Besides, time boxes help to keep test execution focused on the objectives and the rigid time limit ensures prompt feedback for the clients of testing. Scheduling in Stage III is usually an optimization problem of maximizing the number of tests to be executed within the available time of the current test cycle. Part-time resources and test equipment availability are often the major optimization constraints and require a careful alignment of testing work on parallel tracks.

The key decision that has to be made in this stage is the scheduling of the tests for execution.

The result of Stage III is that all work is scheduled without further need for optimization at execution time. However, as practical experience shows, it is often not possible to anticipate all influence factors at the beginning of a test cycle. Therefore in-process monitoring is necessary to improve the output of testing through short-term adaptations of test sequencing. At the end of the fixed-length cycle all planned but unfinished work will be planned in the next cycle.

Figure 42 depicts the two feedback loops in the planning process. While feedback to Stage II is routine to plan the next test cycle based on the results of previous testing, a step back to Stage I shows major changes in design and requirement directions, which influence overall test planning. Allowing changes at project level often enables exploiting new opportunities to realize additional value. An iterative adaptation of the test strategy is therefore a crucial practice to reflect these changes in the value contribution of testing.

An Illustrative Example

A bank intends to introduce a new online service for its customers offering Web access to several legacy capabilities such as trading of stocks, selection of stocks, performance measures of stock options, risk analysis and portfolios, and the simulation of portfolios.

First, stakeholders get together to discuss their value models and to agree on objectives for testing. The stakeholders jointly identify transaction security, performance, and scalability, as well as usability as the most important quality attributes of the system. A risk analysis reveals that a long response time to user commands represents a major risk. Stakeholders also rate the importance of capabilities by considering their business value. Similar to a requirements negotiation workshop (Chapter 7) the stakeholders negotiate testing priorities. Prioritization plays an important role: for each test objective stakeholders need to consider the value of a particular test objective and its feasibility. The prioritization done by the stakeholders ensures that the focus of testing is laid according to the decisions made by the selected stakeholders and appropriately reflects their value propositions. The prioritization allows first budget estimates, which can be compared to the available resources in the project context.

Secondly, the test manager plans several test cycles to propagate the testing objectives from the previous stage. A test cycle focuses testing on a specific release of the system under test, e.g., a build, runs all or a subset of the tests on this release, and completes with reporting the gained insights (Kaner et al., 2002). In our example the test manager defines a test cycle that puts emphasis on transaction security and he plans to focus on performance for "buy and sell options" in the next cycle. Altogether, ten test cycles are planned to cover all testing objectives.

The third step is to detail the test objectives to a test plan for the current test cycle. As the planning uncertainty is high for the first test cycle, the test manager decides to schedule the most valuable tests first so less important ones can easily be deferred if running out of time at the end of the cycle.

While executing the tests of the first cycle, an external change triggers the planned sequence of the cycles. A competing bank announces a graphical visualization to comfortably manage and view portfolios. This new situation leads to a rearrangement of testing cycles in the next step. Instead of performance testing, the next cycle is dedicated to usability tests of the simulation of portfolios to reflect the shift in the business strategy.

Furthermore, when the schedule for the next cycle is planned, different restrictions become dominant. In contrast to the previous testing cycle, this time the scheduling is mainly determined by the availability of the usability test lab and a further optimization of the test execution sequence is not worthwhile.

Finally, after the eighth test cycle, the testing budget is unexpectedly cut back. Instead of the initially planned ten cycles only eight can be accomplished. However, those test objectives that yielded the highest return on investment were successfully covered by the earlier test cycles.

Discussion

The proposed framework emphasizes the value-contributing activities of testing. It encourages decision making based on value considerations and incorporates the practices considered important for value-based testing (see Section 11.3):

- *Requirements-based testing.* Key functions or functional areas and key qualities of the system are determined from stakeholder value propositions (see Stage I and Chapter 7).
- *Risk-based testing.* Based on an initial risk analysis stakeholders determine key potential problems of system operation, risk events, and risk symptoms with significant correlation to the problems and risk events.
- *Iterative and concurrent testing.* The process aims at iterative testing to incorporate changes in the testing context (see overall feedback loops and test cycle planning in Stage II).
- *Stakeholder involvement in testing.* In Stage I stakeholder value propositions are elicited and reconciled. Stakeholders are involved in defining testing objectives and test budget negotiation. Thereby the value objectives are transformed

to testing priorities, which are propagated through Stages II and III to test execution.

- *Testing managed as investment activity.* Stakeholders determine a joint value proposition and also estimate costs of testing for different testing options. This usually includes some form of cost-benefit analysis and trade-off negotiations among the stakeholders similar to investments activities. The process optimizes the deployment of testing effort available from the test budget according to test planning criteria, such as most effective or most efficient approaches first.

11.5 Conclusion and Outlook

Software testing is a very resource-intensive activity in software development. A value-based approach to software testing could help to improve the return on investment of testing and to align testing with stakeholder value contributions. In this chapter we discussed the value contribution of testing by considering soft benefits such as reduced planning uncertainty or lower project risks. We have presented testing from the perspective of buying information. We regarded it as an investment decision to trade off the costs of testing against project risks based on cost-benefit analysis. Hence, to make informed value-based decisions on project planning, a project manager needs to consider not only the cost but also the benefits of testing. Cost-benefit analysis involves estimating tangible and intangible costs (outlays) and benefits (returns) of various project alternatives, and then using financial measures such as return on investment or payback period to assess the relative desirability of the identified alternatives (see also Chapters 1, 2, and 17).

Our approach aims at maximizing the value of testing from the available test budget and at making the value contribution robust to test budget cuts. Therefore, it is rooted in the principles of value-based V&V that were further detailed in characteristic practices of value-based testing: requirements-based testing, risk-based testing, iterative and concurrent testing, stakeholder involvement in testing, and testing managed as investment.

The proposed test management framework comprises following stages: (a) focus of testing value proposition by stakeholders, (b) iterative test cycle construction, and (c) test sequence optimization in a test cycle.

We identified areas that need further research in order to better understand and control the value contribution of testing: Release planning and test planning has to be integrated more tightly; test budget planning and negotiation has to become an integral part of the replanning activities in iterative development; finally, optimizing the test effort needs to better integrated with other quality assurance measures.

Future work includes the validation of concepts described in this chapter in an industrial case study. Based on the case study we will refine our framework to better support rapid and informed decision making in test management.

References

(Amland, 1999) Amland, S.: Risk Based Testing and Metrics. In: *EuroSTAR'99: 5ᵗʰ European International Conference on Software Testing Analysis and Review*, Barcelona, Spain, November 1999

(Bach, 1999) Bach, J.: Risk and Requirements-Based Testing. IEEE Computer, **32**(6), pp 113–114 (June 1999)

(Beizer, 1990) Beizer, B.: *Software Testing Techniques*, 2ⁿᵈ ed (Van Nostrand Reinhold, New York 1990)

(Biffl et al., 2001) Biffl, S., Freimut, B., and Laitenberger, O.: Investigating the Cost-Effectiveness of Reinspections in Software Development. In: *ACM/IEEE International Conference on Software Engineering,* Toronto, Canada, IEEE Comp. Soc. Press, May 2001

(Black, 2002) Black, R.: *Managing the Testing Process: Practical Tools and Techniques for Managing Hardware and Software Testing* (Wiley, New York 2002)

(Boehm, 1988) Boehm, B. W.: A Spiral Model of Software Development and Enhancement. IEEE Computer, **21**(5), pp 61–72 (May 1988)

(Boehm, 2000a) Boehm, B. W.: Spiral Development: Experience, Principles, and Refinements, CMU/SEI-2000-SR-008. Spiral Development Workshop, July 2000

(Boehm, 2000b) Boehm, B. W.: The Art of Expectations Management. IEEE Computer, **33**(1), pp 122–124 (January 2000)

(Boehm, 2003) Boehm, B. W.: Value-Based Software Engineering. Software Engineering Notes, **28**(2), (March 2003)

(Boehm and Basili, 2001) Boehm, B. W., and Basili, V.R.: Software Defect Reduction Top 10 List. IEEE Computer, **34**(1), pp 135–137 (January 2001)

(Boehm and Huang, 2003) Boehm, B. W., and Huang, L.G.: Value-Based Software Engineering: A Case Study. IEEE Computer, **36**(3), pp 33–41 (March 2003)

(Boehm et al., 2001) Boehm, B. W., Grünbacher, P., and Briggs, R.O.: Developing Groupware for Requirements Negotiation: Lessons Learned. IEEE Software, **18**(3), pp 46–55 (May/June 2001)

(Bullock, 2000) Bullock, J.: Calculating the Value of Testing. Software Testing and Quality Engineering, **2**(3), pp 56–61 (May/June 2000)

(Burnstein, 2003) Burnstein, I: *Practical Software Testing: A Process-oriented Approach* (Springer, Berlin Heidelberg New York 2002)

(Cohen et al., 2004) Cohen, C.F., Birkin, S.J., Garfield, M.J., and Webb, H.W.: Managing Conflict in Software Testing. CACM, **47**(1), pp 76–81 (January 2004)

(Crosby, 1979) Crosby, P.B.: *Quality Is Free: The Art of Making Quality Certain* (McGraw-Hill, 1979)

(Ferscha and Mattern, 2004) Ferscha, A., Mattern, F. (eds.): *PERVASIVE 2004: Pervasive Computing*, Second International Conference, Vienna, Austria, Lecture Notes in Computer Science, vol 3001 (Springer, Berlin Heidelberg New York 2004)

(Gause and Weinberg, 1989) Gause, D.C., Weinberg, G.M.: *Exploring Requirements: Quality before Design* (Dorset House Publishing, New York 1989)

(Gryna, 1998) Gryna, F.M.: Quality and Costs. In: *Juran's Quality Handbook*, 5th edition, ed by Juran, J.M., Godfrey, A.B. (McGraw-Hill, New York 1998), pp 8.1–8.26

(Harrold, 2000) Harrold, M.J.: Testing: A Roadmap. In: *The Future of Software Engineering*, ed by Finkelstein, A., 22th International Conference on Software Engineering, Limerick, Ireland, June 2000, pp 63–72

(Hauston, 2002) Hauston, D.: Cost of Software Quality: Justifying Software Process Improvement to Managers. In: Daughtrey, T.: *Fundamental Concepts for the Software Quality Engineer* (ASQ Quality Press, Milwaukee 2001), pp 85–94

(IEEE 610.12, 1990) *IEEE Standard Glossary of Software Engineering Terminology*, IEEE Std 610.12-1990. (IEEE Computer Society, 1990)

(Kaner et al., 1999) Kaner, C., Falk, J., and Nguyen, H.Q.: *Testing Computer Software*, 2nd edition (Wiley, New York 1999)

(Kaner at al., 2002) Kaner, C., Bach, J., Pettichord, B.: Lessons *Learned in Software Testing: A Context-Driven Approach* (Wiley, New York 2002)

(Kruchten, 2003) Kruchten, P.: *The Rational Unified Process: An Introduction*, 3rd edition (Addison-Wesley, Boston 2003)

(McConnell, 1996) McConnell, S.: Rapid *Development: Taming Wild Software Schedules* (Microsoft Press, Redmond 1996)

(Myers, 1979) Myers, G.J.: *The Art of Software Testing* (Wiley, New York 1979)

(Pinkster et al., 2004) Pinkster, I., Burgt, B.v.d., Janssen, D., Veenendaal, E.v.: *Successful Test Management: An Integral Approach* (Springer, Berlin Heidelberg New York 2004)

(PSS-05, 1991) ESA Board for Software Standardisation and Control (BSSC): *ESA Software Engineering Standards PSS-05-0* (European Space Agency (ESA), ESTEC, Noordwijk, The Netherlands, February 1991)

(Redmill, 2004) Redmill, F.: Exploring risk-based testing and its implications. Software Testing, Verification and Reliability. **14**, pp 3–15 (2004)

(Reifer, 2002) Reifer D.: *Making the Software Business Case: Improvement by the Numbers*. (Addison Wesley, New York 2002)

(Rosenberg, 2003) Rosenberg, L.H.: Lessons Learned in Software Quality Assurance. In: *Managing Software Engineering Knowledge*. ed by Aurum, A., Jeffery, R., Wohlin, C., Handzic, M. (Springer, Berlin Heidelberg New York 2003), pp 251–268

(Ruhe and Ngo-The, 2004) Ruhe, G., Ngo-The, A.: Hybrid Intelligence in Software Release Planning. International Journal of Hybrid Intelligent Systems. **1**(2), pp 99–110 (2004)

(Slaughter et al., 1998) Slaughter, S.A., Harter, D.E., Krishnan, M.S.: Evaluating the Cost of Software Quality. CACM, **41**(8), pp 67–73 (August 1998)

(Wallace and Fujii, 1989) Wallace, D.R., Fujii, R.U.: Software Verification and Validation: An Overview. IEEE Software, **6**(3), pp 10–17 (May 1989)

(Weinberg, 2003) Weinberg, G.M.: Destroying Communication and Control in Software Development. CrossTalk, pp 4–8 (April 2003)
(Wells, 2002) Wells, D.: An Introduction to Testing, XP-Style. In: Marchesi, M., Succi, G., Wells, D., Williams, L.: *Extreme Programming Perspectives*. (Addison Wesley, 2002)

Author Biographies

Rudolf Ramler is a senior software engineer and a member of the scientific staff at the Software Competence Center Hagenberg, Austria. His research interests include software testing, quality management, and requirements engineering. He has led research projects on testing of Web-based systems and test management. His experience in software development comprises development of tools for test management, project portfolio management, and engineering of Web-based solutions. Rudolf works as a consultant in industry projects and is a lecturer at the Hagenberg Polytechnic University. He studied Business Informatics and holds a MSc (2001) from the Johannes Kepler University of Linz.

Stefan Biffl is an Associate Professor at the Technische Universität Wien. He studied Computer Science and Business Informatics and holds a PhD from the TU Wien in Computer Science. His research focuses on empirical software engineering applied for project and quality management in software engineering. Stefan Biffl was a visiting scientist at the Fraunhofer Institute for Experimental Software Engineering (IESE, Head Prof. Dr. Dieter Rombach) where he gained further experience with empirical software engineering, in particular with survey planning. Stefan Biffl was the principal investigator of Erwin-Schrödinger J1948 (Software Inspection Techniques to Support Project and Quality Management) project supported by the Austrian Science Fund. He is a member of ACM, ACM SIGSOFT, IEEE, the Austrian Computer Society, and the IFIP Technical Committee on Software Engineering.

Paul Grünbacher is an Associate Professor at Johannes Kepler University Linz and a research associate at the Center for Software Engineering (University of Southern California, Los Angeles). He received his MSc (1992) and PhD degrees (1996) from the University of Linz. In 1999 Paul received the Erwin-Schrödinger research scholarship and worked as a visiting professor at University of Southern California in Los Angeles. In 2001 Paul received his Habilitation degree (Venia Docendi in Angewandte Informatik) for this work on software requirements negotiation. His research focuses on applying collaborative technologies to support and automate complex software and system engineering activities such as requirements negotiation or software inspections. He is a member of ACM, ACM SIGSOFT, IEEE, and the Austrian Computer Society.

Part 3
Applications

VBSE is a fairly new concept and there are not many documented experiences of applying VBSE approaches. The aim of Part 3 is to demonstrate the benefits of VBSE through concrete examples and case studies and to illustrate selected practices presented in Parts 1 and 2 in a more tangible way. Part 3 portrays specific applications of VBSE principles and provides firsthand insights into the applicability of VBSE.

The selected chapters cover different areas of software engineering such as release planning, risk management, software traceability, and the introduction of new technology. The presented examples also show the use of VBSE in different domains and discuss perspectives from different organizations applying elements of VBSE. The chapters in this part form a source of information and inspiration for practitioners and researchers interested in applying value-based software engineering. The chapters also help to better understand current limitations of VBSE approaches.

There are six chapters in this part that cover to the following areas:
- Chapter 12: Decision Support for Value-Based Software Release Planning
- Chapter 13: ProSim/RA – Software Process Simulation in Support of Risk Assessment
- Chapter 14: Tailoring Software Traceability to Value-Based Needs
- Chapter 15: Value-Based Knowledge Management – the Contribution of Group Processes
- Chapter 16: Quantifying the Value of New Technologies for Software Development
- Chapter 17: Valuing Software Intellectual Property

In Chapter 12, *Maurice, Ruhe, Saliu,* and *Ngo-The* present the F-EVOLVE* method that uses net present value estimates of proposed features to support the decision making process in release planning. Following this, in Chapter 13 *Pfahl* presents a simulation-based method to risk assessment, which allows calculating potential losses to the delivered product value. In Chapter 14 *Egyed* discusses how precision, completeness, correctness, and timeliness of software traceability can be tailored to value-based needs supported by an approach to automated software traceability. In Chapter 15, *Dingsøyr* addresses the important issue of how to assign value to the knowledge involved in software development in the context of team building and process improvement. In Chapter 16 *Atkins, Mockus,* and *Siy* describe a method for precise quantitative measurement of the value of software technologies and presents a detailed case study. Finally, in Chapter 17 *Reifer* discusses approaches used to value intellectual property of software assets and a framework allowing software experts to value different forms of intangible assets.

12 Decision Support for Value-Based Software Release Planning

Sebastian Maurice, Guenther Ruhe, Omolade Saliu, and An Ngo-The

Abstract: Incremental software development replaces monolithic-type development by offering a series of releases with additive functionality. To create optimal value under existing project constraints, the question is what should be done when? Release planning (RP) provides the answer by assigning features to a sequence of releases in the most beneficial way within the resources available.

In this chapter, we extend the existing hybrid intelligence-based release planning method called EVOLVE* to accommodate financial value in the form of net present value estimates of proposed features. This extension enables us to perform financial value-based software release planning. The new approach called F-EVOLVE* is illustrated by an example. The results show that the F-EVOLVE* model may be used to decide which features to produce and when based on their financial contributions. Specifically, F-EVOLVE* may be used to determine which features generate the highest returns, with the shortest development time.

Keywords: Value-Based Software Release Planning, F-EVOLVE*, Decision Support, Hybrid Intelligence.

12.1 Introduction

In today's world with rapidly changing consumer demands, informational technology, and competitive marketplaces, the requirements are changing rapidly requiring quicker adaptability by market participants. The critical success factor for vendors is responding to changing requirements quickly while maintaining a focus on their value proposition, which may be a quicker return on investments or an improvement in a public service like health, education, and defense (Boehm, 2003). A value-based approach to software engineering is closely aligned with the business goals and objectives of the organization, and seeks to ensure that every step in the software development process is a *value-making* step. Meeting the needs of customers is as important as justifying the development efforts needed to meet those needs (Poladian et al., 2003).

The need for a value-based approach to software release planning can be justified by the need for a faster time to market, while maximizing stakeholder satisfaction. Stakeholders are defined to be anyone that influences or is influenced by the project plan (Farbey and Finkelstein, 1999), and this includes customers, users, developers, project managers (decision makers), etc. For project success, within a value-based context, it makes more sense that traceability back to the value propositions become more important than traceability back to requirements (Boehm,

2003). Decisions support for release planning plays a key role in identifying value propositions through a careful analysis of the release options and how these options impact value, financial, and human resources.

This chapter will contribute to an understanding of software release planning from a financial perspective with the objective of incorporating a more fine-grained measure of financial value to the original EVOLVE* model, thus creating a new model called F-EVOLVE*. Specifically, this financial measure of value will help to choose among competing features as well as choosing among release plan alternatives when integrated into the F-EVOLVE* model. Currently, value is considered based on a nine-point ordinal scale where the assigned stakeholder performs priority evaluations.

The chapter is organized as follows. Section 12.2 presents background information on release planning, which includes the discussion of existing approaches. Section 12.3 provides information on financially based release planning and the development of the F-EVOLVE* method. Section 12.4 presents an example to illustrate the new method. Section 12.5 concludes the chapter and provides directions for future work.

12.2 Background

A software release is a collection of features that form a new product. Without good release planning 'critical' features are jammed into the release late in the cycle without removing features or adjusting dates. This situation might result in unsatisfied customers, time and budget overruns, and a loss in market share (Penny, 2002). "Developing and releasing small increments of requirements, in order for customers to give feedback early, is a good way of finding out exactly what customers want, while assigning a low development effort" (Carlshamre et al., 2001).

Release planning is an integral part of incremental software development methods. These methods promote faster delivery of small components of the overall software product, where shorter time frames result in an iterative process of design, code, test, and deployment of these components (Larman and Basili, 2003).

Difficulties with Software Release Planning

Release planning is a very complex problem including different stakeholder perspectives, competing objectives, and different types of constraints (Ruhe and Ngo-The, 2004). Release planning is impacted by a large number of inherent constraints. Most of the features are not independent of each other. They typically have precedence or coupling constraints between them that need to be satisfied. Precedence constraint requires that specific features must be implemented before other features, while coupling constraints requires that some features must be implemented together. Furthermore, resource constraints such as effort and budget need to be fulfilled for each release.

The overall goal of release planning is to find a relatively small set of "most promising" release plans so the overall value and the degree of satisfaction of all the different stakeholders are maximized. In essence, the objective is to maximize benefit (or value), but there is difficulty in giving a measurable definition of benefit. This difficulty results in the characterization of release planning as a "wicked" problem (Carlshamre et al., 2001).

The Need for Software Engineering Decision Support in Release Planning

Release planning decisions are not always straightforward as they exhibit difficulties that characterize decision making in natural settings. The inability of humans to cope well with complex decisions involving competing and conflicting goals in software engineering suggests the need for supplementary decision support (Ruhe, 2003). It becomes very hard to find appropriate solutions without intelligent decision support systems when one considers problems involving several hundreds of features and large numbers of widely distributed stakeholders.

Because of the inherent difficulties in planning releases, we cannot expect any solution procedure to offer something like "the best" solution. Instead, there are always implicit or subjective factors that are not reflected in the current model. What is proposed in (Ngo-The and Ruhe, 2004) is to generate a set of alternative solutions from which the human decision maker can select his or her most favored plan.

Existing Value-Based Planning Approaches

Various planning approaches have been adopted in industry with academic research proposing equally as many formal approaches. We focus our discussion on existing planning approaches and also on formal approaches that consider the financial value of features in planning.

Ad hoc Release Planning

Some organizations do not see release planning as a separate activity during the development process. Many release plans focus only on the target release contents, rather than on defining incrementally releasable products. Many organizations have an ad hoc plan that relies solely on the judgment of the project manager who equally acts as the decision maker. An ad hoc approach may be suitable for a relatively small in-house project involving few tens of features, few stakeholders, and relaxed constraints but becomes unsuitable for larger projects with many requirements. In any case, value is addressed therein only implicitly as part of the general stakeholder evaluation.

Cost-Value Based Requirements Prioritization and Release Planning

The cost-value approach for prioritizing requirements proposed by (Karlsson and Ryan, 1997) ranks requirements in two dimensions: according to their relative value to the customer and their estimated cost of implementation. Relative value and cost of requirements to the customers are determined by using the pairwise comparison of the Analytic Hierarchy Process (AHP) (Saaty, 1980). Once these values are computed, the project manager can visualize and inspect these values to prioritize and select requirements.

As an extension of the work in (Karlsson and Ryan, 1997), Jung (1998) argued that the inspection of costs and values in the xy plane, in relation to other requirements, become very complicated when the number of requirements is considerable. It is not a simple matter to determine those requirements that have the highest value and the lowest cost simply by visualization and inspection. Also, this inspection method does not guarantee an optimal solution that simultaneously achieves maximum value and minimum cost because the inspection, as he argues, depends on intuition of the cost-value points in the xy plane. Therefore, inspecting costs and values to decide which requirements to implement first should be replaced by optimization techniques.

Hybrid Intelligence (EVOLVE*)

The driving force behind the hybrid approach, EVOLVE* (Ruhe and Ngo-The, 2004), is the belief that computational intelligence cannot replace the human decision maker and vice versa. Hybrid intelligence explores the synergies between computational intelligence and the human decision maker. The hybrid approach for RP, proposed by (Ruhe and Ngo-The, 2004), is a special application of EVOLVE*. It is designed as an iterative and evolutionary procedure, which facilitates the real world problem of software RP, and the available tools of computational intelligence for handling explicit knowledge and crisp data, and the involvement of human intelligence for tackling tacit knowledge and fuzzy data.

EVOLVE* facilitates the involvement of stakeholders to achieve increments that result in the highest degree of satisfaction among different stakeholders. Two of the prioritization schemas used in EVOLVE* are value-based and urgency-based. For the value-related part, a nine-point scale is given to express the stakeholder priorities; for details the reader is referred to (Ruhe and Ngo-The, 2004).

Incremental Funding Method

The incremental funding Method (IFM) introduced by (Denne and Cleland-Huang, 2004) is a data-driven, financially informed approach to software development. This development approach maximizes Net Present Value (NPV) of software investment by carefully analyzing and sequencing feature delivery. To maximize returns, and NPV, functionality is delivered in carefully sequenced 'chunks' of valued customer features.

The main idea behind IFM is the prioritization of features by their (customer) value called *minimum marketable features* (MMFs) defined as a set of small self-contained features that can be delivered quickly and that provide market value to the customer (Denne and Cleland-Huang, 2004). The authors also introduce the term *architectural element* (AE). AEs are the foundation that supports the MMFs. AEs do not generate revenue; they must be in place to support the MMFs: they facilitate the revenue generation from the MMFs. In many cases, MMFs cannot be deployed unless the AEs are in place.

12.3 Value-Based Release Planning

Release planning, as proposed in EVOLVE*, is one way to ensure that software is developed with important business metrics such as effort and budget in mind. The methodology followed in EVOLVE* for release planning already considers value as an ordinal measure provided by stakeholders. However, EVOLVE* does not consider value in financial terms where ratio-scale measures are taken into consideration when choosing among plans. We propose to add a financial component to EVOLVE* resulting in a modified approach called F-EVOLVE*.

F-EVOLVE* Process Model

Figure 43 shows the F-EVOLVE* process model. The model is an adaptation of the EVOLVE* process model introduced in (Ruhe and Saliu, 2005). The shaded area shows the modification to the EVOLVE* model: instead of being asked to vote, the stakeholders are asked to specify the financial estimates for the features. Three roles that contribute to the process and products of *resource planning* (RP) are identified – project managers, stakeholders, and support environment. Activities occur directly under the roles that are actively involved. For example, project managers and stakeholders' roles are involved in feature elicitation, while a support environment maintains the group of features elicited.

The support environment can vary from a simple spreadsheet to an intelligent tool support, depending on the sophistication of the RP methodology. Major activities of the process model are described by rounded rectangles, while intermediate results of each activity are shown in ovals. The key functions of the model are: feature elicitation, problem specification, resource estimation, stakeholder financial estimation, release plan generation, and evaluation of plan alternatives. These functions work seamlessly together to provide release plan alternatives for the decision maker.

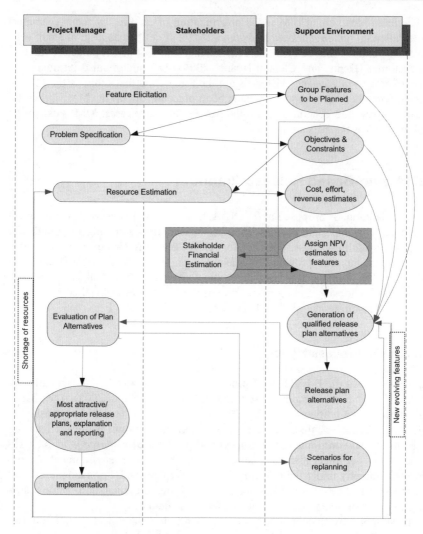

Fig. 43. F-EVOLVE* Process Model

The F-EVOLVE Method*

F-EVOLVE* provides decision support in the generation and selection of release plan alternatives. The model aids in aligning the software development process with the goals of the business: to achieve greater profit in the shortest time possible. It should be noted that F-EVOLVE* does not account for the maintenance of features after they have been developed – it only suggests what should be developed and when. The model can be specified as follows. Let $\Gamma = \{F_1, ..., F_n\}$ be the set of features[11] to be assigned to releases. We consider planning for K releases ahead of time. As decision variables, we use the Boolean decision vectors $x(i) = (x(i,1), x(i,2), ...,x(i,K))$ where $x(i,k) = 1$ if feature i is implemented in release k. By definition each feature can be assigned at most once, these variables must satisfy the following constraints

$$\sum_{k=1..K} x(i,k) \leq 1 \qquad \text{for all } i = 1..n \qquad (1)$$

Developing a feature consumes different types of resources. We assume R types of resource. Development of feature i consumes $resource(i,r)$ units of resource type r. The problem is to offer a most profitable sequence of features under the given resource capacity constraints for each time interval $k = 1,..,K$.

$$\sum_i resource(i,r) x(i,k) \leq Cap(k,r) \text{ for } k=1..K \text{ and } r=1..R \qquad (2)$$

We distinguish two types of dependencies between features. Coupling between two features i_1 and i_2 means that they have to be released at the same time period. Correspondingly, precedence between i_1 and i_2 means that i_2 is not allowed to be released before i_1. Coupling can be easily formulated by the coupling constraints

$$x(i_1,k) = x(i_2,k) \qquad \text{for } k=1..K \text{ and coupled features } i_1, i_2. \qquad (3)$$

Precedence constraints can be formulated by

$$\sum_k (K+1 - k) (x(i_1,k) - x(i_2,k)) \geq 0 \text{ if feature } i_1 \text{ has to precede feature } i_2. \qquad (4)$$

This constraint assures that if the vector $x(i_1,k) = 1$ then $x(i_2,j), j=1..k-1$, cannot be 1, i.e., i_2 cannot be implemented before i_1.

The question of what actually constitutes a good release plan needs careful consideration. The user is expecting features that he or she would need first to get started. But there are different types of stakeholders having different types of expectations and preferences. In our approach, we will consider the net present values from the perspectives of different stakeholders as the basis of the formulation of the problem, i.e., the problem is stated as maximization of NPV within the resource and technical constraints (1)-(4).

For this purpose, we assume the existence of q different stakeholders abbreviated by $S_1, S_2,...,S_q$. Each stakeholder S_p is assigned a relative importance $\lambda_p \in (0, 1)$. The project or product manager typically assigns the relative importance of all involved stakeholders. If it is difficult to actually determine these weights, pair-wise comparison using the analytic hierarchy process (Saaty, 1980) can be used as a support. We assume that stakeholder weights are normalized to 1, i.e.,

---

[11]Without loss of generality we use the concept of features to refer to 'self-contained features' whose financial value stakeholders can elicit.

$$\sum_{p=1,\dots,q} \lambda_p = 1 \tag{5}$$

We further assume that stakeholder S_p estimates the implementation cost and annual revenues generated by the feature i over a certain period of time after its release. Implementation cost estimates are made by technical experts like developers based on their previous experiences with implementing similar features in the past, while customers or marketers (or other personnel with market forecast experience) should be able to use their experiences in similar situations to study the market trend and estimate projected revenues over a period of time. From these data, we can compute the net present values $NPV(i,k,p)$, which is interpreted as "the net present value of the revenues generated by feature i if it is made available in release k as perceived by stakeholder S_p."

Given a feature i, each stakeholder gives his own estimations assuming that only the revenues generated in the first four years (after the launch of a release to the market) are significant, with the additional assumption that feature i can be in release 1, 2, or 3. We emphasize that the time frame of the generated revenues depends on the life cycle of the product and has no relation to the number of releases in consideration.

Feature i should be of appropriate size to provide this estimation. $NPV(i,k)$ denotes the (weighted) average NPV (generated by the implementation of feature i in release k), which reflects the aggregation of all stakeholders' estimates.

$$NPV(i, k) = \sum_p \lambda_p NPV(i, k, p) \text{ for } i{=}1..n \text{ and } k{=}1..K \tag{6}$$

Once these NPVs have been computed, the NPV generated by a plan x can be computed by

$$G(x, K) = \sum_i \sum_k NPV(i,k) \cdot x(i,k) \tag{7}$$

Denote X as the set of all release plan alternatives fulfilling (1)-(7), the financially based release planning problem becomes

Maximize $G(x, K)$ subject to $x \in X.$ $\hspace{4em}$ (8)

Equation (8) represents a specialized integer programming problem. As described in (Ngo-The and Ruhe, 2004), we will generate a set of alternative solutions from which the stakeholder can finally choose his or her most preferred solution that has financial justification.

Providing alternatives for decision makers is a crucial area in decision support. It recognizes that every decision has implications and risk; by providing alternatives a decision maker can choose an option that best fits his preferences in an effort to mitigate the risk, and implications of a bad decision. Chapter 4 also considers decision alternatives as different courses of action that could lead to different consequences while allowing for a dispersion of risk or consequences over the entire life cycle of the project, thereby minimizing the impact of a bad decision. The above method is next applied to an illustrative example to show how features are assigned to release plan alternatives based on their financial value.

12.4 Example

To illustrate the F-EVOLVE* method we present an illustrative example inspired from the Web portal project at EPCOR Utilities Inc., one of Canada's top integrated utilities company The objective of the Web portal is to allow energy customers in Canada to view and manage their billing data online on a Web site.

Background

Currently, EPCOR does not have any formally accepted way of performing its release planning. While it uses incremental development methods to better react on changing customer requirements, there exist several issues:

- *Size and complexity of the problem:* The number of requirements in some projects may go up to hundreds or even thousands. The situation gets worse by the fact that there are usually a large number of stakeholders involved in the project who are either not consulted at all or are not given appropriate relative weights.
- *Changing requirements and other parameters:* If a large number of requirements increase the complexity of the project, their dynamic nature poses another challenge.
- *Requirements are not well specified and understood*: There is usually no formal way to describe the requirements. Nonstandard format of requirement specification often leads to incomplete description and makes it harder for stakeholders to understand the requirements properly.
- *Other constraints:* The project manager has to consider various constraints while allocating the requirements to various increments. The resources may act as a bottleneck for the allocation of some requirements in the same increment.

Application of F-EVOLVE*

This study is performed for three release periods (i.e., $K = 3$). We consider self-contained features as a market deliverable chunk of software similar to what (Denne and Cleland-Huang, 2004) refer to as a minimum marketable feature. This study has two stakeholders and 30 requirements. Stakeholder S_1 is the manager of information technology, and stakeholder S_2 is the project manager. Stakeholder S_1 has a weight of $\lambda_1=0.7$ and stakeholder S_2 has a weight of $\lambda_2=0.3$. Each release occurs on an annual basis. There are three resource types to create the different features: systems analyst (SA), programmer (P), and database administrator (DBA).

Table 20 shows the resource capacities and the effort in person-days for each resource (SA, P, DBA). Table 21 shows the features and their estimated resource consumption.

Table 20. Resource capacities (in person-days for release k)

Release k	Cap(k, SA)	Cap(k, P)	Cap(k, DBA)
1	200	100	60
2	200	80	10
3	80	100	10

Table 21. F-Evolve* data[12]

	Description	SA	P	DBA	NPV(i, 1)	NPV(i, 2)	NPV(i, 3)
F_1	ARC billing interface	80	50	0	36,500	20,750	17,250
F_2	MV-PBS billing interface	90	55	0	40,200	19,100	11,800
F_3	UIS billing interface	110	90	0	33,000	12,900	9,600
F_4	Customer account setup	24	48	0	11,500	16,500	13,000
F_5	Web site enhancement	0	20	0	6,500	3,700	2,300
F_6	Administration options	52	16	0	2,700	6,100	4,700
F_7	Reporting functionality	52	132	0	10,200	5,700	5,700

To ensure that the estimates are "good," all, or most, of the information that impact revenues should be taken into consideration to determine the degree of influence on the estimates. We can minimize the variability in the estimates by ensuring that we have accounted for all relevant information in an effort to minimize variability in the estimates. For example, stakeholders may involve other departments or sources within the organization, such as marketing, accounting, and sales, to determine these numbers, and understand the general trend in the market for the features. A seasoned stakeholder who can exploit information in these sources will generally have a good idea of the value of the feature. The results of applying the proposed F-EVOLVE* method are discussed next.

---

[12]We assume *ceteris paribus* when generating the estimates in Table 21.

Results

It is inappropriate to argue that one plan is better than another if the difference in terms of revenue is insignificant. The reason for that is the fact that preferences are typically not based on just one criterion. Therefore, we consider a small set of solutions that are close enough in terms of NPV. The project manager uses his/own experience and judgment to compare these solutions and makes the final choice (Ruhe and Ngo-The, 2004). In this example, four alternative solutions have been calculated of which the NPVs are within 5% of the optimal value (Table 22). The postponed option means that this feature should not be considered for the next three releases.

Table 22. F-Evolve* example results

$G(x,K)$	Alternative 1 $G(1, K)=84,680$	Alternative 2 $G(2, K)=84,680$	Alternative 3 $G(3, K)=80,480$	Alternative 4 $G(4, K)=80,480$
F_1	3	2	3	2
F_2	1	1	1	1
F_3	Postponed	Postponed	Postponed	Postponed
F_4	2	3	2	3
F_5	1	1	3	3
F_6	2	2	2	2
F_7	Postponed	Postponed	Postponed	Postponed

In Table 22, each column corresponds to an alternative qualified solution, i.e., a plan generating NPV, which is within 5% of the optimality. The first row represents the NPV generated by each solution. The numbers 1, 2, and 3 represent the release to which the feature is assigned in the corresponding plan. For example, at the intersection of column "alternative 1" and row "F_1" we see 3; this means that feature A will be in release 3 according to the plan 1. Due to the lack of resources, certain features cannot be implemented in the horizon of the three releases in consideration; they are marked as "postponed" in Table 22.

Although $G(3, K)$ and $G(4, K)$ have lower NPV, the difference is too small to exclude them from the consideration. We now proceed with the analysis of these alternatives to make the final choice. We observe that among these four alternatives, only three features are assigned differently: F_1 (release 2 or 3), F_4 (release 2 or 4), and F_5 (release 1 or 3). A discussion with the stakeholders shows that F_5 is important and should be included in release 1, i.e., alternatives 3 and 4 are excluded.

Now, the question becomes how to decide between alternative 1 and alternative 2? We look for a criterion to help us making this decision.[13] Here, the only

---

[13]The decision to choose the best plan will be context-specific. Our analysis in no way suggests that there is *one-way* to choose the best plan.

difference relates to the schedule release for F_4 and F_1. The question is then which of F_4 and F_1 should be implemented first. The effort needed to implement F_1 is 130 person-hours, which is higher than the effort required implementing F_4, which is 72 person-hours. But the value generated by F_1 is greater than that generated by F_4. Looking at the risk factor, such as the effort, the project manager realizes that F_1 requires much more effort and is associated with a higher risk of being delayed. To mitigate the risk, it is decided that F_1 should be implemented sooner in order to have more time to deal with this risk. Finally, alternative 2 is chosen for implementation.

Contributions of the F-EVOLVE* Model

The meaningfulness of the results depends on the accuracy of the estimates of cost and revenue that are needed for the net present value calculations.[14] The implicit assumption is that the stakeholders have some market knowledge about the costs and returns for the features so their consolidated input on the estimates could lead to better estimates. Furthermore, the cost of readjustment of estimates, in terms of generating new release plans, would be minimal in this model because the numbers are simply inputs into an integer programming algorithm that can immediately generate new release plans.

The F-EVOLVE* model has several benefits for companies. If there is a limited project budget the F-EVOLVE* model can help to prioritize features that are less costly to develop. Or it can prioritize features based on the value generated in the form of net present value. The F-EVOLVE* model can also show features that generate value earlier rather than later. For example, in the discussion of the results above, we chose alternative 2 for the reason that we wanted to realize value sooner rather than later. For many companies it is a prudent business decision to develop features that deliver value sooner rather than later – this is even truer for highly competitive industries, like the software industry.

12.5 Conclusions and Future Work

In the 1995 CHAOS Report (Standish, 1995), the main causes of project failure are the lack of user involvement, lack of resources, incomplete requirements, unrealistic expectations, lack of executive support, and changing requirements. The F-EVOLVE* model is one way to address these critical issues. Specifically, by establishing a financially informed approach to software release planning the model tries to mitigate the risk of project failure by ensuring that ROI is an explicit part of the decision process.

---

[14]Changes in market condition can of course change estimates but there is an implicit assumption of *ceteris paribus*: all market conditions are held constant at time of estimation.

Software release planning is a critical component of the software development life cycle. Introducing value and financial planning into software release planning is one way to bring the value-based component into release planning. These ideas heighten the awareness that financial considerations must go hand in hand with meeting customer requirements.

The focus of this chapter has been to highlight current value-based approaches to software release planning. The main goal of the chapter was to enhance the existing EVOLVE* approach to accommodate financial value-driven analysis of release planning.

In future, we plan to further investigate the financial planning aspects of F-EVOLVE* and determine how this could mitigate some of the risk involved in software development. Another area to improve is the project management aspect of software development from a value-based perspective. How can project control and monitoring be improved or incorporated in the F-EVOLVE* model? F-EVOLVE* could also be extended to consider the selection of architectures, COTS, etc. Developing software from a financial planning perspective may be one way to improve the way we develop software and may also improve the business of software development. Finally, we suggest a comprehensive empirical evaluation of the proposed method. We need more industrial feedback on the meaningfulness of the proposed research. This will be facilitated by tool support, as is currently available for EVOLVE*.

Acknowledgements

The authors would like to thank the Alberta Informatics Circle of Research Excellence (iCORE) for its financial support of this research.

References

(Boehm, 2003) Boehm, B. W.: Value-Based Software Engineering. Software Engineering Notes 28(2), pp 1–12 (May 2003)

(Carlshamre et al., 2001) Carlshamre, P., Sandahk, K., Lindvall, M., Regnell, B., and Nattoch Dag, J., An industrial survey of requirements interdependencies in software release planning. In: Proceeding of the 5th IEEE International Symposium on Requirements Engineering, pp 84–91, 2001

(Denne and Cleland-Huang, 2004) Denne, M. and Cleland-Huang, J., The Incremental Funding Method – A Data Driven Approach to Software Development, IEEE Software, May/June, 2004

(Farbey and Finkelstein, 1999) Farbey, B. and Finkelstein, A. Exploiting Software Supply Chain Business Architecture: A Research Agenda, In Proceedings of the 1st Workshop on Economics-Driven Software Engineering Research (EDSER-1), 21st International Conference on Software Engineering, 1999

(Jung, 1998) Jung, H.-W., Optimizing Value and Cost in Requirements Analysis, IEEE Software, pp 74–78, 1998

(Karlsson and Ryan, 1997) Karlsson, J. and Ryan, K., Prioritizing Requirements using a Cost-Value Approach, IEEE Software 14(5), pp 67–74, 1997

(Larman and Basili, 2003) Larman, C., and Basili, V., Iterative and Incremental Development: A Brief History, IEEE Computer Society, pp 47–56, 2003

(Ngo-The and Ruhe, 2004) Ngo-The, A. and Ruhe, G., Optimization Algorithms for Generating Largely Diversified Release Plans, University of Calgary, Laboratory for Software Engineering Decision Support, TR 014/04, 22p., 2004

(Penny, 2002) Penny, D. A., An Estimation-Based Management Framework for Enhancive Maintenance in Commercial Software Products, In Proceedings of International Conference on Software Maintenance (ICSM), pp 122–130, 2002

(Poladian et al., 2003) Poladian, V., Butler, S.A., Shaw, M., and Garlan, D., Time is Not Money: The Case for Multi-dimensional Accounting in Value-based Software Engineering, Position paper for the Fifth Workshop on Economics-Driven Software Research (EDSER-5), affiliated with the 25th International Conference on Software Engineering (ICSE'03), May 2003

(Ruhe, 2003) Ruhe, G., Software Engineering Decision Support – A New Paradigm for Learning Software Organizations, Advances in Learning Software Organization, Lecture Notes in Computer Science, 2640, Springer, pp 104–115, 2003

(Ruhe and Ngo-The, 2004) Ruhe, G. and Ngo-The, A., Hybrid Intelligence in Software Release Planning. International Journal of Hybrid Intelligent Systems, 1(2004), pp 99–110, 2004

(Ruhe and Saliu, 2005) Ruhe, G. and Saliu, M.O., The Science and Practice of Software Release Planning, 2005, Technical Report TR-SEDS 23/2004

(Saaty, 1980) Saaty, T.L., The Analytic Hierarchy Process, Planning, Priority Setting, Resource Allocation, McGraw-Hill, New York, 1980

(Standish 1995) Standish Group, CHAOS, http://www.standishgroup.com, 1995

Author Biographies

Sebastian Maurice is a Project Manager at M-Tech Information Technology, Inc., a member of the laboratory for Software Engineering Decision Support at the University of Calgary, and also a member of the Project Management Institute. His general area of research and interest is value-based software engineering. He is the founder and chair of the Software Engineering Consulting Consortium (SECCO) at the University of Calgary, has over ten years of combined professional experience as a researcher, software developer and project manager, and has several publications in International Journals; one of these publications has been recognized as landmark work. Sebastian has a Bachelor of Social Science degree in Economics from the University of Ottawa (1993), a Bachelor of Science degree in Pure Mathematics from the University of Calgary (1997), a Master of Science degree in Agricultural Economics from the University of Alberta (1997), and is completing a Master of Science in Software Engineering from the University of Calgary. He can be reached at smaurice@ucalgary.ca.

Günther Ruhe holds an Industrial Research Chair in Software Engineering at University of Calgary and is an iCORE Professor since July 2001 (see http://www.seng-decisionsupport.ucalgary.ca/). His laboratory comprises 20 researchers focusing on Intelligent Decision Support in Software Engineering. His main results and publications are in software release planning, requirements and COTS selection, knowledge management, measurement, simulation and empirical research. From 1996 to 2001 he was deputy director of the Fraunhofer Institute for Experimental Software Engineering Fh IESE. He is the author of two books, several book chapters, and more than 120 publications. Ruhe is a member of the ACM, the IEEE Computer Society, and the German Computer Society GI.

Omolade Saliu is a PhD candidate and an iCORE scholar in Computer Science Department at the University of Calgary, Canada. He holds a Bachelor of Technology (BTech) degree in Mathematics/Computer Science from the Federal University of Technology, Minna, Nigeria (1998). He obtained his Master of Science (MS) degree in Computer Science from King Fahd University of Petroleum and Minerals, Saudi Arabia (2003). His research interests include Software Metrics and Measurement, Software Engineering Decision Support, Software Process-related issues and Soft Computing. He is a member of the IEEE Comp. Society.

An Ngo-The received his BSc in Mathematics and Computer Science at the University of Ho-Chi-Minh City, Vietnam in 1985 and his MBA at the French-Vietnamese Center for Management Education (CFVG), Vietnam in 1997. He received his DEA (equivalent to MSc) in Decision Support at the LAMSADE laboratory, University Paris Dauphine, France in 1998. He got his PhD in Computer Science (Decision Support in Operational Research) at the LAMSADE laboratory, France and the ESSEC Doctoral Program. Since October 2002, he is post-doc fellow at the Laboratory Software Engineering Decision Support, University of Calgary, Canada.

13 ProSim/RA – Software Process Simulation in Support of Risk Assessment

Dietmar Pfahl

Abstract: In the past decade, several authors have pointed out the potential of simulation as an analysis and decision support tool for software managers. In this chapter, we present a five step simulation-based method to risk assessment, ProSim/RA, which combines software process simulation with stochastic simulation. Although the proposed method is not new as such, it is the first time that it is described systematically and in detail based on an illustrative case example that can serve as a model for similar scenarios. By applying cost functions to the risk probabilities generated by ProSim/RA, the potential losses to the delivered product value can be calculated.

Keywords: ProSim/RA, simulation model, software process simulation, system dynamics, risk assessment, risk management.

13.1 Introduction

Software development projects can become highly risky endeavors and thus need good risk management processes in order to avoid or mitigate events that potentially cause monetary losses due to late product delivery, insufficient product quality, damaged reputation, or any other negative effect.

Prominent software risk management processes typically comprise several phases. The well-known risk management process proposed by Boehm (1991), for example, consists of two phases, i.e., risk assessment and risk control, comprising six tasks: risk identification, risk analysis, risk prioritization, risk management planning, risk resolution, and risk monitoring. These tasks are further subdivided into specific activities. More recent risk management processes are extensions of Boehm's original proposal, for example, Kontio's Riskit model (Kontio, 2001) which puts particular focus on the important role of stakeholders, or Wallmüller's risk management model (Wallmüller, 2004) which advocates an integration of project and risk management.

While software engineering practice and research frequently lacks a value-oriented perspective, Value-Based Software Engineering (VBSE) seeks to integrate value considerations into current and emerging software engineering principles and practices (Chapter 2; Boehm, 2003; Boehm and Huang, 2003). Software-related decisions cannot be extricated from business value concerns in a commercial software development context. A value-oriented approach provides explicit guidance for making products useful to people by considering different people's utility functions or value propositions. The value propositions are used to determine relevant measures for given scenarios.

This chapter addresses the planning and control aspect of VBSE to manage the risk of failing to deliver planned project value to customers. Specifically, simulation techniques are combined and applied to complex project situations in order to account for business value loss due to the combined materialization of typical project risks, such as time and budget overruns or lack of product quality. A somewhat similar approach has recently been proposed by DeMarco and Lister (2003) in the form of their Riskology. The main difference between Riskology and our approach to simulation-based risk assessment is that we propose to use Software Process Simulation (SPS) to adequately represent the complex project reality instead of using more limited static predictive models.

SPS can be used to reason about software value decisions. Simulation can analyze the impact of multivariate risk factors on those project parameters that are of particular interest to the project manager and/or its customers. This approach can be combined with a VBSE decision framework by involving expert opinion. This can happen either on the input side by eliciting expert estimates on the potential variation of risk factors, or on the output side by using expert estimates for constructing loss functions that are applied to the output probability distributions characterizing the risks of late product delivery, low product quality, and project effort overrun. Examples of compatible VBSE frameworks can be found in Part 2 of this book.

In the following sections of this chapter, we present a simulation-based approach to risk assessment, ProSim/RA, which combines SPS with stochastic simulation.

In the past decade, several authors have pointed out the potential of simulation as an analysis and decision support tool for software managers (Christie, 1999a; Pfahl and Ruhe, 2001; Raffo and Kellner, 1999). Kellner and Hansen (1989), and Abdel-Hamid and Madnick were the first to apply simulation modeling in the context of software process and project management (Abdel-Hamid and Madnick, 1991; Lin et al., 1997). The most influential SPS model, the one by Abdel-Hamid et al., comprised:

- Generic project variables, such as workforce level, budget, scheduled completion date, number of errors produced, number of errors detected;
- Managerial-related functions, e.g., staffing, planning, and controlling;
- Production-related functions, e.g., design, development, verification, rework;
- Human-related functions, e.g., productivity, motivation, error rate, whose values are affected by the project's perceived status (schedule pressure) and the penalty-reward structure of the organization.

Typical applications of the Abdel-Hamid model focus on project estimation and the effects of project planning on product quality and project performance.

Since 1991 many new SPS applications in software engineering have been published, focusing on more specific topics within software project and process management, such as multi-project management (Lee and Miller, 2004), concurrent engineering (Powell et al., 1999), requirements engineering (Christie and Staley,

2002; Ferreira et al., 2003; Höst et al., 2000; Pfahl and Lebsanft, 2000a; Stallinger and Grünbacher, 2001), software process improvement (Bandinelli et al., 1995; Birk and Pfahl, 2002; Birkhölzer et al., 2004; Christie, 1999b; Pfahl and Birk, 2000; Raffo et al., 1999; Ruiz et al., 2002; Tvedt and Collofello, 1995), strategic planning (Pfahl et al., 2004; Williford and Chang, 1999), software verification and validation (Aranda et al., 1993; Madachy, 1996; Neu et al., 2003; Raffo and Kellner, 2000; Raffo et al., 2004), software reliability management (Rus et al., 1999), software maintenance (Cartwright and Shepperd, 1999), software evolution (Smith and Ramil, 2002; Wernick and Hall, 2004), COTS software development (Ruiz et al., 2004), global software development (Raffo et al., 2003), software outsourcing (Roehling et al., 2000), open source development (Jensen and Scacchi, 2003), agile software development (Mišic et al., 2004), and software engineering training (Drappa and Ludewig, 1999; Madachy and Tarbet, 2000; Pfahl et al., 2001).

The potential application domain of software risk management, however, has not yet been explored deeply and described in terms of a generally applicable procedure. Apart from an early paper by Weil and Dalton (1992), in which the idea of using SPS for risk analysis was suggested in a very generic way, and two more recent application-specific case examples published by Houston et al. (2001) and Neu et al. (2002), there exists only one comprehensive and detailed description of an approach to simulation-based risk assessment published in the form of a dissertation by Bröckers (1995). Although the work by Bröckers is very useful from the conceptual point of view, the proposed approach has the disadvantage that the SPS-based risk assessment procedures are strongly tool dependent as they are inherently linked to a specific software process modeling language (MVP-L) (Bröckers et al., 1995) and a specific software process enactment environment (MVP-S) (Lott et al., 1995).

The lack of research into the application of SPS for the purpose of risk management tasks is surprising as there are very obvious possibilities to apply SPS models particularly in the area of software project risk assessment.

Regarding risk identification, systematic sensitivity analysis offers a powerful means to explore unwanted levers in the project, which may be considered potential risk factors. Subsequently, sensitivity analysis combined with stochastic analysis can be used to further investigate into the effects of individual risk factors or combinations of risk factors on project performance. Finally, based on the probability distributions constructed upon the simulation results generated for the purpose of risk analysis, risk prioritization can be done by ranking the effects on project performance according to probability of the occurrence of unwanted effects multiplied by the associated estimated loss.

The organization of the chapter is as follows. First, we give a brief introduction into SPS in general and with particular focus on its applicability in the context of software risk management. Then we present the main ideas of ProSim/RA; in particular, its five step procedure to simulation-based risk analysis will be described in detail. The main part of this chapter will be used to illustrate the application of ProSim/RA in a case example and to explain how ProSim/RA can be used to support informed decision making within a VBSE framework. A discussion of the strengths and weaknesses of ProSim/RA and an outlook to future research concludes the chapter.

13.2 Software Process Simulation

Because it is partly based on statistical analyses of data which is produced by a series of simulations, the proposed risk assessment procedure ProSim/RA depends on the availability of a valid project simulation model. Currently, there exists a wide range of SPS modeling techniques. The interested reader can find a concise introduction into the most popular paradigms in (Kellner et al., 1999). In principle, the choice of the simulation modeling technique does not restrict the applicability of ProSim/AR. Nevertheless, some thought should be spent on the selection of an appropriate simulation modeling technique. Due to several positive characteristics, which will be sketched below, we recommend using System Dynamics process simulation models.

System Dynamics (SD) is a continuous time simulation modeling approach (Forrester, 1961; Madachy, 2005) which models the continuous change of system states over time with the help of material flows that are controlled by a causal network of information links. SD simulation models of software development processes are a particularly suited and easy to use means for adequately capturing mental models of software managers about software projects and processes. They are holistic in the sense that they easily combine the three main dimensions that characterize software development: processes, products, and people. Moreover, SD models allow for capturing nonlinear behavior, multi-causality, and feedback phenomena.

SD simulation modeling has the following positive characteristics:

- Top-down approach: SD facilitates quick delivery of an initial SPS model comprising the complete software development process; subsequent refinements help improve validity of the model by stepwise inclusion of necessary detail in a controlled manner; an instructive example of a top-down SPS modeling exercise using SD can be found in (Pfahl and Ruhe, 2003).
- Detailed guidance with particular focus on applying SD in software development organizations (Pfahl and Lebsanft, 2000b; Pfahl and Ruhe, 2003).
- Mature tool support, e.g., Vensim[15], Ithink[16], and Powersim[17] offering a graphical modeling language, mathematical functionality with high analytic power, and comprehensive data import/export interfaces.

Although only the availability of an SPS model and not the choice of the simulation modeling technique with which the SPS model was created is essential for the

---

[15]http://www.vensim.com

[16]http://www.iseesystems.com

[17]http://www.powersim.com

applicability of ProSim/AR, we will rely exclusively on an SD-based SPS model in the remainder of this chapter.

The SD-based SPS model GENSIM (GENeric SIMulator) will be used in a case example in Section 13.4 to illustrate the application of ProSim/RA. GENSIM is a generic SD model representing a waterfall-like software development process. It is a research prototype that was developed for demonstration purposes in the context of project management training (Pfahl et al., 2001). The GENSIM model simulates the software development process from the end of the requirement analysis step through to the end of system testing. A detailed description of GENSIM can be found in (Pfahl, 2001). Although the model is only a research prototype it can be easily calibrated to product and process measures of a specific software organization. For producing the simulation results used in the case example, GENSIM was calibrated to the development process of a "typical" software organization.

The GENSIM model has a modular structure. It consists of five interrelated sub-models:

- Production: This sub-model represents a typical software development cycle consisting of the following sequence of transitions (see Figure 44): set of requirements → design documents → code → tested code. Note that the detection of defects during testing only causes reworking of the code (and not of the design documents).
- Quality: In this sub-model, the defect co-flow is modeled, i.e.: defect injection (into design or code) → defect propagation (from design to code) → defect detection (in the code during testing) → defect correction (only in the code).
- Effort: In this sub-model, the total effort consumption for design development, code development, code testing, and defect correction (rework) is calculated.
- Initial Calculations: In this sub-view, the normal value of the central process parameter "productivity" is calculated. The "normal productivity" represents the productivity that can be observed in standard projects, i.e., in projects of typical size and complexity, and with typical (not extreme) constraints. The normal productivity varies with assumptions about the product complexity (e.g., simple stand-alone software, complex software system without significant hardware interaction, embedded software with complex hardware interaction) and characteristics of the personnel resources available (e.g., developer skill).
- Productivity, Quality & Manpower Adjustment: In this sub-model, project-specific process parameters, like (actual) productivity, defect generation, effectiveness of QA activities, etc., are determined based on a) planned target values for manpower, project duration, product quality, etc., and b) time pressure caused by unexpected rework or changes in the requirements.

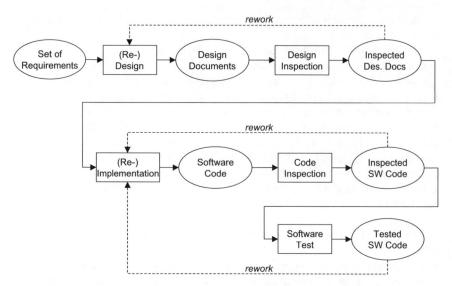

Fig. 44. Product flow captured by the GENSIM production sub-model

The most important input and output parameters and their use in the context of predicting effort, quality, and duration are listed in Tables 23 and 24. The input parameters of the simulation define the project goals (parameters Product_size, Planned_completion_time, and Goal_field_defect_density) and constraints (parameters Average_complexity, Planned_manpower, and Manpower_skill), as well as the process, e.g., the degree to which design and code inspections are applied (parameters Inspection_intensity_design and Inspection_intensity_code).

Table 23. GENSIM input parameters with units

Input Parameters	*Unit*
Product_size	Total number of size units (e.g., Function Points)
Average_complexity	Values: (0.5=low, 1=default, 1.5=high) [no unit]
Manpower_skill	Values: (0.5=low, 1=default, 1.5=high) [no unit]
Planned_manpower (optional)	Number of persons
Planned_completion_time (optional)	Days
Goal_field_defect_density (optional)	Defects per implemented size unit
Inspection_intensity_design	Fixed percentage of total number of size units
Inspection_intensity_code	Fixed percentage of total number of size units

The output parameters represent the simulation results, e.g., size of the work and end products (parameters Design_size, Code_size and Product_size), project duration (parameter Project_duration), effort consumption (parameter Project_effort), and product quality (parameter Field_defect_density).

Actually, the detailed cause-effect structure that underlies each of the submodels, and in particular each of the process stages (design, implementation, test) of the production sub-model, would make it possible to monitor any detail of the project status at any point in time during the project execution, e.g., effort consumption per phase and activity (design production, design analysis, design correction, number of inspections conducted, etc.). For the sake of simplicity, in the following, only a small subset of the analytic potential of the GENSIM model will be exploited.

Table 24. GENSIM output parameters with units

Output Parameters	Unit
Design_size	Total number of designed and inspected size units
Code_size	Total number of implemented and inspected size units
Product_size	Total number of implemented and tested size units
Project_duration	Project total and per phase [days]
Project_effort	Project total and per phase [person-days]
Product_field_defect_density	defects per implemented size units after test

13.3 SPS-Based Risk Analysis Procedure

The proposed simulation-based risk analysis procedure ProSim/RA requires the availability of a simulation model that represents the overall software development process on an adequate level of granularity. Having such a model at hand, ProSim/RA consists of the following five steps.

STEP 1: Define risk factors. Risk factors are attributes of project entities that are supposed to cause losses of a certain amount with a certain probability. In the related project simulation model, such attributes are represented by model parameters.

STEP 2: Define impact factors. Impact factors are attributes of project entities that are supposed to be affected by variations of risk factors and need to be controlled. In the related project simulation model, such attributes correspond with model output variables. Typically, variables representing the dimensions of the "magic triangle" (see Figure 45) are of particular interest. The dimensions of the "magic triangle" are requirements coverage (referring to both functional and nonfunctional requirements), effort (or cost), and time (either time-to-market or project duration).

STEP 3: Define variation of risk factors. In particular, this implies the construction of a distribution function describing the probability of assuming a particular value. One way of constructing such a distribution function is to fit generic probability functions (e.g., triangle distribution, normal distribution) to available data from (similar) past projects, for example, extracted from an Experience Data Base (EDB) (see Figure 46). The fitting can be performed automatically by using tools that employ test statistics such as Chi-Square, Kolmogoroff-Smirnoff, or Anderson-Darling (D'Agostino and Stephens, 1986). If empirical data is not available, expert interviews can be used to construct triangular distributions by asking for estimates of the most probable value (peak), the minimal (min) value, and the maximal (max) value (see Figure 47). If more than one expert is available, the easiest way to define the min, max, and peak values per risk factor is to take the averages of the experts' estimates. Alternatively, group consensus techniques such as Delphi can be used to combine expert judgment values (see also Chapter 5 for hints about related group negotiation support techniques).

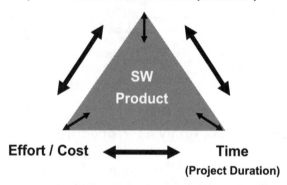

Fig. 45. The magic triangle

STEP 4: Conduct sensitivity analyses. Sensitivity analyses are conducted by repeatedly running the SPS model with values of the risk factor attributes randomly sampled from the probability functions constructed in STEP 3. As a result, the sensitivity analyses generate SPS output distributions reflecting the induced variation of the impact factors.

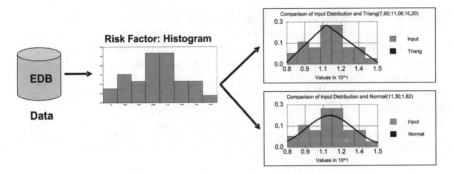

Fig. 46. Data-based construction of probability distribution

STEP 5: Analyze simulation results. This means in particular to check the probabilities of those value ranges that are worse than expected. By combining the
probabilities of the occurrence of unwanted attribute values of impact factors with
their associated estimated losses, rankings can be constructed that may serve as an
input for risk prioritization. Typically, potential losses are associated with late
product delivery (contract penalty), lacking product quality (rework cost), and effort overrun (personnel cost).

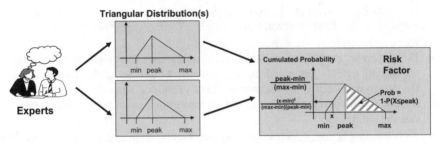

Fig. 47. Expert-based construction of probability distribution

In the following section, we show with the help of a case example, how the
ProSim/RA five-step procedure can be applied in the context of an SE technology
adoption risk assessment.

13.4 Case Example

In software development, we can identify two main sources of project risks:
- Lack of data in early phases (i.e., planning) causing the risk of incorrect project
  estimates (i.e., related to time, effort, quality, functionality)
- High variability of project over time causing the risks of insufficient project
  control and unsatisfactory achievement of project goals (i.e., related to time, effort, quality, functionality)

Having a valid SPS model at hand that accurately represents the important cause-effect relationships between actors in a process, and artifacts produced and consumed in the various process steps, the above identified risks can be analyzed.

In the following case example, we show how one can analyze the risks related to the actual impact of verification (or quality assurance; QA) and validation (or quality control; QC) activities (i.e., inspections and tests) on product quality, project duration, and project effort consumption simultaneously. Using the SD-based SPS model GENSIM, each step of the simulation-based risk analysis procedure ProSim/RA is described in detail.

Define Risk Factors (STEP 1)

As QA-related risk factors, the following SPS model variables can be identified:
- *Nominal_design_error_density* [defects per size unit]: represents the average number of defects per size unit of design documentation generated during design, given that the standard development process is followed and the average skills of the workforce (captured by variable Manpower_skill) are adequate for the project to be performed.
- *Nominal_implementation_error_density* [defects per size unit]: represents the average number of defects per size unit of program code generated during implementation, given that the standard development process is followed and the average skills of the workforce are adequate for the expected project complexity.
- *Design_error_amplification* [no unit]: a multiplier that represents the average number of defects generated during implementation per undetected defect in the design documents; the number of defects resulting from design error amplification is added to the number of defects resulting from nominal defect generation during design.
- *Nominal_inspection_effectiveness* [%]: represents the average percentage of defects that are detected during design and code inspections.
- *Inspection_effort_per_task* [person-days per size unit]: represents the average effort that is needed to inspect one size unit of design documents or program code.
- *Design_rework_effort_per_error* [person-days per defect]: represents the average effort needed to rework defect in a design document detected during design inspection.
- *Implementation_rework_effort_per_error* [person-days per defect]: represents the average effort needed to rework a defect in the program code detected during code inspection.

As QC-related risk factors, the following SPS model variables were identified:
- *Nominal_test_effectiveness* [%]: represents the average percentage of defects that are detected during testing.

- *Test_error_fix_effort* [person-days per defect]: represents the average effort needed to rework a defect in the program code detected during testing.

Table 25. QA/QC-related risk factors

QA/QC-related Risk Factor	Unit
Nominal_design_error_density	defects per size unit
Nominal_implementation_error_density	defects per size unit
Design_error_amplification	- no unit -
Nominal_inspection_effectiveness	%
Inspection_effort_per_task	person-days per size unit
Design_rework_effort_per_error	person-days per defect
Implementation_rework_effort_per_error	person-days per defect
Nominal_test_effectiveness	%
Test_error_fix_effort	person-days per defect
Manpower_skill	- no unit -

Finally, the SPS model variable *Manpower_skill* [no unit] can be identified as a risk factor related to the performance of both QA and QC activities. *Manpower_skill* represents the adequacy of the average skills of the workforce in relation to the difficulty of the project to be performed. If *Manpower_skill* is adequate (i.e., *Manpower_skill* = 1 ["medium"]), then the nominal productivity and defect generation rates apply. If *Manpower_skill* is unbalanced, e.g., too small (i.e., *Manpower_skill* = 0.5 ["low"]), then design, inspection, and test productivity decrease below the nominal values, while defect generation during design and coding increases above the nominal values. The summary list of all QA/QC-related risk factors with their associated units is shown in Table 25.

Define Impact Factors (STEP 2)

The following impact factors are of interest in the case example (see Figure 48):
- *Project_duration* [days]: represents the duration of the project in calendar days from begin of design to end of system test. One calendar day is equivalent to eight hours elapsed working time.
- *Project_effort* [person-days]: represents the effort consumption in person-days from begin of design to end of system test.
- *Product_field_defect_density* [defects per implemented size units]: represents the number of defects per code size unit that remain undetected in the program code after system test.

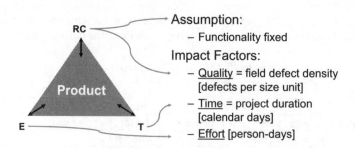

Fig. 48. Impact factors of the case example

It should be noted that in the case example, as indicated in Figure 48, the achievement of the specified functionality is not expected to vary, and thus is not considered an impact factor in the risk analysis.

Define Variation of Risk Factors (STEP 3)

Table 26 below shows the variation of risk factors in terms of fictitious expert estimates for minimum, maximum, and most probable (peak) value.

Table 26. QA/QC-related risk factor variation

QA/QC-related Risk Factors	*Expert Estimates for*		
	Min	*Peak*	*Max*
Nominal_design_error_density	1.30	**1.50**	*1.80*
Nominal_implementation_error_density	0.70	**1.00**	*1.20*
Design_error_amplification	1.50	**2.50**	*3.00*
Nominal_inspection_effectiveness	*0.60*	**0.70**	0.85
Inspection_effort_per_task	0.18	**0.20**	*0.25*
Design_rework_effort_per_error	0.07	**0.08**	*0.10*
Implementation_rework_effort_per_error	0.20	**0.24**	*0.30*
Nominal_test_effectiveness	*0.75*	**0.80**	0.90
Test_error_fix_effort	0.50	**0.60**	*0.80*
Manpower_skill	*0.80*	**1.00**	1.10

The most negative expected outcome with regard to its impact on project performance is formatted in italics. For example, in the case of *Design_error_amplification*, the minimal and maximal possible values are estimated to be 1.5 and 3.0, respectively, while the most probable (peak) value is estimated to be 2.5. Obviously, the maximal value 3.0 will cause more quality problems, effort consumption due to defect identification, and rework than the minimal or peak values.

Conduct Sensitivity Analyses (STEP 4)

Figures 49 to 51 below show the variation of the impact factors "project duration" (GENSIM variable *Project_duration*), "product quality" (GENSIM variable *Product_field_defect_density*), and "total project effort" (GENSIM variable *Project_effort*) when using multivariate Latin hypercube[18] sampling.

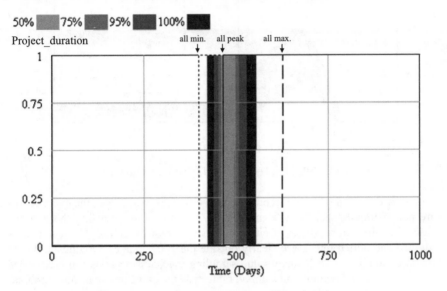

Fig. 49. Simulation output for project duration

The solid line ("peak line") represents the simulation result when assuming the peak value for each risk factor, while the intervals around the peak line represent the areas in which 50% (light gray), 75% (gray), 95% (dark gray), and 100% (black) of all simulation outcomes are located. The dotted and dashed lines represent simulation outcomes for the best and worst cases, i.e., those cases in which either all risk factors are concurrently either most favorable or most unfavorable with regards to project performance.

---

[18]Advice on selecting adequate random sampling techniques can be found in (Vose, 1996). Latin hypercube sampling is generally more precise for producing random samples than conventional Monte Carlo sampling, because the full range of the distribution is sampled more evenly and consistently.

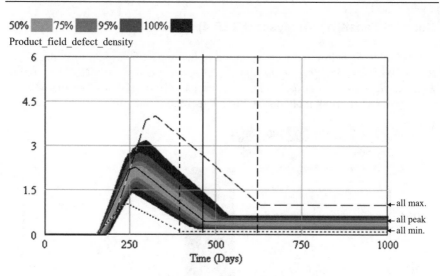

50% ▢ 75% ▨ 95% ▨ 100% ■

Product_field_defect_density

Fig. 50. Simulation output for product quality

As the case example does not represent a specific real-world case, the exact values are not of importance. What is interesting, though, is the fact that the extreme cases, i.e., the combinations of either exclusively best or exclusively worst cases (dashed and dotted lines), are clearly outside the 100% ranges. Obviously, due to the large number of risk factors, the sampling mechanism yields more balanced combinations of favorable and unfavorable risk factor values than the combinations of extremes.

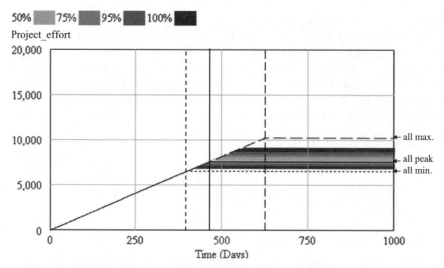

50% ▢ 75% ▨ 95% ▨ 100% ■

Project_effort

Fig. 51. Simulation output for total project effort consumption

On the other hand, there is still some variation of the impact factors that needs to be considered when estimating potential loss of value of the delivered product. Furthermore, it can be seen that the simulated averages of project duration and project effort overrun the all-peak outcomes, while the simulated average of product quality is below the value of the all-peak outcome. This is interesting, because it implies that the risk of loss of business value – or, in other words: the risk of missing the planned product value (i.e., the all-peak values) – is unbalanced.

Analyze Simulation Results (STEP 5)

The simulation results produced in STEP 4 can be used to prioritize risks, to focus investments into risk prevention, risk control, and risk mitigation activities, and to calculate potential losses of product value in the cases of lower than planned project performance.

Losses only occur when at least one impact factor yields a result that is worse than its planned value[19]. Typical examples of costs that induce value losses are cost of late delivery (e.g., contract penalties), cost of lacking quality (e.g., unbudgeted rework cost), and cost of effort overrun (e.g., unbudgeted labor cost). In order to calculate the potential losses for each individual cost category it is necessary to establish a cost function and to combine this cost function with the probability of risk realization.

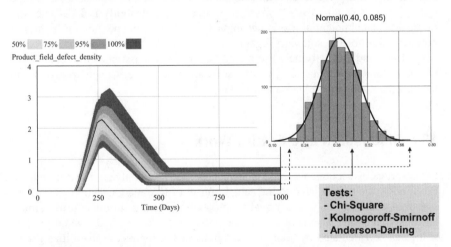

Fig. 52. Construction of the impact factor probability distribution

The probability of risk realization is defined as $1 - P(X \leq$ planned quality$)$ or $1 - F($planned quality$)$ where X is the value of the impact factor and F is the associated

---

[19]The planned values are equal to the peak line, if the project planning is done based on the experts' peak estimates and the SPS model is valid.

probability distribution of X. F can be identified with the help of standard good-ness-of-fit tests (D'Agostino and Stephens, 1986) based on the simulation results. Figure 52 shows the fitted probability distribution of impact factor *Product_field_defect_density* which, in the case example, can be approximated by the normal distribution N(0.40, 0.085).

As an example, for impact factor *Product_field_defect_density*, the potential loss due to lower than planned product quality can be calculated as follows:

$$ExpectedLossProductQuality = \frac{P}{100\%} \cdot S \cdot C \cdot (1 - F(Q)), \text{ where}$$

P denotes the percentage of undetected defects that will surface after delivery,
S denotes the size of the delivered functionality, e.g., in Function Points (FP)
C denotes the correction cost per defect after test,
Q denotes the planned quality after test (e.g., undetected defects per FP), and
F denotes the fitted probability distribution N(0.40, 0.085)

In the case example, the planned (or at least expected) value of impact factor *Product_field_defect_density*, Q, equals 0.45 undetected defects per FP. There-fore, $1 - F(Q)$, i.e., the cumulative probability of missing this threshold equals 0.28. Similar calculations can be conducted for impact factors *Project_duration* and *Project_effort*. For these factors, however, the cumulative prob-abilities of missing the related thresholds are less favorable. For example, in the case of impact factor *Project_effort*, the cumulative probability is 0.72. The sum of the associated potential losses per impact factor gives the potential total loss of product value for the software organization in relation to the expected effective-ness of QA and QC activities. For a comprehensive discussion of the relation be-tween risk and the economic value of a software product, see Chapter 5, or refer to the excellent book by DeMarco and Lister (2003).

13.5 Discussion and Future Work

In the previous section, we have shown how one can analyze with the help of ProSim/RA the risks related to the actual impact of QA and QC activities (i.e., in-spections and tests) on product quality, project duration, and project effort simul-taneously. We have also shown how the potential losses to the delivered product value can be calculated by applying cost functions to the risk probabilities gener-ated by ProSim/RA.

It should be noted that many other scenarios than the one presented in the case example are possible. In particular, the risk of making a wrong decision with re-gards to technology selection can be assessed by applying ProSim/RA, including the calculation of potential loss of product value. A typical scenario is related to making the right decision on selecting the most effective inspection technique with regards to overall project performance (project duration, project effort, prod-uct quality). In a ProSim/RA-based analysis representing this scenario, we compared type-A design and code inspections to type-B design and code inspections, where type-A inspections are supposed to find on average about 60% of all defects with a defect type distribution that is proportional to the distribution of defect types contained in the design and code, while type-B inspections are supposed to find on average only about 50% of the defects contained in the design and code but with a higher proportion of defects difficult to correct (if found in later phases). While type-A inspections can be considered a value-neutral neutral defect detection technique (as they are blind towards the variation of defect types with regards to their difficulty of correction), type-B inspections are value-based because they focus on detection of defects difficult to correct (and thus expensive).

The result of the ProSim/RA-based analysis showed that there was no significant difference between inspection types A and B if they are only applied to 50% of the design and code documentation, while type-B inspections have a more positive effect on overall project performance than type-A inspections if they are both applied to 100% of the documentation. In the latter case, type-B inspections reduce the number of remaining defects (of all types) in the code after test by about 20% and save about 10% effort and time as compared to type-A inspections. As a byproduct the analysis also reconfirmed the claim that using inspections (no matter which type they are) is better than not using inspections as a QA technique in software development. The product value gained by applying inspections can be calculated in a similar way as shown in Section 13.5.

The strengths of the proposed risk analysis procedure ProSim/RA can be summarized as follows:

- *Multi-causality:* The procedure offers the possibility to assess the impact of risk factors not only individually but concurrently. In other words, it is a holistic approach which does not limit itself to monocausal dependencies but facilitates the consideration of complex interdependencies among risk factors.
- *Comprehensiveness:* Similarly, the procedure offers the possibility to asses the impact of risk factors not only on one impact factor but on several impact factors simultaneously, thus allowing for tradeoff analyses and holistic assessment of potential loss to product value.
- *Flexibility:* The procedure offers the possibility to combine statistical analysis with expert knowledge.
- *Adaptability:* The procedure offers the possibility to assess and compare the impact of different SE methods, techniques, and tools by adapting the underlying SPS model. For example, the SPS model GENSIM could be changed to have three defect co-flows for high, medium, and low businesspriority defects, and then be used in combination with ProSim/RA to explore the differences between value-neutral inspection and test strategies versus strategies focusing effort on the detection of high businesspriority defects. Examples of value-based methods of defect reduction can be found in this book, e.g., value-based inspection and testing based on prioritized requirements is discussed in Chapter 7, 9, and 12.

- The weaknesses and limitations of the proposed risk analysis procedure ProSim/RA can be summarized as follows:
  - The costs for SPS model development and maintenance are high.
  - It is difficult to achieve sufficient validity of the SPS model.

In order to overcome the weaknesses and limitations of ProSim/RA even more efficient and effective simulation modeling approaches than the existing ones are needed. Two promising research directions have been identified, i.e., improving reusability of SPS models by offering sets of model patterns, and increasing modeling efficiency by introducing agile development principles into existing SPS model development practice (Angkasaputra and Pfahl, 2004). In addition, to improve validity and maintainability of SPS models, opportunities to better integrate the SPS model with existing organizational experience bases need to be pursued. Initial work in this direction has been done by Münch and Armbrust (2003), and Rus et al. (2002).

In order to better exploit the benefits of ProSim/RA for business planning, a more systematic integration of simulation-based risk assessment with the VBSE framework is still required. The seven key elements of VBSE are (Chapter 2; Boehm, 2003; Boehm and Huang, 2003): benefits realization analysis, stakeholders' value proposition elicitation and reconciliation, business case analysis, continuous risk and opportunity management, concurrent system and software engineering, value-based monitoring and control, change as opportunity. The potential usefulness of SPS for VBSE has been demonstrated by Madachy (2004) who investigated the application of SPS models to assess product quality options and their impact on business value. His work shows how software business decision making can improve with value information gained from simulation experiments. In general, SPS can be used to reason about software value decisions, i.e., it can help find the right balance of activities that contribute to stakeholder value with other constraints such as quality, cost, and schedule.

In contrast to Madachy's research, which focuses on business case analysis, we have been focusing on risk management. So far, however, we have only been able to demonstrate the usefulness of SPS to assess the sensitivity of certain risk factors on important dimensions of project performance and product quality (impact factors). More research is needed to find ways for mapping simulated impact factor values onto generally accepted business value scales. The framework proposed in Chapter 5 might be a good starting point in this regard. In addition, more work will be done to further exploit the analytic power of ProSim/RA. We see two different promising research directions.

Firstly, due to the very generic nature of its five step approach, ProSim/RA could be combined with more specialized techniques that were developed to solve very specific software engineering problems. For example, the F-EVOLVE* method for value-based software release planning proposed in Chapter 12, which is based on comprehensive stakeholder involvement and the execution of genetic algorithms for problem solving, could possibly be connected to ProSim/RA, e.g., by providing a distribution of feasible release plans as one input to a more comprehensive risk assessment task.

Secondly, the five step procedure of ProSim/RA is not necessarily restricted to risk assessment. It could also be interpreted as a procedure that helps explore the opportunities for change, e.g., by analyzing the negative impacts (risks) and positive impacts (opportunities) that the introduction of a new technique or the change of an activity in a process may have. If we find ways to smoothly integrate such an impact exploration tool into regular software development, the seventh key element in Boehm's VBSE framework ("change as opportunity") will move closer to reality.

In conclusion, we see the main benefit of ProSim/RA – and SPS in general – in using simulation outcomes to support informed decision making in VBSE. This may happen either by stand-alone application for risk assessment and improvement opportunity exploration or by synergetic combination with specialized analysis and decision support techniques.

References

(Abdel-Hamid and Madnick, 1991) Abdel-Hamid, T. K., Madnick, S. E.: Software Project Dynamics – an Integrated Approach (Prentice-Hall, 1991)

(Angkasaputra and Pfahl, 2004) Angkasaputra, N., Pfahl, D.: Making Software Process Simulation Modeling Agile and Pattern-based. In: Proc. of 5th International Workshop on Software Process Simulation Modeling, Edinburgh, Scotland (IEE, Stevenage 2004), pp 222–227

(Aranda et al., 1993) Aranda, R. R., Fiddaman, T., Oliva, R.: Quality Microworlds: modeling the impact of quality initiatives over the software product life cycle. American Programmer, May, pp 52–61 (1993)

(Bandinelli et al., 1995) Bandinelli, S., Fuggetta, A., Lavazza, L., Loi, M., Picco, G. P.: Modeling and Improving an Industrial Software Process. TSE 21(5), pp 440–453 (1995)

(Birk and Pfahl, 2002) Birk, A., Pfahl, D.: A Systems Perspective on Software Process Improvement. In: Proc. of 4th International Conference on Product Focused Software Process Improvement, Rovaniemi, Finland (2002), pp 4–18

(Birkhölzer et al., 2004) Birkhölzer, T., Dantas, L., Dickmann, C., Vaupel, J.: Interactive Simulation of Software Producing Organization's Operations based on Concepts of CMMI and Balanced Scorecards. In: Proc. of 5th International Workshop on Software Process Simulation Modeling, Edinburgh, Scotland (IEE, Stevenage 2004), pp 123–132

(Boehm, 1991) Boehm, B. W.: Software Risk Management: Principles and Practices. IEEE Software, pp 32–41 (January 1991)

(Boehm, 2003) Boehm, B. W.: Value-Based Software Engineering. Software Engineering Notes 28(2), pp 1–12 (May 2003)

(Boehm and Huang, 2003) Boehm, B. W., Huang, L.: Value-Based Software Engineering: A Case Study. IEEE Software, pp 33–41 (March 2003)

(Bröckers, 1995) Bröckers, A.: Process-based software risk assessment. In: Proc. of 4th European Workshop on Software Process Technology (1995), pp 9–29

(Bröckers et al., 1995) Bröckers, A., Lott, C. M., Rombach, H. D., Verlage, M.: MVP–L language report version 2. Technical Report 265/95, Department of Computer Science, University of Kaiserslautern, Germany (1995)

(Cartwright and Shepperd, 1999) Cartwright, M., Shepperd, M.: On building dynamic models of maintenance behavior. In: Project Control for Software Quality, ed by Kusters, R., Cowderoy, A., Heemstra, F., van Veenendaal, E. (Shaker Publishing, 1999)

(Christie, 1999a) Christie, A. M.: Simulation: An Enabling Technology in Software Engineering. CROSSTALK, pp 2–7 (1999)

(Christie, 1999b) Christie, A. M.: Simulation in support of CMM-based process improvement. JSS 46(2/3), pp 107–112 (1999)

(Christie and Staley, 2002) Christie, A. M., Staley, M. J.: Organizational and Social Simulation of a Requirements Development Process. SPIP 5, pp 103–110 (2002)

(D'Agostino and Stephens, 1986) D'Agostino, R. B., Stephens, M. A.: Goodness-of-Fit Techniques (Marcel Dekker, New York 1986)

(DeMarco and Lister, 2003) DeMarco, T., Lister, T.: Waltzing with Bears (Dorset House Publishing, New York 2003)

(Drappa and Ludewig, 1999) Drappa, A., Ludewig, J.: Quantitative modeling for the interactive simulation of software projects. JSS 46(2/3), pp 113–122 (1999)

(Ferreira et al., 2003) Ferreira, S., Collofello, J., Shunk, D., Mackulak, G., Wolfe, P.: Utilization of Process Modeling and Simulation in Understanding the Effects of Requirements Volatility in Software Development. In: Proc. of 4th Process Simulation Modelling Workshop, Portland, USA, 3–4 May (2003)

(Forrester, 1961) Forrester, J.W.: Industrial Dynamics, (Productivity Press, Cambridge 1961)

(Höst et al., 2000) Höst, M., Regnell, B., Dag, J., Nedstam, J., Nyberg, C.: Exploring Bootlenecks in Market-Driven Requirements Management Processes with Discrete Event Simulation. In: Proc. of 3rd Process Simulation Modeling Workshop, London, United Kingdom, 12–14 July (2000)

(Houston et al., 2001) Houston, D. X., Mackulak, G. T., Collofello, J. S.: Stochastic simulation of risk factor potential effects for software development risk management. JSS 59(3), pp 247–257 (2001)

(Jensen and Scacchi, 2003) Jensen, C., Scacchi, W.: Simulating an Automated Approach to Discovery and Modeling of Open Source Software Development Processes. In: Proc. of 4th Process Simulation Modeling Workshop, Portland, USA, 3–4 May (2003)

(Kellner and Hansen, 1989) Kellner, M. I., Hansen, G. A.: Software Process Modeling: A Case Study. In: Proc. of 22nd Annual Hawaii International Conference on System Sciences, Vol. II – Software Track (1989), pp 175–188

(Kellner et al., 1999) Kellner M. I., Madachy, R. J., Raffo, D. M.: Software process simulation modeling: Why? What? How? JSS 46(2/3), pp 91–105 (1999)

(Kontio, 2001) Kontio, J.: Software Engineering Risk Management – A Method, Improvement Framework and Empirical Evaluation, Doctoral Dissertation (Helsinki University of Technology, 2001)

(Lin et al., 1997) Lin, C. Y., Abdel-Hamid, T. K., Sherif, J. S.: Software-Engineering Process Simulation Model (SEPS). JSS 38, pp 263–277 (1997)

(Lee and Miller, 2004) Lee, B., Miller, J.: Multi-Project Management in Software Engineering Using Simulation Modeling. Software Quality J. 12, pp 59–82 (2004)

(Lott et al., 1995) Lott, C. M., Hoisl, B., Rombach, H. D.: The use of roles and measurement to enact project plans in MVP-S. In: Proc. of 4th European Workshop on Software Process Technology, Noordwijkerhout, The Netherlands, LNCS, vol. 913 (Springer, 1995), pp 30–48

(Madachy, 1996) Madachy, R. J.: System Dynamics Modeling of an Inspection-Based Process. In: Proc. of 18th International Conference on Software Engineering, Berlin, Germany (IEEE Computer Society, 1996), pp 376–386

(Madachy, 2004) Madachy, R. J.: A Software Product Business Case Model. In: Proc. of 5th International Workshop on Software Process Simulation Modeling, Edinburgh, Scotland (IEE, Stevenage 2004), pp 232–236

(Madachy, 2005) Madachy, R. J.: Software Process Dynamics, in press (IEEE Computer Society, 2005)

(Madachy and Tarbet, 2000) Madachy, R. J., Tarbet, D.: Case Studies in Software Process Modeling with System Dynamics. SPIP 5, pp 133–146 (2000)

(Mišic et al., 2004) Mišic, V. B., Gevaert, H., Rennie, M.: Extreme Dynamics: Towards a System Dynamics Model of the Extreme Programming Software Development Process. In: Proc. of 5th International Workshop on Software Process Simulation Modeling, Edinburgh, Scotland (IEE, Stevenage 2004), pp 237–242

(Münch and Armbrust, 2003) Münch, J., Armbrust, O.: Using Empirical Knowledge from Replicated Experiments for Software Process Simulation: A Practical Example. In: Proc. of the 2003 International Symposium on Empirical Software Engineering (IEEE Computer Society, 2003), pp 18–27

(Neu et al., 2002) Neu, H., Hanne, T., Münch, J., Nickel, S., Wirsen, A.: Simulation-Based Risk Reduction for Planning Inspections. In: Proc. of 4th International Conference on Product Focused Software Process Improvement, Rovaniemi, Finland (2002), pp 78–93

(Neu et al., 2003) Neu, H., Hanne, T., Münch, J., Nickel, S., Wirsen, A.: Creating a Code Inspection Model for Simulation-based Decision Support. In: Proc. of 4th Process Simulation Modeling Workshop, Portland, USA, 3–4 May (2003)

(Pfahl, 2001) Pfahl D.: An Integrated Approach to Simulation-Based Learning in Support of Strategic and Project Management in Software Organisations, Theses in Experimental Software Engineering, vol. 8 (Fraunhofer IRB, Stuttgart 2001)

(Pfahl and Birk, 2000) Pfahl, D., Birk, A.: Using Simulation to Visualise and Analyse Product-Process Dependencies in Software Development Projects. In: Proc. of 2nd International Conference on Product Focused Software Process Improvement, Oulu, Finland (2000), pp 88–102

(Pfahl and Lebsanft, 2000a) Pfahl, D., Lebsanft, K.: Using Simulation to Analyse the Impact of Software Requirement Volatility on Project Performance. IST 42(14), pp 1001–1008 (2000)

(Pfahl and Lebsanft, 2000b) Pfahl, D., Lebsanft, K.: Knowledge Acquisition and Process Guidance for Building System Dynamics Simulation Models: An Experience Report from Software Industry. IJSEKE 10(4), pp 487–510 (2000)

(Pfahl and Ruhe, 2001) Pfahl, D., Ruhe, G.: System Dynamics as an Enabling Technology for Learning in Software Organisations. In: Proc. of 13th International Conference on Software Engineering and Knowledge Engineering (Knowledge Systems Institute, Skokie 2001), pp 355–362

(Pfahl and Ruhe, 2002) Pfahl, D., Ruhe, G.: IMMoS – A Methodology for Integrated Measurement, Modelling, and Simulation. SPIP 7, pp 189–210 (2002)

(Pfahl and Ruhe, 2003) Pfahl, D., Ruhe, G.: Goal-Oriented Measurement plus System Dynamics. A Hybrid and Evolutionary Approach. In: Proc. of 4th Process Simulation Modeling Workshop, Portland, USA, 3–4 May (2003)

(Pfahl et al., 2001) Pfahl, D., Klemm, M., Ruhe, G.: A CBT module with integrated simulation component for software project management education and training. JSS 59 (3), pp 283–298 (2001)

(Pfahl et al., 2004) Pfahl, D., Stupperich, M., Krivobokova, T.: PL-SIM: A Generic Simulation Model for Studying Strategic SPI in the Automotive Industry. In: Proc. of 5th International Workshop on Software Process Simulation Modeling, Edinburgh, Scotland (IEE, Stevenage 2004), pp 149–158

(Powell et al., 1999) Powell, A., Mander, K., Brown, D.: Strategies for lifecycle concurrency and iteration: A system dynamics approach. JSS 46(2/3), pp 151–162 (1999)

(Raffo and Kellner, 1999) Raffo, D. M., Kellner, I. K.: Modeling Software Processes Quantitatively and Assessing the Impact of Potential Process Changes of Process Performance. In: Elements of Software Process assessment and Improvement, ed by El Emam K, Madhavji N. H. (IEEE Computer Society, 1999), pp 297–341

(Raffo and Kellner, 2000) Raffo, D. M., Kellner, M. I.: Analyzing the Unit Test Process Using Software Process Simulation Models: A Case Study. In: Proc. of 3rd Process Simulation Modeling Workshop, London, United Kingdom, 12–14 July (2000)

(Raffo et al., 1999) Raffo, D. M,. Vandeville, J. V., Martin, R. H.: Software process simulation to achieve higher CMM levels. JSS 46(2/3), pp 163–172 (1999)

(Raffo et al., 2003) Raffo, D., Setamanit, S., Wakeland, W.: Towards a Software Process Simulation Model of Globally Distributed Software Development Projects. In: Proc. of 4th Process Simulation Modeling Workshop, Portland, USA, 3–4 May (2003)

(Raffo et al., 2004) Raffo, D., Nayak, U., Setamanit, S., Sullivan, P., Wakeland, W.: Using Software Process Simulation to Assess the Impact of IV&V Activities. In: Proc. of 5th International Workshop on Software Process Simulation Modeling, Edinburgh, Scotland (IEE, Stevenage 2004), pp 197–205

(Roehling et al., 2000) Roehling, S. T., Collofello, J. S., Hermann, B. G., Smith-Daniels, D. E.: System Dynamics Modeling Applied to Software Outsourcing Decision Support. SPIP 5, pp 169–182 (2000)

(Ruiz et al., 2002) Ruiz, M., Ramos, I., Toro, M.: Integrating Dynamic Models for CMM-Based Software Process Improvement. In: Proc. of 4th International

Conference on Product Focused Software Process Improvement, Rovaniemi, Finland (2002), pp 63–77

(Ruiz et al., 2004) Ruiz, M., Ramos, I., Toro, M.: Using Dynamic Modeling and Simulation to Improve the COTS Software Process. In: Proc. of 5th International Conference on Product Focused Software Process Improvement, Kyoto, Japan (2004), pp 568–581

(Rus et al., 2002) Rus, I., Biffl, S., Halling, M.: Systematically Combining Process Simulation and Empirical Data in Support of Decision Analysis in Software Development. In: Proc. of 14th International Conference on Software Engineering and Knowledge Engineering, Ischia, Italy (2002)

(Rus et al., 1999) Rus, I., Collofello, J., Lakey, P.: Software process simulation for reliability management. JSS 46(2/3), pp 173–182 (1999)

(Smith and Ramil, 2002) Smith, N., Ramil, J. F.: Qualitative Simulation of Software Evolution Processes. In: Proc. of WESS'02, Montreal, Canada (2002), pp 41–47

(Stallinger and Grünbacher, 2001) Stallinger, F., Grünbacher, P.: System dynamics modelling and simulation of collaborative requirements engineering. JSS 59, pp 311–321 (2001)

(Tvedt and Collofello, 1995) Tvedt, J. D., Collofello, J. S.: Evaluating the Effectiveness of Process Improvements on Development Cycle Time via System Dynamics Modelling. In: Proc. of Computer Science and Application Conference (1995), pp 318–325

(Vose, 1996) Vose, D.: Quantitative Risk Analysis: A Guide to Monte Carlo Simulation Modelling (Wiley, 1996)

(Wallmüller, 2004) Wallmüller, E.: Risikomanagement für IT- und Software-Projekte (Hanser, 2004)

(Weil and Dalton, 1992) Weil, H. B., Dalton, W. J.: Risk Management in Complex Projects. In: Proc. of System Dynamics Conference, Utrecht, The Netherlands (1992), pp 39–49

(Wernick and Hall, 2004) Wernick, P., Hall, T.: A Policy Investigation Model for Long-term Software Evolution Processes. In: Proc. of 5th International Workshop on Software Process Simulation Modeling, Edinburgh, Scotland (IEE, Stevenage 2004), pp 149–158

(Williford and Chang, 1999) Williford, J., Chang, A.: Modelling the FedEx IT Division: A System Dynamics Approach to Strategic IT Planning. JSS 46(2/3), pp 203–211 (1999)

Author Biography

Dietmar Pfahl is a professor at University of Calgary, Canada. He previously held a position as department head at the Fraunhofer Institute for Experimental Software Engineering (IESE) in Kaiserslautern, Germany. He has more than 15 years of experience in conducting and leading national and international research and transfer projects with the software industry, including organizations such as

Bosch, DaimlerChrysler, Dräger, Ericsson, and Siemens. He has more than 50 refereed publications. He is a regular reviewer and program committee member of scientific journals, conferences, and workshops. His current research interests include quantitative software project management, software process analysis and improvement, and simulation-based learning and decision support.

14 Tailoring Software Traceability to Value-Based Needs

Alexander Egyed

Abstract: Software development generates and maintains a wide range of artifacts, such as documentation, requirements, design models, and test scenarios; all of which add value to the understanding of the software system. Trace dependencies identify the relationships among these artifacts. They contribute to the better understanding of a software system as they link its distributed knowledge. Trace dependencies are also vital for many automated analyses including the impact of change and consistency checking. This chapter compares the problem of manual traceability versus automated traceability with the Trace/Analyzer approach. This chapter also explores how to tailor precision, completeness, correctness, and timeliness to adjust the trace analysis to value-based needs.

Keywords: Traceability, software modeling, trace analysis, trade-off analysis, consistency, impact of change, change propagation, traceability uncertainties.

14.1 Introduction

Software development is a process that involves many stakeholders and generates a range of development artifacts. For example, the requirements are typically captured independently from the design/implementation although it has been recognized that there is a strong, intertwined relationship between them (Nuseibeh, 2001). The design, in turn, is often refined stepwise over several layers to explore the complexity of subsystems. Each such subsystem or layer may be the explored structurally (i.e., class diagrams) and/or behaviorally (i.e., sequence or statechart diagrams) (Rumbaugh et al., 1999).

Handling artifacts independently benefits the concurrent software development (Boehm, 2003) because it separates concerns, reduces complexity, and allows engineers to work independently. However, these artifacts (e.g., requirements, design) must to be linked together to understand their combined impact on the software system. Trace dependencies explicitly describe the relationships among such separately recorded artifacts.

In some form, every software artifact has "some relationship" to every other artifact. We thus define a trace dependency to specifically identify whether two, separately recorded artifacts have the same/similar meaning (i.e., since traces tend to bridge artifacts of different modeling notations it is typically not possible to capture the same/similar artifacts in a uniform manner). However, there are many potential trace dependencies and value-based software engineering (Boehm, 2003; Boehm and Huang, 2003) recognizes that it is not always meaningful to capture all of them without understanding their value. While this chapter does not discuss how artifacts differ in their value, it does stipulate that the quality of trace dependencies should reflect the value of the artifacts they bridge (better quality traces for higher value artifacts). It is thus beneficial to customize traces in terms of their precision, completeness, correctness, and timeliness.

Trace analysis is the process of finding and validating trace dependencies among artifacts. While finding trace dependencies alone is not sufficient to reconcile multiple perspectives, they are the foundation for any such mechanism. Trace dependencies are vital for documentation, program understanding, impact analysis, consistency checking, reuse, quality assurance, user acceptance, error reduction, cost estimation, and customer satisfaction (Antoniol et al., 2002; Biffl and Halling, 2003; Pohl, 1996; Gotel and Finkelstein, 1994; Ramesh, 1993). Their absence usually inhibits automation. This chapter discusses how to generate and validate trace dependencies and how to customize this process to value-based needs. That is, not all traces are equally important and this chapter demonstrates how the trace analysis can be tailored to the importance of the artifacts they bridge. It must be noted that this chapter does not discuss the many uses of trace dependencies (besides some examples).

Not understanding trace dependencies has many negative side effects. Most significantly, it increases the risk that changes are not propagated correctly. And it causes errors in that engineers, ignorant or unaware of the inconsistencies, make decisions on inaccurate information.

Trace analysis is well motivated in value-based software engineering (Boehm, 2003) due to the need to evolve the system and software concurrently. Concurrent engineering implies that changes can happen anytime and anywhere and traces help the engineer in identifying the impact of those changes across all development artifacts (e.g., requirements, design, and implementation). Traces are also vital for value-based monitoring and control (Boehm, 2003) because the engineer needs to understand the mapping between goals and solution. This value benefit has been recognized in the past as there are many standards that mandate trace analysis as a required activity (e.g., DOD Std 2167A, IEEE Std. 1219, ISO 15504, and SEI CMM).

On the downside, trace analysis is a complex activity. Standards encourage trace analysis but they generally do not tell how to do it (Lindvall, 1994; Lindvall and Sandahl, 1996). Also, existing tool support is typically limited to the recording of trace dependencies but not to their identification (Antoniol et al., 2002) (i.e., traceability matrix). As a result, thorough trace analysis is a predominantly manual activity (Card, 1992) that has to cope with many complexities:

- *Non-scalable growth:* up to n^2 trace dependencies for n artifacts (Antoniol et al., 2002; Card, 1992)
- *Syntactic and semantic differences:* hard to identify traces exactly (Övergaard, 1998; Jacobson, 1987).
- *Informal/semiformal languages* (e.g., requirements, UML design): artifacts are described imprecisely (Finkelstein et al., 1991) and cause trace uncertainties (Egyed, 2004).

- *Many-to-many mappings* (Tilbury, 1989): a requirement is often implemented by multiple design elements but these design elements may also implement other requirements.
- *Incompleteness and inconsistencies* (Lindvall and Sandahl, 1996).
- *Different stakeholders in charge of different software artifacts* (Boehm et al., 1998) where no single stakeholder understands them all.
- *Increasingly rapid pace of change* (Moore, 1995): traces change as their artifacts evolve.
- *Nonlinear increase in the number of software artifacts* during the course of the software lifecycle (Cross, 1991) (this feeds to the n^2 complexity)

In summary, no simple, accurate, and automated approach to trace analysis exists to date. The few approaches that support the automatic detection of trace dependencies usually require precise and complete models, i.e., if you make the models precise enough then trace analysis becomes implicit (Jacobson, 1987). However, informal requirements and popular design models (e.g., UML) are not nearly precise enough to benefit from this automation. Therefore, comprehensive trace analysis is largely a manual activity resulting in high cost, incompleteness, and even incorrectness (Cross, 1991). The predominant way of dealing with this complexity is by limiting trace analysis to *some* necessary minimum. Unfortunately, engineers rarely predict accurately which trace dependencies are more important than others.

This chapter introduces a testing-based approach to trace analysis that reduces or avoids all of the complexities discussed above. This chapter also emphasizes value-based tradeoffs during trace analysis. These trade-offs explore:
- what traces are needed (i.e., not all traces are equally important)
- when those traces are needed (i.e., not all traces are needed at the same time)
- what level of precision (detail), correctness, and completeness these traces are needed (i.e., to concentrate on traces that have a higher value)

That is, we demonstrate how to tailor trace analysis to the needs of value-based software engineering by producing better quality traces for higher value artifacts. This saves cost and effort in that unnecessary trace analysis is avoided (or reduced). It must be noted that this chapter does not discuss how to identify high value artifacts (e.g., see Chapters 9 and 12 for information on requirements prioritization techniques) and it does not identify what quality of traces are needed for certain uses (e.g., see Chapter 11 on using traces for value-based testing). This information is expected as input and it is used to guide (tailor) the trace analysis.

In the following, we will demonstrate how to compute traces through transitive observations and, in doing so, how to reduce the quadratic traceability problem to a linear one (where *n* inputs compute up to n^2 results). Precision, completeness, and correctness are tailorable variables during the trace analysis to reduce cost and increase (or maintain) quality. These variables are customizable to individual artifacts to cater to the needs of value-based software engineering (i.e., to support the prioritization of artifacts). That is, since value-based software engineering decides on the importance of artifacts, we will demonstrate how to customize trace analysis to match traceability quality accordingly.

Section 14.2 introduces an illustrative example to discuss the complexities of trace analysis and Section 14.3 presents our testing-based approach. Section 14.4 then generalizes our approach and Section 14.5 discusses various factors that influence the results of the trace analysis.

14.2 Video-on-Demand Case Study

We will demonstrate our approach on a Video-on-Demand (VoD) system[20] that provides capabilities for searching, selecting, and playing movies. The "on-demand feature" supports the playing of a movie concurrently while downloading its data from a remote site.

Software Artifacts (Requirements, Design, and Code)

The VoD system consists of 21 Java classes and uses a large number of off-the-shelf library classes. The VoD system was modeled using various diagrams (e.g., class and statechart diagrams) and textual views (e.g., requirements) (Egyed and Grünbacher, 2002). The purpose of the trace analysis is to uncover the relationships among these requirements, design, and code artifacts.

Table 27. List of VoD requirements

r0	Download movie data on-demand while playing a movie
r1	Play movie automatically after selection from list
r2	User should be able to display textual information about a selected movie
r3	User should be able to pause a movie
r4	Three seconds max to load movie list
r5	Three seconds max to load textual information about a movie
r6	One second max to start playing a movie
r7	Novices should be able to use the major system functions (selecting movie, playing/pausing/stopping movie) without training
r8	User should be able to stop a movie
r9	User should be able to (re) start a movie

Table 27 depicts a subset of the VoD requirements. For instance, requirement *r7* defines the need for an intuitive user interface modeled after a VCR player. Requirement *r6* defines a maximum delay of one second to start playing a movie once it has been selected. These requirements are written in an informal prose and it is generally infeasible to identify trace dependencies among them automatically.

---

[20]Java MPEG Player available at http://peace.snu.ac.kr/dhkim/java/MPEG/

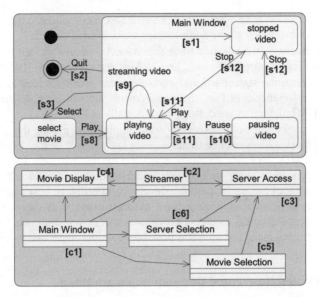

Fig. 53. Class and statechart diagram of the VoD system

The VoD system was modeled in UML and Figure 53 depicts two UML diagrams (perspectives) of its structure and behavior. The statechart diagram (top) describes the behavior of the VoD. A user may select individual movies for playing. During playing, a selected movie may be paused, stopped, and played again. The transitions between these states correspond to buttons a user may press in the VoD's user interface. The class diagram (bottom) shows the coarse structural decomposition of the VoD system. In the following, the model elements are often referred to by their short identifiers. Note that the presented model is a subset of the actual UML model for brevity.

Trace Dependencies and their Complexity

The goal of the trace analysis is to understand how the software artifacts in Table 27 and Figure 53 relate to one another and to the source code. As such, trace analysis should reveal how the statechart elements relate to the classes or how the requirements relate to the statechart and class elements. After all, every state transition describes a distinct behavior and every class describes a different part of the structure that implements that behavior. Thus, they represent two separate perspectives of the VoD system. The goal of the trace analysis is to identify the commonality between them. For example, what state transition requires the *Streamer* class? Or what classes implement the *"Play"* transition? While it might be easy to guess some of these trace dependencies, the semiformal nature of the UML diagrams and the informal nature of the requirements make it hard to identify them completely and virtually impossible to do so automatically.

While the VoD system appears rather small and uncomplicated, it may surprise one that it exhibits many of the complexities we discussed earlier:

- It has factually, 1,012 possible trace dependencies among the ten requirements, six classes, eight state transitions, and 21 Java classes (i.e., $(6+10+8+21)^2/2$).
- The requirements, statechart, and class diagrams exhibit strong syntactic and semantic differences; in fact, the requirements are not even defined formally and the UML diagrams are defined semiformally at best.
- There is no guarantee of consistency and completeness among these artifacts as different stakeholders created them.

How could any trace analysis tool ever understand these development artifacts? And if no such tool can understand the development artifacts, how could they ever identify trace dependencies among them automatically? It is clear that no fully automated approach could do that. This chapter will demonstrate what guidance is required by the engineer and how it is possible to reduce these many complexities.

A Few Samples How Trace Dependencies are Used

Trace analysis does not solve issues such as requirements conflict analysis, impact of changes, or consistency checking. However, trace analysis provides a necessary foundation for doing these and other activities. The following illustrates the use of trace dependencies during some of these activities.

Table 27 exhibits a conflict between two requirements that is not obvious to see at first. Requirement $r6$ is a performance requirement that requires at most a one second delay in starting a selected movie. What is not obvious is that in order to start the movie, the player needs to know about the movie details (i.e., location of file for streaming). We find that the requirement $r5$ allows for a three second response time for downloading the movie info. This is a potential conflict as the downloading of the movie details may take more time than the starting of the movie is allowed to take altogether. Trace analysis should identify a trace dependency among the two requirements. While knowing about this trace dependency, in itself, does not identify the conflict among the two requirements, it nevertheless implies the close relationship between the two requirements which is important for conflict analysis (Egyed and Grünbacher, 2004).

Trace analysis should also identify a trace dependency between requirement $r1$ and the statechart elements $s3$ and $s8$. This trace dependency implies that the selecting and automated playing of a movie is implemented in the "select" and "play" transitions of the statechart diagram. If this requirement changes (i.e., no longer start the playing of a movie automatically after selection) then the transitions $s3$ and $s8$ are affected and may need to be changed also. While trace dependencies alone are not sufficient to describe the impact of changes, it is obvious that they play a vital role during the "impact of a change" analysis.

And trace analysis should identify trace dependencies between the class diagram and the source code. This information is important for consistency checking to, say, validate whether the calling dependencies in the design are implemented correctly. For example, the class diagram defines a calling dependency (arrow) between $c2$ and $c3$. Therefore, the Java classes that implement $c2$ must call at least one of the Java classes that implement $c3$. As before, trace dependencies do not guarantee consistency but consistency checking relies on trace dependencies to understand what to compare.

14.3 Testing-Based Trace Analysis

Trace analysis is the process of identifying trace dependencies among software artifacts. The following discusses a strongly iterative, testing-based approach to trace analysis. We will show that it is possible to largely automate the generation and maintenance of trace dependencies. And we will show that it is possible to reduce and even eliminate all of the complexities associated with trace analysis discussed previously.

Our approach simplifies the trace analysis by using and observing test executions (Egyed, 2002). Testing is a natural process during software development. It is not difficult for an engineer to supply a set of test scenarios (Lindvall, 1994). Of course, an executable software system is needed to test the scenarios but such a (partial) system typically exists early in modern, iterative software development. In addition, the engineer must provide input hypotheses on how these test scenarios relate to the software artifacts. The essential trick is then to observe the runtime behavior of these test scenarios during their execution and to translate this behavior into a graph structure to indicate commonalities. Trace dependencies are then computed on the bases of their degrees of commonality. Note that testing is a validation form that does not have a completeness guarantee (i.e., missing test cases). This naturally affects the trace analysis and thus our approach provides an input language that lets the engineer express these uncertainties (if known).

Our approach requires only a small set of input hypotheses (i.e., the input are essentially trace dependencies between test scenarios and software artifacts but are allowed to be incomplete or incorrect; ergo hypotheses) to generate new trace dependencies. Our approach also validates existing trace dependencies and it identifies incorrect input in some cases. For the engineer, this translates into confidence that the results of the trace analysis are correct. Our approach strongly encourages iterative trace analysis. The following discusses how testing helps in the identification of trace dependencies between:
- Requirements/design and code
- Requirements and requirements
- Requirements and design
- Design and design

Trace Dependencies between Requirements/Design/Code

In order to identify trace dependencies, the approach requires test scenarios that are executable on the source code. Table 28 lists some test scenarios we defined for the VoD system. For example, test scenario 1 uses the VoD system to display a list of movies. The details on how to test this scenario on the system are omitted here for brevity but the test scenario describes how to configure the VoD system and what user interface actions to perform (e.g., which buttons to press) in order to achieve the desired results. We then used the commercial tool IBM Rational PureCoverage to monitor the VoD system while it was executing the test scenario. It detected that the Java classes BorderPanel (C), ListFrame (J), ServerReq (R), and VoDClient (U) were executed while testing the scenario. In the following, we use the single letter acronyms for the 21 Java classes for brevity.

Table 28 also depicts the hypotheses on how the test scenarios relate to the previously mentioned software artifacts (classes, state transitions, and requirements) and Table 29 resolves the footprint acronyms in terms of the Java classes used. For instance, test scenario 1 is about viewing a movie list and it was hypothesized to relate to the state transition [s3] "Movies Button" in the statechart diagram (see Figure 53). This implies that test scenario 1 is a test case for the state transition [s3] and, while executing it on the real system, it was observed to execute the Java classes (code) [C,J,R,U]. Due to the transitivity of trace dependencies, one may conclude that the state transition [s3] is implemented in the source code classes [C,J,R,U]. This is a trace dependency between a design element (e.g., state transition *s3*) and the source code (e.g., classes BorderPanel (C), ListFrame (J), ServerReq (R), and VoDClient (U)).

Table 28. Scenarios and observed footprints

Test Scenario	Artifact	Observed Java Classes
1. view movie list	[s3]	[C,J,R,U]
2. view textual movie info	[s4,s6][r2]	[C,E,J,N,R]
3. select/play movie	[s8,s9][r6]	[A,C,D,F,G,I,J,K,N,O,R,T,U]
4. press stop button	[s9,s12][r8]	[A,C,D,F,G,I,K,O,T,U]
5. press play button	[s9,s11][r9]	[A,C,D,F,G,I,K,N,O,T,R,U]
6. change server	[s5,s7]	[C,R,J,S]
7. playing	[s9]	[A,C,D,F,G,I,K,O]
8. get textual movie info	[r5]	[N,R]
9. movie list	[r4]	[R]
10. VCR-like UI	[r7]	[A,C,D,F,G,I,K,N,O,R,T,U]
11. select movie	[r0]	[C,J,N,R,T,U]
12. select/play movie	[r1]	[A,C,D,F,G,I,J,K,N,O,R,T,U]
13. press pause	[s9,s10][r3]	[A,C,D,F,G,I,K,O,U]

Table 28 defines 12 additional scenarios including one test scenario for every requirement (although multiple may exist). A trace dependency is ambiguous if it does not precisely define relationships between artifacts and code. For instance, test scenario 2 defines the state transitions [s4] and [s6] relating to the code [C,E,J,N,R]. This statement is ambiguous in that it is unclear which subset of [C,E,J,N,R] actually belongs to [s4] and which subset belongs to [s6].

Our approach relies on the abilities of the engineers to relate the test scenarios to the requirements and design elements. Three error types are possible that impact the trace analysis in different ways: (1) the engineer omits a link between a test scenario and a requirement, (2) the engineer creates a wrong link, or (3) there is a mismatch between a requirement and the specified tests (for example, a test case exercises a wrong or a partially wrong functionality). Although the technique has means of detecting inconsistencies among its input (Egyed, 2004), it can be fooled this way and engineers need to be careful when providing their specifications.

Table 29. VoD Java classes and their unique identifiers

A	BitInputStream	H	GOPHeader	O	Picture
B	Block	I	IDCT	P	PictureHeader
C	BorderPanel	J	ListFrame	Q	SequenceHeader
D	DataStore	K	Macroblock	R	ServerReq
E	Detail	L	MacroblockNew	S	ServerSelect
F	FrameImage	M	MacroHeader	T	Video
G	GOP	N	Movie	U	VODClient

The advantage of this approach is that it reveals trace dependencies between any software artifact and source code provided that the engineer is able to define and execute a corresponding test scenario. We will discuss in Section 14.5 why this avoids the many complexities discussed earlier.

Trace Dependencies among Requirements

Pfleeger and Bohner (1990) distinguish between vertical and horizontal trace dependencies where the former identify traces among artifacts belonging to the same level of abstraction (same layer) and the latter identify traces among artifacts of different levels of abstractions. Trace dependencies among requirements fall into the first category.

Our approach identifies trace dependencies among requirements by investigating the requirements to code dependencies identified above. Figure 54 depicts the execution of three requirements schematically with arrows to represent their execution paths (i.e., arrows correspond to the sequence of method executions). For example, the efficiency requirement r6 that the playing of a movie has to start within one second is testable by clicking on the "start movie" button of the VoD player and monitoring its execution path (i.e., path in the upper left). The other two requirements follow their own execution paths during testing. We are not actually interested in what sequence classes/methods where executed but only in *whether they were executed or not*.

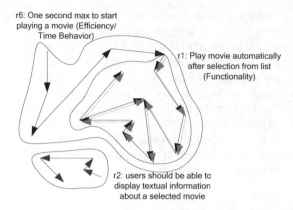

Fig. 54. Execution paths (footprints) of three VoD requirements

Once testing is complete, we infer trace dependencies among the three requirements through their overlapping execution paths (called "footprints"). For example, we can observe in Figure 54 that the footprints of requirements *r1* and *r6*
overlap. This implies some trace dependency between the efficiency requirement
r6 and the functionality requirement *r1* because they execute similar lines of code
during testing and thus their implementation is interwoven (i.e., they share a
common part of the code). Since there is no overlap between the footprints for *r6*
and *r2* we conclude that there is no trace dependency between those two requirements as they are implemented in different parts of the system. Note that *r6* and *r2*
may still affect one another in other ways (i.e., calling or data dependencies) but
these relationships are not of interest here. If more than one test scenario exists for
a requirement then its footprint is simply the union of all individual paths.

The three weaknesses of this approach are: (1) lack of test scenarios which
leads to a footprint that is a subset of the true one, (2) shared utility classes that are
used by different artifacts but do not imply commonality, and (3) code duplication
which leads to fewer overlaps. All three problems have to be dealt with manually
but the engineer is supported by the trace analyzer in terms of the input language
and results generated. For example, an engineer may state that an artifact has "at
least" some footprint if only a subset of test scenarios are available. Or if an engineer provides input that states that two artifacts are unrelated but an overlap is
eventually identified then either the input was incorrect or the overlap is shared
utility code (the choice is presented by the approach but has to be decided upon by
the engineer).

Trace Dependencies between Requirements and Design

Pfleeger and Bohner (1990) define horizontal trace dependencies as linking artifacts of different lifecycle activities. Trace dependencies between the requirements
and the design fall into this category and they are computed in the same fashion as
the ones above. For example, we know that the requirement *r2* (the ability to get

textual information about a movie) executes the Java classes N and R (see Table 28). We also know from Table 28 that the state transition *"Play Button"* (*s9* and *s11*) executes the Java classes [A,C,D,F,G,I,K,N,O,T,R,U]. Thus, there is a trace dependency between [*s9,s11*] and *r2* because the latter is a subset of the execution of the former. In other words, it appears as if the pressing of the play button results in the downloading of textual information about the movie (among other things).

Trace Dependencies within Design and Issues of Uncertainties

Trace dependencies within the design (i.e., between the statechart and the class diagram) are identified on the same principle. However, while investigating the input hypotheses in Table 28 in more detail, we find that there are several examples where the input hypotheses include multiple software artifacts. For example, test scenario 3 is about selecting and playing a movie which was correctly hypothesized as relating to the state transitions *s8* and *s9* (selecting and playing). This implies that *both* state transitions relate to the Java classes [A,C,D,F,G,I,J,K,N,O,R,T,U] but it remains unknown (uncertain) which Java classes relate to *s8* and which ones relate to *s9*. This uncertainty is a problem as is illustrated in Figure 55 (Egyed, 2004).

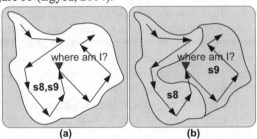

Fig. 55. Grouping uncertainty causes trace dependency uncertainty

Figure 55.a depicts the execution path of test scenario 3 schematically. Since test scenario 3 was hypothesized to relate to both *s8* and *s9*, we may wonder how exactly this region is divided up between them. Imagine we have another design element that overlaps with *s8* and *s9* at the triangle in the middle. We know that this overlap implies a trace dependency but it is incorrect to say that this triangle overlaps with *both s8 and s9*. The grouping of software artifacts is a problem because we only understand the meaning of the elements as a group but not its individual elements. For example, Figure 55.b expands the illustration of the execution path and separates the execution *s8* from the execution *s9*. It is now obvious that the triangle in the middle factually overlaps with *s9* but not *s8*.

We support grouping uncertainty to ease the task of the engineer in providing input hypotheses because there are cases where it is hard to break down a single test scenario into separate pieces as in the case of test scenario 3. Recall that the selection of the movie automatically starts the movie which makes it hard to test the hypotheses separately. Our approach is capable of resolving grouping uncertainties by taking other input hypotheses under consideration. The details are discussed in (Egyed, 2004).

Benefits of Test-Based Trace Analysis

As input, our approach requires (1) software artifacts (i.e., model elements) with unknown trace dependencies; (2) an executable software system; (3) test scenarios; and (4) hypotheses on how the artifacts relate to the test scenarios. By monitoring the lines of code executed during the testing of the scenarios, overlaps are identified. These overlaps imply trace dependencies among the test scenarios and subsequently among the artifacts that are hypothesized to relate to those scenarios.

Clearly, all of the input items are reasonable during software development. Software artifacts and the executable software system are the products of software development. So are test scenarios. Even the relationships between software artifacts and test scenarios are defined by engineers as they are needed during validation and verification. If this input is available then the benefits are extensive:

1. Only n input hypotheses are required to infer n^2 trace dependencies: a model element has trace dependencies with potentially every other model element (n^2) but a model element has only one trace dependency to the system (n).
2. Collaboration among engineers is reduced: engineers only need to investigate their own artifacts and how they relate to the source code. There is no need to understand any other engineer's artifacts. Also there is no need to understand the semantic and syntactic differences among artifacts because the artifact to code mappings can be done independently for all artifacts.
3. The use of informal, partial, nonstandardized notations is less of a problem because these differences do not have to be understood in the context of other models or by other engineers.

The key benefit of our approach is that the engineer only needs to understand the individual relationships between any artifact and the system (i.e., source code). These relationships can be investigated fully independently for every artifact.

Another benefit of our approach is that it measures the completeness and correctness of the generated trace dependencies (this is discussed in detailed later). That is, incomplete and (potentially) incorrect input also produces incomplete and (potentially) incorrect trace dependencies as a result. By being able to measure completeness and correctness, we can guide the engineer in what additional input is needed to make the result more complete or more correct. This fits well with value-based software engineering where software artifacts have different levels of importance. Thus, by simply prioritizing our guidance according to the importance of the artifacts, it is possible to customize our approach in producing more complete/correct trace dependencies for more important artifacts. It must be understood that generating complete/correct traceability is very expensive. Even with the improvements of our approach, the trace analysis is still hard. Being able to tailor the trace analysis to the high value artifacts is thus an effective way of dealing with this problem.

However, there is also an issue of timeliness. The software system and corresponding test scenarios are not available early on during the software lifecycle. Thus, the value-based benefits outlined above are not applicable to the entire software lifecycle. Furthermore, our approach detects trace dependencies only among artifacts that can be mapped to source code. Thus, the approach is only applicable to product models that describe software systems. This includes requirements, design models, and architecture models but excludes process or decision models.

This trade-off is not unreasonable during software development but may not be acceptable always. It has been argued that trace dependencies are not that important early on during the software lifecycle because the complexities are still manageable and few stakeholders are involved (Lindvall, 1994). Since the approach is applicable to implementation, testing, and maintenance, it is actually applicable to most of the software lifecycle because these stages consume more than two thirds of all development cost (Boehm et al., 2000). However, if trace dependencies are needed early on, a pure testing-based approach to trace analysis will not suffice. To get around this problem, the following investigates value-based trade-offs of a variation of this approach.

14.4 Trace Analysis through Commonality

Our approach works on the commonality principle. That is, if model element A traces to some source code and model element B traces to the same source code then A and B are similar elements because both A and B are interwoven in the implementation. We thus use overlaps among lines of code during test execution to infer commonality and subsequently trace dependencies. This results in a significant reduction of the complexity of the trace analysis because instead of having to define trace dependencies among all software artifacts (Figure 56.a), one only has to define them between the software artifacts and the source code (Figure 56.b). As output, the approach then generates the traces in Figure 56.a based on their overlaps in Figure 56.b. In other words, the linear input generates a quadratic number of trace dependencies as its output.

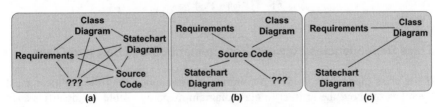

Fig. 56. Trace analysis based on commonality

It is important to observe that there are really two factors that contribute to the simplification of the trace analysis problem: (1) the use of the source code as a common ground and (2) the use of testing to ease the artifact to code mapping of the input hypotheses.

In other words, the source code is a common ground for identifying commonalities among artifacts and it is a testable item. Both factors contribute to the simplification of the trace analysis but it is its use as a common ground that has the more significant effect in this equation. The use of a common ground changes the network (many-to-many) structure in Figure 56.a to a simple, linear star (many-to-one) structure in Figure 56.b. The use of the common ground thus simplifies trace analysis to a linear problem instead of a quadratic one.

Testing is an added benefit in providing the linear input. Instead of requiring the engineer to guess the artifact-to-code mapping directly, we allow the engineer to break down this task into (a) finding test scenarios for artifacts and (b) testing these artifacts.

Testing is thus an aid to the trace analysis but not a requirement. This opens our approach to other possibilities. For example, could we use the class diagram (instead of the source code) as a common representation for the trace analysis? Figure 56.c depicts this case. If it were possible to use the class diagram as a common representation then engineers would need to define their input in terms of artifact to class diagram mappings (e.g., requirements to class diagram and statechart diagram to class diagram). While this alternative sacrifices the use of testing as a simplification, it benefits from the use of the common representation. The following explores the trade-offs of this option.

Table 30. Artifact to class mapping

Artifact	Classes
r0	c2
r1	c2,c3,c4,c5
r6	c2,c3
r5	c3
s3	c3,c5
s8	c2,c3
s9	c2,c3,c4
s2	c1
s1	c1,c4

Trace Dependencies between Requirements/Statechart and Class

If the class diagram is used as a common representation then the engineer must hypothesize about the artifact to class diagram mapping. Table 30 identifies such hypotheses for some requirements and statechart elements. For example, requirement *r0* (download movie data on demand while playing a movie) is a functionality that has to be implemented inside the class *Streamer* (*c2*). Or the statechart transition *s3* (select movie) is likely about the classes *Server Access* and *Movie Selection* (*c3* and *c5*).

Trace Dependencies between Requirements/Statecharts

Trace dependencies can now be established on the basis of their commonality in the class diagram. For example, there is no trace dependency between the requirement *r0* and the state transition *s3* because they are implemented in different classes in the class diagram. On the other hand, there is a very strong overlap between the classes of requirement *r6* and the state transition *s8* which implies that there is a trace dependency between the "one second max to start playing a movie" and the state transition "play" implying that the state transition has to implement the performance requirement. The class diagram also serves as a good common representation for trace dependencies among requirements. For example, we see that requirement *r6* is realized in a subset of the classes that requirement *r1* is realized with. This implies that the "one second max to start playing a movie" is still a sub-requirement to the "play movie automatically after selection."

Trade-Offs During Class-Based Trace Analysis

Using the class diagram instead of the source code as a common representation brings with it another set of trade-offs. On one hand, we lose testing as a simplification on how to provide input hypotheses (mapping between artifacts and class diagram). On the other hand, we gain in two ways:

1. it is easier to define input hypotheses in terms of six classes in the class diagram than 21 classes in the source code. This shifts the granularity of the trace analysis in favor of fewer elements to consider (i.e., less complexity).
2. the class diagram is available earlier in the software lifecycle than the source code. This shifts the timeliness of the trace analysis in favor of early risk assessment.

On the surface, the use of the class diagram is thus a trade-off in less automation (i.e., no testing) and also less complexity and earlier availability. The reduction in complexity may well offset the loss of automation but it has the added advantage of its earlier availability in the software lifecycle.

Even better, the results of this earlier trace analysis also benefits the finding of input hypotheses for later phases when source code is available. As such, we then only need to find test scenarios for the classes in the class diagram and, through transitivity, get the traces from requirements/statechart to source code for free. For example, if the class *c3* maps to the Java classes [A,D,G,I,K,R] (i.e., we may find out through testing at a later time) then we may conclude that requirement *r5* must also trace to [A,D,G,I,K,R] because the Table 30 defined *r5* to trace to *c3*.

Unfortunately, there is another drawback that must be considered. The use of the class diagram changed the granularity of the trace analysis. Overlaps are now determined based on the commonality of the six classes in the class diagram instead of the 21 Java classes in the source code. This shift in granularity may result in false trace dependencies. Consider the following example: the requirement $r5$ (three seconds max to load textual information about a movie) overlaps with the state transition $s9$ (playing) which is rather odd (see Table 30). Of course, it is necessary to load textual information to start playing but, once the movie is playing, it is no longer necessary to load textual information about the movie. On closer investigation, we find that the class $c3$ implements interfaces for two different servers: the first interface deals with the movie server that handles movie lists and textual details and the second interface deals with the http server that handles the streaming media. The requirement $r5$ uses a different server than the state transition $s9$ but both servers were packaged into the one class $c3$.

Therefore, the downside of less granularity during trace analysis is that distinct concerns are packaged together although they may not always be used together. Because $c3$ now packages two kinds of servers, it is no longer possible to identify which server, in particular, is being used. During trace analysis this implies that artifacts are related even if they use different servers. We refer to the effects of changing granularity during trace analysis as *precision*. The use of the class diagram instead of the source code lowered precision.

For a stakeholder, lower precision means a higher likelihood of false positives (wrong trace dependencies) but not false negatives (missing trace dependencies). This is acceptable in cases where errors happen because of the lack of traces but not their abundance. However, if there are many more false trace dependencies than correct ones, then this is a problem also.

14.5 The Tailorable Factors

The required quality of traces is determined by their usage. For example, during impact analysis it may be acceptable to have a trace with false positives whereas during consistency checking they may be inappropriate. It is thus vital for trace analysis to be guidable and our approach can be guided in terms of the completeness, precision, timeliness, and even correctness of the resulting trace dependencies; on both a global level affecting all results and a local level affecting the traces among particular software artifacts. This ability to guide the trace analysis is vital for value-based software development as it allows the engineer to minimize the cost/effort of trace analysis.

This chapter discussed trace analysis as a trade-off among four contributing factors: precision, completeness, correctness, and timeliness. As we find often, it is hard (and expensive) to get the best of all four factors at the same time. The following thus discusses the value trade-offs among some variations.

Precision, Completeness, Correctness, and Timeliness

Precision (introduced in the previous chapter) is a tailorable factor that depends on the granularity of the common representation. The more granular the common representation the more precise is the trace analysis. We demonstrated that the use of the 21 Java classes results in a more precise trace analysis than the use of the six-class diagram. It is even significant whether we perform trace analysis on the 21 Java classes or its hundreds of individual methods as, sometimes, classes merge methods that are not always used together. The lack of precision has the negative side effect of false positives in that the trace analysis will identify more trace dependencies than factually exist. In an extreme case, where the common representation exists of a single element only (e.g., the system), all artifacts will map to this single element and thus there would be trace dependencies among all artifacts.

Completeness (i.e., an input is complete if we know the artifacts relationship to every code element) is a tailorable factor that depends on the input hypotheses. The fewer the hypotheses, the less complete is the trace analysis. We demonstrated this effect on the grouping uncertainty where it made a difference not knowing exactly what artifact traces to what part of the common representation (i.e., if *a* and *b* trace to *1* and *2* then we do not know whether *a* traces to *1* or *2* or both). The lack of completeness has the negative side effect of incomplete results. Thus, the trace analysis will not be able to define exactly how two artifacts relate to one another if it does not know exactly how these artifacts relate to the common representation. In an extreme case, where there is only one input that states that all artifacts map to the entire common representation, the trace analysis could not define any trace dependencies.

Correctness is a tailorable factor that also depends on the input hypotheses. It was not much emphasized in this chapter as its effects should be obvious: the less correct the input, the less correct the resulting trace dependencies. The lack of correctness may result in both false positives and false negatives (i.e., wrong trace dependencies and missing trace dependencies). However, our approach is capable of detecting incorrect input as a trade-off among multiple inputs. This capability was not discussed here for brevity (Egyed, 2004). Correctness is affected by testing (i.e., testing is a halfway automation of the input hypotheses which positively affects correctness) and by granularity (i.e., the complexity is reduced with less granularity).

Finally, timeliness is a tailorable factor that depends on both the input hypotheses and the common representation. Timeliness is affected indirectly in that a testable, common representation (i.e., source code) may be substituted by another common representation that, typically, benefits timeliness but not precision (because of granularity) and not completeness (because of lack of testing).

Trade-Offs among the Tailorable Factors

To understand the effects of precision, completeness, and correctness, we have to investigate them in relationship to the common representation. Figure 57 depicts the common representation and its relationships to individual artifacts (e.g., requirements, class, and statechart). Since the trace analysis determines overlaps among artifacts in terms of their effects on the common representation (CR), it follows that the tailorable factors of the individual inputs have to be combined to understand their effects on the results. For example, the trace analyzer generates trace dependencies between artifact 1 (A1) and artifact 2 (A2) by investigating the overlap among the trace dependencies between A1 and the common representation (A1-CR) and A2 and the common representation (A2-CR). The following explores how the quality of the individual input hypotheses affects the value of the output trace dependencies.

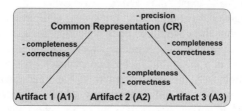

Fig. 57. The effects of the input on the trace analysis

Precision is a property of the common representation (directly) as input hypotheses are defined in a level of granularity that matches the common representation. Since all artifacts share the same common representation, it affects all resulting trace dependencies among all artifacts (A1-A2, A1-A3, and A2-A3). Completeness and correctness are properties of the input hypotheses of individual artifacts (e.g., A1 to common representation). Since these two factors belong to individual artifacts, they only affect those resulting trace dependencies that include these artifacts (e.g., A1 to A2 trace dependencies are affected by A1-CR and A2-CR qualities but not by A3-CR qualities).

The output trace dependencies are only as good as the product of the quality of the input trace dependencies. For example, if the A1-CR mapping is 100% complete and the A2-CR mapping is only 50% complete then the resulting A1 to A2 trace dependencies will be 50% complete only (i.e., the output cannot be more complete than its individual inputs). The correctness factor exhibits the same effect. Not surprisingly, 100% complete and precise output requires 100% complete and precise input (see Table 31). Note that the values are averages in that a 50% input mixed with another 50% input is 25% complete on average.

Table 31. Effect of input completeness/correctness on output

	Completeness/Correctness					
	A1	A2	A1	A2	A1	A2
	100	100	100	50	50	50
A1-A2	100		50		25 on average	

For example, the input of the VoD system was defined with an unknown level of completeness and correctness. However, after the trace analysis (based on the input in Table 28), we learn that we have almost complete knowledge of the mapping from state s9 to the code (>90%) but still rather incomplete knowledge of the mapping from s8 to the code (<50%). If an engineer values s9 higher than s8 then the engineer also values the traces derived from s9 higher than those from s8. Assume that we have complete knowledge of the footprints of the requirements (100%). The trace analyzer thus generates output traces between the requirements and s9 that are 90% complete while the ones between the requirement and s8 are less than 50% complete.

This property has several benefits. First, we can predict the quality of the result based on the quality of the input. Second, not all input must be defined 100% complete if the output is not required to be 100% complete also. Value-based software engineering places different levels of importance onto different artifacts. Our approach can thus be guided by the required level of importance.

While completeness and correctness are independent value factors, we observed that the more complete the input the more likely our approach detects incorrectness. In essence, our approach uses constraint-based reasoning to identify incorrectness, and the more the input the more constraints.

Table 32. Effect of precision on completeness and correctness

		Completeness or Correctness			
	x	100	75	50	25
Precision	x/2	100	87	75	62
	x/4	100	94	88	81

In principle, the effects of precision are independent from the effects of completeness and correctness. This is because we measure completeness and correctness relative to the granularity of the common representation. However, doing so ignores a side effect: if an input is 50% complete for a given precision then the same input becomes 75% complete (on average) if the precision is cut in half (i.e., completeness gets grouped with incompleteness which gives the wrong appearance of more completeness). That is, correctness and completeness evolve relative to the precision of the common representation as is illustrated in Table 32. It must be noted that Table 32 depicts the relative effects of completeness and correctness within a single application only. This table cannot be used to predict completeness/correctness for other applications.

Table 33. Input vs. output trade-off during trace analysis

Input and Output Trade-Off		Output (Results of the Trace Analysis)		
		False positives	False negatives	Incomplete-ness
Input	Precision	Yes		Yes
	Completeness	Yes		Yes
	Correctness	Yes	Yes	

Table 33 summarizes the effects of the tailorable input factors on the output. More input precision reduces false positives and incompleteness. The same is true about more input completeness. More correctness reduces both false positives and false negatives but does not affect completeness. Our approach can measure the level of input/output completeness and it can indicate input incorrectness.

14.6 Conclusions

Value-based software engineering places different values on different software artifacts. It is important for cost-effectiveness to adapt the quality of trace dependencies among these artifacts according to their importance. This paper discussed the complexity of trace analysis and the many benefits of a testing-based approach to trace analysis (e.g., quadratic reduction in trace input, irrelevance of syntactic and semantic differences among artifacts). Furthermore, this paper discussed the factors that affect the quality of the trace dependencies (output) generated by the trace analysis (e.g., precision, completeness, correctness, and timeliness).

The engineer can influence these factors to accommodate the needs of value-based software engineering in terms of what traces are needed, when traces are needed, and of what level of quality traces are needed. It is future work to calibrate the quality trade-offs discussed in this chapter on other case studies. Also, it is future work to investigate the effects of using different kinds of common representations (e.g., the class diagram) as our findings are limited to date.

References

(Antoniol et al., 2002) Antoniol, G., Canfora, G., Casazza, G., De Lucia, A., and Merlo, E.: Recovering Traceability Links between Code and Documentation, IEEE Transactions on Software Engineering, 28(10), pp 970–983

(Biffl and Halling, 2003) Biffl, S. and Halling M.: Investigating the Defect Detection Effectiveness and Cost-Benefit of Nominal Inspection Teams, IEEE Transactions on Software Engineering, 29(5), pp 385–397

(Boehm, 2003) Boehm, B. W.: Value-Based Software Engineering, Software Engineering Notes, 28(2), pp 1–12

(Boehm and Huang, 2003) Boehm, B. W. and Huang, L.G.: Value-Based Software Engineering: A Case Study, IEEE Computer, 36(3), pp 33–41

(Boehm et al., 1998) Boehm, B. W., Egyed, A., Kwan, J., and Madachy, R.: Using the WinWin Spiral Model: A Case Study, IEEE Computer, pp 33–44

(Boehm et al., 2000) Boehm, B. W., Abts, C., Brown, A.W., Chulani, W., Clark, B.K., Horowitz, E., Madacy, R., Reifer, D., and Steece, B.: Software Cost Estimation with COCOMO II, (Prentice Hall, New Jersey, 2000)

(Card, 1992) Card, D.N.: Designing Software for Producibility, Journal of Systems and Software, 17(3), pp 219–225

(Cross, 1991) Cross, G.M.: Requirements and Traceability Management, Proceedings of the International Conference on Software for Guidance and Control, pp 4/1–4/4

(Egyed, 2002) Egyed, A.: A Scenario-Driven Approach to Trace Dependency Analysis, IEEE Transactions on Software Engineering (TSE), Volume 29, Number 2, pp 116–132

(Egyed, 2004) Egyed, A.: Resolving Uncertainties during Trace Analysis, Proceedings of the 12th ACM SIGSOFT Symposium on Foundations of Software Engineering (FSE), 3–12

(Egyed and Grünbacher, 2002) Egyed, A. and Grünbacher, P.: Automating Requirements Traceability – Beyond the Record and Replay Paradigm, Proceedings of the 17th International Conference on Automated Software Engineering (ASE), pp 163–171

(Egyed and Grünbacher, 2004) Egyed, A. and Grünbacher, P.: Identifying Requirements Conflicts and Cooperation: How Quality Attributes and Automated Traceability Can Help, IEEE Software, 21(6), pp 50–58

(Finkelstein et al., 1991) Finkelstein, A., Kramer, J., Nuseibeh, B., Finkelstein, L., and Goedicke, M.: Viewpoints: A Framework for Integrating Multiple Perspectives in System Development, International Journal on Software Engineering and Knowledge Engineering, pp 31–58

(Gotel and Finkelstein, 1994) Gotel, O.C.Z. and Finkelstein, A.C.W.: An Analysis of the Requirements Traceability Problem, Proceedings of the First International Conference on Requirements Engineering, pp 94–101

(Jacobson, 1987) Jacobson, I.: Object Oriented Development in an Industrial Environment, Proceedings of the International Conference on Object-Oriented Programming Systems, Languages, and Applications (OOPSLA), pp 183–191

(Lindvall, 1994) Lindvall: A Study of Traceability in Object-Oriented Systems Development, PhD Thesis Tech Report No 462, Linköping University, Institute of Technology, Sweden

(Lindvall and Sandahl, 1996) Lindvall, M. and Sandahl, K.: Practical Implications of Traceability, Journal on Software – Practice and Experience (SPE), 26(10), pp 1161–1180

(Moore, 1995) Moore, G.: Inside the Tornado, (, Harper Collins Publishers, 1995)

(Nuseibeh, 2001) Nuseibeh, B.: Weaving Together Requirements and Architectures, IEEE Computer, 34(2), pp 115–117

(Övergaard, 1998) Övergaard, G.: A Formal Approach to Relationships in the Unified Modeling Language, Proceedings of the Workshop on Precise Semantics for Software Modeling Techniques (PSMT'98), pp 91–108

(Pfleeger and Bohner, 1990) Pfleeger, S.L. and Bohner, S.A.: A Framework for Software Maintenance Metrics, IEEE Transactions on Software Engineering, 16(5), pp 320–327

(Pohl, 1996) Pohl, K.: PRO-ART: Enabling Requirements Pre-Traceability, Proceedings of the 2nd International Conference on Requirements Engineering (ICRE), pp 76–85

(Ramesh, 1993) Ramesh: A Model of Requirements Traceability for Systems Development, Technical Report, Naval Postgraduate School, Monterey

(Rumbaugh et al., 1999) Rumbaugh, J., Jacobson, I., and Booch, G.: The Unified Modeling Language Reference Manual, (Addison Wesley1999)

(Tilbury, 1989) Tilbury, A.M.: Enabling Software Traceability, In IEE Colloquium on the Application of Computer Aided Software Engineering Tool, London, UK

Author Biography

Alexander Egyed is a research scientist at Teknowledge Corp. His research interests include requirements engineering, incremental and iterative software modeling (transformation and analysis), traceability, and simulation. He received his PhD in Computer Science from the University of Southern California. He is a member of IEEE, IEEE Computer Society, ACM, and ACM SIGSOFT.

15 Value-Based Knowledge Management: the Contribution of Group Processes

Torgeir Dingsøyr

Abstract: Knowledge management has recently received much attention in software engineering, but the main focus has been on information systems to support learning. For most software companies, the most valuable knowledge remains in the people, and this knowledge needs different methods to be managed. In this chapter, we discuss the learning contribution of two people-oriented methods: postmortem reviews and process workshops.

Keywords: Postmortem reviews, process workshop, knowledge management, learning software organization, group process, software engineering.

15.1 Introduction

Software development has a history of cost and time overruns. Knowledge management has been proposed as an approach for solving these problems recently (Aurum et al., 2003; Lindvall and Rus, 2002). Developing software is a typical example of what Peter Drucker has called "knowledge work"; where "value is ... created by 'productivity' and 'innovation'" (Drucker, 1999). Knowledge is a scarce resource in software development – much more than other "means of production" like computer hardware and software, office buildings, or capital.

There has been much work on knowledge management in software engineering, or learning software organizations. However, much of the work has concentrated on information technology to support knowledge sharing, where few studies indicate impact on software development practice (Dingsøyr and Conradi, 2002). One reason for this might be that the knowledge represented in the tools has not had sufficient value to the users. In this chapter, we discuss two techniques that rely on group processes to share knowledge, are lightweight, and focus mainly on documenting only the knowledge that the contributors see as having the greatest value.

Software development is usually performed in projects. Projects are time limited, producing one time outputs that are "non-repetitive in nature and involve considerable application of knowledge, judgment and expertise" (Cohen and Bailey, 1997). There are, however, similarities between projects, and learning from one project has the potential of improving the next. A company's own portfolio of projects is more likely to be the source of relevant knowledge than what can be provided in courses and bought in competence. To better manage knowledge in projects we will present and discuss postmortem reviews (Dingsøyr, 2005) as a method for analyzing past projects for the benefit of future projects.

Software development processes are another important concept. These processes are often quite general and need to be tailored to suit either specific projects or types of projects. We will discuss a method for defining work processes for software companies, called process work-shops (Dingsøyr et al., 2005). The output of such workshops are usually electronic process guides (Scott et al., 2002) available on a company intranet which provides a "how to" reference manual for people involved in projects.

The common denominator for these two techniques is that they rely on group processes using some of the same brainstorming techniques. We will later discuss the impact of brainstorming techniques on group effectiveness.

We believe good techniques for developing the knowledge required in projects through postmortems and developing the cross-project knowledge in processes can add substantial value to a software company – what some call increasing the intellectual capital of the company.

A major leverage point in value-based software engineering is to stimulate stakeholders to achieve more compatible and improvement-oriented utility functions via team building, participation in decision making, and development of shared goals and mutual trust; what Boehm (Boehm, 2003; Chapter 1) calls "value-based people management." Both collaborative processes in this chapter and the stakeholder win-win processes in Chapter 7 (also discussed in Chapter 2) address this leverage point in complementary ways. Additional complementary strategies include prototyping team-oriented versus individual rewards and group-oriented collaboration tool support as discussed in Chapter 10.

The methods presented in this chapter are also alternatives to the Experience Factory (Basili et al., 1994), which is suggested as a tool for value-based monitoring and control of projects and organizations. Postmortem reviews and process workshops are lightweight, or agile, methods that rely much on sharing knowledge orally, and consume little time to carry out. In small companies, a postmortem can be carried out in four hours, and running a workshop on a process such as "blast-off" can be carried out in less.

The rest of this chapter is organized as follows: In the next section we define knowledge and discuss broad issues in how knowledge can be managed. We introduce postmortem reviews and process workshops as group processes to work on project and process knowledge from software companies. We then present an action research study from a company where we used postmortem reviews and from another company where we used a process workshop. In the discussion section, we discuss how these techniques can assist in learning and eliciting knowledge. We conclude with what we see as implications for practice for software companies.

15.2 Managing Knowledge

Davenport and Prusak (1998) define knowledge as: "a fluid mix of framed experience, values, contextual information, and expert insight that provides a framework for evaluating and incorporating new experiences and information. It originates and is applied in the minds of knowers. In organizations, it often becomes embedded not only in documents or repositories but also in organizational routines, processes, practices, and norms."

We often divide knowledge into two types, tacit and explicit knowledge. By tacit knowledge (Polanyi, 1967) we mean knowledge that a human is unable to express, but is guiding the behavior of the human, like much of the organizational routines, norms, practices, and inner beliefs. Webster's dictionary defines tacit as "under-stood without being openly expressed" (Webster's, 1989). Explicit knowledge is knowledge that we can represent, or "codify," for example, in documents and repositories.

Nonaka and Takeuchi claim that tacit knowledge can be transferred between people through a process called socialization, which can involve observation and discussion (Nonaka and Takeuchi, 1995). Newcomers will typically need to spend time with others in an organization to get into the routines, norms, and practices that exist.

When knowledge is articulated so that it can be represented in text or pictures, we say that knowledge is externalized. Brainstorming can be one technique to facilitate articulation of knowledge in order to share how "things are done."

Important assets for software companies are the employee's knowledge, and the routines that exist in the company. Often, little of this knowledge is codified, but exists in the heads of the employees and in work practices.

In order to spread knowledge in an organization from individuals to groups, we depend on what has been called "organizational learning". This differs from individual learning in two respects (Stata, 1996): First, it occurs through shared insight, knowledge, and shared models. Second: it is not only based on the memory of the participants in the organization, but also on "institutional mechanisms" like policies, strategies, explicit models, and defined processes.

Hansen et al. (1999) define two strategies for knowledge management. "Codification" is to depend on explicit, codified knowledge, typically in databases – which require heavy investments in information technology. The competitive strategy for companies choosing codification is to "provide high-quality, reliable and fast information systems implementation by reusing codified knowledge." The other strategy is referred to as "personalization," which depends on the tacit knowledge in the company – the strategy involves developing networks to link people to share tacit knowledge. The competitive strategy for companies choosing personalization is to "provide creative, analytically rigorous advice on high-level strategic problems by channeling individual experience."

The stimulation of shared goals and tacit knowledge is also critical to coping with increasingly rapid rates of unpredictable change in software projects. This is a major theme in the use of agile methods (Abrahamsson et al., 2003; Cohen et al., 2004).

Both these strategies apply to software companies, but the research on knowledge management in software engineering has mainly been concentrated on information technology support for codification (Dingsøyr and Conradi, 2002). We will now present two group processes to promote sharing of knowledge, which mainly support the personalization strategy, namely postmortem reviews and process workshops. Note that the processes could also support a codification strategy if more emphasis is made on the resulting documentation.

Postmortem Reviews

Postmortem reviews are processes organized when projects are completed in order to discuss what can be learned from the project (Dingsøyr, 2005). One way to organize postmortems (Birk et al., 2002) is to invite all project participants, and organize a postmortem meeting where a facilitator uses two techniques for first identifying issues, and then for analyzing the causes of the issues with the highest priority.

For a focused brainstorm on what happened in the project, a technique named after a Japanese ethnologist, Jiro Kawakita, can be used (Scupin, 1997), called "the KJ Method." The technique involves giving participants a set of "post-it" notes, and asking them to write one "issue" on each. After some minutes, the first participant presents a note by attaching it to a whiteboard and saying why this issue was important. Then the next person presents a note and so on until all the notes are on the whiteboard. The notes are then grouped and renamed. This is done for "what went well" in the project, and for "what did not go well." This technique leaves a set of issues in both categories, and usually the most important ones are selected by allowing all participants to vote. One way of organizing this is to give each participant two votes, which can be placed on the categories the voter thinks were most important in this project, or the categories the voter thinks the team is most likely to influence in the next project. The most important issues are then analyzed using the next technique.

Root Cause Analysis (also called Ishikawa or fishbone diagrams) (Straker, 1995) can be used to analyze the causes of an important issue. We draw an arrow on a whiteboard indicating the issue being discussed. We then attach arrows to this arrow. These represent issues perceived by the participants as causes for the main issue. Sometimes, we also explore the subcauses for some of the causes and attach arrows for those as well.

As a group process, the postmortem allows everyone participating in a project to know what other participants thought were important issues. It also allows for both positive and negative criticism of actions taken, processes followed, and products delivered from the project.

Process Workshops

Process workshops (Ahonen et al., 2002; Dingsøyr et al., 2005) are made in order to discuss how work is to be carried out in the organization. The output is descriptions of "best practice" in an area, for example, in software development. A typical process workshop consists of the following five steps:

1. *Identify activities.* Find the main activities of the process using a group brain-storm (KJ process).
2. *Define the sequence of activities.* Take the activities from the previous phase and make a sticker for each. Place them on the activities field of the process worksheet (see Figure 59 for an example worksheet), where time goes from left to right. Find a suitable workflow between the activities.
3. *Define input and output.* Find the documents or artifacts that must be available (and possible preconditions that exist) to start the process, and the documents (and possible postconditions) that mark the end of the process. Use stickers with other colors than for the activities to mark input and output, and attach them to the process worksheet on the wall alongside the activities. Conditions that must be satisfied to begin or exit the process can be described in checklists.
4. *Define roles.* Find the roles (developer, project leader, manager, etc.) that should contribute to each activity – and define responsibilities.
5. *Find related documents.* Identify documents that already exist in the company, and new documents that could be helpful in carrying out the activities. Such documents can be templates, checklists, and good examples of input or output documents.

The result of a process workshop is a draft process guide based on a minute of the workshop. The next step would be to assign someone the task of preparing a more readable process guide based on the first draft. In the end, the process guide is a workflow-oriented document available on the company intranet. This is usually a tool which can be used voluntarily, and is intended to assist people in developing software effectively.

15.3 Example: Postmortem Review and Process Workshop

We present an example postmortem review from a company we will refer to as "Delta," and a process workshop in another company "Gamma." Both techniques were used in an action research (Greenwood and Levin, 1998) project where researchers and company representatives tried out techniques, and together reflected on the results.

An Example Postmortem

This postmortem was done on a project to develop a Web-based ticket ordering system for a major transport company in Norway. The project was critical for the transport company, as it introduced fundamental changes to their revenue management process. The project team from Delta at the end of the project consisted of eight people, who all took part in the postmortem meeting (the project had involved three more people earlier, but they were removed from the project because of costs). The company that was running the software project is a large software house with approximately 500 employees.

The postmortem analysis followed the approach described earlier (Birk et al., 2002) except for starting with a timeline-exercise (Kerth, 2001), as the project had lasted for almost two years. This exercise was done by asking all participants to remember key events, and write down the names of the events on stickers and attach them to grey paper on a wall, rectangular stickers for events and round stickers for dates. Important events in this project were tasks like: choosing platform, deciding on coding standard, choosing the database, intense work period, etc. Participants were asked to write down up to four positive and negative experiences they faced during the project. These notes were then put on a whiteboard and grouped into categories or themes. Issues that went well were: team spirit, competence development, human competence, will and ability to solve problems, customer responsibility, good products and improved customer relation. Issues that were problematic were: testing, technical investments, lack of knowledge, and immature technology.

We will now analyze two of the issues that went well and two that did not work out well more in detail. We will show excerpts of what people said about the issues, and what we found to be possible causes for these issues in this project.

Team spirit: "If you look at the people involved in this project, you see that we are very different, but are anyway able to work well together. I think that has been unbelievable, I see so many other places that this does not work," "I would also like to emphasize that it has been very nice socially in the project, although there have not been much [activities] after working hours ... professionally there have been people whom you could ask [any relevant question], ... people have not had enough with their own problems."

Testing: "The greatest mistake we made is that we said 'no' to more load testing before we went to production." "I think we ought to have done more automatic testing earlier, and should have done load testing earlier. We also should have had a better understanding of what load testing means – we have at least two different views of it."

To determine the contributing factors for critical issues, we did root cause analysis, using fishbone diagrams (Straker, 1995). In the root cause analysis, main causes for team spirit were found to be good mix of people, solution-oriented people, collocation of the project team, ownership to solutions, and that it was easy to have a good overview of the group. Similarly, we found the following reasons for problems with testing: lack of automated tests, difference in development and production environment, test process was not followed, and testing did not measure the right features. Upon completion of the postmortem analysis, two facilitators wrote an 18 page report, which was organized with an introduction giving background on the project and the purpose of the postmortem, which was to share experience from the project in a structured manner. Then, the report explains how the work was done, which activities were performed during the postmortem meeting. The results are presented as seven issues that went well, and then the most important (after voting) were described in more detail with quotes from transcripts of the postmortem meeting. In this report we used mind maps to document root causes for the main issues as in Figure 58 (fishbone diagrams were used during the postmortem meeting).

Fig. 58. Mind map showing reasons for issue "competence development"

The seven issues that did not work out well are described in the same manner as the issues that went well.

The company invested 32 hours in this postmortem in addition to approximately 20 hours used by the facilitators, in total 52 hours. A further discussion of this postmortem can be found in (Desouza et al., 2005).

An Example Process Workshop

The satellite software company Gamma, where a series of process workshops were performed (Dingsøyr et al., 2005) delivers turnkey ground station systems, consultancy, feasibility studies, system engineering, training, and support. The company has been working with large development projects, both as a prime contractor and as a subcontractor.

Customers range from universities to companies like Lockheed Martin and Alcatel to governmental institutions like the European Space Agency and the Norwegian Meteorological institute.

Most of the software systems that are developed are running on Unix, many on the Linux operating system.

The company possesses a stable and highly skilled staff, many with Master's degrees in computer science, mathematics, or physics, and have what we can describe as an "engineering culture." Approximately 60 people are working in the company, and the majority is working with software development. Projects are managed in accordance with quality routines fulfilling the European Space Agency PSS-05 (European Space Agency, 1991) standards and ISO 9001-2000 (Cianfrani et al., 2001).

The company had an extensive quality system, but the system was cumbersome to use because of the size – and because it existed partly on file and partly on paper. As a part of being certified according to ISO 9001-2000, the company decided to document all main processes in the company.

In a process workshop on the initiation phase of projects, we identified three subprocesses: "offer," "follow up," and "blast off."

As the initiation of projects is an interface between different parts of the organization, it was important to bring together people from marketing, quality assurance, and the development department. We started the workshop by giving a 15 minute presentation of what we were going to do, and put a large sheet with a figure of the process worksheet (as in Figure 59) on the wall – one for each process that would be discussed in the meeting.

For each subprocess we wanted to define, "offer," "follow up," and "blast-off," we went through the steps mentioned earlier, to identify activities, define the sequence, and define input/output, roles, and related documents. The main activities identified in this step for the "blast-off" subprocess were:

- Appoint project manager
- Organize "hand over" meeting
- First project analysis
- Allocate resources
- Prepare for kickoff meeting
- Internal kickoff

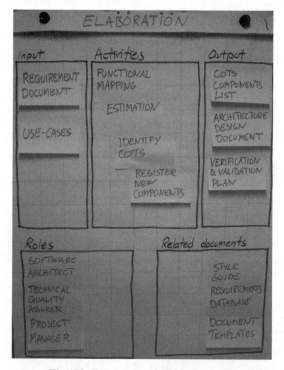

Fig. 59. Process worksheet example

We brainstormed on which roles should contribute in each activity and found the following roles for the "blast off" phase: project manager, quality assurance, development leader, technical leader, product committee, bid manager, purchasing manager, and logistics expert.

We identified related documents that either already existed in the company, or new documents that would be helpful in carrying out the activities. Such documents were templates, checklists, and good examples of input or output documents.

We found it helpful to ask the people who participated in the process workshop to read the result and comment on it (see (Shull et al., 2000) for an example of such a technique in requirements inspection). We assigned the most typical roles that were involved in the processes to people – and asked them to find if there was information that was lacking or irrelevant for this role in the description. This reading resulted in a number of modifications and clarifications on the process description.

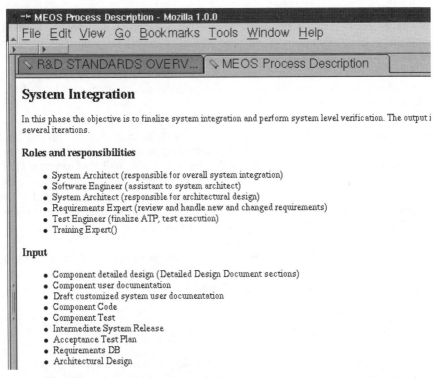

Fig. 60. A screenshot of a part of the resulting electronic process guide

Finally, two people in the company were responsible for making a draft process guide, based on the overall description of the processes which were developed in the workshop. Each activity was then described in much more detail than what appeared in the workshop minutes – the participants gave feedback on these before the processes were implemented in the process guide, as shown in Figure 60. The main part of the final process guide is the description of the activities. For the example shown in Figure 60, the subprocess for system integration lists the following initial activities: "1. Finalize system integration (install scripts, finalize system configuration), 2. Perform dry-run loop (build and test installation, log and correct bugs, raise requirement changes, update architecture design if necessary) ...".

The company invested 168 hours in seven process workshops, another 40 hours in preparation and afterwork, and 208 hours in developing the process guide tool based on the minutes from the workshops, in total 416 hours. The company intends to develop several tailored versions of the process guide, for ad hoc projects to large development projects. The project manager is always responsible for tailoring an original process description to the needs of the project.

15.4 Discussion

We have described two methods for conducting postmortem reviews and process workshops, both relying on group processes as a central element. The methods produce discussions which should lead to reflections among participants, and some of the main discussion points are documented in minutes. It is the participants who decide what are the most important issues to concentrate on in analysis and in documentation.

In software engineering, the critical elements are how many hours it takes to develop the software, that the customer gets the right functionality, and that the software system has the desired quality. Deciding to invest in knowledge management should be because of a belief that the investment will lead to better efficiency and effectiveness in software development; better understanding of customer requirements, greater insight in factors that lead to high or low quality of software. In the context of value-based software engineering, this is to extend the traditional focus on cost, schedule, and product to also involve issues that are of value to the software development organization.

In this context we ask, what is the effect of managing knowledge through group processes? We will investigate this question by examining studies of project work and group processes, and use examples from the cases of Delta and Gamma.

Group Processes and Group Effectiveness

To what extent can management of knowledge influence the effectiveness of software development? From studies of team effectiveness we find that team members rate the performance of the team high if the team has "healthy internal processes, such as collaboration and resolution conflict" (Cohen and Bailey, 1997). We also find that group cohesiveness – how united the team is – is related to performance (Cohen and Bailey, 1997). A survey article on brainstorming research (Faure, 2004) cites several brainstorming studies that report satisfaction with the group (increased cohesiveness) as an outcome of a brainstorming session. Also, the survey reports that there is "abundant evidence that nominal groups (i.e.,

groups of individuals working together independently, but in the presence of another) outperform interactive groups (i.e., groups where ideas are generated
through face to face discussions) in both the quality and the quantity of ideas generated in brainstorming sessions." Reasons why nominal groups outperform interactive groups are that in interactive groups, having to state ideas orally makes it
possible for only one person to present an idea at a time; also, fear of negative
evaluation from group members and "free riding" – reducing effort when individual contribution is not identifiable – has been suggested. Note that when using
electronic tools in the brainstorming process, the picture changes: interactive
groups outperform nominal groups (Dennis and Valacich, 1993; Nunamaker et al.,
1991). For an overview of experiments on computer-supported decision making
see (Fjermestad and Hiltz, 1999).

In the example from Delta, the group agreed on seven categories of issues that
went well, and four categories of issues that did not work out well.

The results from the fields of research above indicate that group processes using brainstorming techniques such as the KJ process used in postmortems and
process workshops has a positive effect on the performance of the participants.
Also, we think that techniques for postmortem reviews can be seen as a "healthy
internal process" that can lead to conflict resolution and better collaboration because team members get better insight into other team members' views. Having a
postmortem process can then lead to a perception of better effectiveness in the
team.

The postmortem at Delta led to a praise of the project team in the session on issues that went well. Also, agreeing on the four issues that did not work out well
and their importance is something we can see as a "healthy" internal process
where criticism is allowed, and critical opinions are discussed.

In the process workshop at Gamma, the discussion on the blast-off phase involved people from different parts of the company: from the marked and software
development departments. Sharing views on the interface between the departments
is likely to lead to better understanding of others' work, and a lower risk of cooperation problems later.

Studies of group performance do, however, state that team effectiveness is perceived differently by internal project members and external stakeholders such as
managers: "Team members tend to rate the team's performance high if the team
has engaged in healthy internal processes, such as collaboration and resolution
conflict. Managers ... rate a team highly according to more external factors like
the amount of communication the group has with external agents" (Cohen and
Bailey, 1997). However, a high perception of effectiveness is likely to lead to better motivation within the team.

There are, however, some problems that are often referred to in group work,
those of group bias ("group think"), group pressure, and political preferences. An
indication of these problems is if people express other opinions in the group than
individually after the group work. As for group bias, the KJ process is a method
that makes everyone prepare their work individually – and then present it to the
rest of the group. It could happen that individuals focus their brainstorm in a way
they think is politically correct in the organization, and into issues that they also

think their group peers will agree to. In order to remove this effect, one solution is to present the ideas of each person anonymously – so that a facilitator collects all stickers, and presents them in random order. Such a procedure would make sorting of ideas afterward a bit more cumbersome, because they would have to be rewritten on new stickers in order not to reveal the source from the handwriting. You would also lose the context behind each idea on a sticker, as the facilitator usually is someone who is not intimately familiar with the project. We have not done any tests to check if the result of the postmortem given in the example from Delta differs from personal opinions. But some of the issues presented were provoking to the project manager, which could indicate limited self-censorship. Also, people knew that the final report would not relate opinions to individuals.

An argument for the suggested group processes are findings on the importance of conducting work in the project according to tailored processes. The survey on team effectiveness reports that "projects where the coordination mechanism fit the newness of the project resulted in products that were higher in quality, were more likely to achieve sales objectives, and reached their break-even point sooner than those projects whose coordination mechanisms were too bureaucratic or too informal given the newness of the product." Also, the survey report that "when team design and processes are properly fit to product characteristics, performance can be high, but when they are not so, performance will suffer." Organizing process workshops in a company is a way to make the work processes adapt more to the real problems in the company than using a more general available model. But we could also easily imagine that using the process described at Gamma, which, for example, prescribes eight roles to be present in the blast-off meeting, would be a far too high burden on very small projects.

In addition to the implications on effectiveness we have discussed, we have a possible effect of sharing the knowledge with other projects in the company that might be in similar situations and could benefit from avoiding mistakes or reusing work products. The example postmortem from Delta reports on problems with testing: "I think we ought to have done more automatic testing earlier, and should have done load testing earlier" was a statement from one participant. This was probably not something that was new to the project team. But it was stated and generally agreed on that it should have been handled differently in this project which would have increased the probability of better testing in the next project.

As value-based software engineering techniques, postmortem reviews and process workshops focus on the development team, and can contribute to team-building and the management of expectations.

Group Processes to Improve Product Quality

In order to improve product quality, there are two possible effects from postmortems and process workshops. There have been many claims in software engineering about the relationship between development process and product quality. In order to ensure that the process influences quality, the development process of course needs to take place in action – not only be described. Process workshops are a method to discuss the work processes, which could then influence how the processes are used in practice. We have not found evidence for this claim in the software engineering literature, but we are currently working with research on the hypothesis that process workshops – which means user involvement – leads to a higher degree of process conformance.

Another possibility to improve quality comes from the postmortem – to ensure that problems that happened in producing one product do not happen again when producing something similar. In the example from Delta, testing is one issue which is likely to be dealt with differently after the project postmortem.

An experiment on group processes for software effort estimation reports that groups outperform individuals in making less optimistic and more realistic estimations of required effort (Moløkken-Østvold and Jørgensen, 2004).

Benefits and Limitations

What was the value delivered from the postmortem and process workshop methods at Delta and Gamma? Do they justify the cost of performing the methods? At Delta the outcome of the postmortem for the company as a whole was an 18 page report. For the group it also meant better insight into what other people in the project thought about it, and a chance to reflect on the project. The cost was 52 work hours, which is less than 1% of the total cost of the project. Taking, for example, the issue on testing, we could imagine that a more optimal test process could save 52 hours of debugging after release in a future project. As for the organization as a whole, the total result depends on how they are able to use what they learned in this project for the benefit of the whole organization. We will return to this point in the next section.

At Gamma, the benefit was a documented development process, as well as a better understanding of other people's tasks which were leveraged in the workshops. It is too early to say if this investment of 416 work hours has paid back, but this effort is also less than 1% of the total staff time in the company. One positive indicator was that the company had zero deviations in an ISO revision after the process guide was introduced thus satisfying the company goal of having less than four deviations. We describe what we will do to follow the introduction of the process guide in this company in Section 15.5.

We have described what we see as the benefits of the methods. What about the limitations? As for the postmortem review, doing it in a four hours session as described at Delta makes it focus on the broad picture rather than the details. If a company has specific problems then this method is not something that can provide a good solution. The postmortem can rather uncover issues, which usually have to be analyzed better in order to make corrective actions for the company as a whole. A postmortem is also heavily dependent on a good atmosphere in the project and a willingness to share experience. Internal competition for positions is a factor that might reduce this willingness, as seen in software consulting companies (Orlikowski, 1992). As for the process workshop, this is a method that only documents what the participants think is the best way to carry out a series of tasks. To optimize a process or to make innovative processes tailored to solving completely new problems would require other approaches.

As group processes, both process workshops and postmortems require a skilled facilitator who can make sure that all participants are able to contribute, and that the issues agreed on reflect the attitudes of the whole group.

Organizational Learning

In the introduction, we defined knowledge management and what we called organizational learning. We defined the latter term as having two conditions: "shared insight, knowledge, and shared models" and based on the "institutional mechanisms" like policies, strategies, explicit models, and defined processes.

We think group processes is a good mechanism to achieve shared insight, knowledge, and shared models, and it can also be a good starting point for documenting experience and defining processes. However, achieving organizational learning also requires the methods to have an impact on the organization as a whole, which is something we have not discussed here. Following up on the results of a postmortem and introducing a process guide in a company are natural future activities.

15.5 Conclusion and Further Work

We have discussed two methods to facilitate learning in software companies, namely postmortem reviews and process workshops. We have argued on the value of the group processes in the methods by examining work on project team effectiveness and brainstorming research. We have found support for claims that such processes can lead to more efficient project work and more satisfied project teams. There are also indications that such activities influence the product quality. We have further shown how the methods contribute to important goals in value-based software engineering by achieving consensus on experience and work processes, and focusing on improvement. Such techniques can be an important foundation for organizational learning, which require little of a project or company's resources.

In the future, we plan to do more studies of both postmortem reviews and process workshops. The focus for postmortem reviews will be to study the effect of the postmortems on an organization – does it lead to organizational learning, and what critical factors needs to be in place to ensure it. Another interesting topic in postmortem research would be to use group support systems in order to make the brainstorming process more effective. As for process workshops, we are currently studying the infusion of the resulting electronic process guide in the company Gamma, through surveys, semi-structured interviews, analysis of usage logs, and revision of projects.

Acknowledgements

I am very grateful to colleagues at the SINTEF ICT software engineering group for discussions about postmortem reviews and process workshops: Tore Dybå, Tor Erlend Fægri, Geir Kjetil Hanssen, Nils Brede Moe, and Hans Westerheim. This work was supported by the SPIKE project, partially funded by the Research Council of Norway.

References

(Abrahamsson et al., 2003) Abrahamsson, P., Warsta, J., Siponen, M.T., and Ronkainen, J., New Directions on Agile Methods: A Comparative Analysis, in Proceedings of the 25th International Conference on Software Engineering ICSE'03: (IEEE Press, 2003)

(Ahonen et al., 2002) Ahonen, J.J., Forsell, M., and Taskinen, S.-K., A Modest but Practical Software Process Modeling Technique for Software Process Improvement, Software Process Improvement and Practice. 7(1), pp 33–44

(Aurum et al., 2003) Aurum, A., Jeffery, R., Wohlin, C., and Handzic, M., Managing Software Engineering Knowledge. (Springer, Berlin 2003)

(Basili et al., 1994) Basili, V.R., Caldiera, G., and Rombach, H.D., The Experience Factory, in Encyclopedia of Software Engineering, vol. 1, ed by Marciniak, J.J. (John Wiley, 1994), pp 469–476

(Birk et al., 2002) Birk, A., Dingsøyr, T., and Stålhane, T., Postmortem: Never leave a project without it, IEEE Software, special issue on knowledge management in software engineering. 19(3), pp 43–45

(Boehm, 2003) Boehm, B. W., Value-Based Software Engineering, ACM SIGSOFT Software Engineering Notes. 28(2)

(Cianfrani et al., 2001) Cianfrani, C.A., Tsiakals, J.J., West, J.E., and West, J., Iso 9001: 2000 Explained: (ASQ Quality Press, 2001)

(Cohen and Bailey, 1997) Cohen, S.G. and Bailey, D.E., What Makes Teams Work: Group Effectiveness Research from the Shop Floor to the Executive Suite, Journal of Management. 23(3), pp 239–290

(Cohen et al., 2004) Cohen, D., Lindvall, M., and Costa, P., An Introduction to Agile Methods, vol. 62. (Elsevier, Amsterdam 2004)

(Davenport and Prusak, 1998) Davenport, T.H. and Prusak, L., Working Knowledge: How Organizations Manage What They Know: (Harvard Business School Press, 1998)

(Dennis and Valacich, 1993) Dennis, A. and Valacich, J., Computer Brainstorms – More Heads are Better than One, Journal of Applied Psychology. 78(4), pp 531–537

(Desouza et al., 2005) Desouza, K., Dingsøyr, T., and Awazu, Y., Experiences with Conducting Project Postmortems: Reports vs. Stories and Practitioner Perspectives, Hawaii International Conference on System Sciences (HICSS 38), 2005

(Dingsøyr, 2005) Dingsøyr, T., Post Mortem: Purpose and Approaches in Software Engineering, Information and Software Technology. 47 (to appear)

(Dingsøyr and Conradi, 2002) Dingsøyr, T. and Conradi, R., A Survey of Case Studies of the Use of Knowledge Management in Software Engineering, International Journal of Software Engineering and Knowledge Engineering. 12(4), pp 391–414

(Dingsøyr et al., 2005) Dingsøyr, T., Moe, N.B., Dybå, T., and Conradi, R., A workshop-oriented approach for defining electronic process guides – A case study, in Software Process Modelling, Kluwer International Series on Software Engineering, ed by Acuña, S.T., Juristo, N. (Kluwer Academic Publishers, Boston, 2005), pp 187–205

(Drucker, 1999) Drucker, P.F., The coming of the New Organization, in Harvard Business Review on Knowledge Management: (Harvard Business School Press, 1999)

(European Space Agency, 1991) European Space Agency, PSS-05-0 Issue 2, ESA Software Engineering Standards 1991

(Faure, 2004) Faure, C., Beyond Brainstorming: Effects of Different Group Procedures on Selection of Ideas and Satisfaction with the Process, Journal of Creative Behavior. 38(1), pp 13–34

(Fjermestad and Hilz, 1999) Fjermestad, J. and Hiltz, S.R., An assessment of group support systems experimental research: Methodology and results, Journal of Management Information Systems. 15(3), pp 7–149

(Greenwood and Levin, 1998) Greenwood, D.J. and Levin, M., Introduction to Action Research: (Sage Publications, 1998)

(Hansen et al., 1999) Hansen, M.T., Nohria, N., and Tierney, T., What is your strategy for managing knowledge? Harvard Business Review. 77(2), pp 106–116

(Kerth, 2001) Kerth, N.L., Project retrospectives: a handbook for team reviews. (Dorset House Publishing, New York, 2001)

(Lindvall and Rus, 2002) Lindvall, M. and Rus, I., Knowledge Management in Software Engineering, IEEE Software. 19(3), pp 26–38

(Moløkken-Østvold and Jørgensen, 2004) Moløkken-Østvold, K.J. and Jørgensen, M., Group Processes in Software Effort Estimation, Journal of Empirical Software Engineering. 9(4), pp 315–334

(Nonaka and Takeuchi, 1995) Nonaka, I. and Takeuchi, H., The Knowledge-Creating Company: (Oxford University Press, 1995)

(Nunamaker et al., 1991) Nunamaker, J., Dennis, A., Valacich, J., Vogel, D., and George, J., Electronic Meeting Systems to support Group Work, Communications of the ACM. 34(7), pp 40–61

(Orkikowski, 1992) Orlikowski, W.J., Learning from Notes: Organizational Issues in Groupware Implementation, Proceedings of the Conference on Computer-Supported Cooperative Work, Portland, Orgeon, USA, 1992

(Polanyi, 1967) Polanyi, M., The Tacit Dimension, vol. 540. Garden City, (Doubleday, New York, 1967)

(Scott et al., 2002) Scott, L., Carvalho, L., Jeffery, R., D'Ambra, J., and Becker-Koernstaedt, U., Understanding the use of an electronic process guide, Information and Software Technology. 44(10), pp 601–616

(Scupin, 1997) Scupin, R., The KJ Method: A Technique for Analyzing Data Derived from Japanese ethnology, Human Organization. 56(2), pp 233–237

(Shull et al., 2000) Shull, F., Rus, I., and Basili, V.R., How Perspective-Based Reading Can Improve Requirements Inspections, IEEE Computer. 33(7), pp 73–79

(Stata, 1996) Stata, R., Organizational learning: The key to management innovation, in How organizations learn, ed by Starkey, K. (Thomson Business Press, London, 1996), pp 316–334

(Straker, 1995) Straker, D., A Toolbook for Quality Improvement and Problem Solving: (Prentice hall International (UK) Limited, 1995)

(Webster, 1989) Webster's, Encyclopedic Unabridged Dictionary of the English Language. (Gramercy Books, New York, 1989).

Author Biography

Torgeir Dingsøyr is a research scientist at the Department of Software Engineering at SINTEF in Trondheim, Norway. He wrote his doctoral thesis on "Knowledge Management in Medium-Sized Software Consulting Companies" at the Department of Computer and Information Science, Norwegian University of Science and Technology. He has worked on several large software process improvement and knowledge management in national and international projects as a researcher and consultant. He has published papers on knowledge management in software engineering, case-based reasoning, and software engineering education. He is a co-author of the book "Process Improvement in Practice – A Hand-book for IT Companies," published by Kluwer Academic Publishers.

16 Quantifying the Value of New Technologies for Software Development

D. L. Atkins, A. Mockus and H. P. Siy

Abstract: Introducing relevant software technologies may provide significant advantages to a software organization. Unfortunately, the value the technology may provide is almost never quantified. We describe a methodology for precise quantitative measurement of the value a software technology may add to the project in terms of the impact on quality and lead time. The methodology employs measures derived from version control and problem tracking repositories to determine the value of technology. We illustrate this approach in a detailed case study on the impact of using two particular technologies – a version-sensitive source code editor and a domain engineered application environment – in a telecommunications product. In both cases use of technology had a strong positive impact on the considered quality measures. The methodology relies on information commonly available in project version control and problem tracking systems and, therefore, can be widely and easily applied.

Keywords: Statistical models, empirical studies, case studies, software change database, software metrics, software quality, development lead time, version-sensitive editing, domain engineering, large-scale software development, technology transfer, technology evaluation.

16.1 Introduction

New technologies – languages, tools, methodologies – are constantly being introduced in the hopes of improving quality, decreasing lead time, or increasing productivity. While they have the potential to greatly improve the quality and maintainability of software, deploying and maintaining a new technology in a large organization can be an expensive proposition. We explore how to quantify the effects of assimilating software engineering technologies into ongoing large-scale software projects, presenting a simple methodology that correlates technology usage with field defects and lead time based on analysis of the change history of a software project.

Quantifying the impact of a technology on software development is particularly important in making a case for transferring new technology to the mainstream development process. Technology transfer involves significant effort spent in training developers and integrating the technology with the existing development process. It also carries the risk of decreasing developer productivity due to the inevitable learning curve. (Rogers, 1995) cites observability of impact as a key factor in successful technology transfer. Observability usually implies that the impact of the new technology can be measured in some way. Most of the time, the usefulness of a new technology is demonstrated through the best subjective judgment. This may not be persuasive enough to convince managers and developers to try the new technology. By having a methodology for quantifying the value added by the new technology, early adopters can be assured that an objective evaluation can be performed after trying it out. Furthermore, having quantified results from other projects gives interested practitioners an opportunity to gauge whether the new technology has potential for a positive return on investment in their environment.

Previously we have reported on a methodology to estimate the savings in terms of effort to perform a software change provided by new technologies in (Atkins et al., 2000; Atkins et al., 2002). We now extend this methodology to also estimate the impact of the new technology on defect and lead time reduction – two qualities that are likely to prove more valuable (Boehm, 2003) to a software organization than developer effort savings. Furthermore, instead of estimating these two qualities for individual software changes, we estimate these for units that add business value. In our case, these are called features – customers buy products or upgrade to new software releases contingent on the on-time delivery of certain features that have passed their rigorous acceptance tests.

While still focusing on the analysis of changes to the software, our estimation methodology is modified accordingly to deal with features. First, we obtain a number of change measures, such as size, lead time, and technology usage, from the change history of the source code. Then we add a new step where we aggregate changes into their associated features. Finally, we fit statistical models that relate defects and lead time in the considered units to the predictor that indicates usage or non-usage of the technology. We also have an additional four years of data to verify the trends observed in previous reports.

As we will see, the methodology is largely automatic, inexpensive, nonintrusive, and applicable to most software projects using version control systems. Furthermore, it can be applied to an entire software project in its actual setting as we do here to measure the effects of a version-sensitive source code editor and of a domain engineered application environment. Despite fairly simple general features, there are a number of differences between the ways the methodology is applied to estimate the impact of various technologies. The goal of this paper is to highlight and summarize these differences to make the methodology easier to use in practice.

We start by briefly describing the software project under study, software changes, and data sources in Section 16.2. Section 16.3 describes the two technologies under consideration. Section 16.4 describes the step-by-step application of our methodology. Finally, we conclude with a relevant work section and a summary.

16.2 Background

The case study here revolves around a large telephone switching software system developed over more than two decades. Lucent Technologies' 5ESS® switch is used to connect local and long distance calls involving voice, data, and video communications. The 5ESS source code is organized into subsystems with each subsystem further subdivided into a set of modules. Each module contains a number of source code files. The change history of the files is maintained using the Extended Change Management System (ECMS) (Midha, 1997), for initiating and tracking changes, and the Source Code Control System (SCCS) (Rochkind, 1975), for managing different versions of the files.

We present a simplified description of the data collected by SCCS and ECMS that are relevant to our study. ECMS, like most version control systems, operates over a set of source code files. An atomic change, or delta, to the program text consists of the lines that were deleted and those that were added in order to make the change. Deltas are usually computed by a file differencing algorithm (such as the Unix diff), invoked by SCCS, which compares an older version of a file with the current version.

ECMS records the following attributes for each change: the file with which it is associated; the date and time the change was "checked in"; and the name and User ID of the developer who made it. Additionally, the SCCS database records each delta as a tuple including the actual source code that was changed (lines deleted and lines added), login of the developer, MR number (see below), and the date and time of change.

In order to make a change to a software system, a developer may have to modify many files. ECMS groups atomic changes to the source code recorded by SCCS (over potentially many files) into logical changes referred to as Modification Requests (MRs). There is one developer per MR. An MR has an English language abstract associated with it, provided by the developer, describing the purpose of the change. A timestamp of when the MR was opened is also recorded in ECMS.

We also obtained a complete list of identifiers of MRs that were done using the domain engineered application environment and/or using the version-sensitive editor. Thus, for each MR, we were able to obtain the following information:

- who made the change (developer login)
- size of the change (number of lines added and deleted)
- number of deltas
- duration (dates of first and last deltas)
- indicator if the change was done to fix a problem in a released version of the software
- number of files touched
- whether the change was done using the technology under consideration.

16.3 Applications

In this section we describe two technologies we evaluate. The first one represents a source code editor that is designed to show a desired version of the source code. The second example describes a domain engineered application environment including a special language and a GUI-based code generator.

VE: A Version-sensitive Editor

The *Version Editor* (VE) is used by 5ESS developers to simplify the view of source code as they make changes. The software project for these programmers requires the concurrent development and maintenance of many sequential versions as well as two main variants for domestic and international configurations of the product (Perry et al., 2001). The 5ESS source code may be common to more than two dozen distinct releases of the code, which may be deployed products in maintenance mode, or new product versions under active development.

As described in (Atkins et al., 2002), the software releases form a complex version hierarchy with the often conflicting project management goals of isolating deployed releases from current development changes yet maximizing commonality to promote the automatic flow of software fixes to future releases.

```
Before . . .
  routing = getRoute(routing);
  #version (4A)
  dest = getDest(routing);
  if (dest.port == 0)
  return (ConnectLocal(routing));
  #endversion (4A)
  Connect(routing);

After . . .
  routing = getRoute(routing);
  #version (4A)
  dest = getDest(routing);
  #version (!5A)
  if (dest.port == 0)
  #endversion (!5A)
  #version (5A)
  if (dest.port == 0) || dest.module == 0)
  #endversion (5A)
  return (ConnectLocal(routing));
  #endversion (4A)
  Connect(routing);
```

Fig. 61. Example: Before and after a Release 5A change (in bold)

The implication is that, at any given time, several releases of the software are in the field and are actively being supported. Several versions of the source code needed to be maintained. Since the industrial source code management technology of the early 1980s did not have good support for branching and merging, source code was kept common among many releases with release-specific differences delineated by a special embedded `#version` directive. This directive is similar to a C preprocessor `#if` where a symbol (corresponding to the release) is used for control and the symbol may be negated.

This system permits a single source file to be extracted to produce a different version for each software release. Software development environment tools verify the consistent use of these constructs according to a release hierarchy maintained by the system and perform the extraction of the source code for building each software release. For example, the first frame in Figure 61 shows a source file where three lines of code are specific to the 4A release. The system guarantees that these lines will not appear in earlier releases but will appear in later releases. Also, the lines will not appear in isolated releases (the domestic and international configurations are all isolated from each other).

A developer adding new code must target the change for a specific release and then bracket it by the appropriate `#version` constructs. When existing code is changed, it must be logically deleted with a `#version` construct using the negation of the target release. Figure 61 shows how these constructs are used to change the expression in an if-then statement for Release 5A. The original if-then statement was inserted for Release 4A.

This simple example shows how even a one line code change requires the developer to add five lines to the file (four control lines and the changed code line). In addition to this extra overhead for a logical one line code change, the version control lines make the source file more difficult to read and understand. In the project being studied there are several dozen distinct releases and some core source files may contain `#version` directives for most of these releases. In worst-case files, only 10% of the lines of the file are the extractable source code for a release, with 50% of the lines being `#version`/`#endversion` lines and the other 40% being source that extracts for other releases.

```
routing = getRoute(routing);
dest = getDest(routing);
if (dest.port == 0 || dest.module == 0)
    return (ConnectLocal(routing));
Connect(routing);

MR 12467 by dla,97/9/21 [Local routing]
"route.c" [modified] line 67 of 241
```

Fig. 62. Release 5A view in VE with change in bold

The version-sensitive editor VE (Coplien et al., 1987; Pal and Thompson, 1989; Atkins, 1998) was made available to make this situation more manageable for the developer. This tool allows the developer to edit in a view that shows only the code that will be extracted for the release being changed and performs the automatic insertion of any necessary control lines.

The developer's view is of normal editing in the extracted code; VE manages the changes to the #version constructs according to the described constraints. Figure 62 shows the view presented by VE for the file from Figure 61. The developer only has to use standard vi or emacs editing commands, and VE inserts the required #version directives (behind the scenes).

The use of VE by developers is entirely optional. The usage of VE may be detected, because VE leaves a signature on all of the #version/#endversion control lines that it generates (see (Atkins et al., 2002) for more details.) Thus we can distinguish when VE was used to make a change involving #version lines from when the change was made using an ordinary editor.

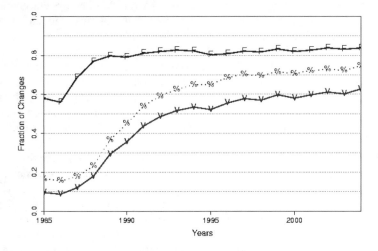

Fig. 63. VE usage over time

Figure 63 shows the history of VE usage in the considered project, which consists of approximately 1.2M MRs. The three lines show the fraction of MRs that were done with VE (V: MRs such that at least one delta of the MR contained #version lines with the VE signature), that involved #version line (F: MRs such that some delta of the MR contained a #version line), and fraction of #version MRs that involved VE (%: V/F). The usage of VE increased dramatically over time.

Figure 64 shows the history of VE usage in terms of the fraction of developers that use it. The three lines show the fraction of developers that used VE (V: developers such that at least one delta within a year contained #version lines with the VE signature), that made changes with #version line (F: developers such that some delta within a year contained a #version line), and ratio of the quantities above (%). The figure indicates that 60% of developers make changes involving #version lines and 70% of them use VE.

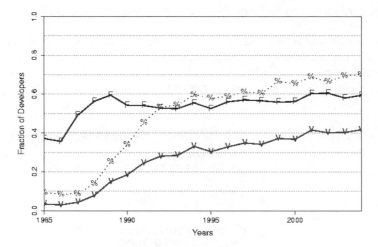

Fig. 64. VE usage over time

Domain Engineering

Traditional software engineering deals with the design and development of individual software products. In practice, an organization often develops a set of similar products, called a family or product line (Weiss and Lai, 1999). Traditional methods of design and development do not provide formalisms or methods for taking advantage of these similarities. As a result the developers practice some informal means of reusing designs, code, and other artifacts, massaging the reused artifact to fit into new requirements. This can lead to software that is fragile and hard to maintain because the reused components were not meant for reuse.

Domain Engineering (DE) (Weiss and Lai, 1999; Coplien et al., 1998; Cuka and Weiss, 1998) approaches this problem by defining and facilitating the development of software product lines rather than individual software products. This is accomplished by considering all of the products together as one set, analyzing their characteristics, and building an application engineering environment to support their production. In doing so, development of individual products (henceforth called Application Engineering) can be done rapidly at the cost of some significant up-front investment in analyzing the domain and creating the environment.

The process is summarized in Figure 65. In this figure, DE is further divided into domain analysis and domain implementation and integration. Domain analysis identifies the commonalities among members of the product line as well as the possible ways in which they may vary. Usually, several domain experts assist in this activity. Also, the application engineering environment is designed and built. This usually involves creation of a domain-specific language, a graphical user interface front end, and a source code generator back end. Domain implementation and integration deploys the DE-based process, making necessary adjustments to product construction tools (makefiles, version control systems, etc.) and to the overall development process.

Several teams have used the DE-based process to reengineer specific domain areas within the 5ESS software (Ardis and Green, 1998). We conducted a study to evaluate the impact of the AIM project, a DE effort to reengineer the software and the process for developing the multiplicity of screen interfaces to the 5ESS switch database.

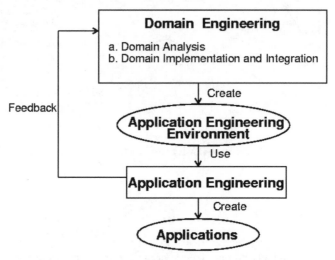

Fig. 65. Domain engineering and application engineering

The problem faced by the screen developers was that most clients who purchased the 5ESS switch required customization of their screen interfaces. In the old process, screens were customized by inserting #ifdef-like compiler directives into existing screen specification files. Over time, the specification files have become difficult to maintain and modify.

The AIM project used DE to identify commonalities and variabilities in different clients' interface requirements. These results provided input to the development of a GUI tool for assisting in the design of and keeping track of the customized screens. Information gathered through the GUI was saved in files whose format was specified by a domain-specific language. During the product build process, a code generator would then take these files and generate the screen specification files.

More details on the AIM study is published in an earlier paper (Siy and Mockus, 1999). In some sense, the problem here is not unlike the problem addressed by VE which facilitates the maintenance of multiple versions of code. However, the creators of AIM undertook a higher level, domain-specific solution in an attempt to achieve even higher productivity.

16.4 Impact Assessment Methodology

We outline here a general framework for analyzing the impact of a software technology. We have previously investigated effects on effort spent on individual changes (Atkins et al., 2000; Atkins, at al., 2002). Because the technology may affect the definition or granularity of changes and also quality and lead time, here we focus on modeling the lead time and quality impact on software features, the units that provide added value to software by providing additional functionality that may be compelling to the customer and provide revenue to the software provider. More specifically, features add value to the software because they generate revenue and enhance competitiveness of the product. We assume that on average, all features implement a similar amount of value. This is a reasonable assumption since we have a large number of features under both conditions and we do not have any reason to believe that the definition of a feature changed over the considered period. Consequently, even a substantial variation of functionality among features should not bias the results. A more precise measure of impact could be obtained by assigning weights corresponding to the actual or projected revenue corresponding to each feature. To approximate such revenue we used the size or complexity of the feature.

The analysis framework consists of the following steps:

1. Obtain measures of changes. Identify the changes made to the software entity of interest and whether or not the technology was used.
2. Group changes into software features or other relevant units that add value. The grouping also involves rolling up the measures of individual changes to the feature level.
3. Select a subset of these rolled-up measures to predict feature quality and lead time. The minimal subset typically includes the size of the change and an indicator as to whether the technology was used or not. Verify independence of predictors.
4. Fit and validate a set of candidate models. Models that explain more variation in the data and have fewer parameters are preferred. Our goal is to select simple models with predictive power rather than complicated models that account for all the variations of the response variable but are difficult to interpret. The fitted models are used to test the significance of the effect of technology.

The following sections explain each step in detail.

Change Measures and Technology Use

The basic characteristic measures of software changes include: identity of the person performing the change; the files, modules, and actual lines of code involved in the change; when the change was made; the size of the change measured both by the number of lines added or changed, the number of deltas, and the number of files touched; and the purpose of the change including whether the purpose of the change was to fix a field defect. Many change management systems record data from which such measures can be collected.

The information on files, modules, and lines changed is usually sufficient to determine if the software entity of interest was touched by the change. The determination of technology involvement in the change might be more complicated. We first discuss how to determine if the technology was used and then if it was not used.

In real life situations developers work on several projects over the course of a year and it is important to identify which changes they performed using the technology of interest. There may be several ways to identify these changes. In our VE example the tool left a trace in the SCCS files. In the AIM example the domain engineered features were implemented in a specific set of code modules (we refer to them as AIM paths).

Finally, to perform the comparison, we need to identify changes to a software entity that were done without the use of the technology. In the case of VE the information was available directly from SCCS except for a subset of changes that had no #version lines. Consequently we had two types of MRs: changes done using VE and changes done without VE. In the AIM example, the source code to the previously used screen specification files had a specific set of directory paths. We refer to those paths as pre-AIM paths. Based on AIM and pre-AIM sets of paths we classified all AIM MRs into two classes: MRs that touch at least one file in the AIM path and MRs that do not touch files in the AIM path, but touch at least one file in the pre-AIM path. In both cases there are two categories of changes that we label:

- TECH: MRs on the software entity that involve use of technology
- no-TECH: MRs on the software entity not involving the use of technology

We excluded features where technology could not be used (code not relevant to AIM functionality) or could not provide benefit (changes with no #version lines).

Aggregating Change Measures

Since our primary concern is to assess the technology impact on software value, we need to combine software changes into groups, each of which is providing comparable value. In the considered organization such groups were referred to as software features. Each feature was designed to provide functionality that could be sold. While the software code was common to all customers, only the licensed features were enabled.

Therefore, we wanted to measure technology impact on defect and lead time reduction on each feature. Because larger and more complex features may take more time and have more defects, we may need to adjust for their size and complexity better to discern the effects of a technology.

To measure feature size and complexity we aggregate the MR measures to the feature level:
1. NMR – number of MRs
2. NDelta – number of delta
3. NLOC – number of lines added
4. NDEV – number of developers who participated
5. NFILES – number files modified
6. whether or not there were changes involving technology use
7. interval from first to last delta
8. if there were MRs fixing field problems

The last two measures were our response variables measuring lead time and presence of field problems.

Variable Selection

Naturally, the size and complexity of a change may have a strong effect on the lead time or probability of a fault. In the case of VE, such covariates were included because there is no reason to assume that the use or nonuse of VE affects the number or complexity of the changes needed to implement a feature. Thus, we chose the number of developers, the number of MRs and the number of added lines as the covariates for predicting feature lead time and quality. We used Spearman correlations due to the highly skewed nature of the observed data. Other measures we collected had correlations above .8 with the number of developers making interpretation of the regression results difficult. The correlation between these three measures and the indicator of VE usage ranged from .2 to .3.

In the AIM case, the programming language was different. Additionally, the changes involving technology were done using a special GUI environment instead of editing the source code in individual files. These reasons suggest that the number, size, or complexity of changes to implement a feature would vary depending on whether or not AIM technology was used. Furthermore, due to previously reported dramatic effort savings, fewer developers may be needed to implement a feature. Therefore, inclusion of change size and complexity covariates may not be applicable when measuring the impact of AIM. After all, AIM was designed to simplify and streamline the changes. Thus, we did not include any covariates in the AIM models.

Models, Interpretation, and Validation

In this step, we are ready to fit the models and interpret the results. Due to the highly skewed nature of the software change data it is important to transform all three predictor measures and the lead time response variable via logarithms. The presence of the fault is such a rare event that we modeled it as a boolean variable (zero or not). For the lead time we use multiple linear regression and for the faults we use logistic regression suitable for the binary response variable.

It is essential to validate software repository data. See, for example, (Atkins et al., 2002; Herbsleb and Mockus, 2003; Mockus et al., 2003; Mockus and Votta, 2000; Mockus and Weiss, 2000) for more details. The key is to understand and validate how the derived attributes of changes relate to the actual software process and exclude computer generated or data collection artifacts. It is important to have several operationalizations of a measure and check for consistency among them.

The statistical aspects involve using appropriate transformation of the variables, excluding strongly correlated predictors, and using appropriate statistical models and procedures.

Other aspects of validation include realization that some technologies may impact the change measures directly, in addition to affecting the outcome variables as happens to be the case with AIM. Finally, the external validation of measures and estimates is performed by presenting and discussing the results with the organization and individuals involved in the study.

16.5 Results

We present the technology impact on feature lead time and quality. We start with the lead time, then investigate quality, and, finally, inspect the hypothesised AIM impact on the number of individuals that are needed to implement a change.

Feature Lead-time

Our response variable is the natural logarithm[21] of calendar time between the first and last delta in a software feature. We exclude infrastructure features that are not "sellable" to customers but are an integral part of the system because they add a different type of value that may be impossible directly to express in terms of additional revenue.

This response variable represents development lead-time, which can be automatically collected from system repositories. We chose this part of the total interval because development lead-time is most likely to be affected by the technologies we are evaluating. To validate such measure of lead time, in previous investigations of the same product we compared a sample of such automatically derived development lead times with the total lead times reported in project management records and found strong and consistent relationship where the total lead time was a constant multiple of the automatically derived development lead time measure.

The predictor variables are the use of technology and the applicable covariates in case of VE application. The regression formulas are as follows:

---

[21]All logarithms in this chapter use the natural logarithm function.

$$E(\log\ time\ ) = \alpha + \beta_1 \log\ NDev + \beta_2 \log\ NMR + \beta_3 \log\ NLOC + \theta_{VE} \quad (1)$$

$$E(\log\ time\ ) = \alpha + \theta_{AIM} \quad (2)$$

In these formulas, we use θ_{TECH} (where TECH is AIM or VE) as a shorthand for $I(TECH)\theta_{TECH}$, where $I(TECH)$ is 1 if the feature involves the use of technology and 0 otherwise. Table 34 presents the results of the regression using formula (1).

Table 34. Feature lead time regression, VE impact

15,953 features, R2 = 0.4

	Estimate	Std. Error	t value	Pr(>|t|)
(Intercept)	12.54	0.04	303.76	0.00
log(NDEV)	0.46	0.02	19.68	0.00
Log(NMR)	0.21	0.02	12.54	0.00
log(NLOC)	0.23	0.01	30.50	0.00
VE	-0.10	0.03	-3.64	0.00

These estimates indicate that the lead time for a feature with median number of developers (3), median number of MRs (3), and median number of lines (725) is 11% longer when VE was not used. Not surprisingly, larger features with more developers, MRs, and lines added consume longer lead times. Table 35 presents the results of the regression using formula (2).

Table 35. Feature lead time regression, AIM impact

2,908 features, R2 = 0.02

	Estimate	Std. Error	t-value	Pr(>|t|)
(Intercept)	14.04	0.04	350.87	0.00
AIM	-0.65	0.09	-7.64	0.00

The R^2 value in Table 35 is very low due to large variability in the size of a feature. The estimate indicates that lead times for features not using AIM are 92% longer.

Feature Defects

The response variable is a binary indicator on whether the feature had any field problem-related MRs. The logistic regression formulas were as follows:

$$E(P(Fault\ )) = \frac{1}{1 + e^{-\alpha - \beta_1 \log\ NDev\ -\beta_2 \log\ NMR\ -\beta_3 \log\ NLOC\ -\theta_{VE}}} \quad (3)$$

$$E(P(Fault\ )) = \frac{1}{1 + e^{-\alpha - \theta_{AIM}}} \quad (4)$$

Table 36 shows the result of regression using formula (3).

Table 36. Feature quality logistic regression, VE impact

15,953 features, null deviance 9,778, residual deviance 7,812

	Estimate	Std. Error	z value	Pr(>|z|)
(Intercept)	-2.53	0.12	-20.61	0.00
Log(NDEV)	1.01	0.07	15.11	0.00
Log(NMR)	0.50	0.05	10.92	0.00
log(NLOC)	-0.30	0.02	-12.08	0.00
VE	-0.23	0.09	-2.67	0.01

These estimates indicate that, for features with median number of logins (3), median number of MRs (3), and median number of lines (725), the probability of having field faults is 25% higher when VE was not used. While, as expected, features with more developers and MRs have an increased probability of having field faults, the number of lines (after adjusting for other factors) appears to decrease that probability. The large number of lines may be an indication of features that are implemented mostly outside the legacy code base where changes are easier to make and, therefore, more code is typically added.

Table 37. Feature quality logistic regression, AIM impact

2,908 features, null deviance 962, residual deviance 955

	Estimate	Std. Error	z value	Pr(>|z|)
(Intercept)	-3.08	0.10	-30.08	0.00
AIM	-0.72	0.29	-2.50	0.01

To interpret the estimate, the features not using AIM were twice as likely to have a fault.

Impact on Change Properties

The introduction of AIM was believed to have another value affecting impact: the reduction of developers. We investigate this hypothesis in this section. The regression formula is:

$$E(\log NDEV) = \alpha + \beta_1 \log NMR + \beta_2 \log NLOC + \theta_{AIM} \tag{5}$$

Only the number of files had correlation less than .8 with the number of MRs for the AIM related features. The results are in Table 38.

Table 38. Number of developers in a feature, AIM impact

2,908 features, R2 = 0.59

	Estimate	Std. Error	t value	Pr(>|t|)
(Intercept)	-0.01	0.01	-0.97	0.33
log(NMR)	0.46	0.01	39.88	0.00
log(NFILE)	0.10	0.01	15.62	0.00
AIM	-0.10	0.02	-6.02	0.00

We can see that even adjusting for the size of feature, the usage of AIM does appear to significantly decrease the number of developers involved in a feature. Thus, the technology enabled the production of features with fewer developers.

16.6 Related Work

The framework to evaluate the effects of a tool on development effort is described in (Atkins et al., 2002). The methodology to assess the impact of Domain Engineering application environments is given in (Siy and Mockus, 1999). In this paper we extend and unify both frameworks to create a general approach for evaluating the impact of any software technology on lead time and quality. We focus on practical applications of the approach by performing a detailed step-by-step analysis of two types of new technology.

This technique is very different in approach and purpose from other quality estimation techniques such as COQUALMO (Chulani, 1999), which make use of algorithmic or experiential models to estimate total project defects. Our approach is to estimate impact after actual development work has been done, using data primarily from change management systems. In addition, our approach is well-suited for quantifying the impact of introducing new technology to existing development processes.

We have previously investigated effects of these two technologies on effort spent on individual changes (Atkins et al., 2000; Atkins et al., 2002). Here we focus on modeling the lead time and quality impact on software features, the units that provide added value to software by providing additional functionality.

16.7 Discussion

We present a methodology to quantify the impact from use of a software technology exemplified by a case study of a tool and an application engineering environment. We calculate the beneficial effects on the development of features, units that add business value. We find that by not using VE the lead time increased by approximately 10% and the probability of field defect in a typical change increased by 25%. This is consistent with the design goals of the tool to make code more clear by hiding irrelevant code.

The use of the AIM application engineering environment resulted in halving the probability of a field defect in a feature. It also roughly halved the lead time of the feature. Furthermore, the use of the environment was associated with the reduction of the number of people that work on a feature, consistent with previous results indicating significant effort savings and with the design goals of the technology.

Presently, the impacts are quantified in terms of reduction in the lead time and the probability of finding field faults. It would be useful to calculate the return-on-investment from introducing such technologies. We cannot obtain revenue data from features due to its proprietary nature, but we can estimate the savings to the organization. Reduction in lead time translates to savings in staffing costs due to the need for fewer developers and the expectation of freeing them up sooner to work on other features. Reduction in the probability of finding field faults translates to savings from fixing fewer faults. These savings offset the investment cost of introducing new technologies into the development process, and will be quantified in future work.

The described methodology is based on automatically extractable measures of software changes and should be easily applicable to other software projects that use source code version control systems. Since most of the change measures are kept in any version control system, there is no need to collect additional data.

This methodology is subject to a few limitations. Data to assess the impact of technological changes is only available after a few years of use. It is also difficult to identify predictors that leave little if no imprint in the change database, for instance, technologies aimed at improving software testing.

We described in detail all steps of the methodology to encourage replication. We expect that this methodology will lead to more widespread quantitative assessment of software productivity improvement techniques. We believe that most software practitioners will save substantial effort from trials and usage of ineffective technology, once they have the ability to screen new technologies based on a quantitative evaluation of their use on other projects. Tool developers and other proponents of new (and existing) technology should be responsible for performing such quantitative evaluation. It will ultimately benefit software practitioners who will be able to evaluate appropriate productivity improvement techniques based on quantitative information.

Acknowledgements

For all statistical modeling and graphics we used the R package that is maintained and enhanced by a large group of volunteers worldwide. We also thank the anonymous reviewers for their helpful comments.

References

(Ardis and Green, 1998) Ardis, M. A. and Green, J. A. Successful introduction of domain engineering into software development. Bell Labs Technical Journal, 3(3):10–20 (September 1998)

(Atkins, 1998) Atkins, D. L.: Version sensitive editing: Change history as a programming tool. In: Proceedings of the 8th Conference on Software Configuration Management (SCM-8), pp 146–157. Springer-Verlag, LNCS 1439 (1998)

(Atkins et al., 2000) Atkins, D., Mockus, A., and Siy, H.: Measuring technology effects on software change cost. Bell Labs Technical Journal, 5(2):7–18, (April–June 2000)

(Atkins et al., 2002) Atkins, D., Ball, T., Graves, T., and Mockus, A. Using version control data to evaluate the impact of software tools: A case study of the version editor. IEEE Transactions on Software Engineering, 28(7):625–637 (July 2002)

(Boehm, 2003) Boehm, B.W.: Value-based software engineering. ACM SIGSOFT Software Engineering Notes, (2003)

(Chulani, 1999) Chulani, S. COQUALMO (constructive quality model) a software defect density prediction model. Project Control for Software Quality, (1999)

(Coplien et al., 1987) Coplien, J. O., DeBruler, D. L and Thompson, M. B: The delta system: A nontraditional approach to software version management. In International Switching Symposium (March 1987)

(Coplien et al., 1998) Coplien, J., Hoffman, D., and Weiss, D.: Commonality and variability in software engineering. IEEE Software, 15(6):37–45 (November 1998)

(Cuka and Weiss, 1998) Cuka, D.A. and Weiss, D.M.: Engineering domains: executable commands as an example. In Proc. 5th Intl. Conf. on Software Reuse, pp 26–34, Victoria, Canada, June 2–6 1998

(Herbsleb and Mockus, 2003) Herbsleb, J. D. and Mockus, A. An empirical study of speed and communication in globally-distributed software development. IEEE Transactions on Software Engineering, 29(6):481–494, June 2003

(Midha, 1997) Midha, A. K.: Software configuration management for the 21st century. Bell Labs Technical Journal, 2(1):1997

(Mockus and Votta, 2000) Mockus, A. and Lawrence, G. Votta. Identifying reasons for software change using historic databases. In International Conference on Software Maintenance, pp 120–130, San Jose, California, October 11–14 (2000)

(Mockus and Weiss, 2000) Mockus, A. and Weiss, D. M.: Predicting risk of software changes. Bell Labs Technical Journal, 5(2):169–180 (April–June 2000)

(Mockus et al., 2003) Mockus, A., Weiss, D. M. and Zhang, P.: Understanding and predicting effort in software projects. In: 2003 International Conference on Software Engineering, pp 274–284, Portland, Oregon (ACM Press, May 3–10, 2003)

(Pal and Thompson, 1989) Pal, A. and Thompson, M.: An advanced interface to a switching software version management system. In: Seventh International

Conference on Software Engineering for Telecommunications Switching Systems, (July 1989)

(Perry et al., 2001) Perry, D., Siy, H. and Votta, L. Parallel Changes in Large Scale Software Development: An Observational Case Study. ACM Transactions on Software Engineering and Methodology, 10(3):308–337, (July 2001)

(Rochkind, 1975) Rochkind, M.J.: The source code control system. IEEE Transactions on Software Engineering, 1(4):364–370:1975

(Rogers, 1995) Rogers, E. M. Diffusion of Innovation (Free Press, New York, 1995)

(Siy and Mockus, 1999) Siy, H. and Mockus, A.: Measuring domain engineering effects on software coding cost. In Metrics 99: Sixth International Symposium on Software Metrics, pp 304–311, Boca Raton, Florida, (November 1999)

(Weiss and Lai, 1999) Weiss, D. and Lai, R. Software Product Line Engineering: A Family-Based Software Development Process (Addison-Wesley, 1999)

Author Biographies

David Atkins is an assistant professor in Computer Science at the American University in Cairo. He came to Egypt from the University of Oregon, and for most of his career, he was a member of technical staff in the Software Production Research Department at Bell Labs in Naperville, Illinois. His research interests include programming languages and software version management. He received a B.A. in mathematics from the College of Wooster in Ohio and a PhD in mathematics from the University of Kansas in Lawrence.

Audris Mockus conducts research on quantifying, modeling, and improving software development. He designs data mining methods to summarize and augment software change data, interactive visualization techniques to inspect, present, and control the development process, and statistical models and optimization techniques to understand the relationships between people, organizations, and characteristics of a software product. Audris Mockus received B.S. and M.S. in Applied Mathematics from Moscow Institute of Physics and Technology in 1988. In 1991 he received M.S. and in 1994 he received PhD in Statistics from Carnegie Mellon University. He works in the Software Technology Research Department of Avaya Labs. Previously he worked in the Software Production Research Department of Bell Labs.

Harvey Siy received the B.S. degree in Computer Science from University of the Philippines in 1989, and the M.S. and PhD degrees in Computer Science from University of Maryland at College Park in 1994 and 1996, respectively. He is a Member of Technical Staff at Lucent Technologies doing capacity and performance engineering for the 5ESS product. He was previously with the Software Production Research Department of Bell Labs, where he conducted empirical studies of large-scale, industrial software engineering processes.

17 Valuing Software Intellectual Property

Donald J. Reifer

Abstract: In this chapter, we discuss approaches used to value software intellectual property. We start by outlining current intellectual property valuation practices. Next, we outline a valuation framework that permits software experts to value all forms of intangible assets when involved in acquisitions, litigations, and disputes. The framework takes advantage of current theory and best practice to derive a fair value for use in valuing intellectual property utilizing the currently accepted cost, income, or market approaches. We conclude by focusing on the barriers that software experts will have to overcome when presenting their findings to non-software participants (executives, venture capitalists, judges, attorneys, juries, etc.).

Keywords: Valuation framework, real options theory, intellectual property valuation.

17.1 Introduction

As firms have used more and more information technology to run their businesses, valuing software and other forms of intellectual property has become more of an issue. That's because such property represents large expenditures that may not be accurately represented in the company's books (i.e., according to the American Institute of Certified Public Accountants (AICPA, 1998), software may have been expensed instead of capitalized and therefore appears as a liability instead of an asset on the firm's income statement). For example, take a firm that has developed software that fuses customer satisfaction data together to provide executives with a true and accurate picture of how well their support processes are viewed as working in the field. Because this software helped the firm improve its level of customer satisfaction, it is viewed by management positively as a marketplace discriminator. However, the same software package may be viewed by the financial community as an unnecessary expense due to the fact that management has elected not to derive income by selling the software commercially because it provided them with a competitive advantage. Undoubtedly, management may want to value the software so that its true value appears on the books. They may also try to protect the intellectual aspects of this software using licenses, patents, copyrights, and trade secrets. Management's goal is to keep the algorithms and other unique properties of this software out of the hands of their competitors.

As license, patent, copyright, and trade secret terms and conditions have been violated, attorneys have become involved in software litigation. While license breaches have proved relatively easy to value (ASB, 2002), determining the worth of patents, copyrights, and trade secrets has been much more difficult (Damiano,

2002). Some of the many issues that make valuation difficult include, but are not limited to, the following:

- Traditional approaches to determine value focus on market price and do not include adequate allowances for appreciation of assets, market growth or technology, and functional, physical, and economic obsolescence (Cole et al., 2002).
- The "fair value," "fair market value," "market value," "acquisition value," or "use value" of an intangible asset is difficult to determine especially in light of current economic conditions. Fair value is defined as the amount in terms of dollars that a willing and able buyer would pay for these assets under current market conditions (Reilly and Schweihs, 1998).
- Determination of value under the "highest and best use" principle is hard to determine as legal, physical, financial and maximum profitability conditions vary greatly depending on premises of value (e.g., value in place, value in exchange, value in continued use, etc.) (Reilly and Schweihs, 1998).
- The range and profitability of the use of intangible assets are difficult to determine in light of future competition and market conditions (Mard, 2001).
- States treat valuation of intangible assets like software trade secrets differently and the case law is nonuniform (Loud and Reilly, 2000).
- Few cases involving valuing intangible assets like software trade secrets are available to establish precedence in a court of law (Goldenberg and Tenen, 2001).

In light of these issues, a framework is needed to help experts develop reasonable value estimates for software intangible assets, especially trade secrets. This framework needs to portray value in a manner that communicates the software's true worth to the many communities trying to assess either the assets' market potential or potential to the firm (e.g., for the case of the software that acts as a marketplace discriminator).

17.2 Software Intellectual Property Protection Mechanisms

The primary ways for owners to protect their software as intellectual property are copyrights, patents, and trade secrets. These safeguards are used to protect the software owner's property rights relative to the ownership, transfer, and use of algorithms, data, designs, and processes used in the design, development, and production of software masters (i.e., configuration managed master copies of the software). Because software managers tend not to understand the advantages and disadvantages associated with the use of each of these protection approaches, we will briefly summarize them at this point in the chapter.

Copyrights

Copyrights are the most frequent form of intellectual property protection for software. They enjoy the advantages that they are easy to use and have an unlimited life. In general, they grant the owner of the copyright with the following exclusive rights for the work being protected:

- The right to reproduce the copyrighted work.
- The right to create derivative works from the copyrighted work.
- The right to distribute and display the copyrighted work.
- The right to display the work publicly, directly, or by means of film, TV, slides, etc.

These rights are violated when anyone copies, excerpts, adapts, or publishes the copyrighted works without permission. Although federal registration is not needed to obtain copyright protection, it is required if the owner decides to litigate because of infringement.

Copyrights provide limited protection because their scope is limited to the tangible expression of an idea and not to the idea itself. In other words, copyrights can be used to prevent the unauthorized copying of source code. They cannot be used to protect either the design concepts or algorithms used in that source code from improper use.

Patents

Unlike copyrights, patents provide their owners the exclusive right for a period of 20 years from the date of the patent application to make, use, offer to sell, and sell the invention covered by the claims of the patent. In general, patents protect the technological "application" of an "idea." A patent precludes "practice" of an invention by others, even if they develop the idea independently. However, the requirements for patents are very stringent. The invention must be useful, novel, and non-obvious compared to prior discoveries (the "prior art") that are patented, in the public domain, or otherwise widely known. While publication is not required for copyright, a patent is granted in exchange for "full disclosure" of what the inventor considers to be the best way of implementing or practicing the invention (OTA, 1990).

The advantage of patent protection for a software invention is that the patent will protect all the claims for the invention, taken as a whole, so long as they are taken in scope. This is an important consideration because many of the processes involved in the patent may not be protected under a copyright as they would be considered part of an unprotected idea.

Patents have not been commonly used in the past for protecting rights in computer software because they are complicated, time consuming, expensive to prepare, and difficult to obtain. One of the major drawbacks of securing patents is that you must prove that your invention is novel and not obvious to the U.S. Patent and Trademark Office (PTO). Another drawback is that you must carefully word your "claim" so that the scope is appropriate; e.g., neither too broad nor too narrow.

Trade Secrets

The final form of intellectual property protection is trade secrets. The Uniform Trade Secrets Act defines trade secrets as information, including formulas, patterns, complications, devices, methods, techniques, or processes, that: (1) derive independent economic value, actual or potential, from not being generally known to the public or to other persons who can obtain economic value from their disclosure or use; and (2) are the subject of efforts that are reasonable under the circumstances to maintain their secrecy. As an example, Coca Cola's formula is protected as a trade secret because its secrecy is protected in all of their dealings with third parties. The claimed secret is indeed kept secret. An idea need not be patentable in order to receive trade secret protection. Its disclosure needs to controlled and limited.

Trade secrets have significant advantage over patents because they can be protected indefinitely as long as the subject mater of the trade secret is kept confidential. The disadvantage of trade secret rights revolves around maintaining confidentiality. Disclosures to outside parties must be limited and procedures must be implemented within the firm to protect proprietary information from inadvertent disclosure.

In determining trade secrets, courts focus on the value of the information and the efforts maintained to keep them confidential. Courts typically consider the following questions when deciding whether information qualifies as a trade secret:

- How extensively is the information known outside of your company?
- How extensively is the information known within the company?
- How easily can the information be independently acquired?
- How novel is the secret?
- Have you made a conscientious effort to protect the information from inadvertent disclosure both inside and outside of your company?

The best way to distinguish between patents and trade secrets is to understand that patents require an "invention" while trade secrets require a "discovery." The other major differences between patents and trade secrets are summarized as follows:

- Patents require disclosure while trade secrets are kept secret.
- Patents award monopoly rights for 17 years while trade secrets provide protection for an unlimited duration.
- Courts have shown more willingness to enjoin patent infringement than a trade secret violation. The reason for this tendency is that patents are well defined while what constitutes a trade secret may not be so precise.

Selecting Protection Mechanism for Software

Because intellectual property usually signifies something tangible, the legal system has had difficulty in applying laws to software. While copyrights, patents, and trade secrets have been used for protection, the courts have had a difficult time administering the law. The reason for this is simple; software is an intangible commodity and its value principally as a product and an enabling technology is hard to put a price on. To establish value, technologists must be able to teach judges and juries software economics. To do this, most practitioners resort to analogies because lay people typically do not understand what it takes to make, market, and manufacture software products. To come up with the numbers, these practitioners must eliminate the magic and mystery.

17.3 Licensing

Licenses are used to spell out the terms and conditions under which software products and services are sold in most industries. In addition, licenses spell out ownership rights along with the terms and conditions of use. For example, they explain things like whether you can transfer a license or if you can copy the software (e.g., for backup purposes). They also specify in detail how litigation will proceed should you violate any of the intellectual property protection statutes cited in the license agreement. Finally, they limit the owner's liability for damages incurred due to use and misuse of the software typically to replacement of the software.

A software license grants a user the right to employ a software program typically on one or a group of machines for a specified time period. Licenses can be granted to individuals, groups, organizations, and enterprises. They can be issued on an annual, semiannual, or indefinite period. They can be issued for one or multiple copies. Their issuance sometimes comes with (although often without) user support bundled with the price. Licensing computer software is like leasing a car in the sense that there are ongoing requirements that determine how and under what conditions the software can be used. These requirements include such things as deployment eligibility, distribution, transferring software to other users, and downgrading to earlier versions of the software.

As an example, Microsoft software licenses generally come with one of two kinds of agreements which specify how you may use the software. The first kind, and the one most users are familiar with, is an End User License Agreement (EULA). If you have ever acquired a license for software from a retailer or purchased a new computer with software already installed, then you have probably seen a EULA. The EULA generally either comes in the box on paper or cardstock or pops up on the screen when you install new software. You typically must accept the terms and conditions before installing the software. Often, the agreement limits damages to replacement of the software. It does not provide any allowances for damages that the software may inflict through error on the user's data, equipment, or other software. The second agreement type, Product Use Rights (PUR) is similar to the EULA except that it pertains to software licensed through Microsoft's Volume Licensing program. The PUR, together with the Microsoft Volume Licensing program agreement under which the license is acquired, governs the use of the licensed software.

The point of this section is that licenses are mechanisms used to provide intellectual property protection. They do this by specifying the terms and conditions of use of this property including the legal liabilities of all parties to the agreement. Licenses are important because they spell out the rights and obligations of all the parties to the agreement. And, if these agreements are breached, they spell out what either party can do legally to correct the situation. Licenses also provide the basis for valuing what the breach is worth. For a simple breach, the payment terms of the license could be used to compute value using lost income as the basis. But, things get more complicated when intellectual property is pilfered. Valuation in the case of intellectual property like software must be accomplished using practices and frameworks that have been shown to work in the courts, not the laboratories.

17.4 Valuation Process

Erdogmus, Favaro, and Halling provide an excellent introduction to the concept of value for software in Chapter 3 of the book. They argue that one must take uncertainty into account and go well beyond cost-benefit analysis to determine the true value of software. They also discuss how to incorporate flexibility as decisions are made by assessing options using risk management techniques (Boehm, 1991) and real options theory (see (Favaro, 1999; Erdogmus, 2001) for examples).

The eight step process that many non-software valuation experts use to determine the worth of software intellectual property is shown in Figure 66. It starts with answering the questions "why" are you conducting the appraisal and "what" are you going to do with it. It then goes through a number of selection steps aimed at deciding which practices to use in the appraisal. As expected, the process ends by producing a value for the intellectual property. Unlike work in software valuation, the process neither explicitly takes uncertainty into account nor does it investigate options.

Let us now look at what is involved in successfully completing each of these steps in the process. The first step is

Step 1 – Define the Appraisal's Purpose and Scope

The first step is taken to establish the objective of the appraisal. To determine value, the appraiser needs to answer the following basic questions:

- What specific intangible assets are being appraised and why? For example, you might be appraising the value of a software patent because you may be interested in acquiring the firm that developed it and its intellectual property.
- Who is going to use the appraisal and for what purpose? For example, the appraisal might be used in a litigation to establish a fair value for breach of an intellectual property agreement.

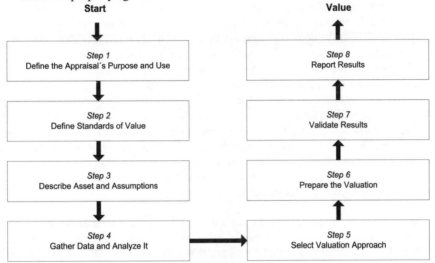

Fig. 66. Valuation process

You should write down the purpose of the valuation exercise once it has been established so that there is no confusion over what you are trying to accomplish and why.

Step 2 – Define Standards of Value

The second step is taken to define exactly what value is represented by the particular asset being valued. Some of the more common standards of value that exist include:

- *Fair value:* The amount that would compensate the owner when involuntarily deprived of the use of the asset. The appraisal here is aimed at estimating a fair and reasonable amount to compensate the buyer for loss of the use of the asset or for inappropriate use.
- *Market value:* The probable amount that a willing buyer would pay to purchase a like asset on the open software marketplace. This can often be determined by researching what similar products cost on the marketplace.
- *Acquisition value:* The amount that a buyer would pay to acquire the rights to use, sell, or distribute the asset on the open marketplace. Appraisers must be able to estimate the costs/benefits associated with use, sale, or distribution of

the property in order to come up with a number. For example, determination of whether the use of a highly efficient software search algorithm would enable a buyer to capture a larger share of the Internet market would have to use forecasts of any additional service revenue to determine whether the costs associated with the acquisition were justified by this added income and increased market share.

- *Insurable value*: The amount of insurance you would need to replace the asset with similar functionality and income producing capability. Appraisers often find it difficult to come up with a value in such cases because just replacing software does not produce like capabilities. The appraiser must be able to value the customization and added work that the firm seeking insurance had done to adapt these software products to their work processes and operational environment in order to derive a fair value.
- *Collateral value*: The amount that a creditor would advance with the asset serving as collateral for the loan. Appraisers again frequently have difficulty with this task because software is an enabling technology whose book value is not always a true indicator of its overall worth to a firm. For example, when an order entry system goes down for a day, the value of the lost sales should count, not the replacement costs for the software.

The selection of the standard then has a direct effect on the estimate of value derived. For example, insurable value for an asset is typically higher than collateral value. The reason for this is that banks are reluctant to highly value an asset when it is used for collateral purposes.

Step 3 – Describe Asset and Assumptions

The third step is taken to fully describe the intangible asset being appraised. This description should completely describe the intellectual property in question. Should proprietary information be involved, all parties to the valuation should sign nondisclosure agreements that allow the property to be described so that there is no question about what is and what isn't being valued by the appraisal. For example, if market value is in question, the owner should identify existing marketing channels, their value, current sales, anticipated sales, market penetration and growth statistics, and other pertinent but proprietary facts. The appraiser will need this data to understand what the true value of the asset is along with any assumptions that have a direct influence on the appraisal. Such assumptions should include items like the date of valuation (start of the license year, etc.), cost of money as of that date (assumed discount rate), the legal rights associated with use of the asset (license privileges, etc.), and the premises of value. The premises of value describe the conditions under which the value of the asset will be determined. The most popular such premise taken into account in appraisals is "highest and best usage" because it represents the best case under which the asset can be valued. Other premises of value include value in place, value in exchange upon disposition, and value in continued use.

Step 4 – Gather Data and Analyze It

The fourth step is taken to gather the data needed to value the asset. The typical valuation information is available from a wide variety of sources. These include the owner of the asset, trade publications, scholarly journals, and court cases. Some of the types of information that you would need to glean from these sources are as follows:

- License terms including limitations on use of the software and any copyrighted, patented, or trade secret protected item.
- Financial terms associated with the license and the sale or disposition of any competitive products or like assets on the open marketplace (including the firms themselves when an acquisition is being contemplated).
- A compilation of practices used to protect trade secrets should they be the subject of the valuation (procedures used, copies of nondisclosure agreements signed, etc.).
- Detailed accounting records that identify the costs involved in the development and the sales records for the asset in question.
- Detailed financial forecasts related to future sales of the asset and associated licensing rights.
- Copies of relevant marketing, training, and purchasing information.

Relevant history should be assessed over the last five year period to identify trends and to be considered relevant.

As part of this collection and analysis step, you will want to interview key management, marketing, engineering, support, and customer personnel to validate that the information you have collected and the results you have developed are reasonable and proper. You will want to make sure that these personnel do not influence your opinions. What you are looking for is independent confirmation that you haven't misunderstood or misconstrued the facts.

Step 5 – Select Valuation Approach

The fifth step is taken to select one of the following three primary approaches for valuing the intangible assets and intellectual property associated with software:

- *Cost approach*: Uses the principle of substitutions to predict how much a prudent investor would pay to either replace or reproduce the asset. For example, an appraiser might estimate the cost to develop a functionally equivalent piece of software when developing a replacement cost for a package that was appropriated by a litigant using nefarious means.
- *Income approach:* Measures the future economic benefits associated with the asset according to the selected premise of value ("highest and best" use, etc.) discounted using present value. For example, an appraiser might use a litigant's public growth data to forecast the income lost due to inappropriate use of the

asset under value in place premises (e.g., the software may have been installed and used on 50 seats in addition to the ten that were licensed).

- *Market approach*: Compares the asset with similar items that have been sold or listed for sale in the appropriate primary and secondary markets using the selected premise of value. For example, the appraiser might use empirical marketing data from a public source to develop future revenue forecast assuming best-case conditions to develop a projected income stream for use in determining the value of a firm being considered for acquisition.

There are many factors to consider when making a choice between these three alternatives. Selection is a function of what is being appraised, why, and for what purpose (see Step 1). For valuing software, the cost approach is often chosen because it focuses on either replacement or reproduction costs. For valuing a business, the income and/or market approaches are often used because they forecast the earning potential of the firm both in the present and future. For valuing a license, the lost income approach would be preferred. In all cases, the present worth of the investment needs to be computed. Obsolescence and salvage values need to be considered along with the tax implications of the investments (using accounting conventions blessed by the appropriate tax agency; e.g., the Internal Revenue Service (IRS) in the United States).

Of course, the devil is in the details when it comes to valuing software (Tockey, 2004). For example, you might use actual salary and overhead information to compute cost to ensure that your estimates are reasonable. You might also factor in an obsolescence factor into your cost computation to ensure that your replacement cost estimate isn't overly optimistic. You might have to assume some useful life for the asset and compute the life cycle costs or market value.

Step 6 – Prepare the Valuation

The sixth step, preparing the valuation, can be taken once all of the preparatory steps have been completed. The framework is established and now the numbers have to be generated. The valuation should consider the uncertainty associated with the decision variables (interest rates, etc.), asset value uncertainty and the available options when framing the alternatives to be considered using any of these three approaches. Performing such a valuation can be achieved using classical approaches (Reifer, 2001) or may take option pricing into account (Smith and Nau, 1995).

There are numerous tools that could be used to assist in developing the financials associated with the alternatives being considered. The most useful of these provided as a function of the software valuation approach selected are summarized in Table 39.

Step 7 – Validate Results

The seventh step is taken to validate the results. This step is normally accomplished by comparing the results derived using several methods for reasonableness. If benchmarks (Reifer, 2004), they can also be used to cross-check the numbers to establish their validity. If they do not, most experts would compare the alternatives to some base financial option to determine the reasonableness of the analysis. For example, they would immediately suspect the results of a purchase versus lease analysis if the payback period of the lease were either six months or 12 years (e.g., the normal payback period is three to four years when initial payments and buyout options are considered as part of the study).

Table 39. Tools by software valuation method

Valuation Method	Tools	Discussion
Cost	- Analogy Models - Cost Estimating Models - Productivity Models - Trend Lines & Graphs	There are mature estimating models like COCOMO II that can be used to estimate the replacement costs for software across the full life cycle.
Income	- Discounted Cash Flows - Depreciation Models - Net present value	Discounted cash flows that compute the net present or future value of discounted cash flows are the primary tools used here.
Market	- Analogy Models - Balanced Scorecard - Forecasting Models - Market Growth Models	Lots of models that take current sales and predict future growth can be used along with a balanced scorecard (Kaplan and Norton, 1996) for presenting the results understandably.

Step 8 – Report Results

The eighth and final step is taken to generate the valuation report. This document summarizes the results of the other steps and puts a value on the intellectual property in financial terms (dollars and cents in the United States). It states the value and discusses the approach used to develop it.

There is an established format for such reports when working with the legal valuation community (Reilly and Schweihs, 1998). The reason for this is simple; i.e., such reports are used by the courts to establish the value of the intellectual property being disputed.

17.5 Valuation Framework for Intellectual Property

As noted, valuation experts currently use the cost-, market-, and income-based approaches, the last of which employs discounted cash flow methods, to value intangible assets. Valuation is done using cost and/or income projections to develop and use a fair value estimate as a standard for compensation. To augment these approaches for valuing trade secrets, we have enhanced the following valuation framework developed by Pitkethly (Pitkethly, 1997) at Oxford for patents as follows in Figure 67 to include options that address changing risk (e.g., due to market and other conditions). Such risk determinations are needed to get a good handle on feasible options. Once these are scoped, we recommend that the option space be enlarged to investigate nontraditional alternatives that could occur due to non-controllable events like market growth or vendor abandonment of support for a product or product line.

Typically, software intellectual property is protected using copyrights, patents, and trade secrets. A trade secret is defined as information, including formulas, patterns, compilations, programs, devices, methods, techniques or processes that (1) derives independent economic value, actual or potential, from not being generally known and (2) is the subject of efforts that are reasonable under the circumstances to maintain its secrecy (Pitkethly, 1997). The last sentence in this definition is critical as efforts to protect the trade secret are paramount.

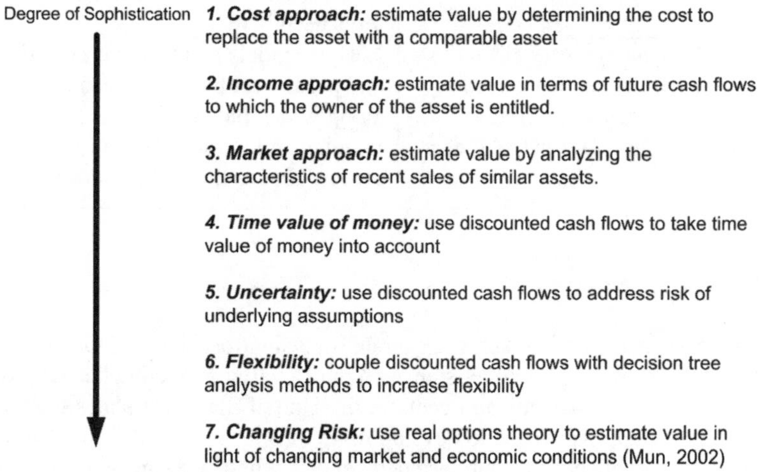

Degree of Sophistication

1. Cost approach: estimate value by determining the cost to replace the asset with a comparable asset

2. Income approach: estimate value in terms of future cash flows to which the owner of the asset is entitled.

3. Market approach: estimate value by analyzing the characteristics of recent sales of similar assets.

4. Time value of money: use discounted cash flows to take time value of money into account

5. Uncertainty: use discounted cash flows to address risk of underlying assumptions

6. Flexibility: couple discounted cash flows with decision tree analysis methods to increase flexibility

7. Changing Risk: use real options theory to estimate value in light of changing market and economic conditions (Mun, 2002)

Fig. 67. Valuation framework for intellectual property

A Simple Licensing Valuation Example

To illustrate the conceptual use of the valuation framework, let us value a license using the income method based on the following three available alternatives:

(1) introduce the product immediately without concern to quality; (2) improve the product quality by spending an additional year or more if the market conditions a year from now are not favorable in testing before releasing the product to market; and (3) wait and introduce the product when market conditions are best (i.e., when the potential income from product sales is the greatest).

Valuation experts would value income by discounting income projections using Net Present Value (NPV) to take the cost of money into account. The formula used to discount some future sum of money F assuming interest rate i over N periods: $NPV = F(1 + i)^{-N}$.

Table 40 identifies the potential income derived from each of these three alternatives over a five year decision horizon assuming that interest rates will vary as a function of a tightening economy (i.e., interest rates are rising to control spending and limit inflation). Alternative 1 introduces the product immediately to market to try to derive as much income as possible. Because the product has some quality issues, expenses to repair and stabilize the product are high in early years. In addition, sales revenues are lower than the alternatives because of quality issues. Alternative 2 spends \$250,000 during the first year of the decision horizon to stabilize the product and improve its quality. The hope is that the increased sales derived by focusing on quality would offset the investment. Alternative 3 waits until market conditions are favorable before introducing the product to market. This choice invests in quality improvement as it waits, but not at the level of Alternative 2. For all cases, the sales projections and expenses have been adjusted to reflect loss of market share because of quality concerns. All alternatives assume that marketing and product release costs are factored into the sales forecasts.

Alternative 2 can involve real options. For this alternative, the real option occurs after beta testing is finished at the end of year 1 because the release of the product can be postponed at this time. For this choice, the exercise date of the underlying real option is fixed like an American call option, a year from the current date. Because such options represent a subset of those available in Alternative 3, we will not analyze these options in our further discussions. We will just note that they exist.

Alternative 3 involves real options. For this alternative, the investment decision to release the product can be made in the future. Like a European call option, the choice can be exercised when either the return on investment or income in our case is deemed best.

Using the results summarized in Table 40, valuation experts would value the license based on the income derived via Alternative 2 because it represents the "highest and best use" of the asset in question. They would establish the replacement cost for the lost license income based on results of Alternative 2.

Table 40. License valuation example

Alternatives	Cost account	Decision Horizon (Years)					Total Return
		1	*2*	*3*	*4*	*5*	
Alt. 1. Introduce now	NPV	146K	306K	406K	513K	562K	$1,933K
	Net	150K	325K	450K	600K	700K	
	Sales	250K	400K	500K	650K	750K	
	Expense	100K	75K	50K	50K	50K	
Alt. 2. Beta test, then release	NPV	-244K	424K	541K	641K	722K	$2,084K (assuming that beta tests go well)
	Net	-250K	450K	600K	750K	900K	
	Sales		500K	650K	800K	950K	
	Expense	250K	50K	50K	50K	50K	
Alt. 3. Wait and see	NPV	146K	377K	496K	598K	682K	Function of when the real option is exercised
	Net	150K	400K	550K	700K	850K	
	Sales	250K	500K	650K	800K	950K	
	Expense	100K	100K	100K	100K	100K	
Interest Rate (i)		2.5%	3.0%	3.5%	4.0%	4.5%	

Uncertainty Assessment Using Decision Trees

The use of variable interest rates tries to take changing economic conditions into account in our basic example. But, there are many other variables that influence the market conditions that may exist over our planned five year decision horizon that must also be taken into account. The uncertainty associated with these market conditions can be factored into our analysis in a number of ways. First, we could use econometric models to determine the potential sales variations due to market conditions. Second, we could assess the uncertainties associated with each of our alternatives statistically. Third, we could use more advanced mathematical techniques like time series analysis (Box, 1994) and stochastic differential equations (Øksendal, 2002) to more fully assess the impact of the many variables in our decision space on market and financial conditions. However, use of these techniques requires time, effort, and specialists.

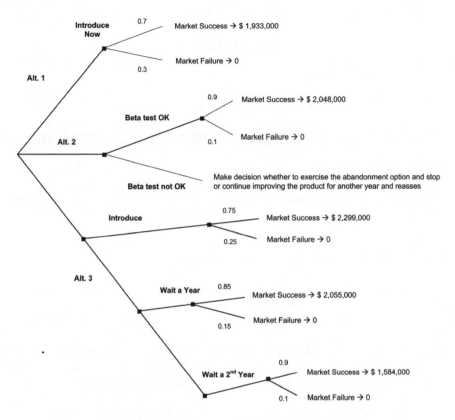

Fig. 68. Decision tree for licensing example

For simplicity's sake, we could use the concept of decision trees to assess uncertainty. As discussed earlier in the book and illustrated in Figure 68, decision trees allow you to account for uncertainty by adjusting the forecasted sales revenue for each licensing option using an associated probability of marketplace penetration success. Such probabilities can be determined using either qualitative techniques like expert judgment or quantitative approaches like statistical sales forecasting models and Monte Carlo simulations (i.e., techniques used to assess the range of potential impacts for marketplace phenomena). To use decision trees properly, we must assume that branches represent mutually exclusive alternatives.

For our licensing example, we can assign a probability of marketplace penetration success to each of the alternatives based on a poll of consumers that took into account their assessment of product quality versus marketplace penetration considerations. These probabilities along with the respective returns taken from Table 40 are illustrated in Figure 68.

It should be noted that computation of the second-year projections for the "wait and see" alternative expenses $100,000 during each option year considered instead of adding income into the projected net revenue stream. When these expenses are incorporated into the tallies, they reduce the NPV of the revenue stream during the year in which they are considered.

It should also be noted that for simplification purposes we truncated the decision tree for Alternative 2 in Figure 68 and made our calculations based on an assumed favorable beta testing result.

We can now make our selection between alternatives by comparing NPV of returns with similar probabilities of market penetration success. We can eliminate Alternative 1 because it provides a low return with a relatively low probability of market success. Based on our analysis, we would then choose Alternative 2 because its return with 90% market penetration success is $2,048,000 compared with $1,584,000 for Alternative 3. We can also discontinue examining Alternative 3 beyond the introduction delay of two years in Figure 68 because the incremental increase in probability of market penetration success does not seem worth the additional investment of $100,000 per year and potential loss of revenue.

More Advanced Analysis – Trade Secrets

As mentioned earlier in this chapter, trade secrets are defined as information, including formulas, patterns, complications, devices, methods, techniques, or processes, that: (1) derive independent economic value, actual or potential, from not being generally known to the public or to other persons who can obtain economic value from their disclosure or use; and (2) are the subject of efforts that are reasonable under the circumstances to maintain their secrecy. Because what constitutes a trade secret is hard to determine, many practitioners have difficulty in valuing them. For example, what is the value of a formula like convolutional coding with Viterbi decoding (i.e., the basis of a forward error correction technique used in cellular phones called Code Division Multiple Access) (Viterbi, 1995)?

Let us take our licensing example a step further and assume that embedded in the software you are licensing is an algorithm that you are protecting as a trade secret. You have taken reasonable precautions to protect information about this algorithm. Access to the algorithm is also limited as you have protected it in the code through encryption. Let us further assume that you licensed the software to a third-party and provided it access to the source code for maintenance purposes with adequate safeguards to protect your intellectual property (nondisclosure agreements, marking of materials as proprietary, etc.). You would have a breach of your license agreement should the licensee disclose information about the algorithm to some outside party. If you went to court over the breach, how much would you claim in terms of value for the algorithm?

To determine the value of the trade secret, you would probably claim lost income using the fair value for the asset. You would discard the cost approach to valuation because it would be inappropriate to use replacement or reproduction costs to establish the value of the asset. In addition, you would most likely reject the use of market approach to valuation because it is highly improbable that you could get realistic data about a like algorithm sold on the marketplace.

To determine the worth of the lost income, you would value feasible scenarios using real options as noted in Figure 67 to address changing risk when appropriate. You will have to carefully delimit your decision space need because those experts who will be hired to discredit your work will contend that your valuation is neither reasonable nor customary.

The scenarios that we have developed to value our trade secrets are summarized in Figure 69 using weightings to reflect the uncertainty associated with the outcome at a given point in time. Probabilities in this example are provided by a panel of experts and reflect the probability that the alternative will occur in the future. The probabilities are time dependent and change as a function of market conditions. The numbers portrayed are based on conditional probabilities because the alternatives are not mutually exclusive (e.g., nonlinear growth may make the firm more attractive for either venture funding or purchase). Table 41 provides backup information about how the NPV is calculated. Once the scenarios are assessed, you will again use the principle of "highest and best use" of the asset to determine value.

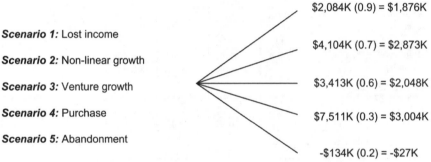

Fig. 69. Weighted returns for trade secrets example

Our first scenario computes the loss of income using traditional means by assuming a sales forecast, decision horizon (5 years), and cost of capital as in the previous licensing example. For the sake of simplicity, we have carried this alternative over as our first option. Scenario 2 assumes a growth model where the algorithm is used to penetrate aligned markets creating nonlinear growth rates. Our third scenario being evaluated assumes that our sales growth attracts venture funding that is used to propel the firm forward. Scenario 4 assumes that increased sales attract various buyers who offer to purchase the firm in the future for the sum of $8 million. Our fifth and final scenario assumes that we do not realize our sales projections and have to seek bankruptcy protection. Because sales projections will vary as a function of market conditions, each of these scenarios should be valued several times during the decision horizon.

Scenarios 3 and 4 can involve real options. In Scenario 3, the option to offer equity to venture capitalists in exchange for funds needed to grow the firm at some future time can be continuously assessed in order to determine when to exercise this option. In Scenario 4, management can take control of those factors that can influence the potential purchase price for the firm at a future time. For example, they can minimize expenses to reduce overhead to make their Profit and Loss statement look good.

Table 41. Trade secrets valuation example

Scenarios	Cost account	Decision Horizon (Years)					Total Return
		1	2	3	4	5	
Scenario 1 Lost income	NPV	-244K	424K	541K	641K	722K	$2,084K
	Net	-250K	450K	600K	750K	900K	
	Sales		500K	650K	800K	950K	
	Expense	-250K	-50K	-50K	-50K	-50K	
Scenario 2 Nonlinear growth (year 3)	NPV	195K	377K	812K	1,190K	1,530K	$4,104K
	Net	200K	400K	900K	1,400K	1,900K	
	Sales	300K	500K	1,200K	1,500K	2,000K	
	Expense	-100K	-100K	-300K	-100K	-100K	
Scenario 3 Venture growth (year 3)	NPV	195K	377K	451K	1,030K	1,360K	$3,413K
	Net	200K	400K	500K	1,200K	1,700K	
	Sales	300K	500K	1,000K	1,500K	2,000K	
	Expense	-100K	-100K	-500K	-300K	-300K	
Scenario 4 Purchase (year 4)	NPV	-244K	424K	541K	6,790K		$7,511K
	Net	-250K	450K	600K	7,950K		
	Sales		500K	650K	8,000K		
	Expense	-250K	-50K	-50K	-50K		
Scenario 5 Abandon (year 4)	NPV	-244K	424K	541K	-855K		-$134K
	Net	-250K	450K	600K	1,000K		
	Sales		500K	650K	800K		
	Expense	-250K	-50K	-50K	-1,800K		
Interest Rate (i)		2.5%	3.0%	3.5%	4.0%	4.5%	

Of course, our analysis of alternatives is neither complete nor completed. There are many linked events that could transpire that need to be added to the decision framework because many of the options are not independent of one another. Therefore, staging of options to take events that could occur into account is essential to our evaluations.

In addition, real options as explained in other chapters of this book can be examined as offers are extended to purchase the firm and withdrawn (Black and Scholes, 1973). For example, the timing of purchase offers could impact determination of the value (or price) offered for the firm. The offers represent the option price. For these cases, income streams from payment options and royalties or cash outlays need to be analyzed as an extension of NPV which remains the point of departure for our assessment. Of course, buyers want to value the firm low while sellers want to do the opposite. It is like playing a game like chess where the timing dictates the strategy that you will use to win the match.

There are many other approaches that have been advanced with this book for valuing intellectual property like trade secrets. Selection of the most appropriate value-based decision making technique is a function of why you are developing a value and who will use it once it is published. Within the context of the legal system, a simple approach is better because the results will have to be explained to both a judge and a jury. Because the valuation expert will also be called to defend his or her work, the results must be pragmatic, free of errors, and indisputable.

17.6 Potential Uses of the Valuation Framework

The valuation framework has a great deal of utility because it can be used to put a value on different forms of software intellectual property including: copyrights, goodwill, human capital, knowledge assets, and technology. Its advantage is that it does not rely only on classical discounting techniques to derive value. Instead, it forces the valuation expert to look at the value of options that can be taken within the expected time frame of the decision to compute what the intellectual property is truly worth. In times of either inflation or recession, timing is its own strategy especially when firms that view information as capital are assessing options in terms of recouping their investments. Under such circumstances, more traditional valuation methods can underestimate or overestimate the value especially when timing of the strategy is not considered. The framework takes risk into account to address these and other considerations using both traditional and advanced risk management techniques.

17.7 Future Shock

As we look into the future, we can visualize many barriers to developing a representative value for an organization's intellectual property. Chief among these concerns are the movement within the information technology business area to open source, outsourcing, and the internationalization of the industry. The industry seems to have no boundaries as products are developed and serviced by teams who reside in many nations.

As we have seen in our example, it is difficult to derive a value for a patent or trade secret. It even complicates matters further by having third parties abroad use the property without protection afforded by international law. Disclosure issues dominate as employees drift from a firm. In some instances, foreign employees might even set up their own firm to compete with yours using similar ideas. This is the situation that exists in some nations who do not enforce copyright, patent, and trade secret protection laws.

Now think about where technology is going in our business. The Internet is making it easy to telecommute. Access is seamless and wideband pipelines exist that make computing ubiquitous in many nations. Limiting access within a multinational firm to intellectual property is difficult even under the best of circumstances. Additional protection limitations exist especially as organizations try to guard their intellectual property against piracy and industrial espionage.

To answer these challenges, additional forms of intellectual property protection need to be developed. They must be capable of preventing unauthorized access to the golden nuggets (algorithms, rule sets, designs, private or classified data, etc.) which form the basis of all software protected assets. Research is needed as are redefinitions of the law that encompass the new technology. Engineers, lawyers, and valuation experts must work together to define these changes in ways that minimize impact on established valuation procedures. Otherwise, transition to their use will be difficult and preventive violations of the law will occur.

Just relying on legal safeguards is not enough. Technical defenses need to be strengthened as more and more protection is built into systems to limit unauthorized access to software assets. Research is needed to determine which defenses work, when, and under what conditions. In addition, we need to explore additional means to capture forensic evidence of break-ins like honeypots.

17.8 Summary and Conclusions

In this chapter, we discussed how to value intellectual property like copyrights, patents, and trade secrets. We started by outlining current intellectual property valuation practices. We next provided a valuation framework that permits experts to value all forms of intangible assets when involved in acquisitions, litigations, and disputes. The framework takes advantage of current theory to derive a fair value for use in valuing intellectual property using the currently accepted cost, income, and market approaches. Under certain conditions, the framework takes advantage of real options theory to address risk when warranted. We conclude by focusing on the barriers that software experts will have to overcome when presenting their findings to non-software participants.

Our hope is that the framework will prove useful to those engaged in valuation exercises. We encourage trial and error and innovation. Our real goal is to make those involved in valuation think about the alternatives. Just developing a value by rote is not enough. Your clients deserve more.

References

(AICPA, 1998) American Institute of Certified Public Accountants: Accounting for the Costs of Computer Software Developed or Obtained for Internal User, AICPA SOP-98-1 (1998)

(ASB, 2002) Appraisal Standards Board: Uniform Standards of Professional Appraisal Practice (2002)

(Black and Scholes, 1973) Black, F. and Scholes, M.: The pricing of options and corporate liabilities. Journal of Political Economy, 81, pp 637–659 (1973)

(Boehm, 1991) Boehm, B. W.: Software Risk Management: Principles and Practices. IEEE Software, pp 32–41 (Jan. 1991)

(Box, 1994) Box, G.: Time Series Analysis: Forecasting and Control (3rd Edition), Prentice-Hall (1994)

(Cole et al., 2002) Cole, R. J., Barnes, and Thornburg: Valuing IP Assets: The Legal Aspects, In: ICLE Spring (2002)

(Damiano, 2002) Damiano, K., "Valuing Intangible Assets under SFAS 141," In: Insights, Winter 2002, Willamette Management Associates (2002)

(Erdogmus, 2001) Erdogmus, H.: Management of license cost uncertainty in software development: a real options approach. In: Proc. 5th Annual Conference on Real Options: Theory Meets Practice, UCLA, Los Angeles, CA (2001)

(Favaro, 1999) Favaro, J.: Managing IT for Value. In: Proc. National Polish Soft. Eng. Conference, Warsaw (May 1999)

(Goldenberg and Tenen, 2001) Goldenberg N. and Tenen, P.: Legal Briefs: Intellectual Property, In: Casenotes (2001)

(Kaplan and Norton, 1996) Kaplan, R. and Norton, D.: The Balanced Scorecard, Harvard Business School Press (1996)

(Loud and Reilly, 2000) Loud, A. and Reilly, R.: What is a Trade Secret Worth? In: Insights, Willamette Management Associates, (2000)

(Mard, 2001) Mard, M.: Intellectual Property Valuation Challenges, In: The Licensing Journal (2001)

(Øksendal, 2002) Øksendal, B.K.: Stochastic Differential Equations, Springer-Verlag Telos (2002)

(OTA, 1990) Office of Technology Assessment: Computer Software & Intellectual Property Background Paper, Report OTA-BP-CIT-61, U.S. Government Printing Office (1990)

(Pitkethly, 1997) Pitkethly, R.: The Valuation of Patents, In: Judge Institute Working Paper 21/97, Judge Institute of Management Studies, Cambridge, England (1997)

(Reifer, 2001) Reifer, D.: Improvement by the Numbers: Making the Sofware Business Case, Addison-Wesley (2001)

(Reifer, 2004) Reifer, D.: Industry Software Cost, Quality and Productivity Benchmarks, In: The DoD SoftwareTech News (2004)

(Reilly and Schweihs, 1998) Reilly, R. and Schweihs, R.: Valuing Intangible Assets, McGraw-Hill (1998)

(Smith and Nau, 1995) Smith, J.E. and Nau, R.F.: Valuing risky projects: option pricing theory and decision analysis. Management Science 41(5) (1995)

(Tockey, 2004) Tockey, S.: Return on Software: Maximizing the Return on Your Software Investment (Addison-Wesley, 2004)

(Viterbi, 1995) Viterbi, A.J.: CDMA: Principles of Spread Spectrum Communications, (Prentice-Hall, 1995)

Author Biography

Donald J. Reifer is an expert in the fields of software engineering and management with over 35 years of progressive management experience in both industry and government. For the past five years, Mr. Reifer has specialized in the area of Information Operations and Anti-Tamper technology. He has conducted vulnerability assessments, developed a language to represent hacker attack scenarios, devised game theory algorithms to respond to attacks in real-time and led efforts to develop new and novel technologies to implement defense-in-depth protection strategies.

Glossary

Absolute Risk Aversion. A measure of investor reaction to uncertainty relating to absolute currency changes in the investor's wealth. (Chapter 3)

Acceptance Testing. Testing conducted to determine whether or not a system satisfies its acceptance criteria and to enable the customer to determine whether or not to accept the system. [IEEE Std 610.12-1990] (Chapter 11)

Additive Weighting Methods. A class of methods for making decisions with multiple criteria, in which weights are used to represent the preferences of the decision maker. (Chapter 4)

Agency Conflicts. Agency conflicts occur if project stakeholders have private incentives that differ from the common project goals. (Chapter 3)

Alternatives. Possible courses of action a decision maker can take. In a decision problem, there are at least two alternatives, otherwise, no decision needs to be made. When formulating a decision problem, two properties of alternatives must be fulfilled: the set of alternatives must be complete, i.e., all alternatives (including the alternative of doing nothing) must be considered, and alternatives must be mutually exclusive, i.e., one and only one alternative must be selected. (Chapter 4)

Ambiguity and Risk. In many decision problems, outcomes of alternatives are not known with certainty. In decision analysis, two classes of decision problems are distinguished: in decisions under risk, the probability distribution of outcomes is known, while in decision problems under ambiguity, only the possible states of nature which lead to different outcomes are known, but not their probabilities. (Chapter 4)

American Option. An option that can be exercised at any time before the final exercise date. (See European option.) (Chapter 3)

Artifacts. Pieces of information that describe a software system (or part thereof). Artifacts include requirements, architecture, and design elements, structural and behavioral descriptions, test scenarios. Artifacts are often maintained by different stakeholders. Trace dependencies (also known as traces or traceability): identify the commonalities among the distributed artifacts of a software system. Trace dependencies are needed for understanding and analyses. Trace Analysis: the activity of generating and validating trace dependencies. (Chapter 14)

Aspiration-Level Methods. A class of methods for making decisions with multiple criteria, in which the preferences of the decision maker are specified via desired levels of the criteria. (Chapter 4)

Behavioral Model. A model of human behavior, the purpose of which is to describe what people actually do when they make decisions, rather than what they should do. (Chapter 8)

Best Alternative To Negotiated Agreement (BATNA). This is an alternative one can obtain if the current negotiation terminates without an agreement, i.e., with a breakdown. Any offer which is higher than the BATNA is better than an impasse. No offer should be accepted that is worse than BATNA. (Chapter 7)

Bundle of Software Requirements. A bundle of software requirements is an informal package of software requirements. The requirements are bundled together based on specific criteria. (Chapter 9)

Business Goals. System qualities are generally defined as nonfunctional requirements which include attributes such as reliability, usability, maintainability, cost, etc. Many of these attributes originate at the business level and thus these are treated as business goals. Achieving business goals is crucial for software product success. Therefore it is important to examine, within a wider business context, how system requirements change, as well as to align them with business goals. (Chapter 9)

Call Option. Option to buy an asset at a specified exercise price on or before a specified exercise date. (Chapter 3)

Capital Asset Pricing Model (CAPM). The CAPM is the most influential equilibrium asset pricing model. An asset pricing model is a theory for valuing real or financial assets based on behavioral assumptions regarding the general economy, capital markets or specific sectors, and investors or other decision makers. Among other assumptions CAPM assumes that investors directly care about the mean (expected returns) and variance (risk or volatility) of asset returns. (Chapter 3)

Certainty Equivalent. A risk-free cash flow that has the same expected value as a particular risky cash flow. (Chapter 3)

Change Propagation. Defines how changes have to be propagated across artifacts. It may query the user for guidance if multiple options for propagation are available. Trace Uncertainties: incomplete knowledge on how software artifacts trace to one another. Uncertainties limit the understanding of the connectedness of software artifacts and impair automation. (Chapter 14)

Cognitive Science. A science concerned with the study of minds and other intelligent systems. It is interdisciplinary in nature, bringing together researchers such as anthropologists, computer scientists, educators, linguists, neuroscientists, philosophers, and psychologists. Cognitive science has a broad span and includes cognitive architectures, culture, development, instruction, language, learning and memory, neuroscience, pattern recognition, perception and attention, philosophical foundations, reasoning, and representation. [Adapted from a statement from the editor of the Journal of the Cognitive Science Society] (Chapter 8)

Collaboration Engineering. A design approach for recurring collaboration processes that can be transferred to groups that can be self sustaining in these processes using collaboration techniques and technology. (Chapter 10)

Competitive Position. The economic profitability and growth rate of a particular business unit relative to that of the average competitor in its product market, produced by its differentiation position and relative economic cost position. (Chapter 3)

Conflict. Perceived divergence of interest; a belief that one's own aspirations are incompatible with others' aspirations. (Chapter 7)

Consensus Building. As a group, to move from less to more agreement; to let a group of mission-critical stakeholders aim for mutually acceptable commitments; to align goals. (Chapter 10)

Contingent Claim. A claim whose value depends on ("is contingent on") the value of another asset. (Chapter 3)

Contingent Claims Analysis (CCA). Analysis of the value of a claim on a real or financial asset, where the underlying asset is disposed of or acquired when certain conditions hold and often at the discretion of the acquirer or seller. Option pricing and decision trees are examples of techniques used for CCA. (Chapter 3)

Convergence. As a group, to move from having many concepts to a focus on and understand to fewer concepts that are worthy of further attention. (Chapter 10)

Copyright. Refers to the protection given to authors of original literary works, and motion pictures from unauthorized copying or performance. The Library of Congress registers copyrights which last for the life of the author plus 70 years. (Chapter 17)

Cost of Quality. The cost associated with the quality of a work product. Cost of quality (CoQ) has two main components: Cost of conformance and cost of non-conformance. Cost of conformance is the total cost of ensuring that a product is of good quality, e.g., cost of testing. Cost of non-conformance is the total cost of re-work (such as finding and correcting defective work) and any further post-delivery costs (such as loss of business, legal redress). [Adapted from http://www.isixsigma.com/dictionary/glossary.asp] (Chapter 11)

Decision Criteria. Decision criteria are numerical thresholds or targets used to determine the need for action or further investigation, or to describe the level of confidence in a given result. Decision criteria help to interpret the results of measurement. Decision criteria may be calculated or based on a conceptual understanding of expected behavior. Decision criteria may be derived from historical data, plans, and heuristics, or computed as statistical control limits or statistical confidence limits. [ISO/IEC 15939] (Chapter 8)

Decision Response. The outcome from an act of decision making. The outcome may be a decision to act, a decision not to act or a decision to wait until further decision stimuli are received. (Chapter 8)

Decision Stimulus. One or more indicators characterizing an object of interest to the decision maker that stimulate them to commence an act of decision making. (Chapter 8)

Decision Tree Analysis. A technique for modeling project outcomes and management decisions using state changes to model uncertainty, actions, and outcomes contingent on these state changes, and probabilities associated with them. (Chapter 3)

Decision making. A cognitive process in which a person uses a mental model to evaluate a decision stimulus according to a set of decision criteria and make a decision response. (Chapter 8)

Defect Testing. To discover faults or defects in the software where the behavior of the software is incorrect, undesirable, or does not conform to its specification. Defect testing is concerned with rooting out all kinds of undesirable system behavior, such as system crashes, unwanted interactions with other systems, incorrect computations, and data corruption. (Chapter 11)

Derivative. An asset (e.g., option or futures contract) whose value is derived from the value of another asset. (Chapter 3)

Derived Measure. A measure that is defined as a function of two or more values of base measures (based on the definition in International Vocabulary of Basic and General Terms in Metrology, 1993). Derived measures capture information about more than one attribute or the same attribute from multiple entities. Simple transformations of base measures (for example, taking the square root of a base measure) do not add information, and thus do not produce derived measures. Normalization of data often involves converting base measures into derived measures that can be used to compare different entities. [ISO/IEC 15939] (Chapter 8)

Development Testing. Testing conducted during the development of a system or component, usually in the development environment by the developer. [IEEE Std 610.12-1990] (Chapter 11)

Discount Rate. Compound rate used to calculate the present value of future cash flows that represent income or expense streams. May be "risk-free" or "risk-adjusted." The discount rate typically captures the cost of capital to the investor. (Chapter 5 and Chapter 3)

Discounted Cash Flow (DCF). A valuation technique based on adjusting income and expense streams occurring at different points in time using a compound rate that captures the risk borne by the streams. The compound rate, called the discount rate, takes into account time value of money. (Chapter 3)

Distributive Negotiation. Negotiations concerned with the division of a single good. (Chapter 7)

Divergence. As a group, to move from having fewer to having more concepts to consider. (Chapter 10)

Diversifiable Risk. See *unsystematic risk.*

Diversification. Refers to an investor's ability to reduce risk exposure by spreading the total investment over multiple risky assets. The resulting reduction in overall risk impacts the value of the investor's portfolio. In order to quantify the risk reduction, one must know the correlation among the investment opportunities or asset classes in the portfolio. The impact of diversification is largest if the different investment opportunities are negatively correlated (tend to move in the opposite direction in response to external events) and it is smallest if they are positively correlated (tend to move in the same direction in response to external events). (Chapter 3)

Economic Value (of the firm). The economic worth of a commercial organization is the sum of all its future profits, discounted for time and risk. (Chapter 5)

European Option. Option that can be exercised only on the final exercise date. (See American option.) (Chapter 3)

Evaluation. As a group, to move from less to more understanding of the benefit of concepts toward attaining a goal relative to one or more criteria. (Chapter 10)

EVOLVE*. EVOLVE* is a problem solving paradigm for ill-structured or wicked problems. It is designed as an iterative and evolutionary procedure to exploit available tools of computational intelligence for handling explicit knowledge and crisp data, and the involvement of human intelligence for tackling tacit knowledge and fuzzy data. There are three phases at each iteration: modeling, exploration, and consolidation. The expected result of applying the paradigm is a better understanding and description of the problem settings and the ability to provide appropriate solutions meaningful in the real-world context. (Chapter 12)

Exercise Price (Strike price). Price at which a call or put option may be exercised. (Chapter 3)

F-EVOLVE*. Refinement of EVOLVE* with focus on financial attributes. Considers value in financial terms where cardinal measures are taken into consideration when choosing among plans. This financial component is added to EVOLVE* as a cardinal metric that will help users choose among plans based on this financial metric. (Chapter 12)

Facilitator. Being impartial, the facilitator is responsible for the preparation, structuration, and moderation of group interaction and collaboration in order to help a group realize the desired outcome of the group process. (Chapter 10)

Financial Assets. Pieces of paper, documents, recorded agreements, or contracts that represent claims on real assets. (Chapter 3)

Financial Option. An option on financial assets (such as stocks). (Chapter 3)

Financial Risk. A measure of likelihood of the receipt of a particular sum of money in the future. Notably, financial risk does not consider just the likelihood of receiving less than a certain sum of money, but also the likelihood of receiving more than a certain sum of money. In financial circles, investors want to know exactly what they are going to receive, since underestimating can result in a misapplication of funds just as easily as can overestimating. (Chapter 5)

Future Value (FV). The value of a flow of money, at some time in the future. For example, the Future Value of a collection of $100 monthly payments is $2,400 in 24 months. The Future Value may also reflect interest payments. (Chapter 5)

Group Support System (GSS). A suite of collaborative software tools that can be used to focus and structure a team's deliberation, while reducing cognitive costs of communication and information access and minimizing distraction among teams working collaboratively toward a goal; an electronic meeting system. (Chapter 10)

Image Theory. A behavioral model of decision making (developed by psychologists Beach and Mitchell) that suggests that the goal of measurement is to foster the creation of a set of images in the mind of the decision maker about the situation, process, service, product, or event that is being measured. This set of images should be so clear that it captures the attention of the decision maker. When necessary, the images should stimulate the decision maker to consider taking action. The images should be rich enough to enable the decision maker to make an appropriate choice from among the available actions. Following this decision, the images should then enable the person to receive feedback on its consequences in order to allow for refinements and corrections. (Chapter 9)

Impact Analysis. Describes the exact nature (impact) of a change. For example, what design and implementation artifacts are affected by a requirement change. Impact Analysis is often integrated with Change Propagation. (Chapter 14)

Incremental Funding Method. It is a data-driven, financially informed, approach to plan iterations in incremental software development. This development approach maximizes Net Present Value (NPV) of software investment by carefully analyzing and sequencing feature delivery. (Chapter 12)

Incremental Software Development. Offers a series of releases with additive functionality to create optimal value under existing project constraints. This promotes faster delivery of small components of the overall software product to incorporate early user feedback into the system. (Chapter 12)

Independent Verification and Validation (IV&V). Verification and validation performed by an organization that is technically, managerially, and financially independent of the development organization. [IEEE Std 610.12-1990] (Chapter 11)

Information Asymmetries. Occur in situations where some project stakeholders have superior or private information not available to others. (Chapter 3)

Information Need. The insight necessary to manage objectives, goals, risks, and problems [ISO/IEC 15939] (Chapter 8)

Information Product. One or more indicators and their associated interpretations that address an information need (for example, a comparison of a measured defect rate to planned defect rate along with an assessment of whether or not the difference indicates a problem) [ISO/IEC 15939] (Chapter 8)

Integrative Negotiation. Negotiations where the parties make use of their capabilities and resources to generate more value. (Chapter 7)

Intellectual Property. Refers to intangible value created by human creativity and invention, and includes copyrights, trademarks, and patents. (Chapter 17)

Interdependence. Interdependence means that each party in the negotiation shares has or wants something that the other party has or wants. Without interdependence, there would be no need for negotiation. (Chapter 7)

KJ. A technique to structure information, typically after a brainstorm. Keywords are written on stickers and organized according to group. The technique is named after Japanese ethnologist Jiro Kawakita. (Chapter 15)

Knowledge-Based Economy. As the world continues its profound transition from an industrial economy to an "Information-Age Economy, " knowledge and technology have become central to the economic development which strongly depend on production, distribution, and use of knowledge and information. Knowledge is the driver of productivity and economic growth, leading to a new focus on the role of information, technology, and learning in economic performance. The term "knowledge-based economy" is the result of a fuller recognition of the role of knowledge and technology in economic growth. (Chapter 10)

Market Risk (systematic risk). Risk that cannot be diversified away (e.g., in a portfolio of holdings). (Chapter 3)

Model Uncertainty. Relates to the validity of the specific models used (e.g., the suitability of a certain distribution to model the defects). (Chapter 3)

Model. An idealized, simplified representation of a real object, system, or any other subset of reality, which is still similar with respect to certain properties. (Chapter 13)

Monte Carlo Simulation. A computer-intensive technique for assessing how a statistic will perform under repeated sampling. (Chapter 13)

Natural Uncertainty. Directly relates to variations in the environment variables (e.g., the variation in the number of defects in a software product). (Chapter 3)

Negotiation Analysis. The science and art of collaborative decision making. It is a mostly prescriptive approach to advise negotiators to understand the intricacies of the problems they face, to make decisions confidently in the face of complexity, to justify decisions and to ultimately conduct negotiations. Negotiation analysis is based on decision analysis, behavioral decision making approach, and game theory. (Chapter 7)

Negotiation. A form of conflict behavior that seeks to resolve divergence of interests by means of a verbal exchange between parties. (Chapter 7)

Net Present Value (NPV). A project's net contribution to wealth. Given by the present value of future cash flows minus initial investment. Alternatively, the present value of future income net of immediate investment and the present value of future expenses. (Chapter 3 and Chapter 5)

Organization. As a group, to move from less to more understanding of relationships among concepts; to provide structure among a set of concepts. (Chapter 10)

Outranking Methods. A class of methods for making decisions with multiple criteria, in which a special relation between alternatives (the outranking relation) is constructed. (Chapter 4)

Parameter Uncertainty. Relates to the estimation of parameters (e.g., the reliability of the parameter representing average number of defects). (Chapter 3)

Patent. Refers to property right granted by a government to an inventor "to exclude others from making, using, offering for sale, or selling the invention or importing the invention" for a limited time in exchange for public disclosure of the invention when the patent is granted. (Chapter 17)

Positivist Behavior Model. A label attached to a particular model of human behavior. The concepts underlying this model can be summarized as: (a) Human action is intentional and "rational," (b) Humans interact in stable and orderly ways, and (c) Conflict is dysfunctional and must be eliminated. (Chapter 8)

Postmortem Review. A collective learning activity which can be organized for projects either when they end a phase or are terminated. The main motivation is to reflect on what happened in the project in order to improve future practice – for the individuals that have participated in the project and for the organization as a whole. (Chapter 15)

Preferences. In decision analysis, preferences of decision makers are always formulated with respect to outcomes of decision alternatives, not with respect to the alternatives themselves. Thus, two alternatives which always lead to the same outcomes are considered to be identical. Preferences can be measured at different levels of scales. In ordinal scales, only the information that one outcome is preferred to another outcome is available. In difference scales, it is assumed that the decision maker is also able to rank differences between outcomes, e.g., that moving from outcome A to outcome B is a greater improvement than moving from outcome B to outcome C. In ratio scales, it is assumed that the decision maker is able to provide ratios of the outcomes, e.g., stating that outcome A is twice as good as outcome B. (Chapter 4)

Present Value (PV). The current value of a sum of money, payable or receivable at some point in the future. Discounted value of a future cash flow representing income or expense. (Chapter 3 and Chapter 5)

Prioritization of Software Requirements. Software requirements may be prioritized based on different criteria, to be included first in a bundle and then later in a requirements package. (Chapter 9)

Process Guide. A structured, workflow-oriented, reference document for a particular process, exists to support participants in carrying out the intended process. Usually describes activities, artifacts, roles, and tools. (Chapter 15)

Process Workshop. A workshop where employees with key roles such as project managers, developers, and system architects are invited to define work processes to be disseminated in a process guide. (Chapter 15)

Process. A method of doing or producing something following a sequence of steps. (Chapter 13)

Product Value. The value of a product is a function of the quality of the inputs utilized to create it. The value of a product might be interpreted in different ways by different customers and software developers. (Chapter 9)

Put Option. Option to sell an asset at a specified exercise price on or before a specified exercise date. (Chapter 3)

Quality Management. A systematic set of activities to ensure that processes create products with maximum quality at minimum cost of quality. The activities include quality assurance, quality control, and quality improvement. [http://www.isixsigma.com/dictionary/glossary.asp] (Chapter 11)

Quality Risk Management. The process of identifying, prioritizing, and managing risks to the quality of the system under test, with the aim of preventing them or detecting and removing them. (Chapter 11)

Quality Risk. The possibility of undesirable types of behaviors, or failure modes, in which the system under test does not meet stated product requirements or end users' reasonable expectations of behavior; in plain terms, the possibility of a bug. (Chapter 11)

Random Sampling. A sampling procedure that assures that each element in the population of interest has an equal chance of being selected. (Chapter 13)

Real Assets. Tangible and intangible assets used for doing business. Real estate and a software project's income stream are examples of real assets. (Chapter 3)

Real Option. A contingent claim on real assets such as capital investment opportunities in projects. See also *contingent claim* (Chapter 3 and Chapter 17)

Real Options analysis. A set of techniques used to value options on real assets by examining the underlying active and passive waiting strategies and using option pricing and decision tree techniques. See also *real option, contingent claim,* and *contingent claims analysis* (Chapter 3 and Chapter 17)

Relative Risk Aversion. A measure of investor reaction to uncertainty relating to percentage changes in the investor's wealth. (Chapter 3)

Release Planning. Release planning for incremental development assigns features to releases such that the most important technical, resource, risk, and budget constraints are met. Poor release planning decisions that result (i) in unsatisfied customers not getting what they expect, (ii) in release plans unlikely to be performed within given schedule, quality and effort constraints, and (iii) in plans not offering the best business value out of the taken investments. (Chapter 12)

Return on Investment (ROI). A measure of the financial performance of an investment. Usually expressed as the return divided by the investment. For example, a $1,000 investment that yields a $100 return has a 10% return on investment. (Chapter 5)

Risk Analysis. All management activities that are related to assessing the potential impact of identified risks. This includes the quantification of the probability of risk occurrence and the description of potential loss (qualitatively or quantitatively). (Chapter 13)

Risk Assessment. All management activities that are related to risk identification, risk analysis, and risk prioritization. (Chapter 13)

Risk Management. A practice with processes, methods, and tools for managing risks in a project. It provides a disciplined environment for proactive decision making to assess continuously what could go wrong (risks), determine which risks are important to deal with, and implement strategies to deal with those risks. (Chapter 13)

Risk Premium. An extra amount added to a discount rate to reflect the financial risk of the investment's return. (Chapter 5)

Risk. The possibility of suffering loss. (Chapter 13)

Risk-adjusted Discount Rate. The discount rate that applies to uncertain cash flows. The more uncertain a cash flow is, the higher the risk-adjusted rate. (Chapter 3)

Risk-Based Testing. (1) Prioritizing tests according to the probability that the tested part fails and the impact of the failure, if it does fail. Risk is used to manage testing, mainly for validation testing. (2) Using risk analysis to identify problem areas for designing tests with a high probability to uncover resulting errors. Risk is used for test design, mainly for defect testing. (Chapter 11)

Risk-free (Discount) Rate. A discount rate that does not reflect any financial risk and that applies to cash flows with no or minimal uncertainty. This rate can be observed in the markets and often equated with the interest rate provided by short-term government-backed securities such as treasury bills. (Chapters 3 and 5)

Root Cause Analysis. Also called Ishikawa or fishbone diagrams, are used to structure discussions on the causes of important issues by drawing a line for an issue, and arrows for causes and sub-causes. (Chapter 15)

Simulation. The process of conducting experiments with a model. (Chapter 13)

Socio-technical systems. Systems that are situated in a social context and where some elements of the system depend on human abilities to think and work in groups, while other elements of the system are provided through the use of technology. (Chapter 8)

Software Engineering Decision Support. Intelligent decision support is mainly required in situations characterized by the following factors: complexity, uncertainty, presence of multiple stakeholders, large quantities of (organization-specific) data, and/or rapid changes in problem parameters and related information. Support here means to provide access to information that would otherwise be unavailable or difficult to obtain; to facilitate generation and evaluation of solution alternatives; and to prioritize alternatives by using explicit models that provide structure for particular decisions. (Chapter 12)

Software Process Simulation. A computer-intensive technique for imitating behavioral aspects of real software development behavior with a set of mathematical models representing the software development process. (Chapter 13)

Software Process. A method of developing or producing software. (Chapter 13)

Software Requirements Package. This refers to the formal packaging of software requirements, i.e., it is the formalization of bundles after having prioritized requirements. A package acts as a non-devisable unit that is delivered to a project. However, several packages may be input to a development project and the intention is that a specific package should be implemented as a whole, without removing any of the requirements within a package. (Chapter 9)

System Dynamics. A methodology for studying and managing complex feedback systems, such as one finds in business and other social systems. (Chapter 13)

System. A collection of elements that operate together for a common purpose and appears as a self-contained unit with a defined structure. (Chapter 13)

Systematic Risk (Un-diversifiable risk). A type of risk to which all companies, or projects are exposed. For example, since the ability to attract and hire good engineers is essential to any project, we might consider "hiring good people" to be a systematic risk factor. (Chapter 5)

Test Cycle. A partial or total execution of all the test suites planned for a given test phase as part of that phase. A test phase involves at least one cycle (usually more) through all the designated test suites. Test cycles are usually associated with a single release of the system under test, such as a build of software. Generally, new test releases occur during a test phase, triggering another test cycle. (Chapter 11)

Test Management. Activities for planning, executing, analysis, and control of testing. (Chapter 11)

Test Planning. The process of identifying the means, resources, and actions necessary to accomplish the testing objective. (Chapter 11)

Testing. The process of operating a system or component under specified conditions, observing or recording the results, and making an evaluation of some aspect of the system or component. [IEEE Std 610.12-1990] (Chapter 11)

thinkLet. A scripted facilitation technique to create a pattern of collaboration. All a facilitator needs to know to reproduce one predictable, repeatable pattern of collaboration among people working together toward a goal. (Chapter 10)

Trade Secret. Refers to any information, whether or not copyrightable or patentable, that is not generally known or accessible and that gives competitive advantage to its owners. (Chapter 17)

Undiversifiable Risk. See *systematic risk.*

Unsystematic Risk (Specific, Private, or Diversifiable Risk). A type of risk specific to an individual company or project. For example, it may be important to have a medical domain expert available for consultation while a software project entailing a CAT scan system is underway. This would be viewed as unsystematic, or specific risk, since the need for such a domain expert is not a risk factor shared with other projects. (Chapter 5)

Usability Evaluation. Usability evaluation considers the user, the tasks, the equipment, and the environment, and the relationships among them (Bevan and Macleod, 1994). Usability evaluation includes multiple methods to evaluate the usability of a system including usability testing. (Chapter 10)

Usability Heuristics. A common set of criteria used to evaluate software usability. (Chapter 10)

Usability Testing. Usability testing determines whether a system meets a predetermined, quantifiable level of usability for specific types of users carrying out specific tasks. (Chapter 10)

Usability. The extent to which a product can be used by specified users to achieve specified goals with effectiveness, efficiency, and satisfaction in a specified context of use. (Chapter 10)

User Interface. The part of the system through which the user interacts with the system either physically, perceptually, or conceptually. (Chapter 10)

Utility Functions. A utility function is a mathematical representation of preferences. An outcome A is preferred to outcome B whenever $u(A) > u(B)$. Depending on the scale level of preferences, different functional forms of utility functions can be used. It should be noted that utility functions are mainly a technical device for preference representation, and are not meant to represent the "inherent value" of outcomes to the decision maker. (Chapter 4)

Validation Testing. To demonstrate to the developer and the customer that the software meets its requirements. For custom software, this means that there should be at least one test for every requirement in the user and system requirements documents. For generic software products, it means that there should be tests for all of the system features that will be incorporated in the product release. (Chapter 11)

Valuation Horizon. Period over which cash flows are captured in order to compute a firm's valuation. Typically five to ten years. (Chapter 5)

Valuation. The act of valuing, or of estimating current value or worth of intellectual property for the purpose of acquisition, appraisal, and/or other purposes. (Chapter 17)

Value Creation. To remain competitive in an era of increasing uncertainty and market globalization in the third millennium, software companies have begun focusing on the value of different customers and markets when developing products. Value creation is about building and growing business by creating value for the customer and delivering this effectively. It involves identifying core competencies of the organization and connecting these to its future vision. This is essential in any business, including software companies, as it help them to achieve long-term strategic gains. (Chapter 9)

Value Measurement. Value is a "measurable concept" that satisfies some information need. By this it is meant that value can be indirectly measured once there is agreement about what the concept means. In this, it is similar to other "measurable concepts" such as quality, productivity, efficiency, effectiveness, and client satisfaction. Value cannot be directly measured in the way that mass, volume, and time can be measured, chiefly because it is a multi-attributed, personal construct. Instead base measures must be collected of the agreed attributes of value, using agreed measurement methods and scales, and combined with other base measures according to an agreed measurement model to produce derived measures that, by agreement, act as indicators of value. (Chapter 8)

Value. The numerical or categorical result assigned to a base measure, derived measure, or indicator [ISO/IEC 15939] (Chapter 8)

Value-Based Decision Making. Values are a driving factor in personal and organizational activities. Value-based decisions, such as value analysis, are meant to assist software developers in their decisions. For example, whether enhancing software performance, improving flexibility, or improving data integrity and consistency will increase the lifecycle cost and strengthen communication between stakeholders. (Chapter 9)

Verification and Validation (V&V). The process of determining whether the requirements for a system or component are complete and correct, the products of each development phase fulfill the requirements or conditions imposed by the previous phase, and the final system or component complies with specified requirements. [IEEE Std 610.12-1990] (Chapter 11)

List of Figures

List of Tables

Index